# The
# Daily
# Planet

# The Daily Planet

A Critic on the Capitalist Culture Beat

**PATRICIA AUFDERHEIDE**

University of Minnesota Press

Minneapolis • London

Published by the University of Minnesota Press
111 Third Avenue South, Suite 290
Minneapolis, MN 55401-2520
http://www.upress.umn.edu

Library of Congress Cataloging-in-Publication Data

Aufderheide, Patricia.
    The daily planet : a critic on the capitalist culture beat / Patricia Aufderheide.
        p.    cm.
    ISBN 0-8166-3341-X — ISBN 0-8166-3342-8 (pbk.)
    1. Mass media.   I. Title.
    P90.A857 2000
    302.23—dc21                                                    99-044814

Printed in the United States of America on acid-free paper

The University of Minnesota is an equal-opportunity educator and employer.

11  10  09  08  07  06  05  04  03  02  01  00        10  9  8  7  6  5  4  3  2  1

For Stephan

# Contents

## Part IV.  Living with the Media

# Introduction

Critics walk a woozy line between the dilatory and the portentous. In the end, if we're lucky, a bit of wit saves us. Listen to Henry Adams, whose description of his work continues to be a beacon to my own. "The press," he wrote in his autobiography,

> was still the last resource of the educated poor who could not be artists and who would not be tutors. Any man who was fit for nothing else could write an editorial or a criticism. The enormous mass of misinformation accumulated in ten years of nomad life could always be worked off on a helpless public. The press was an inferior pulpit; an anonymous schoolmaster; a cheap boarding school. But it was still the nearest approach to a career for the literary survivor of a wrecked education.

For decades, that quote has hung above my desk as I furiously typed (and, later, keyboarded). While it works well to puncture incipient punditry, it also reminds me, as does the life of the estimably interstitial Henry Adams himself, that we writers play public roles in public spaces, however rough-hewn those spaces may be.

Sometimes, we carve them out ourselves. As a cultural critic, I've had the good fortune to work in the worlds of journalism, advocacy, and the academy, without ever having to give up my freedom. Rarely have my colleagues in one environment had the faintest clue of my existence in another. It has been like an inverse case of multiple personality disorder, in which all of my working selves are actually great friends, but each of which is unknown to the friends of the other. I am hoping this collection of my work will help introduce everybody all around and also make a case for cultural criticism as an enterprise.

What I do, wherever I do it, is to explore the culture of daily life under capitalism and the ways in which our media help or hinder the project of a civilization in which all of our children can live well, together, in freedom. There are themes: expanding access to information; fostering public life and democratic process; understanding the subtle and not-so-subtle implications of imperial relationships; overcoming victim and identity politics in a polycultural society; finding ways in which art can take us past the glaze of the familiar, the daze of despair, and the caviling of the helpless and inspire hopefulness about the human project. I have always been as interested in how business and government structures condition opportunity for expression and communication as I have been in the kinds of expression that emerge. And I have always hoped to talk to people about these themes in ways that would connect with their daily lives.

## Who, Me?

When the term *public intellectual* started to get bandied about, I felt an enormous sense of relief. Finally, a name for what I was doing! And one that was a little more dignified, or at least more generic, than terms like *thumbsucker, policy wonk, gadfly,* and *pundit*—all those slyly contemptuous inside-the-Beltway pigeonholes, none of which fits me. Unfortunately, the term has come to be cloaked in piety. Among communications academics, it is often reduced to mean a popularizer of our knotty truths to those vulgarians in the press. It now also has its stars, what critic Carlin Romano calls, with his great ability to detect naked emperors, "publicity intellectuals." I suppose the sound-bite-ization of the term was inevitable, but it's a pity, because it is a nicely non–career-specific term for symbolic analysis within the context of public life. And it distinguishes such work from the much more common practice—privatized intellectual work conducted by the myriad handmaidens to power in memos, briefs, consultants' reports, and strategizing behind closed doors.

Another reason why my heart leapt up at the idea of the term *public intellectual* was that it implied a commitment to the common good and a common conversation, and not merely ideological thrusts and parries between dueling think tanks. Not that I thought I was standing on neutral ground. My work is all colored by my commitment to fairness and to "strong" democracy, and by my conviction that we can cultivate better civilizational habits than the ones we inherited. These concerns, when I started out writing, placed me somewhere gently left of center of American politics. As politics have shifted with capitalist restructuring, my spot on the landscape has become much more of a left outpost. I think it will probably, even in my own lifetime, come to look more centrist again, as people begin to reorganize themselves along new lines. My fascination with the arts intersects with those concerns, without being congruent with them.

Yet another reason why I liked that label so much was that it distinguished intellectual life in public from politics. If there's one thing that journalism ought to teach you, it's the difference between acting within and on political structures and reporting on culture. Intellectual work can, obviously, sometimes also be political action. My policy writings—some samples are included in the second part of this book—were mostly political acts, at least when they started out. But my critical and journalistic writings are written to fuel public conversation, reaching beyond true believerdom, and that's a different process with different actors. So it's irritating to be neatly filed away under the rubric "left critic" by my pals on the arts beat, since I know full well that left critics are to critics as military music is to music. It's just as annoying to be labeled a "radical academic," since confusing education with political action is just the kind of thing that leaves the professoriat vulnerable to sniping both from the more-working-class-than-thou folks and the Right.

Finally, that term *public intellectual* has the great advantage of crossing institutional boundaries, without disparaging them. Although I value my autonomy, I'm also grateful for the resources and collegiality of the institutions through which I've worked. Much of the journalism I have gratefully conducted within the orbit of *In These Times*. The weekly newspaper is the 1974 creation of left historians, especially James Weinstein, who joined a commitment to social equity with a passionate aversion to cant and dogma and a conviction in the force of properly informed argument. Much of my academic work has been done at American University's School of Communication, where Dean Sanford Ungar convinced me that returning to academe was a good idea. As an advocate, I worked at the United Church of Christ, long noted for its progressive activism, with a wide-open mandate from Beverly Chain, and with great encouragement from her predecessor, the Reverend Everett Parker. All of these creative administrators found an intersection between their organization's needs and a cultural critic's curiosities.

## Cultivating Curiosity

Cultural criticism, when the culture is capitalism, has no neat career trajectory. I began by dashing off movie reviews for a student paper as a diversion from my research as an aspiring historian of capitalist culture. As an undergraduate I studied with special interest the rise and decline of the English in India and China. As a graduate student I focused, with the help of eminent scholar Stuart Schwartz, on the colonial cultures of Spain and Portugal. I came to understand them as the pioneer empires of the capitalist era that has now become our "natural" universe. I gained a great respect for the ways in which capitalism has gradually become global, for how it has both transformed and been transformed by cultures, and for its vitality and adaptability.

This work showed me the limitations both of traditional top-down historical methods and the then-fashionable Marxism that relegated all the interesting questions about why we do what we do to "superstructure." It gave me respect for insights of structuralist and semiotic analysis, and also renewed my admiration for the humanist tradition in scholarship and criticism. It allowed me to travel to and live in Mexico, Central America, Brazil, and Portugal, where I first really came to terms with the cultural implications of power and specifically of imperialism and neo-imperialism, both in the lives of the long-dead people I studied and in my own.

And it left me with too many questions about how things work, how culture is formed, to settle down into the academic subculture of colonial history. When I was offered the job of building the cultural section of *In These Times*, I saw an opportunity to take my curiosities about culture and power and marry them to my will to contribute to a more just democracy. I wanted the section to be able to interpret not just the drawbacks but the possibilities of a consumer society to readers who, by and large, already worked in some social reform movement.

When I just got too tired of working with no budget, I went on to the monthly magazine of the American Film Institute, *American Film*, in Washington, D.C. The magazine soon moved, without me, to New York, in the first of a series of buyouts. I stayed, having been captured by Washington, D.C., where power was on parade, even if artlessly disguised as tedious policy process. Charmed by the fact that the policy process was all, putatively, open to a public that by and large had no idea even where that open door was, I worked up some basic expertise. Moving briefly from journalism to advocacy, in the mid-1980s I was a policy analyst for the United Church of Christ (UCC) Office of Communications. It was heady and sometimes terrifying to design UCC's communications policy agenda, especially when the whole operation was conducted out of a corner of my bedroom. We tried to disguise its bare-bones quality, but I did wince once when at a reception an industry lawyer leaned over his wine to ask, "All I want to know is, when is the United Church of Christ going to upgrade from a dot-matrix printer?" I was caught between the thrill of knowing he'd read our comments in a current FCC docket and the embarrassment of being caught out barefoot at the ball. Just printing them out in regular dot-matrix format had taken me the better part of a day, coaxing each page out of the cantankerous machine; if I had used the fine format, we might not have made the deadline. But those guys had already gone laser, and they had paralegals to babysit the hardware.

After a few small successes, one big one, and one too many lunches with telephone company flacks, and with a mild but not unconquerable sense of guilt, I left advocacy, returned to journalism, and was eventually invited to teach at American University in the School of Communication. Teaching gave me new contact with the children of our commercial culture, and new opportunities to extend my own cultural analysis.

## Telling the Story

Whatever the subject matter, I approach it as a reporter (armed, of course, with those research skills that historians get). The world has always seemed to me so much more surprising than any kind of prediction about it, that I always want to measure argument against reality—to find out exactly what does happen, for instance, when people launch video distributors, make independent films, finally get their own TV channel, or are asked by the federal government exactly how they might use reserved spectrum for noncommercial use. My conversations with artists and builders of what I call "electronic public spaces" have told me much more than I could have imagined about the challenge of finding something to say and someone to say it to and with. Some of my best sources have been business reporters and corporate executives.

Although my critical writing has a variety of forms and audiences, I try always to write as clearly and simply as I can. Just how clear and simple that can get depends on subject and audience, as well as on my own frail abilities. I remember once when we were all working on telephone policy, a friend called me up to crow, "I just wrote 1,200 words without a *single acronym!*" I was very impressed. My reader is the intelligent lay person, someone who probably would see the beauty and importance in a subject that I see if I could explain it clearly.

My relationship with that intelligent lay reader is different, though, in different places. When it comes to movies and television, people read with a sense of self-confidence and open curiosity that is unequaled in any other critical form. Readers never seem to feel any deference toward reviewers, no matter how erudite; they know how they reacted to the movie, and they'll flay you for pretension. They also love you for putting your finger on something, even if it's something they never considered. Furthermore, and even better, they will soon consider it theirs.

My policy analysis, conducted for foundations, nonprofits (including public television), and government agencies, has been an entirely different relationship. There, I can speak with and to people who have the power to shift resources. It was something of a shock to me when I watched the Reagan-appointed head of the Federal Communications Commission inaugurate a new telephone welfare service for poor people, after we (and our allies at the Consumer Federation of America) had argued it was the decent thing to do.

My academic work has perhaps most surprised me, in terms of audience. Having come to adulthood within academe, I had cultivated many of its self-dismissive poses, its frustrations with all the academic excesses and pretensions. But my academic journal articles, several of which are republished here, have reverberated far beyond their original venues. They have been entered in court cases, they have been dragged into FCC dockets, they have been assigned in courses, spurred arguments among other academics, and been used by activists and even journalists.

In the academic articles, I began to explore more consistently than in my journalism the idea of electronic public spaces. I think this concept is wonderfully rich, if more a suggestion than a reality. It draws on notions of the public in John Dewey's work, of civil society in the work of Antonio Gramsci, of the public sphere in Jürgen Habermas's work, and on the connections that James Carey has made with all these thinkers and more in his work on communication. Each of these authors takes a different approach to the architecture of public relationships, but they share the conviction that a healthy, self-governing society needs specifically public relationships and activities.

In one sense, it is simply astonishing to me that any society, even one that prides itself on its democratic aspect, lets people like me have a public platform. I have taken great pleasure in publishing in free weeklies and in prestige dailies. I am surprised that a television series I worked on, *Signal to Noise,* has been shown in all major markets in the United States. It always delights me to discover how many old friends I rediscover on every soundprint I leave on National Public Radio. But I'm also impressed with the low tolerance level, not only for my voice but for anything in the same ballpark as my perspective or project, in mainstream media. Commercial radio and television have scant space for conversation in any ordinary meaning of the term. Magazine journalism caters religiously and obsequiously to the logic of demographics, with the frail last bastions of serious opinion journalism shrunk to a space about equal to the closest friends of the editor du jour. Newspapers are extraordinarily politically sensitive both at the level of office politics and at the level of institutional power.

Will it all be different as the information age dawns? When I started out, aspiring writers built up their finger muscles, in order to hit the keys hard enough to make two clear carbon copies. I have since been stationed permanently on the cutting edge of the communications revolution, although rarely by choice. Writers with multiple clients and bosses have been, whether we wanted to be or not, the debuggers of technologies that later became user-friendly and part of our lives. As well, I have watched entire industry patterns morph and morph again. I am now watching all of old media shudder before the challenge of networking. There is a lot to learn, during this wrenching transition, from how people have faced the introduction of new technologies in the last half of the twentieth century, and what they have used them for. I believe that the concerns for fairness and democracy that have shaped my explorations into media over the past decades will continue to be central in a networked era.

I am grateful to the staff of the University of Minnesota Press, including Micah Kleit and Carrie Mullen; to reviewers, including Larry Grossberg, Barbara Abrash, Steve Schwartzman, and an anonymous reviewer, for a process that always kept the goals of my project in the center; to my colleagues at American University, who have supported me in ways that have turned colleagues into friends; and to my family, always an inspiration. I would also like to acknowledge the importance, throughout my working life, of the inspirational example provided by people who combine generosity of spirit and critical judgment. Many people blessed with this gift have supported my endeavors, too many and in too many ways to itemize here. I owe them each a particular debt of gratitude, which must be paid in the promise to keep working in the spirit of their example.

**Part I. Popular Culture in Context**

# Capitalist Culture

# and

# the Left

When I was first hired as cultural editor of *In These Times* in 1978, I asked the editors what they expected of the cultural section of a left-wing weekly. "That's what we expect you to show us," one said. "What we know is that politics isn't the same thing as culture."

It was a real challenge, meeting that expectation over the course of the next decade.

For *In These Times*, politics is the prosaic complex of institutions, structures, and actions through which people organize consciously for social change, not the ideological milieu implied by the New Left slogan "The personal is the political," or the environment proposed by post-Foucauldian arguments on the pervasive inscription of power. The newspaper was founded with a commitment to nonsectarian approaches toward democratic socialism, approaches that avoid self-marginalization and political fundamentalism. Richard Rorty would put it in the Reformist Left category. It is read largely by leftists who do organizing or other practical political work, through labor unions, universities and schools, churches, nonprofit organizations, and local and regional government. These are smart people, many of whom are not intellectuals, and who mostly come home late and tired.

The newspaper's perspective neatly demystifies political action—that is, it separates political actions from oppositional attitude and subcultural personal gesture. But it leaves a cultural editor out there alone, between organizers who justifiably sneer at academic fops and intellectuals who rightly disdain the unproblematized.

But I gradually honed a notion of what our job as critics was, in the cultural section at (of course) the back of the book. It wasn't, in my conception, a small task, and certainly not as small as our resources, which approached zero. Just as the Left has social change toward greater equity as a mandate, I reasoned, the left critic's job is to chart how culture is shaped, so that we can understand how it changes and seize opportunities to change it in ways that create possibilities for greater social justice. Culture, in this sense, doesn't just mean the arts, but the assumptions, attitudes, and actions that make up our lives as we experience them. The arts create cultural texts in which those tissues of the social fabric are finely woven.

I figured that it wasn't my or my writers' job just to offer a consumer guide, to judge what is good or bad, but rather to explore how the concepts "good" and "bad" are constituted. It's all too easy to substitute for the good art/bad art judgment one based on good politics/ bad politics or good intentions/bad intentions. At the same time, I thought we still had the responsibility to exercise the moral judgment inherent in all criticism, but often unspoken in criticism that operates at the center of cultural hegemony. We tried to create ways for people to think about both mainstream and marginalized cultural expressions in social terms—as processes and results of social relationships, and with implications for them.

## Suspicion and Desire

It was much, much easier to set that broad critical agenda than to exercise it. The reasons were several, but the simple and obvious fact that there was no single left aesthetic was an overarching one. Balkanized political and cultural experience cripples the debate that is the critic's field of play. Our readership did, of course, share a suspicious attitude toward commodity culture. In fact, that may have been, in my experience, their broadest shared conviction—which is a problem, since it signaled the fact that commodity culture was their cultural common denominator. By *commodity culture* I mean the production of meaning through commodities, tangible and intangible, with the profit objective overriding everything else—MTV and the McMansion phenomenon and the sport utility vehicle (SUV) and cell phones as much as *Star Wars* and Godzilla licensing and Spice Girls. This is the process that gained momentum after World War II and now seems capable of sweeping us entirely away. People like Jackson Lears and Tom Engelhardt and Joshua Meyerowitz are just some of the people whose telling of pieces of that story *In These Times* readers and I enjoyed during my years there; Thomas Frank among others has since stunningly continued the story. Commodity culture, then, conditions the terms under which any alternatives to it can emerge. By *alternatives,* I mean activities that construct meaning with a primary objective that is not profit, and that address the potential audience primarily as something other than a consumer.

The fact that leftists lacked a shared aesthetic wasn't that surprising. After all, there wasn't—and still isn't—a broad leftist *political* movement in the United States. There was no milieu in which such expression could be fostered, even though many people shared, as they share today, a distrust of big government, big business, and market-oriented solutions. It's an ugly little circle. Cultural balkanization follows on political balkanization and reinforces it in turn. This wasn't a pattern exclusive to the Left, of course.

I did not lack for a range of habits and tastes on the Left. Among *In These Times* readers, virtually absent is the stern demand for "politically correct art" that typifies sectarian approaches. In my tenure, I found cautiously conservative and sentimental taste quite common, especially among union people, but it was far from universal. A vocal contingent of academics, professionals seasoned in the 1960s, was always ready to pounce on the lack of subtlety, creeping cheerleading, or sentimentality. Their critical acuteness, however, often seemed exercised for the satisfaction of intellectual one-upmanship; when I begged them to write, point me to other writers, serve on the board, there was almost always a stunned silence. Even today, I treasure the people who didn't turn me down, like Michael Kazin, Judith Kegan Gardiner, and Joel Schechter.

There was an old guard of leftists for whom being able to experience high art—theater, dance, visual arts—was a mark of victory against the limits put on the working class. Many of these people once participated in left sectarian movements of the '30s and '40s, which did create subcultures of their own. Some of them, like the wily sportswriter Lester Rodney and the generous scriptwriter Walter Bernstein, had that rarest and most treasured of characteristics, a sense of humor. That generation now is passing, and I miss their zest.

There was a group of readers who lived "alternative" lifestyles, in cooperative arrangements, shared jobs, searching out products and services from like-minded people. These people typically were formed in the days of the New Left; they leaned toward the moralistic and the earnest, in a long American tradition. And there was a budding crop of young people nurtured on an environmental-feminist ethic.

Many of these people were white and heterosexual. The cultures of color in America—blacks (as the term was then), Chicanos, Neoricans, Japanese Americans, and other premulticulturalist categories—shaped the habits and expectations of each of these groups in ways that might or might not intersect with an agenda of social equity. Too often, I encountered one of the twin evils of cheerleading and paternalism—your coverage of black film is bad because you're white; it's an important novel because it was written by a Hispanic; you're homophobic because you won't let our activists cover our events—and too infrequently I found ways to showcase the cultural construction of ethnicity and gender in American culture.

The Left has had its moments of cultural identity. Consider Communist Party–led culture of the '30s and '40s, or the New Left counterculture of the '60s and '70s. Both were set in motion by political movements—resistance to the Depression, civil rights—and both were strongly marked by the historical juncture and the nature of the political movement. The former collapsed from a kind of involution, following the same fate as the party's sectarian politics. The counterculture, both resistance to and expression of a postwar youth culture, eventually became engulfed by commodity culture, which can use as many revolutions per minute as are fed into the marketing machinery. Both cases were exceptional moments in American left history.

The problem of a variety of cultural habits could be seen in my tenure at the newspaper in the absence of two frequently suggested features: a recipe column and a gossip column. The brown rice casserole one reader wanted to see would surely have offended the reader who only had fifteen minutes to cook (out too late organizing!) and wanted a cans-in-a-pan special. One reader's hot gossip tip would draw a blank with another and offend a third. And almost every attempt at humor or satire that we tried in the cultural section plunged *In These Times* into a swamp of misunderstanding. Once during the Sandinista era in Nicaragua (an era that we covered scantily, to the horror of many of our readers), we ran a satirical sketch, "The American Leftists (*Progressivus Sandinistis Supportoris*)." The typical characteristic of this peculiar animal included "Know some of the words to 'The Internationale'" and "Love Thai food and greasy diners." Indignant letters poured in. The problem wasn't that "the Left can't take a joke," but that there was no single entity, "the Left," to take it.

This cultural balkanization was highlighted for me as well in the tenuous relationship between artists and leftists. The New York art scene was full of people who felt—or at least that's how it seemed to me—that they were probably too good for the likes of us, but that we should cover them anyway. Our readership may have been their first encounter with audiences significantly different from themselves. There were artists like authors Alice Walker and Marge Piercy, dramaturge R. G. Davis, singer-songwriters like Pete Seeger, Si Kahn, and Holly Near, producing work that emerged from the experience of a coherent left aesthetic of another era or subculture. And some artists, such as filmmaker Errol Morris, story-teller Spalding Gray, and novelist Evan Connell, didn't see themselves as part of a political movement, although their work was interesting to people concerned with how we interpret and change the world around us.

It was our job to locate the aesthetic challenge put forward by these different people to readers who often understood artists as an instrumental resource, perhaps to produce an organizing tape or a poster. These were readers who railed against commercial crap but were irritated by anything that seemed obscure, potentially offensive (perhaps not to them but to their constituencies), or "homemade." The most common notion of the cultural section that I met from our board members was that it should be a lure to readers in order to get them to pick up the newspaper and read the "real" news.

Leftists may not like *Seinfeld,* or the *Titanic,* or John Grisham. But they know by brand name who and what they're rejecting. They practically can't help it. It blares out at them from the supermarket checkout counter. Our criticism and cultural reporting on mainstream culture—TV programs, advertisements, popular movies—ended up being a central feature of the section, and it was very popular with *In These Times* readers. Often they wanted their own opinions confirmed, which is typical of consumer-guide review readers generally and can make for interesting dialogue. They were also interested in behind-the-scenes reporting, just like anybody else who watches *Entertainment Tonight.*

### Entertainment, Every Night

So maybe the greatest challenge I faced was designing a program for constructive criticism of mainstream culture and its expression in the arts. The sharp-tongued critic can have a field day with the dead heart of mainstream commodity culture, in terms of style. It's fun to mock the

New Age sentimentality of a *The Horse Whisperer*, or the bloated corpse of a *Godzilla*. I had a wonderful time with *Gandhi*, one of the most patently colonialist costumers I ever saw. But it's also too easy to get glib or complacent in one's carping, as I learned when a blizzard of angry letters arrived to complain that I had been mean to a movie that meant well. Anyway, that caviling approach fits too well within the terms of commoditized criticism, whether the opinion-nuggets mixed with image-nuggets that TV reviewers provide or the slick opinions and pictures retailed in *Vanity Fair*. The focus is on products, not processes, and on what's hot and what's not.

The hard part was stripping commodity culture of its apparent naturalness to reveal its social construction, and not simply pointing fingers and decrying the hand of capitalism at work. We were always hungry for the kind of article we could never pay for, one that could explain popular culture's popularity, taking business, art, and the audience all seriously. The landscape was full of likely targets. Consider, for example, the long-range success of broadcaster Paul Harvey and the splash success of Howard Stern, neither explained alone by the vagaries of the radio business and both dismissed only at one's peril. Howard Stern is a creature of broadcast deregulation, and also a troubling icon of postmodern masculinity. Paul Harvey's success is a particularly fascinating personal trajectory across a changing landscape of commodity culture; he is the lost soul of the domesticated American incarnate (see "Paul Harvey and the Culture of Resentment").

I found that a historian's training stood me in good stead and helped me to avoid the teleological curse in leftist analysis inherited from the Frankfurt School, in which reified abstractions such as capitalism inevitably grind out *Lethal Weapons*. It helped me to appreciate how volatile commodity culture is, and how its constant permutations are not purely a result of innovations, opportunities, and challenges strictly within its terms. Television's look, for instance, has been greatly altered by the work of video artists experimenting with new technologies, as MTV demonstrates. It is hard to imagine a *Cosby*, with all its limitations, occurring before civil rights changed the racial landscape. *China Beach* and *Tour of Duty* provided peculiar resolutions to the conflicts still alive in the United States about the Vietnam War. But their existence alone, as prime-time TV series, testified to the importance of those conflicts (see "Vietnam Grunts R Us"). The growth of *X-Files* fanaticism measures inelegantly the sense of disconnection between citizens and their governments, and provides an interesting contrast to other eras in science fiction (see "When Any Alien Looks Good").

Within the terms of commodity culture, surprising stuff gets made, and it's been worth signaling it where it happens, and even asking how it did. *Bulworth*, Warren Beatty's simply astonishing film about what politicians don't and can't see and say, defies all the ordinary marketplace logics. John Sayles's movies, such as *Lone Star*, operate within the expectations of the mall cineplex but center on social tensions and conflicts. The too-little-seen film by Jonathan Kaplan *Heart like a Wheel* has as its driving narrative the struggle of a woman to become her own person (it's the true story of Shirley Muldowney, top award-winner in drag racing). *A World Apart* showed, unlike *Cry Freedom*, that one could make an anti-apartheid movie featuring whites, and one that did not divorce political issues from human drama. Films like *Hour of the Star* and *Sugar Cane Alley*, in styles that owe much to neorealism but also to the dramatic traditions of international feature film, put names and faces and psychological intensity to social issues of poverty in Latin America. *Mississippi Masala*, *Bhaji on the Beach*, and *Hate* are part of a film trend that testifies to the coalescing of transborder cultures. As interesting as the formal properties of these works are the stories of their distribution and reception.

At *In These Times* in those early days, it was important for us to look not only at products but at institutions, including those bastions of traditional "high culture," museums. What difference does it make if museums reframe the past? That's a good question for a critic. Smithsonian exhibits that built a reputation for public history, such as "Field to Factory" (about black northward migration) and "A More Perfect Union" (about Japanese American internment during World War II), followed by the debacle of the *Enola Gay* controversy, all provided good material for us.

### Beyond the Well-Intentioned

If there's one word I would like to collect a nickel for every time I heard it while I was an editor, it's *empowerment*. Everybody knows that cultural expression is empowering; everybody wants it; but nobody really wants to read about somebody else's empowerment, especially when it's just asserted and not proved. And there was little consensus about who were the important, interesting, relevant artists outside the mainstream. So our coverage of out-of-mainstream artists had to overcome hurdles of disinterest tinged with mild guilt ("I ought to care about Holly Near or Dario Fo or the Labor Heritage festival, but I don't"). Our coverage also had to counter suspicion on the part of many readers who would spy cultural

Stalinism or in-group cheerleading in any positive coverage of Left-oriented cultural expression.

In covering alternative, independent, or subcultural expression, our main problem was avoiding softhearted good will on the one hand, and preemptive cynicism on the other. When we were faced with a video project done with a tenants group in New Jersey or with black schoolchildren in Chicago, or locally staged dramas drawn from rural tradition in Kentucky, or a photographic display in the Museo del Barrio in New York, we needed to set the scene as well as evaluate the work. We needed to give our readers context, to make them care. What obstacles were faced, what techniques used to overcome them, and did they work? We wanted not merely to find noble or interesting examples but to highlight strategies that might be interesting to our organizing-oriented audience, even if they would never see the performance, the exhibit, the slide show. Regional media arts workshop Appalshop; the Deep Dish TV enterprise; Service Employees International Union; and Oil, Chemical and Atomic Worker plays, videos, and other cultural projects; and New Day Films distributors were all examples of cultural work that we featured.

Inevitably, there was a sobriety about this kind of criticism and cultural reporting. It lacks snap. Of course it does. It can't depend on celebrities, and certainly not on ironic references, comparisons with similar but more familiar work, and perhaps most important, on the assurance that the readers share something in common in their approach to the work. But the real job was the same one we faced in criticism of commodity culture: to locate work within the appropriate context and to create reader interest in the challenge that faced the creators.

## Business as Usual

Even in order to chart an agenda like this, it was critically important to learn about the terms of doing business in the entertainment industry, which now produces the second-largest export product in the United States. Business conditions affect public access to communication and therefore the options for cultural change. Trade magazines like *Variety, Editor & Publisher,* and *Broadcasting & Cable* gave me a crash course in the business side of commodity culture. And it quickly became obvious that in electronic media especially—broadcasting, cable TV, and increasingly the Internet—you can't get far understanding the terms of doing business unless you understand the role of government. Regulatory agencies, Congress, arts and humanities entities, the courts: I came to see each of them as a richly informative site of struggle over who will control what we take to be reality. Reading legal briefs and FCC (Federal Communications Commission) dockets, I came to feel like a spy in the culture wars.

I never thought it was our job to tell readers that capitalists make entertainment products for profit, although they sometimes complained that we didn't. But I figured they already knew that coming in. The trick was to make the business news meaningful. What effect do mergers and takeovers have on the quality of network and local news, if any? If the FCC blithely deregulates broadcasting, does public service at the local level suffer? (See "After the Fairness Doctrine.") What implications do funding guidelines at the endowments have for works that express American cultural diversity? Does the privatization trend in European TV threaten U.S. independent filmmakers, who have long depended on sales to public TV there? If cable companies achieve First Amendment claims against municipalities, what is the fate of public access cable? (See "Access Cable TV as Electronic Public Space" and "Access Cable in Action.")

One of my beats became public broadcasting because it's an institution that could provide, on a community-wide and even nationwide scale, alternatives to commodity television culture. Public TV has over the past two decades so lost a sense of mission, however, that it has imperiled its reason to be publicly funded. I wanted my articles both to document problems and to keep in mind what was at stake, and why it was worth caring about (see "The What and How of Public Broadcasting" and "Public Television and the Public Sphere").

## The Left and the Rest

This approach to cultural reporting and criticism was not, I came to believe, something that was merely appropriate for a left-wing publication. Our readership was, and still is, particularly inclined to cast a critical eye on the status quo. But it is also typical of the general population in other ways. Like it or not, everyone participates in commodity culture. Also, underneath the shimmering surface of consensus brought to us twenty-four-seven, the general population increasingly suffers the experience of social balkanization that was so boldly evident on the left.

I think there are many people who would ask questions about the way the world is organized, or would take a step out of their private daily routine to participate in a social action, group, or movement, or would simply stand up in a work situation to say that they think something is wrong—if they didn't think they were all alone. There are many people who would rather take some kind of positive action in their own communities than mutter in disgruntlement about the anonymous systems in which their lives seem to be trapped—if they thought it was reasonable and possible.

The naming involved in cultural expression is a powerful counterforce to the rootless anxiety that seems to mark our era and cripple action. The cut-up quality of modern life can too easily lead to a dulling of the conviction that what we do and who we become matters. Challenging criticism and sound cultural reporting can let people know that having principles, integrity, critical voices, and projects that resist the impetus toward greed, self-indulgence, ignorance, and cruelty is important, right where we are, within our communities. The meager demonstration of that kind of critical project that we were able to do at *In These Times* is only one small experiment in what can be a much larger journalistic project: making capitalist culture a reportorial beat that shares pride of place with other front-page news informing a democratic public.

# Growing Up

# Is Hard to Do

# in Kidpix

*Movies are products of intensive, collaborative effort to ride cultural waves, so it's no wonder critics spy social meaning in popular movie trends. I was grateful to my insightful editor, Craig LaMay, at what was then the Gannett Center Journal for asking me, as the '90s began, to look back at a wave of '80s movies about suburban high school kid culture.*

Through a funhouse mirror, '80s movies set in high school reflected disturbing social realities—about the power of commercial youth culture, about authority, about the powerful dividers of class and race. And they could make you feel downright sorry for the teacher.

Of course, it's only a movie. The troubling part comes when you realize that movies draw, if not on reality, on widespread perceptions of reality, in order to sell. It gets worse when you realize that sometimes not only the kids but our nation's educational leaders seem to be more in sync with Hollywood than with the problems of their own local schools.

In the late '70s and early '80s a subgenre bloomed, the comedy or drama set in a middle-class high school. Kidpix, as they were known in the trade, were a product of marketing demographics—big ones. Teen spending in the United States was becoming a significant category. Indeed, by the early 1990s it matched the size of the Argentine national economy.

13

Soon after *American Graffiti* became a monster hit in 1973, the hand-writing was on the wall, or on the concession stand: the money was in the twelve-to-twenty-four crowd, especially the teens, who go to the same movie repeatedly and who have unprecedented spending power. Then *National Lampoon's Animal House* hit the kid jackpot in 1978. Kidpix—movies like *Fast Times at Ridgemont High* (1982), *Risky Business* (1983), *The Breakfast Club* (1985), among so many others that their titles and images blur in the mind—raked in dollars for the entertainment indus-try during the '80s. Of course, the not-yet-married have always been the staple audience of theatrical movies. But pre–youth culture, when young people were still second-class citizens in the marketplace, they wanted to see movies about adults.

It only makes good marketing sense that kidpix put the focus on the kids. And not just on them, but on the separate and lucrative commercial culture they're immersed in—from bedroom hideaways with beamed-in music videos, to their jobs and social life at the shopping mall. Education often isn't even in the picture; it's the irritant, the pointless information that clogs up a perfectly good weekend, hallway romance, or impish adventure.

What may raise an eyebrow is that in kidpix, usually set in a perpetu-ally sunny, generic middle-class America, social conflict is a driving ele-ment. That might seem surprising, not only in a society where most poll respondents self-identify as middle class but in an industry where the cardinal rule still is, "If you want to send a message, call Western Union." But it makes sense if you're looking to propel a drama enclosed by the world of middle-class high schoolers.

The American high school has been celebrated as "the last classless so-ciety," the last social moment in most American lives when people of dif-ferent social tiers mix. To some degree, given residential patterns and seg-regation, that's always been a fiction. But it's true that high school—the institution that serves that demographic creation of industrial society, adolescence—is a society unto itself, and that its world is as much about socialization as it is about formal education. And it's more classful than classless. As John Sayles's *Baby, It's You* (1983), a cross-class high school love affair set in the '60s, showcased, the social tensions of the wider so-ciety are enacted there more intensely than people have to experience them before or after in their lives.

But in the pre–youth culture era, teachers along with parents and par-ents' associations acted vigorously as a governor over the furnace of social conflict. They had a crucial advantage: the students' own aspiration to be adults. They were, willy-nilly, role models as well as enforcers.

Eighties kidpix handily abolished this element. At their bubbliest, they not only put the kids in the center of their stories but made authorities the butt of the joke, often not even giving them the dignity of a weighty villain. At their darkest, movies like *River's Edge* (1986) and *Suburbia* (1983, also known as *The Wild Side*) bleakly showcased middle-class adolescent nihilism, predicated on a despair about adults and adulthood generally. (*River's Edge*, drawn from a real-life murder incident, appealed more to critics than to teenagers, though; and the independently made *Suburbia* sank into a distribution black hole.) Either way, they sold the image of a hermetically autonomous adolescence.

## Kids in Charge

In these films, students wage their social battles on their own, with the weapons of consumer culture: fashion, celebrity, attitude. (Not often drugs, though—in the Hollywoodized middle-class high school, that's the big unmentionable.) Attitude is that endlessly transmutable feature of teen identity, to which all the commercial accoutrements contribute.

The kids, not the teachers, are in charge of their own education. As the heroine (Winona Ryder) of the black comedy *Heathers*—one-stop shopping for teen-film stereotypes, and a punchy satire of the subgenre—says of the most viciously popular girl in school: "Heather says she teaches people how to live." The teachers, by contrast, function as convenient enemies and buffoons, icons of the bleak promise of adulthood and the separate reality of youth culture.

Classroom learning is patently irrelevant. New Deal policies, the Russian Revolution, the Platt Amendment, frog dissection—it's all just dropped in to signal that stuff we have to get right for the test but that has no relevance to our lives. (Quick, what *was* the Platt Amendment?) And it's not even a question of making it relevant. Let the eponymous hero (Matt Broderick) of *Ferris Bueller's Day Off* (1986) explain it, as he faces the prospect of studying about European socialism: "I don't plan on being European. They could be fascists or anarchists; that wouldn't change the fact that I don't have a car."

Good thing Ferris didn't go on *Bill and Ted's Excellent Adventure* (1989)—although, come to think of it, it might not have made much difference in his attitude. In that helium-weight comedy, a garage band duo are plunged, by a character from the future, into the past, European and elsewhere, so that they can pass their history oral report. They capture

Socrates, Genghis Khan, and Lincoln among others, who are dazzled by mall culture and finally boogie for the student assembly. In a music-video-like performance, Lincoln delivers a parody of the Gettysburg Address, with the rousing finale: "Let's party, dudes!" Indeed, not only the present but the future belong to the lunkish Bill and Ted: their guardian has rescued them from imminent separation (Ted's policeman father wants to send him to military school if he doesn't pass history class) because in the future, entire society is built around worship of Bill and Ted's heavy metal band.

If learning is irrelevant, so are the teachers, universally nerds, jerks, or tyrants. Authority is the traditional butt of American movie comedy, of course, but here when authority is funny, it is because it's vacuous. When authority is the enemy, it's because it's petty, arbitrary, irrelevant to the passions and issues of the kids. Even the tyrants are only tyrants up to the parking lot (and their cars aren't nearly as nice as those of the students). The occasional good adult authority, like the mad scientist of *Back to the Future* (1985), is a nonestablishment figure, an idiosyncratic fringe element who resonates to the kids' self-perception.

The teachers are mere obstacles—some more amusing buffoons than others—to the real business of life. They certainly have no relation to the students other than prison guard or torturer. Take the history teacher of *Fast Times at Ridgemont High*, who shows up in the poster-decorated bedroom—which looks strangely like one of the MTV video-jockey sets—of the gonzo surfer on the night of the big dance, solely in order to grill him on the American Revolution and thus take his revenge for the surfer's insolence. (Only a movie made from a teen perspective would show a teacher wasting his own weekend evening to grill a sloucher.) In *The Breakfast Club*, a cruelly authoritarian teacher—he's forgotten how to be a kid—interns the students with sneering contempt and then grouses to the janitor, a failed but resigned '60s idealist, about how the kids are "worse" every year. And in *Back to the Future*, the teacher's only role is to shred the self-esteem of the hero (Michael J. Fox). "You've got a real attitude problem," he says, adding that the boy's father did too. "No McFly ever amounted to anything in Hill Valley."

The teachers who try to get on the kids' wavelengths make the best butts of jokes. Take the touchy-feely ex-hippie of *Heathers*—a self-professed '60s idealist who evokes even the other teachers' scorn. (The near past is the most passionately rejected.) Faced with mounting apparent suicides in the school, she asks her students to join her to "connect this cafeteria into one mighty circuit." She's also alerted the media, of course, and exhorts the students: "On TV, let's show them how you *feel!*" The students mount a spectacle the irony of which bypasses the teacher, caught up in her own narcissistic dreaminess.

Ineffectual authority at school—Ferris Bueller's dean of students rails about his capacity to "govern this student body," making gaffe after gaffe—is echoed at home. But these parents aren't misguided authorities who need to wake up, like the parents of the 1955 *Rebel without a Cause.* Sometimes they're simply thugs, insensitively barking orders and criticism. Sometimes they're self-indulgent and neglectful. And sometimes they're patronized innocents, hapless dependents of their own children—or simply, pleasantly, absent. In any case, the old adolescent complaint, "They don't understand me," becomes in these movies, "They'd never understand us." Even in *The Breakfast Club,* where parents and teachers are responsible for the kids' misery—one kid says he stirred up trouble "for my old man; I wanted him to think I was cool" and another, asked why her parents are so bad, says in a whisper, "They ignore me"—the kids reject the teacher's command to write an essay on the theme "Who am I?" They ask, "Why do you care?" without expecting an answer, instead finding self-realization in a spontaneous group therapy session with each other.

The kids, who shop or work (or both) at the mall, struggle toward a sense of self in relation to each other and the challenge of the go-go '80s: making it. In the works of John Hughes, who either wrote or directed the major hits of this minigenre (*16 Candles* [1984], *Pretty in Pink* [1986], *The Breakfast Club, Some Kind of Wonderful* [1987]), that means climbing the social ladder one's peers have erected without losing your integrity. His '80s films (he recently directed *Home Alone*) usually featured some kind of hermetic class conflict, in which the heroes are the hard-working, misunderstood, poor kids, often in love with someone from the disparaged wealthy crowd. From locker room to high school hallway to the mall and back to the high school dance, the romance is pursued to a happy ending, when common decency is rediscovered and the myth of the universal middle class reaffirmed.

Success is sometimes romantic resolution, sometimes prestige, sometimes business, and sometimes all at once. The hero (played by Tom Cruise) of *Risky Business* overexemplifies the '80s when he manages to mount a successful prostitution ring out of his parents' upper-middle-class home, and even draws the Princeton recruiter into it. Other kids aspire to solvency, through hard work at the mall burger shop. Ferris Bueller's a hero because he's a consummate con man. At the end of *Back to the Future,* the hero achieves the ultimate success: he redesigns not only his life but his entire family's by altering the past, gaining upscale professional parents *and* a cool car of his own.

But it's hard work being cool, and they know it. The heroine of *Heathers* explains to the young psychopath who asks her why she hangs around with girls she doesn't like, "They're people I work with, and our job is being popular and shit." And the ultimate self-dramatizing melodrama, suicide, is always an option.

No wonder the teachers don't count. What do they know about popularity or '80s star Pat Benatar? What's the Platt Amendment compared to an abortion, suicide—or being without a car? Gone in these movies is the angst of *Rebel without a Cause,* where the James Dean character longed for proper patriarchy. These kids are playing on their own, for real, and for cash.

The kidpix explosion created a galaxy of new young stars, most of them (Molly Ringwald, Ally Sheedy, and Winona Ryder apart) male: Tom Cruise, Michael J. Fox, Sean Penn, Matt Broderick, Emilio Estevez, among others. These actors' stars rose with the popularity of the images they projected. The male characters, either bright screwups or cheerful dim bulbs, were droll wiseacres, seemingly juvenile but in reality new leaders of an insouciant youth culture. Their great achievement is one of performance, a bold, daring self-presentation. (It's interesting that the one high school film of this era that was interracial and cross-class, *Fame* [1979], was about a school of performing arts. There, teachers *could* exercise authority because they were a gateway to a life of performance.) Girls, in these films, win autonomy only in two gender-segregated arenas: fashion (among girls), and feeling (with the boys). The image of the white, middle-class teen world in these movies may be divorced from that of adults, but some things, like gender roles, don't change.

With the more sober and recessionary moment of the early 1990s, as well as with a shrinking teenage population, the gas went out of kidpix. They spoke as much to the bubble of false prosperity generally as they did to the power of the middle-class teen marketplace. The wryly anti-ideal nuclear family—think of *Married . . . with Children, The Simpsons,* and *Roseanne* on TV—launched a new trend. Kidpix also echoed, in teen terms, a pervasive '80s disillusionment among American consumers with authority, seen elsewhere, for instance, in the rash of films about Vietnam and its aftermath.

They also took populist, often self-contradictory myths of middle-class mobility—anyone can make it; being rich is bad, but getting rich is great;

the past is prologue; do it yourself; thumb your nose at authority and also get in charge; look for the individual solution to social problems—and put them to work within the malled confines of commercial youth culture. Maybe it's that rather lumpy collection of myths that then–Secretary of Education William Bennett responded to when, at the height of college student demonstrations for institutional disinvestment in South Africa–related stocks, he advised prospective college students, rather, to consider "disinvestment" in their stereo systems and spring vacations. And maybe it's that collection of myths that made it possible for Hollywood to trust—with good evidence at the box office—that films about the white middle class would appeal across racial and class lines among youthful audiences.

## Rich and Poor

Eighties movies about high school life at the upper and lower ends of the social spectrum more directly commented on the roiling tensions over education and its social function. What's scary is how well they echoed Republican rhetoric about the educational crisis among America's disadvantaged.

These movies—at the upper end of the scale, *Dead Poets Society* (1989), and at the lower end, *Stand and Deliver* (1987) and *Lean on Me* (1989)—were not pitched to the teen market, but to adults. They not only took place within school but were about school, and even about the classroom. In those movies, teachers were important, even life-saving, role models.

Of course, the goals of education are entirely different for the different classes. For the rich and white, it's about self-fulfillment, self-expression, stimulating the life of the imagination. For the poor and people of color, it's about discipline.

In the prep school of *Dead Poets Society*—set in a hazily post–World War II past—the putative protagonist is the boy who will eventually commit suicide, plagued by his rigid father's elite aspirations for him. But his central problem, as that of the film, is one of authority properly wielded, and that puts the teacher at the crux of the drama.

This is not a high school with teeming hallways. It's a small school, rich in tradition (the boys see pictures of their fathers on the wall). The boys are cowed by the combined authority of rigid masters and demanding parents, until Mr. Keating comes along. As played by Robin Williams, he's a sprite, but a sprite with bite. When he tells his students to tear out the pedantic introduction to their poetry books, by God they do it. When he tells them to jump up on his desk, they hop up there. When he commands them to have imagination, they produce it.

Mr. Keating's command to imaginative liberation takes place in the same intellectual universe that William Bennett so touted, first at the National Endowment for the Humanities and the Department of Education: in the safely splendid world of stamped-and-approved dead white male writers. No danger of ugly questions of multiculturalism or Afrocentric curricula here. These kids, ensconced not only in an all-white, all-male prep school but in the precomputer, predrugs era, rebel (on order by Keating, of course) by studying the Romantics and not the Realists. It's a timid example of Bennett's generous claim that the five-foot shelf could be expanded a foot or two if necessary. Although Keating presumably heralds the same imaginative wave that brought us the beatniks (and one of the kids wears a token beret), there's not a hint of the brewing cultural upset. And so *Dead Poets Society* offers a two-hour return to a spurious past, in which the educational questions boil down to more or less conformity within unquestioned confines.

Bennett also loved the heroes of two films about ghetto school teachers: Jaime Escalante in Los Angeles *(Stand and Deliver)* and Joe Clark in New Jersey *(Lean on Me)*. He heralded them, along with other charismatic figures who had a strong, disciplinary, pull-yourself-up-by-your-bootstraps message, for producing exemplary school environments "that work."

Escalante, a Bolivian immigrant and math teacher in the Los Angeles schools, has gotten students in a low-income, primarily Hispanic school to pass advanced placement calculus tests, with strong discipline and motivational methods that include cheerleading and prizes, personal attention to students' home lives, and Saturday sessions. His techniques have drawn fire from colleagues and teachers' unions because they require a much greater workload than normal. Indeed, however charismatic a teacher Escalante is, he's hardly a one-man solution to endemic educational problems among the Hispanic poor, a third of whom drop out before completing high school—the highest dropout rate in the country, and one that's growing.

Joe Clark, an African American teacher, came into a down-at-the-heels New Jersey school plagued with drug and discipline problems, and used harsh disciplinary methods, including expelling troublemakers and symbolized by his carrying a baseball bat in the halls. Proudly calling himself a dictator and likening high school to a plantation, he succeeds temporarily in bringing about order and improving test scores (mostly by kicking out the lowest scorers), but at the cost of a sky-high dropout rate and record-breaking teacher turnover.

Betting on a succession of tough-love educational Supermen and Rambos to turn the educational system around may not be much of an educational policy, especially if high schools are run like large factory prisons, with huge populations and class sizes. But it's great movie material. Hollywood does love a hero. And the minority poor, especially the young, are easy targets for a savior. They can be patronized like the white middle-class kids—subjects of the films pitched to them and their allowances and salaries—could never be.

*Stand and Deliver* is sensitive to the complexities of the teacher-student relationship, while still tub-thumping the bootstraps message. Made partly with public television money for PBS's *American Playhouse* by director Ramon Menendez, it's a low-key ensemble film, in which a provoking subdrama is that of the testing board's refusal to accept the high scores, portrayed as a case of institutional racism. Escalante—played by Edward James Olmos, who also had a significant role in the script—is bulwarked by a rich supporting cast, including then-rising stars Lou Diamond Phillips and Andy Garcia. Although we learn little about calculus—the story is about kids coming to realize they can make something of themselves—we do enter into the thick texture of personal relationships Escalante has with the students. Some of the film's heroes are the kids who despite awesome odds get a little taste of success.

*Lean on Me,* directed by the same John Avildsen who gave us *Rocky* (1976) and *The Karate Kid* I and II (1984, 1986), doesn't bother with subtleties. It openly cheerleads for tough-love policies, and if its hero (played by Morgan Freeman) goes a little overboard, it's all justified in the end. He's pitted not only against drug dealers (with the poor, Hollywood can acknowledge drugs) but the school board and the mayor; he "adopts" a boy and a girl student who are set straight. "This is not a damned democracy!" he shouts. "We are in a state of emergency, and my word is law." The students endorse him: "Mr. Clark believes in us!" "He's like a father!" The film ends with a face-off at the mayor's office between bureaucrats and kids, with Clark triumphant, Rocky-like, at the top of the steps.

In *Lean on Me,* the hero is Clark, who tramples namby-pamby liberals in his crusade for discipline. And here, discipline *is* education. Leave the quest for self-expression, the small groups, and the intimate and exploratory conversations to the prep school kids. In fact, what was the problem in *Dead Poets Society* is the solution in *Lean on Me.* Of course, neither the problem nor the solution even enters the equation in films pitched to teens themselves.

You expect the movies to thrive on heroes, stereotypes, and happy endings. So it's not surprising that in '80s high school movies, middle-class heroes were the teens themselves; upper-class heroes were emotional liberators; and lower-class heroes were law-and-order types. It's not surprising either that the movies should dramatize social tensions that infuse the high school experience. You might even see in '80s teen movies disturbing truths refracted about a collapse of faith in a future that proceeds, in anything but a miraculous way, from the recent past.

But in the end, it's only a movie, and in real life high schools, education, equity, and the challenge of authority properly wielded are still at issue. In real life, there's no way to go back to the future.

# Is Educational

# Children's TV

# Possible?

*This article began as a study, conducted with the Center for Media Education, of the 1993 syndication market in children's television. When we presented it in Congress—part of an assessment of the Children's Television Act of 1990—the National Association of Broadcasters howled and said we had unfairly blamed broadcasters for the behavior of syndicated program distributors. But in fact our research revealed even deeper problems than the ones we raised in Congress. I was delighted to be able to share with the journalistic audience of the* Media Studies Journal, *thanks to then-editor Ted Pease, both the research results and the larger issues. The syndication market has since evaporated in children's TV, poofed away by vertical integration in media businesses, but the marketing and programming trends described here have only intensified.*

It doesn't take getting up early too many Saturday mornings with the kids to convince yourself that there isn't much educational and informational programming for them on commercial broadcast TV, and that what there is, by and large, isn't very inspiring. And yet it can't be that hard, you might find yourself saying, to make programs that will do more for kids than convince them to buy brand-name paraphernalia (GI Joe guns! Pokémon cards! Mulan and Mighty Morphin Power Rangers birthday paper plates!) or take a ride on an action-packed roller coaster of slapstick events.

You might think that maybe you're just not looking in the right place, because after all Saturday morning is playtime, not schooltime. But you won't find much educational and informational on during the week either. In fact, most of the good-for-you stuff is shown on the weekend.

Or you might think you're just not watching at the right time. And there you'd be right, because you probably can't wake up early enough—before 8 or even 7 A.M.—to see a substantial minority of good-for-you shows.

But most probably, and like most Americans, you are not going to think much of anything about kids' TV. The furthest most of us get is an offhand discussion with an exercised conscience: "I watched a lot of TV and it didn't hurt me, I think"; "TV is a part of our culture that they'd better understand"; "They don't watch that much, and if I didn't have the TV while I'm making dinner, I'd go crazy." Most of us don't think of television as a potential educational resource, at all. We think of television the way it has come to us over the years, cheerfully complacent in its vulgarity and its bottom-line objectives. And if it's good enough for us . . .

Peggy Charren didn't have that reaction when she began her campaign for good kids' television three decades ago, founding Action for Children's Television and striking fear into network executives. She thought it was an outrage that a civilized society would let television do nothing more than hawk junk to kids—sitting ducks for pitchmen—when it wasn't plain ignoring children. And it's hard to disagree. Television isn't the only influence on our children's lives, but it's one captivating one. Broadcasters are in a for-profit business, but they're also licensees of the public airwaves and required to serve the public interest.

Charren's dogged persistence finally pushed the Children's Television Act of 1990 into existence, over the objections of a Republican president. It was to be her organization's swan song; she retired in 1993. The act says that broadcast stations (the part of the TV industry directly beholden to Congress for licenses) must carry some educational and informational kids' programming and must show the Federal Communications Commission (FCC) at license time what they did for kids.

The Republican-led FCC at the time the law was passed wrote the kind of wink-wink regulations that made it easy for broadcasters not to take the law seriously. It wasn't until Charren's inheritors, the Washington-based Center for Media Education (CME), motivated legislators and regulators in the new Clinton administration to reexamine the market and the law that the act took on substance.

One of the things that CME, in conjunction with Georgetown University's Center for Public Representation, did to insist on compliance was to study broadcasters' license renewals and to publicize the sillier things they found. Some stations claimed, for instance, that shows like *Leave It to Beaver, The Jetsons,* and *GI Joe* were educational. Publicizing those claims put egg on broadcasters' faces. If they hated the public shaming, and the attention it brought from Congress and the Clinton-era FCC, they also decided—this was in late 1992 and early 1993—to start putting on programs they could defend without looking ridiculous.

In early 1994, CME asked me to look at the commercial broadcast marketplace for educational and informational children's programs over the past year, to see how broadcasters had risen to the challenge. I decided to talk to the providers of programming, as well as to some key decision makers at the four major networks, to get a better understanding of how it works. I ended up talking to around fifty people.

It was pretty easy to figure out what had happened in 1993. Everybody who had a program remotely plausible as an educational/informational show—or as they instantly became known, "FCC-friendly," a term that let everyone know just how cynical people inside the industry were about the law—immediately hauled it to a market or took out an ad. The industry magazines made comprehensive lists of these shows—there were more than seventy-five—by midsummer.

Stations went shopping and made sure they had at least one show they could wave before the FCC. If they were affiliates, they might get it through a network, since each of them had at least one FCC-friendly show (CBS's science show *Beakman's World*; NBC's teen show on careers, *Name Your Adventure*; ABC's science show *Cro*; Fox's geography show *Where on Earth Is Carmen Sandiego?* belatedly replacing *Bobby's World*, with its prosocial values) cleared by their own lawyers for the season. Or they might buy something from a syndicator.

The syndicators' deals virtually all worked on what's known as barter. A syndicator splits the advertising time with the local station. The local station gets the revenues from ads it can place—usually local. The syndicator gets to place national ad time, potentially lucrative if the syndicator can get enough stations in enough markets to place the program at a good enough time for children to watch.

The barter deal in kids' programming really began to flourish once the FCC lifted, in 1984, its strictures against program-length commercials like *He-Man* and, in short order, *Strawberry Shortcake* and *My Little Pony* and *Transformers.* That was when every gimmick promoter in the country leaped to the chance to use TV to sell to kids.

Of course, the concept of using the show as the advertisement for the stuff was not new. Not one aging baby boomer who can remember the Mickey Mouse Club watches ("Good things come in small packages") and the product hyping on *Romper Room* in the old days will be shocked by the notion. In fact, this was what had brought forth the FCC stricture in the first place. But that was pre-Reagan, before it was common knowledge that, as Reagan-appointed FCC head Mark Fowler put it, the public interest is what the public is interested in, and that the market would answer our society's needs as well as anything was going to.

The 1993 market in educational and informational programming for kids arrived as if to show the Reagan ideologues—if belatedly—that there are some areas of life that the marketplace simply does not provide for very well.

The problem with the barter notion for educational and informational kids' programming, as far as I could figure out, was that without a serious licensing sideline—a My Little Pony, a Transformer, a Smurf—the whole thing was a gamble on hitting around 75 to 80 percent of the nation's markets (including the top three, New York, Los Angeles, and Chicago) in order to make national ad revenue pay the rest of the costs. And to do that you needed lots of stations, and good time slots from each of them. The good time slots were mostly taken up by shows for other and more lucrative demographics; by sports; and by other kids' shows with more money to bid on the spots because they had the promise that kids would buy mountains of junk if the show were just on TV.

Things were a little better at the networks, but even there many affiliated stations had better things to do with the best time slots than give them to the educational and informational shows. And networks themselves sometimes placed them in spots virtually guaranteed to be preempted. *Beakman's World*, for instance, was preempted much of the first half of 1994 on the West Coast because of CBS's Olympics and other sports coverage.

When good shows were placed at good times, they got good ratings. But they didn't make as much money as other programs could in other ways.

As I began to figure out the scene, I became fascinated not only by what people said but by the way they said it. Many people clearly liked kids and were fascinated by the challenge of engaging them seriously. Others talked as if the consciousness, the curiosity, the passion to learn about our children—the same kids who one day will vote on our Social Security and medical care payments—were either fodder to their money-making machine or simply not real enough to worry about.

In talking to me, people didn't usually bother to cloak their descriptions in the kind of exculpatory verbiage that lawyers haul out for congressional and FCC testimony. Take Howard France (personal communication, January 6, 1994), a syndicator who had picked up a kids' fitness show:

> In December 1992, a producer brought *Scramble* to us. He was in it for the money because it was a unique merchandising opportunity, because of Randall Cunningham, a famous football player. [*Unique merchandising opportunity* means you can sell a lot of toys, doodads, placemats, and key rings branded with the name of the show and star.]
>
> He said, "Without TV, I'm nothing." [The TV show is the ad for the stuff.] I said, "It'll be a difficult show to clear [i.e., to get enough markets to make a national-reach claim to advertisers]. Maybe we can clear it by touting it as FCC-friendly."
>
> This was all the rage among distributors because the station wants to put on *Morphin* and cartoons that make them money. Educational TV doesn't make any money historically. Is a show FCC friendly? How do you know? The FCC so far says, "We won't define it, but we'll know it when we see it."
>
> The strategy worked out fairly well because we were one of the first ones there when it hit the fan at NATPE [an industry trade show, where it sank in that the FCC was considering revamping the rules] last year, and the spring and winter of '93.
>
> The show has been canceled but it was 72 percent [clearance] at its peak. It was canceled in December. Why? Because nobody watched it.
>
> I think a big contributing factor was the time of the show. Stations reserved their best time periods for the shows most important to them, cartoons. They had this government incentive, these threats, to put this kind of programming on, but they don't give this programming the best time period. Also, the show had weaknesses.
>
> The profit margin in barter is tiny. If you've got a *Mighty Morphin* with a 6 or a 7 rating, you can make a decent amount of money, but in kids' TV you can't expect that kind of breakout. You have to hope you do a 2 rating. There's not much money to be made there. There has to be another angle, dolls or lunchbuckets or something, which is only valuable if the show is valuable in the first place.

This far, Howard France had done an admirable job of demonstrating the kind of match made in hell created by the FCC's wink-wink regulation. A guy whose highest ambition was to move product stamped with his celebrity's logo had found a distributor savvy enough to know that stations needed something that would convince the FCC it had fulfilled minimal obligations to get a license renewed. Everyone was depending on the rules staying loose, and on a shared contempt for the spirit of the law.

What he said next sounded familiar: "The FCC is telling you you have to put boring TV on. The primary focus has to be educational not entertaining. You know kids: they don't want to go to school all week. If they don't want to watch it, who's gonna make 'em? The government can't pass a law to make people watch shows."

Practically everyone I talked to, and especially all the network people, managed to work into their chat a discussion of how kids don't want to be educated with television, and how no one can force a person to watch boring programming. For instance, here's Jenny Trias, then head of children's programming at ABC, with a story that may indeed have really happened to her but also seems to have happened, with minor variations, to several other people I talked to: "I've done focus groups over my fifteen years here, and I will always remember that one little boy said, 'I go to school Monday to Friday. Saturday morning is *my* time.' The most important thing should be entertainment, and if we can add educational elements, it's icing on top of the cake."

Again and again, distributors and programmers had told me that, sad as it might be to admit, the problem was that kids just didn't want to learn when they weren't in school. They just wanted to be diverted and distracted.

This attitude seemed to assume that kids came preset into the dismal work-versus-leisure-time mode their parents had grown into. This attitude assumed that learning was, and should be, the same thing as schooling. It pretended that kids didn't learn from entertainment—even if it was what we might not want them to learn. And it overstated the case, as if not making as much money as other programming was the same thing as not making money. It flew in the face of evidence like *Sesame Street* and other hits from Children's Television Workshop, which had ridden public TV to financial success of its own (including a major business in licensed products); and the long histories of *Captain Kangaroo* and *Mr. Wizard*, which had managed not to lose money while also speaking to children's curiosity. It shrugged off the promotional and brand-identity value of a feature like *Schoolhouse Rock*, whose jingles are still indelibly imprinted in many adult minds today.

Nonetheless, this sentiment was so well known that people said it semiautomatically, explaining the obvious to an outsider. And that's how

Howard France said it. But he had just finished explaining to me in some detail how he had successfully taken up space and time in a station's schedule with low-budget programming whose objective wasn't to teach anything or even to entertain but merely to sell. If this is routine procedure—and in 1993 it was—then no wonder kids don't watch the stuff.

Not that quality can't happen. *Cro, Beakman's World,* and *Where on Earth Is Carmen Sandiego?* are all examples of network shows with production values and some investment in research into the educational side of the show. And when they're on in good time slots, they get good ratings. In syndication, there's *Bill Nye the Science Guy,* which, like *Cro,* used about a million dollars of taxpayer money in grants to do that research. Bill Nye also launched the show at a public TV station, thus adding to the public investment in his program, which Disney is now syndicating. In local programming, you can look at *News for Kids,* a snappy and self-possessed little news show produced at KCNC-TV in Denver, a station with a powerful community role. *News for Kids* uses a low-low budget, but it has the backing of the station and in-house resources to accomplish much more than what most stations are doing.

But even when a show gets a decent budget and maybe even network support, the schedule is usually still a problem. And when a show isn't on when kids can see it, the ratings fall. The self-fulfilling prophecy kicks in: kids somehow just "don't want to watch it."

What's keeping the stations from running shows like this at good times and promoting them the way they do other shows is that nobody's making them do it, and there are more lucrative options. For people who were trying in good faith to make interesting programs for kids, often against great odds—and I talked to at least a dozen of these folks—this was completely crazy-making. Kent Takano, producer of the now-defunct *Scratch,* a show for teens, said, "I work out of a station, so I understand the dollars and cents, but when you see how some stations treat it, you want to say, 'Why take it at all?'"

Squire Rushnell, an independent producer who had been head of children's programming at ABC through the *Schoolhouse Rock* era of the '70s, brought about when Charren and other mothers had raised consciousness, explained why he's discouraged in this market: he couldn't put together the licensing deals that would pay for a show. And then, there was dealing with the stations:

> You need to have a program that's paid for, but then you also need to get stations to clear it. *Sonic the Hedgehog* doesn't make it because it's a

good program. It makes it because [game company] Sega is willing to put in extra dollars for advertising and promotion. So if you're going, say, to a station in Chicago, the company has to be ready to put more advertising dollars into that market [i.e., promise the station it will spend more advertising dollars elsewhere in the broadcast week on that station] because otherwise, the station might go with a [toy company] Hasbro-related program.

Allen Bohbot, a plain-talking distributor of animated and action-oriented kids' programming ("Some people call it violence, I call it action," he says) confirmed that paying over the top for a good time slot had become standard practice: "It has become so competitive that people are doing everything to get their programs in a good time slot, if it means pledging advertising, if it means doing incentives, whatever it takes. It's been ongoing for four or five years. It's not a good practice, but it's reality."

In Bohbot, I figured I had finally found the person I could quiz about the clash between market priorities and social values that I felt so strongly, someone who could counter my liberal perspective. But when I asked him about whether he'd ever tried to distribute programs with an educational side, he launched into a rather disturbing reflection. He said he wasn't trying not to be educational. It just didn't pay:

> The kids come home and the last thing they want to do is be educated. They want entertainment. And we keep pushing further and further what that means. We look for ways to entertain that push that fine line.
>
> It scares the daylights out of me. If I were a parent, I'd be very concerned. Not just what gets to the air but what succeeds scares the daylights out of me.
>
> I think TV is mirroring what they see in their daily lives. I think we kid ourselves if we ignore that. The greater problem is the society as a whole. As things get worse and worse for kids in their daily lives, the entertainment seems to follow that. Disney ratings are down 55 percent in the last three years, in some of the classic animated shows. Those animals are not real world. *Mighty Morphin Power Rangers*, that seems more accepted by them, what they want, so you'll see a lot more of that stuff.
>
> That doesn't make it right. Most of us are conscientious adults; we've done all kinds of shows like *Gulliver's Travels*, and they're the lowest rated shows we've ever had. The better return isn't on the socially acceptable program but on where the kids are glued to the set, and that's where we raise the bar a little higher each time.

Where does it stop? I don't know. Is it in the wrong direction? Yes. Is
it where people are tuning in? Yes. Sounds cynical, but it's the truth.

This view of a descent into a social hell, lit dimly by the flickering of
action on the tube, is maybe what I should have expected from a syndicator, who's out on the do-or-die front lines of business reality. The network people, living a more comfortable though still insecure life, always
in our discussions infused their language with social concern.

But hyperbole or no, I thought Bohbot's comments gave a vivid picture of what anyone who wants to come into today's marketplace with
educational/informational programming will compete with. There was
no way I could see, without some help from regulators who would shape
and constrain market conditions, that kids would see the kind of programming the 1990 act mandated.

The Center for Media Education's codirector, Kathryn Montgomery,
and I wrote up the results of the study, after she did further research and
more interviews. CME presented the study at a congressional hearing
and then took the results to the FCC, which eventually wrote stricter
guidelines. Needless to say, the industry didn't agree with us, and in an
FCC filing said, among other things, that we overstated our case and that
there were better and more programs that year than last (there were).

The sparring will go on—it's a basic part of the policy-making process. It is encouraging to see networks making an effort, but I'm very sure
that they wouldn't be if legislators and regulators weren't looking over
their shoulders.

# Paul Harvey

# and the

# Culture of

# Resentment

*Resentment, that small, stifled, and suffocating emotion, seems to have gradually pervaded the national culture. For a while, political conservatives marketed it well, but by now almost anyone can lay claim to an amorphous sense of grievance and disgruntlement. It was the late Erwin Knoll, editor of* The Progressive *and someone whose graciousness and generosity provided a bracing alternative to resentment, who gave me the chance to look at this phenomenon close up, by asking me to examine the career of ubiquitous, common-man celeb Paul Harvey.*

"Stand by ... for news!"

It's not an announcement, it's an incantation. Paul Harvey is about to perform his daily ritual, sorting out the messy business of worldly events.

Paul Harvey—the man who is credited with inventing the words *skyjacker, guesstimate,* and *Reaganomics*—is perennially the hottest news commentator in America.

Paul Harvey is always on the air. Every morning, as harried commuters rush to their cubicles and terminals, they catch a last-minute lift from his morning news. "I'm supposed to be at my desk at 8:30," says one avid listener, "but I'll sit in my car and listen to him."

He gives his fans headlines. Pulled without attribution from such sources as the *Wall Street Journal,* the *New York Times,* and the AP wires, they mingle international crises with murder-and-mayhem police reports. Random information ("A baby killer whale was born yesterday . . . seems fine"), "bumpersnickers" ("Stay in North Dakota; Custer was healthy until he left"), and country music lyrics ("And when your phone don't ring, it'll be me") spice up the broadcast.

Then come the little stories that are pure Harvey: a couple in a nursing home have been unjustly separated by unfeeling bureaucrats, then reunited by their love and the outrage of their friends; a dog that rescued a couple from certain death in a fire; sly naked-lady and toilet-humor jokes.

At midday, as they run errands, open thermos jars, or rush home to make the kids' lunch, listeners hear Harvey's noon-hour broadcast, with more prefab folk humor buttressing the news bulletins. On the way home, they can relax into "The Rest of the Story," Harvey's common-man version of history. And while out shopping on Saturdays, they can listen to Harvey's weekend broadcast.

His audience is enormous: his radio shows have a weekly reach of 25 million. While 40 percent are retirement age, a surprising number—nearly half—are between twenty-five and forty-nine. Men and women listen in equal proportions, and the bulk of his listeners make less than $40,000 a year. The older half, though, has advertising clout: people over fifty account for half the discretionary spending in the United States. And Harvey's reach is national, with listenership in the Midwest and South slightly higher than average. In brief, Paul Harvey talks to America.

Yet he goes unnoticed by media analysts and historians. He may get showered with grateful attention by the likes of the American Legion, and construction industry moguls may pay him big money to speak at their conventions, and the account managers at various advertising agencies may pray nightly for his continued health. But look to the history books, to the clip files, to the studies of the power of mass-media news, and the man who strolls the top of AM radio's ratings charts is nowhere to be found.

Even many regular listeners dismiss him. "He's a trivia-type person," says one woman who catches him in the car on the way home from her aerobics class. "I can't take him seriously," says a thirty-two-year-old secretary. "I love to listen to him because he makes me laugh. But I never remember his stories for more than a day."

But he is not after a place in the history books, especially those of historians who focus on the public and the political. His authority derives from being the voice of invisible Americans, the representative of their emotion in the face of cruel and complex pseudorationality.

America doesn't just listen; it talks back. At thirteen hundred radio stations around the country, staffers know the routine by heart. Right after the broadcast, the calls start. Callers rarely ask about hard news, nor do they complain. They want to know more about those tasty tidbits from small towns, and they want to talk to Paul Harvey. They are sure he's at the station. All are referred to his central office in Chicago, as are the thousands of letters he receives each week. When Harvey says something that's particularly opinionated, he can expect to get twenty-five thousand letters and calls.

In a crazy world where crises erupt daily in countries we've never heard of, and news anchors change lines and faces as if they were hair fashions, Paul Harvey is to listeners a real person, a touchstone of the real homegrown America. He engenders trust and affection.

"He's so positive," says a longtime listener. "He tells you about the news you don't usually hear. Usually you'll hear about the man who died from cancer, but not the five who were saved."

"He's not sensational," says another. "He sticks to the facts, and he's not fake like Dan Rather."

"You can tell he believes what he says," explains still another. "It's his own writing."

With his gruff-grandfather style and curmudgeonly attitudes toward bureaucrats, intellectuals, and foreigners, Paul Harvey seems old-fashioned, a simple do-it-yourselfer. Off the air, however, Mr. America is a state-of-the-art millionaire. With his unique formula, Harvey has become the richest broadcaster in the nation, and a one-man media empire. Aside from the radio programs, he has a syndicated TV show and several books.

The man who hawks work gloves on the air dresses in silk at the office, goes home to one of several mansions—in the basement of one are complete broadcasting facilities—and travels in private jets to his weekly speaking engagements, which carry a five-figure price tag. ABC news executives tremble at the mere thought of his departure.

In fact, this staunch defender of tradition is a thoroughly modern phenomenon of media-made reality. Harvey is a precursor of the "infotainers" who soothe the anxieties of working Americans, like NBC weatherman Willard Scott, Prairie Home Companion's Garrison Keillor, television talkmeister Phil Donahue, and increasingly, our celebrity-conscious national politicians.

He appears to lead the ultimate in open lives. After all, a nation of listeners has shared a father's delight in the first steps and favorite toys of his son Paul Jr. (He works with the Harvey operation, writing "The Rest of the Story.") It has tracked the family's sojourns to its farm in the Ozarks and basked in Harvey's reverential affection for his wife, Lynne, a.k.a. Angel, the icon of American wife-and-motherhood.

But it's not easy to find out who Paul Harvey is when he's not on the air. Reporters go through the same channels that listeners do; calling the Chicago office, they must convince Harvey's stern secretary that the Harvey operation will benefit from paying them some attention. I didn't even rate a press packet.

Those who do get interviews share a common experience: After looking in on Harvey's preparations for the morning show, which begins at 5 A.M., the reporter visits the Harvey family in its plushly decorated home, where Paul Jr. and Angel pose with Paul for a family portrait. The result is some version of the slogan Harvey uses when he autographs books: "Paul Harvey . . . Good News!" Almost never does a story mention the upscale side of the Harvey life—the affluent trappings, the luxury hideaway in Arizona (the family never goes to the Ozarks anymore), Angel's socialite friends and big-business deals, Paul Jr.'s adjoining mini-mansion, Harvey's position on the board of the MacArthur Foundation. It's not that reporters want to lie. There's just no percentage—no market—in that side of Paul Harvey.

Behind the slick packaging is a story. It starts in Tulsa, Oklahoma, in 1918, when Paul Harvey Aurandt is born into a family full of preachers, and it gets rocky with his father's death in a hunting accident when Paul is six. (He will later claim that his father was killed in the line of duty as a police officer on Christmas Eve.)

As an eager teen-age volunteer and then as a low-paid staffer, he worked at a variety of local radio stations. At one of them, he met his future wife, Lynne Cooper, a schoolteacher with a radio program and a driving ambition. To quote Harvey today, she wanted "to be married to a network news commentator." She also had sharply conservative political opinions: "If you think I'm right-wing," he likes to say, "you should see Angel. She thought Douglas MacArthur should have been president." Angel also brought to the marriage an ace business sense and a zest for high-style socializing. It is Angel who runs the Harvey enterprises and has pushed Harvey into new media and technologies.

The story begins to go wrong during World War II when, after working for several years in the Office of War Information, twenty-six-year-old Paul Harvey Aurandt is drafted. Only a month later, he was in an Army hospital, having wounded himself in an apparent fit of depression.

Doctors declared him emotionally unstable. After more bizarre episodes during the following two months, he got a medical discharge for psychological reasons. After a couple of weeks in a veterans' hospital, he left to try his broadcasting luck in Chicago. And there he began to create a new man. He dropped his family name, under which the grim Army records were filed, and made friends with people who needed Harvey just as much as—or more than—he needed them.

When Paul Harvey began broadcasting, radio was still the dominant news medium for most Americans, but it would soon be badly shaken by two forces: the advent of television, which accounted for a dramatic plunge in radio's ratings in the years 1948 to 1951, and anti-Communist hysteria.

In the 1920s, radio's early news broadcasts threatened the then-dominant newspaper interests. Intermedia treaties were in place by 1933, barring advertising from radio news and allowing news only as a public service. But commentators were not bound by the treaties, and commentary shows flourished. A colorful range of political views clashed on the air, from the liberal Edward R. Murrow to the sober, from-the-front voice of Lowell Thomas to the vituperative, up-from-the-gutter sound of Walter Winchell to the bulletins of Gabriel Heatter.

By 1942, the treaties were relics, and 73 percent of Americans polled said they got their news from radio. But what kind of news was it? In the words of Lowell Thomas, "We're really entertainers. My talks are planned as entertainment, not education."

When television began to take over, radio sought refuge in more narrowly targeted audiences. But Paul Harvey's popular Chicago broadcasts for ABC gave a network desperate for national advertising that increasingly rare item in radio: a program with a truly mass audience.

The Red Scare was on, and blacklists shadowed radio figures. The anti-Communist newsletter *Counterattack*, founded in 1947, quickly became required reading for broadcasters. In 1950, *Counterattack* issued a book, *Red Channels: The Report of Communist Influence in Radio and Television*, listing 150 entertainment-industry figures tainted by political activities ranging from attendance at Communist Party–organized meetings to signing a Spanish Civil War petition. Some commentators, such as Drew Pearson, bucked the tide. Others vociferously joined the anti-Communist cause, and Harvey was one of them. He was not then the homey curmudgeon of today. He was a crusader, drawing lessons from ancient imperial histories for Americans in danger of losing their spirit of freedom.

But business interests and anti-Communist leaders cultivated the young man with the righteous radio voice. Harvey got his big break in broadcasting, he says, from friendly chats he and Angel had with Joe Kennedy, the owner of the Chicago Merchandise Mart, which housed the ABC studios. Kennedy had caught a whiff of Harvey's neopopulism on the air and recommended that he be promoted to a national show.

Paul and Angel Harvey catered to the right contacts. He made friends with Joe McCarthy. J. Edgar Hoover became one of the show's heroes, especially after Harvey bungled his one foray into investigative reporting. He raised the ire of the FBI with his pursuit of a story about poor security at a nuclear installation near Chicago. In the investigation of Harvey himself that resulted, he needed the conservatives on his side, and they came through. Right-wing Congressman Fred Busbey testified for him, and Harvey's reputation and job were rescued. The right-wing Heritage Foundation published the first of two books compiled from his broadcasts.

Harvey was too smart, however, to fall into the trap of politics-of-the-moment. His message was not about villainy but decadence. His demon was not so much Communists—his isolationism already encompassed most foreigners—but Franklin D. Roosevelt, whose New Deal had begun an insidious process making us dependent on Big Government and sapping our independent spirit. Harvey found a way to ride the tide of anti-Communism, but to preach a still more fundamentalist message, based on a vision of an America that could stand alone, at once world empire and nation of yeoman individualists. His version of "no entangling alliances" was uniquely domestic. It was to stop, finally, at the garage door. Harvey became the apostle of isolationism for new and would-be suburbanites.

In 1952, he explained it to his listeners in classic Harvey style: "No one came to this country originally or since to found a government. We came here to get away from government!" And he underlined it with a historical parable:

> They were not cowards . . . men of failure and frustration . . . academic theorists. They were successful men of business and agriculture, but they were scared. . . . They wanted little government . . . big people. And with freedom in their hearts and old buckskin shirts on their backs they headed off over the mountains.
>
> There was no TVA out there . . . no price supports . . . no price control. No job for sure . . . no guaranteed rocking chair. . . .
>
> It's 1776 again. Right now!

Behind the promise of social welfare, he could smell Communism, through the softening effect of affluence: "We have passed already from abundance to selfishness to complacency to apathy," he railed in 1954. "Cannot we conceivably hold back the clock?" he asked. "Continue our technological progress without allowing our character to decay away?"

Harvey was building with political rhetoric a postpolitical position—inventing an attitude for people who wanted safe havens from the complexities of postwar empire. He brilliantly and intuitively discovered an audience and a need. His target was the hardworking chemical engineer who told me he may often disagree with "Paul" but feels a kinship with him. "I feel he speaks for me on some issues," the man says. "I don't think people should go hungry, but I'm against long-term welfare because I think it creates a weakness in our society."

"A weakness in our society." That has been Harvey's constant theme. It's as if he had discovered a bruise on America's conscience and learned how to poke it to get attention. The bruise is the uneasy fit between the mythic image of the individualist producer American and the reality of an emerging consumer society. Harvey's central constituency was the new lower middle class, a class learning to define itself not in terms of production but consumption, people with unprecedented postwar aspirations to a steady job, a suburban home, a car, a toolshed. He filled the drive time of the new commuters with the sound of legitimacy. His persona melded victim and survivor. His news commentary simultaneously registered grievance and optimism.

Paul Harvey's American was somebody who was so intrepid, so trustworthy, so respectable that he didn't need the structure of government. It could only get in the way of opportunity. Bureaucrats of all kinds became his bad guys.

Harvey never saw a contradiction between his work-shirt voice and his affection for the wealthy. What makes America great, he would claim, long before Ronald Reagan did, is the capacity to get rich.

As the Paul Harvey image has been burnished, the routine has become ritual, the tone more chronically belligerent and less anguished. The crusader has become a kind of Cassandra, his sound of alarm now a cantankerous refrain. But the format remains the same, and the audiences continue to grow.

"He's so positive." That's the single most common reason people young and old give for listening to Paul Harvey. "He gives you the nice side of the news," people say. To those who hear the caviling edge in his intonations, the calculated exasperation, the resentment toward profes-

sional authorities and bureaucrats, the multifarious charges of ungrate-
fulness, it seems an odd claim. But what Paul Harvey is positive about is
his conviction that it is still possible for America to be great, through a
combination of little government and big people, if only the experts
would get out of the way.

He still has the same economic policy he started with. As he put it in a
typically adulatory interview in *USA Today*, he was a supply-sider while
Reagan was still a Democrat. He is relentlessly upbeat in his bulletins on
economic revival: "Sitka, Alaska! American Indians will move one big
step away from welfare today . . . [with] a nonprofit corporation."

His spin on the news can set traditional reporters' teeth on edge. When
he told one of his apocryphal stories—this one about a Raleigh, North
Carolina, cop who, while arresting a drunk, left his car for long enough to
let the confused drunk drive home in it—the *Raleigh News & Observer*
investigated the tale. Raleigh police denied it, and the paper published
news stories and an editorial condemning Harvey's piece as slipshod
journalism. Associate editor Farrell Guillory said, "He advertises what he
does as news. But if he's not checking his facts, you wonder if he should
call himself something else."

But Guillory's readers by and large disagree. The paper was besieged
by readers who complained that all Harvey had done was to stretch the
truth—and besides, they knew of a similar case in another county. "It's
not important that it's not true," explained an older secretary to me.
"That is, unless it defames somebody or gets them in trouble." She says
she learns from him: "He gives you insight into people elsewhere in the
world." Whether or not the story is true, for her it is the insight that
counts. For Harvey's supports, there's a human being behind the voice.

In taking on Harvey, the *News & Observer* displayed a certain courage.
Harvey's listeners are fiercely loyal to the man who has become the voice
of their ever-endangered pride. Harvey can depend on that. He never
counters his critics; he engulfs them. He told the newspaper that since the
story didn't hurt anyone, it didn't matter whether it was true. And what
he did to a couple of "good-old-boy" broadcasters at a Washington radio
station was better still. He incorporated them into his own folklore.

Frank Harden and Jackson Weaver's morning drive-time program on
WMAL became over decades a staple of the D.C. area listening routine, a
cheerful amalgam of wire-service oddities, weather and traffic updates, and
backchat. Harvey's morning news comes on in the middle of their show.
Harden and Weaver would make affectionate fun of the commentator's

conservatism, with remarks like, "Harvey graduated from the Attila the Hun Military Academy."

Off the air talking with me, they were both franker about Harvey, whom they described as a savvy opportunist—"He's latched onto a real moneymaker"—but not a newsman. "I'd put him as an entertainer," said Harden. "He's like an evangelist. You don't call an evangelist a theologian."

"He takes his stuff off the wires, and so do we, and many times we use it before he does, so you can see the difference," said Weaver. "He'll embellish it to the point where it's hardly recognizable. Accuracy is a minor detail to him."

But they learned to be gentle with Harvey on the air. "His listeners are very loyal—the switchboard will light up immediately if the time of his broadcast is changed for some reason. Sometimes they think it's deliberate sabotage," Harden explained. "And if we've kidded him, someone will call up and holler, 'He's a better American than you are!' and slam the receiver down. We're in the popularity business, you know, and we can't afford too much stuff like that."

Harvey's loyal listeners in fact began writing in righteous indignation to Harvey about Harden and Weaver's on-air joking. But Harvey's reaction, when they called him, was genial. "Do I know who you are?" he said. "Boy, do I know who you are. But keep it up!" Harvey could recognize good publicity, and he could dish it out. He even featured Harden and Weaver and inserted their jokes into his broadcasts.

Paul Harvey often feels good. "Sixty-one percent of American families are together each night for dinner," he discovers in a poll. "It is a precious time, carefully reserved at our house, but I thought it rare anymore." (One wonders how he manages to be home for dinner so often, what with his weekly speaking schedule.)

He finds amazing personal-achievement stories: "She begins every day with twenty-five push-ups and then jumps rope. For more exercise she moonlights as a hula dancer for a Hawaiian band. Nattie DeLera is 90." Sixty-year-old marriages get a glory mention on his broadcasts. But like the rest of his news, the characters in the upbeat tales are embattled. They stand in shining contrast to the worldly realities of lonely dinners, stress-related diseases, and divorce.

In recent years, Harvey has turned more often to animal stories to color his broadcasts. Animals, especially house pets, have the values he treasures—loyalty, simplicity, generosity—in a world of constant betrayal. He retails stories of pets who save their owners from certain death and brings alarming news that animals given as "unwanted Christmas gifts" are flooding the animal-welfare societies.

The story of Pigby is a prime example of why Harvey loves animal news. Pigby was the runt of a litter of pigs. Nursed and raised among dogs, Pigby now thinks he is one and travels everywhere with the farmer's wife. "She says a day never passes that she's not thankful for the comical little companion who's made himself a member of the family," Harvey discourses. "She says farmers have a lot of extra worries these days. Pigby helps her forget hers." And that's what Pigby does for us as well.

In the Paul Harvey world, where politics is an unpleasant intrusion, the listeners—whom he hails with his opening greeting, "Hello, Americans!"—are portrayed as yeomen or small entrepreneurs but treated as consumers. He takes the question of consumer choice with a kind of seriousness other newsmen reserve for the headlines.

Harvey has always claimed the right to make his own commercials, and he has turned them into a vehicle for the Paul Harvey image. He will begin a news program with the words, "The following is a commercial announcement, but if it were not, it might be the best news in the program." He claims only to promote products he uses himself. For example, Harvey does not do pain-reliever commercials, because he never gets headaches.

He does, however, seem to have a roach problem (he promotes Copper Brite Roach-Pruf) and chapped skin (Neutrogena). He plays heavily on the personal endorsement: "Your Hoover dealer and I are as excited about this as you will be—I want you to at least see the Hoover 1000. Will you? Thank you." And the response is awesome. The sales of Roach-Pruf, for instance, went up 40 percent in ninety days.

Harvey also does advocacy advertising. When buffing the utility corporations' image for the Electric Information Council, he turns one of the biggest businesses in America into a populist celebration, praising the company linemen and hailing a wildlife rescue program sponsored by power companies.

He sees no jarring line between the news and advertising, and no need for one, because Paul Harvey is the citizen-consumer's authority on everything from hand cream to budget cuts. The same voice that sells products with a combination of resentment and resignation ("You and your things were not meant to be moved around . . . but when for professional reasons you must, Mayflower is there") sells self-righteous resistance to social management. And if his facts are wrong, his attitude is right.

"He's a throwback to the days of the old radio commentators," says an older broadcasting executive. "It's like he's been frozen in ice and thawed out again." But Harvey's news and commentary are dramatically different from the genre of the generation that preceded him. Rather than information for public debate, his message is reinforcement, moral uplift, support for the understandable desire not to understand complexity.

His lessons from the past, the famous, the foolish, those who triumph from adversity, and those who are felled by underhanded foes are the gems of "The Rest of the Story." A boy who wants to be an evangelist more than anything grows up to be Vincent Van Gogh. The eager war correspondent turns into Sir Winston Churchill. A hypochondriac woman, we discover, becomes Florence Nightingale.

History becomes a collection of "Believe It or Not" facts. Anne Boleyn had six fingers on her left hand. Eau de cologne started out as a medicine against the plague. "The Rest of the Story" is an expert mix of the arcane and the universal. And the hero of the tale often has the poignant plight of the misunderstood innocent that the Harvey persona exemplifies.

The genius of Paul Harvey is that he is sincere. He may have invented himself on the air, but the invention has integrity. And he has stood by his principles—his fundamentalist populism—even when they run counter to orthodox conservatism. He has repeatedly taken stands against U.S. foreign policy, when imperial ambition runs afoul of his notion that nations, like people, should be do-it-yourselfers and that American moral purity must be preserved at all costs.

During the Korean War—or "police action"—Harvey developed his foreign-policy position: bomb 'em or get out. Either commit yourself to the maximum and fight the moral battle with flags waving, or disentangle yourself from sordid military governments. Korea left him deeply disillusioned, horrified at American support for a corrupt government—support that might contaminate America's innocent purity.

Then came Vietnam, for him an ugly replay of Korea. After years spent urging Americans on in broadcasts that made him the best friend of the hawks in Congress, he began to back off around 1966. He rejoiced in Richard Nixon's election and celebrated Spiro Agnew's attacks on the media. But with the discouraging sight of American forces bogged down, of American support for yet another corrupt government, and some say, the prospect of seeing his son drafted while remembering his own experience in the Army, he began openly to express his disagreements.

In the spring of 1970, the United States invaded Cambodia. Harvey opened his broadcast the next day with the words, "Mr. President, I love you, but you are wrong." He had become the major antiwar voice in the silent majority. His decision was hard on his listeners; tens of thousands of angry, wounded letters arrived within the week, and white feathers floated out of some of the envelopes. But conservatives like to say that Harvey's change of heart was a more potent force on public opinion than the antiwar movement.

The Reagan administration, too, came under Harvey's fire, especially over Central America, where he argued that the anti-Communist domino theorists are wrong, building on the same misconceptions that "motivated our dead-end involvement in Vietnam." He wanted the United States to stay out of unwinnable wars in Central America, to disentangle itself once again from untrustworthy allies and corrupt dictators.

Harvey is a hawk. It's just that he wants to win. But for him, the real war is still the one at home, in the hearts and minds of Americans.

Back in 1970, when his stand on the war in Southeast Asia shocked the nation, he frankly acknowledged that his approach was less political than evangelical. "I guess I'm a political fundamentalist," he told the *New York Times*, "although I'm not sure what that means. I thought of myself as a conservative until I woke up one morning in 1966 [and] came out against the war in Vietnam."

Harvey's search for the moral beyond the political in the news has found rich material in terrorism stories. Terrorists sit on the same side of the moral and social fence as do criminals, the greedy rich, selfish pet owners, and corrupt evangelists. Like Reagan, he inveighs against them. But where Reagan had to work in the messy world of international diplomacy, Harvey indicts halfway measures and uses them as proof of bureaucratic bungling and untrustworthy alliances.

One broadcast essay on the state of the national psychic health revealed Harvey's understanding that American society has irrevocably changed, and also demonstrated his faith in the power of the media to help ordinary Americans endure the transformations:

> In my years as a professional observer I have never seen less polarization than now. Less friction left and right, black and white, young and old. . . . Today's sociological collision is not between colors, cultures, and convictions. It's between right and wrong. The bad guys are as numerous as ever, and more effectively armed, whether they are foreign terrorists preying on political enemies or homegrown terrorists preying on our own elderly. . . .
>
> Some days, engulfed in the muddy, bloody, cruddy news, you and

I reach out for some of the old values that used to stabilize us, and we find them unstable. Religion. On any given day on forty-odd places on planet Earth people are killing people in the name of religion. Or we reach out for the security of home and family, and often they are not what they were.

And so we turn on the TV and turn off the news and tune in some fantasy, and if only for a little while we can feel we're conquering our nation's last frontier. When the program's done and the credits are run, we're back in a world where Miami vice is nothing like *Miami Vice*, but skillful program producers have filled our need, providing us if only for a little while a refuge where right prevails and justice is being done and decent people live happily ever after.

No one should know better than Paul Harvey about the work of "skillful program producers." In this survey of the American psyche, he found as intense a need for something to assuage the pain of the search for "the old values that used to stabilize us" as when he arrived on the scene in 1951. And every day he answers that need with love and affection, with a supreme loyalty to the mass of people who suspect that those in charge somehow feel superior to them while taking advantage of them. Harvey exploits that sentiment with the passion of someone who feels it acutely himself. And as the split between the myth of the yeoman American and the reality of the consumer caught in the spokes of late capitalism becomes ever wider, Paul Harvey paints over the contradictions with "good news," creating a refuge "where right prevails and justice is being done and decent people live happily ever after."

Paul Harvey ushered us into an age in which the difference between public and private information is fuzzy, in which the voice of authority has become a ventriloquist's trick, and what matters is not accuracy but attitude. It is Paul Harvey who originally found the way to express the forlorn and embattled spirit of hope in a postwar America where image is everything, as real as that remarkable phenomenon, "Paul Harvey."

# Vietnam

# Grunts

# R Us

*For someone whose early adulthood was shaped by the social turmoil around the Vietnam War, the Vietnam War films that were released in the late '80s and early '90s held a grim fascination. This analysis of these films benefited beyond measure from the editorial guiding hand of Tom Engelhardt, another person whose life was reshaped by anti–Vietnam War activism. Post–*Saving Private Ryan *and in the midst of a nostalgic revival of World War II in games, toys, and tales, I see these films as indeed having accomplished a certain social amnesia, or at least a rewriting of historical memory, which permitted a return to heroic postures of war.*

Rain or shine, weekday or weekend, they file into the trough of the Vietnam Memorial in Washington, D.C. They emerge somber and shaken from this monument to inchoate sorrow, and there are always more behind them. Some, hoping to make a connection, leave behind mementos; more than twelve thousand personal objects left there are now archived in perpetuity. Nothing better symbolizes how Vietnam has hovered in the American popular consciousness—unavoidable but inexplicable, a horror to be grasped only at the level of adding up the dead one by one.

It took Americans until 1982 to erect a monument to the Vietnam War. It took longer still for the makers of American movies and television programs—those avenues through which history becomes part of popular consciousness—to find a way to transform discordant political passions and unbearable images into entertainment. Only in the later 1980s, after periods of filmic silence and false starts, did the war become the subject of a subgenre, one that could be called the "noble-grunt film."

The noble-grunt films have been widely heralded as a sign of the maturing of the American audience—an audience finally ready for brutally frank images of the war the way it was really fought. But they are better seen as reconstructing the place of Vietnam in American popular history, away from a political process and toward an understanding of the war as a psychological watershed. Indeed, they speak more eloquently to the psychological plight of the average moviegoer than to any reality of the war years. Just as the Vietnam Memorial enabled a public acknowledgment of personal mourning, films and TV shows of the later eighties evinced a sense of loss and a recognition of the need for grief.

These films had often been in the works for years, even decades. They got made, though, only when public opinion turned toward sympathy for Vietnam vets, and when Vietnam had become a topic for retrospectives and for academic research (Auster and Quart 1988; Calloway 1986; Gitlin 1988b; Rollins 1984; Silverman 1988). By 1979, four-fifths of Americans agreed that "veterans who served in Vietnam are part of a war that went bad." Welcome-home marches for vets in New York in 1985 and in Los Angeles in 1987 showcased that sentiment (U.S. Senate 1980, 87). And this shift in the social mood occurred as it was becoming apparent that America's international role had changed, when not even calling for "morning in America" could obscure the onset of imperial twilight.

We waited a long time to begin this transformation of Vietnam into a digestible element of popular consciousness. The war itself, *New Yorker* writer Jonathan Schell noted in 1969, was strongly marked by a sense of dreamlike unreality: "This may be partly because Vietnam is the first war to be shown on television, but we believe that there are more important reasons. A man dreaming is caught up in a reality that is entirely his own creation" (in Schell 1989). The self-created reality to which Schell referred was grounded in assumptions so deep they often appeared simple fact until they were challenged. Novelist and vet Philip Caputo recalled, "America seemed omnipotent then; the country could still claim that it had never lost a war, and we believed that we were ordained to play cop to communist robbers and spread the political faith around the world" (in Auster and Quart 1988, 83). Historian Loren Baritz neatly summarized the beliefs with which Americans had entered the war: "Our national myth showed us that we were good, our technology made us strong, and our bureaucracy gave us standard operating procedures. It was not a winning combination" (1985).

No, it wasn't. The Vietnam War took the easy confidence out of America's self-image as a good-neighbor world cop, the Lone Ranger of international policy, a cowboy tall in the saddle against a world teeming with sneaky Indians. Even when President Reagan later evoked these images, there would be invisible quote marks around them, as if foreign policy were only a late-night movie.

The war also bitterly divided social groups and generations, and out of the social turmoil surrounding the war came a deepening of cynicism and disbelief in an effective relationship between citizenry and government. The crisis of American international authority so boldly symbolized by the taking of hostages in the American embassy in Iran, and the Iran-Contra scandal, deepened a sense of rupture without signaling new directions.

The Vietnam War marked a messy end point to "the American century" in popular culture. "The sixties" has become a talismanic reference to that rupture in expectations and self-image. As Todd Gitlin put it, "History was ruptured, passions have been expended, belief has become difficult; heroes have died and been replaced by celebrities. The 1960s exploded our belief in progress, which underlay the classical faith in linear order and moral clarity. Old verities crumbled, but new ones have not settled in" (Gitlin 1988a, 1). The sixties reevaluation that hit late-eighties media always referred to Vietnam (Gitlin 1988b). You could see it in the movies—for instance, in *The Big Chill* (1983), all about people caught up in the era without having been actors in it and nostalgic about antiwar atmospherics. The film's popular reception testified that millions who were merely present in the era remained psychologically unaccounted for long afterward.

In the late eighties that very sense of confusion became the psychological center of films and TV programs about the war. Films as different as *Platoon* (1986), *Full Metal Jacket* (1987), *Good Morning, Vietnam* (1987), *Hamburger Hill* (1987), *Gardens of Stone* (1987), *84 Charlie MoPic* (1989), *Off Limits* (1988), *Dear America* (1988), *Casualties of War* (1989), and TV series like *Tour of Duty* and *China Beach* have carried into film what author C. D. B. Bryan described for literature as "the Generic Vietnam War Narrative" (Bryan 1984). This generic narrative features combat units in tales that chart "the gradual deterioration of order, the disintegration of idealism, the breakdown of character, the alienation from those at home, and finally, the loss of all sensibility save the will to survive." There is something terribly sad and embattled about these films and TV shows, even in their lighter and warmer moments. They celebrate survival as a form of heroism, and cynicism as a form of self-preservation.

The noble-grunt films collectively recast the war as a test of physical and, much more important, psychological survival of the person who had no authority and too much responsibility. The war is seen from the viewpoint of the American soldiers in the barracks and bars, in the jungles and the paddies (rarely in the air or on water). The war is confined to the years in which the most ground troops were present. The battlefield has been internalized, and the enemy is not so much the Vietnamese as the cold, abstract forces of bureaucracy and the incompetence of superiors.

Vietnam, in these movies, becomes a Calvary of the powerless—not just for the grunts, but also for the viewers. The American moviegoer—a citizen-consumer who, like the soldier in Vietnam, is far from decision making yet still accountable for its consequences—can find much to empathize with here. The moviegoer, too, is plagued with a nagging sense of guilt and suffused with a dull anger for carrying that burden. And, like the movie grunts, he or she has learned contempt for the bureaucrats above, whether at work or in government. Vietnam has thus become a powerful metaphor for tensions in American society since the war, especially over questions of personal responsibility for social conflict and political decisions. Watching the noble-grunt films, viewers can identify with characters who are misunderstood, confused, idealistic, well-intentioned, and betrayed from above.

## The Civil War of the Soul

The plots and styles of these films range widely, although they share a common focus and theme. In Oliver Stone's sentimental, elegiac *Platoon*, a young naif (much like Stone himself, a Yale dropout and Vietnam enlistee) joins a platoon in which two archetypal warriors, the saintly, dope-smoking Elias and the bleak killer Barnes, vie for his soul. Barry Levinson's *Good Morning, Vietnam*, in a style that borrows something from sitcom rhythms and draws heavily on the talents of comedian Robin Williams, uses the character of hip, reckless army deejay Adrian Cronauer to poke fun at official stuffed shirts and to wring poignancy out of the Americans' search for friends across culture and politics. *Gardens of Stone*, directed by Francis Ford Coppola, nostalgically evokes (and embalms) 1968 in an honor guard; a young recruit chafes at favors and begs to go to Vietnam, while his NCOs, heartsick veterans, try to stop him. Patrick

Duncan's deliberately crude *84 Charlie MoPic* is told entirely from the point of view of the naif behind the camera. He is recording, ostensibly for a training film, a day on patrol with a crackerjack squad whose routine tour in the bush becomes a confrontation with death and with moral questions in fighting "Charlie's war." *Casualties of War,* directed by Brian De Palma in his characteristic florid style, recounts the rape and murder of a Vietnamese farm girl by a battle-crazed squad, the newest of whose members brings them to court-martial. *Dear America: Letters Home from Vietnam,* made by Bill Couturie for HBO (which backed many cable ventures about Vietnam in the days when Michael Fuchs, a vet, headed it), draws on music video. Its images are outtakes from network news footage, including many close-ups of soldiers; its script is a collage of letters written to relatives from the field; its sound track comes out of a still timely jukebox. The earnest TV series *Tour of Duty* dramatizes the conflicts of and relationships between field soldiers; the stylistically hipper *China Beach* sets its dramas in a field hospital next to an R&R station and prominently features the role of women who served as nurses and support staff. Stanley Kubrick's chilling *Full Metal Jacket* both fits within and breaks the noble-grunt convention, since it uses the elements of this subgenre to shape a critique of it. Hapless boys are turned into killing machines in boot camp, where one—a recruit—kills his sergeant in despair; fellow recruit Joker goes off to war and to battle during the 1968 Tet offensive.

The viewpoint of the noble-grunt film is not, in any one instance, inaccurate, although it is partial. Taken together, these films revise, even erase our understanding of what was, historically, not so much a military as a political process. They replay history as an emotional drama of embattled individual survival.

Entertainment movies, of course, stand or fall on their ability to act powerfully on viewers' emotions. Recall Samuel Fuller's comment in Jean-Luc Godard's *Pierrot le Fou*: "A film is like a battleground. It's love, hate, action, violence, death. In one word, emotion." Successful films tap something in the feelings of millions of viewers and express them in a way that all can share. What these films offer is the revisioning of history as personal tragedy of a particular kind. It's the agony of having the emotional battleground itself destroyed, leaving the fighters without a way to express their own pain.

In these films, close-ups of the grunts' faces are a regular feature. *Dear America*'s editors, for instance, combed archives' worth of footage to find fresh faces. Often the grunts talk directly to the viewer, either in voice-over, as in *Platoon*, or, as in the interview sequences of *84 Charlie MoPic* or in *Full Metal Jacket*'s, frontally into the camera in self-reflexive sequences. These are the voices and faces of people who insist on finally being heard and seen. The sound and image come at the viewer with a faint whiff of the grunts' resentment at having been overlooked, and also with a certain bravado for daring to risk recognition and, ultimately, self-acknowledgment.

If this focus recognizes and validates the suffering of the men (and sometimes women) who fought, it is also the result of the filmmakers' search for acceptable heroes. That fact was made explicit by liberal journalist and Vietnam vet William Broyles Jr., who codesigned the concept of *China Beach*, which featured women. "No matter how involved you get with the tangled purposes of the war and its moral confusion and its unhappy end," he said, "what they did was purely heroic" (in Morrison 1988). And the search for acceptable heroes is also the search for an acceptable vision of Vietnam, one that allows for the empathic union of character and audience. (The movie industry, after all, is in business to sell tickets, not critical history.) So these films arrange reality to fit the Hollywood grunts' perspective.

Consider the portrayals of the Vietnamese. Those portrayals show boldly that we, as citizens and moviegoers (not to mention moviemakers), don't know why we were in Vietnam and are no longer afraid to admit it. Nor are we interested in finding out, in a political sense. Such questions lie with others—politicians, pundits, bureaucrats—who have already lost our trust.

Vietnam was not only an overseas war but a civil war, which Americans first entered as advisers. It was also a war fueled by anti-Communist rhetoric, both in Vietnam and in the United States. In these movies the civil war virtually disappears; differences between North and South, civilian and military, "our" Vietnamese and "theirs," evaporate. From this filmic point of view the Vietnamese are all inscrutably Other, a pervasively untrustworthy population (except as victims)—not because filmmakers have suddenly accepted the proposition that the conflict was a true people's war, as the North Vietnamese claimed, but because the whole struggle is presumed meaningless. As a soldier in *Casualties of War* puts it, the first three weeks you're "in country," you're likely to be killed because you don't know; the last three weeks, it's because "you don't care."

And so the civil war simply moves inside the platoon, where ideology and the survival of peoples are replaced by lifestyle, careerism, and the survival of individuals. The war itself appears typically as a chaotic, maddening exercise in tracking a mostly invisible enemy. In the absence of community or mission, the only real job left to the grunt is his search for individual integrity.

The Vietnamese typically become part of the backdrop of paranoia into which innocents are lowered, or act as plot triggers to the problem of individual responsibility in the absence of social cues. When the Vietnamese function as victims, their mortal suffering is often a trigger for the central issue, the moral suffering of the grunts. What precipitates *Platoon*'s crisis, for instance, is a My Lai–type massacre, but the massacre itself is portrayed as the direct result of unbearable tension and paranoia in the platoon—fueled when the troops uncover a Vietcong guerrilla hidden in the village.

It's the war for the soul of *Platoon*'s naive hero Chris that really occupies the two warrior-gods Elias and Barnes. Elias is a superlative fighter whose guerrilla tactics make him a potent warrior; Barnes's nihilistic style is far more dangerous to the group. Elias puts a stop to the massacre, overriding the death-happy Sergeant Barnes, but Barnes gets his revenge by killing Elias. Although Chris kills Barnes, there's no satisfaction in it; the civil war in the platoon has eaten away at the warrior mission. At the end of the movie Chris says in mournful voice-over, "We didn't fight the enemy, we fought ourselves, and the enemy was in us." As Oliver Stone put it in the introduction to the published screenplay, Elias and Barnes were meant to illustrate two views of the war: "The angry Achilles versus the conscience-stricken Hector, fighting for *a lost cause* on the dusty plains of Troy. It mirrored *the very civil war* that I'd witnessed in all the units I was in" (Stone 1987, 9, emphasis added).

In *Casualties of War,* American atrocities lead back to American casualties. The farm girl's suffering—filmed in a style that makes it, horrifyingly, a pornography of pity—is the vehicle leading us to the film's central tragedy: the collapse of a moral framework for the men who kill her. The spectacular agony of her death is intended to stir not the audience's righteous anger at the grunts—that role is already filled in the film itself by the moralistic new recruit Eriksson—but empathy for the ordinary fighting men who have been turned into beasts by their tour of duty. De Palma himself said as much: "It's not really [a] political [movie]. It's very emotional, and full of sorrow." The sorrow was for the soldiers; he called the court-martial scene a moment that revealed that "these are all casualties of the war." The film was for him about America's emotional legacy from Vietnam: "To me, the Vietnam experience is the sore that will never

heal. So many things happened to these kids, and marred their lives for-
ever, and there's no rational way to explain it" (in Weber 1989, 24).

## Our Vietnamese, Ourselves

Not that the Vietnamese can't be worthy enemies in these movies, but as
such they are likely to be flags for questions of conscience, responsibility,
and conflict within the platoon. In *84 Charlie MoPic* the squad members
have the highest respect for the Vietnamese as soldiers. "It's Charlie's
war," they say. They don't even conceive of the war as a moral or political
battlefront between them and the Vietnamese; political issues are incon-
sequential for men trying to survive a day in the bush. The Vietnamese,
not only setting the terms of the war but fighting it well enough to
threaten the Americans, set a standard for what a real warrior is. They are
even enviable, for having real community and purpose, while the squad
members must create community in the field and mostly out of oppositional sentiment directed against their own superiors. For most of the
film the Vietnamese presence is registered only as ominous rustlings,
small figures in the distance, or by booby traps, until one Vietnamese soldier is captured. The squad leader, a ferociously serious black man, forces
the white, careerist lieutenant to kill the man with a knife, literally driving home the point that war means killing real people.

   Thus, conflicts within the army are acted out on the Vietnamese soldier's body. This acting-out occurs again at the end of *Full Metal Jacket*,
when the squad finally locates the lone hidden sniper who has decimated
the patrol. The soldiers' arguments over killing the girl (who in the
screenplay is an Amerasian) revive again the bitter divisions within the
American fighting unit. In Kubrick's vision these divisions are not neatly
drawn between grunts and officers but exemplify the contradictions
within the values that fueled the American war effort.

   The therapeutic mission of the noble-grunt subgenre—to rehabilitate,
through confrontation with one's own pain, both grunts and viewers—
comes out even more clearly on television, where subtleties take second
place to sentimental drama. Vietnamese appear occasionally in the TV
series *China Beach*, but they function as mere triggers of the series's central concern: how to maintain your humanity in the midst of chaos and
pointlessness. One episode of *Tour of Duty* ends with an aborted discussion of the U.S. role in Vietnam: "The war is wrong," says one grunt.
"That's not the point," says the other. And in context, of course, it's not—
the point is the grunts' survival, not just physically but as caring human
beings.

As vehicles back into the problems within the U.S. armed forces, the Vietnamese can sometimes be shown sympathetically, since they reveal the grunts' plight. For instance, in *Good Morning, Vietnam* the major Vietnamese characters function primarily to show how Cronauer, a Huck Finn–like individualist, is betrayed by higher-ups in his own army, and how Cronauer can hear what his superiors cannot. He forms a romantic attachment with a young Vietnamese woman and then an even deeper emotional bond with her younger brother. The boy cries out to him, "We're not the enemy—you're the enemy." When Cronauer does end up in danger, it's his own officer who is the real culprit, and the young boy— who works for the Vietcong but loves Cronauer—saves the hero. And so the boy's act reveals conflict within the Army. The minor Vietnamese characters who fill Cronauer's goofy English classes show us that the Vietnamese can be just like us, except poorer and with funny accents; they learn ghetto jive and play improvised softball, only with melons, and endear themselves to Cronauer and the audience. We know they will soon become boat people. *Full Metal Jacket* showcased the complacent imperialism of such attitudes, in the remark of a colonel to Joker: "We are here to help the Vietnamese, because inside every gook there is an American trying to get out."

Vietnamese characters are more often the displaced object of grunt rage at the meaninglessness of their mission. These Vietnamese are sneaky, and they don't play fair. *Casualties of War,* for instance, opens with two battle episodes, one nighttime and one daytime, that showcase guerrilla tactics and provoke virulently racist comments from the grunts. The sergeant offers a relatively sympathetic explanation: "See, these people here are confused themselves—are they Cong or not Cong."

America's Vietnamese allies are also often shown in a way that reflects the American soldiers' cynicism and dismay. For instance, in Christopher Crowe's *Off Limits,* a film noir set in wartime Saigon, the corrupt South Vietnamese police are "mice" to the hard-bitten U.S. Army detectives. In *Full Metal Jacket* the grunts frankly despise their Vietnamese allies. Their hostility is worked out on, among others, Vietnamese prostitutes. In interviews with a Canadian television crew one says, "We're shootin' the wrong gooks." Or Vietnamese can simply become invisible, as in *Gardens of Stone,* where Vietnam is seen only in one murky jungle shot. And sometimes they're erased, for a reason. In the making of *Dear America* HBO simply struck references to Vietnamese deaths, according to the director, for fear that such comparisons would be invidious.

The grunts, and the viewers, are almost invariably plunged into a

Vietnam of alien beauty and ever-present danger, without clear boundaries. The war is murky in most battle scenes, such as in *Platoon,* where the thick jungle metaphorically overwhelms the grunts rather than sheltering them, as do the warm dens of their barracks. (*Full Metal Jacket,* whose urban battle scenes take place during the atypical 1968 Tet offensive, is the exception.) If the field is impenetrable jungle, Saigon—symbol of the failure of the rear guard to back its field soldiers—is all riotous overcrowding and crass commercialism. Cronauer's Saigon is sunny daytime in *Good Morning, Vietnam,* while the *Off Limits* detectives mostly see it by neon-lit night. But either way, it's an unpredictable universe, seeded with booby traps, time bombs, and bad faith. In this sea of uncertainty the only real relationships, for good or evil, are among the American fighters.

### Placing the Blame

Portrayals of the Vietnamese thus point to the way in which, for these films, the war isn't about "us versus them" as much as about "us versus Them within us." The "Them within us" is carefully confined. The focus is on someone up above, but not too high—not, for instance, anybody in particular in the State Department or the White House. In *Good Morning, Vietnam* the bad guys are the creep who runs the radio station and his superior, who can't see that the war is changing and that he might need someone with Cronauer's ability to help boost morale. Above them, though, is a good general, who does recognize Cronauer's value and who intervenes in the end to rescue him. In *84 Charlie MoPic* the bad guys are middle-level officers. Careerist "L.T." delivers a speech in which he describes how combat duty is a stepping-stone to a military career. "L.T. thinks being a war hero will give him an edge as a junior exec," director Duncan said, "but the rest of the guys know they've been earning that for him." The detectives of *Off Limits,* pursuing the serial killer of Vietnamese prostitutes and their Amerasian babies, find out that their culprit is an American officer. Although the detectives precipitate his death, his crimes go undenounced because his peers protect him. In *Casualties of War* get-along-go-along officers, both black and white, block the outraged Private Eriksson's pleas for justice. It's only when the Lutheran Eriksson runs into a chaplain—a moral voice that transcends the system—that court-martial becomes a possibility. *Hamburger Hill's* subject, the taking of a pointless strategic objective, where soldiers suffered 70 percent casualties, carries its implicit indictment of military officers into every scene. In TV series incompetent and corrupt officers and embassy officials punctuate the hard life of the grunts and the medical and R&R staff—a seemingly bold, but contained, criticism of higher-ups.

Grunts may be self-righteous in their contempt for the higher-ups, but they are still true to their roles and jobs. Fragging (the killing of officers by their men) is a rarity in these films, as it was not in the war. *Platoon* is the primary case, and there the murders of first Elias and then Barnes occur within the platoon's civil war. Only in *Full Metal Jacket,* where the deranged recruit murders his officer because he takes the drill sergeant's pronouncements literally (this is a "world of shit"), is fragging portrayed as a revolt against the stated mission. As in Kubrick's earlier antiwar films, *Paths of Glory* and *Dr. Strangelove,* in *Full Metal Jacket* arrogant officials carry the brunt of the director's misanthropy, although his bleak view of human folly includes the culture of the grunts—and the audience.

So the noble-grunt subgenre features intense immediate conflict and skirts attacks on the decision makers higher up. That makes sense, of course, given the movie grunts' point of view (although real-life grunts often had a larger perspective). Even the documentary *Dear America,* which might be expected to have looser narrative constraints than a fiction feature, carefully limits its view. It does feature documentary footage of civilian officials, including the presidents, making pronouncements. But they are mere black-and-white punctuation, dramatic images of faraway authorities giving cryptic orders.

The invisibility of the real war-makers is thus built into the premise of these films. That distancing is the expression, in filmic narrative, of a long social process of erasure set in motion by President Nixon in 1972. As public protest grew over massive bombing raids and the mining of the Haiphong harbor, threatening to precipitate more huge demonstrations, and as the presidential election grew near, Nixon announced the existence of a "secret plan" to end the war. Early in 1973 U.S. troops were withdrawn. The TV networks seized on the United-States-leaves-Vietnam theme (Epstein 1974). The war, however, continued, as did U.S. involvement. Within twenty-four hours of the peace announcement, more than a hundred U.S. bombing raids had been conducted over Laos and Cambodia, and within Vietnam the civil war continued.

The "Vietnamization" of the war was a policy designed to get the war out of the sight of U.S. citizens without ending U.S. involvement in Southeast Asia. Aided by mainstream media, the strategy successfully dampened public protest, which declined with the end of U.S. troop involvement. But the out-of-sight policy did not put the experience of the war out of mind for Americans; it merely left its import unresolved.

Nor do the noble-grunt films attempt to resolve the questions swept under the rug by Vietnamization. Rather, they probe the pain of living with that lack of resolution. In their narrowly limited perspective the war becomes as confusing as it may have ever appeared to a nineteen-year-old recruit from Oklahoma.

In fact, these films do not just express but validate that confusion, partly through their very claim to you-are-there-in-the-swamps authenticity. It's perhaps most boldly asserted in *84 Charlie MoPic*, whose camera style and ambient-noise sound track are meant to convince you that you are watching unedited real life. However accurate the films may be—and the battle scenes from *Platoon* and *Hamburger Hill* (directed by John Irvin, who was a BBC film director in Vietnam), among others, have won high praise—their claim implicitly goes further than telling us what some combat soldiers suffered. They claim to tell us "the real truth" and, finally, how to feel about the war.

### Sullen Grievance and Self-Preoccupation

How we feel, by and large, is aggrieved. Aggrieved righteousness was not an attitude that began with the Vietnam War, of course. It had been building in American culture since the first flowering of consumer society (see "Paul Harvey and the Culture of Resentment"). The resentful attitude toward authority that these grunts express can be seen as an oblique commentary on the gutting of a national democratic process in a consumer society. Antiauthoritarianism is a strong tradition in American popular culture, but the antiauthoritarianism that suffuses these films is of a special sort. It has nothing to say about authority badly wielded and evidences, instead, a collapse of faith in "the authorities." Distrust of politics in general is the corollary to that collapse of faith. Sullen grievance and self-preoccupation are accompanying attitudes—attitudes that were key to President Reagan's personal popularity and to the success of the cartoonish movie figure Rambo. They reflect, at a personal level, a sociopolitical reality. The public—increasingly seen even by national political party officials as a collection of demographic-marketing categories—may be polled, may even vote, and carries responsibility for and the onus of decisions made by elected officials. The decisions themselves, however, are executed by those far from the citizen-consumer.

And so the grunts in these films can do something normally forbidden to entertainment movies: lecture the audience. When they do—when the squad members bark out harsh and undeniable truths in *84 Charlie MoPic* or respond with frank vulgarity to the camera in *Full Metal Jacket*—they are, unlike their higher-ups, ready to pay for the consequences of their acts. If the fighting men are angry about the position they have been put in, it is anger on behalf of all those who, as foot soldiers in life, suffer without reward.

The grunt becomes the underdog in the war, even taking on some characteristics of the Vietnamese. The best fighters are guerrilla fighters, like *Platoon*'s Elias and the sergeants of *84 Charlie MoPic* and *Casualties of War*. They fight at the level of the Vietnamese; this time around, the Vietnam War is a ground war.

The air war that, with defoliation, made Vietnam today an ecological disaster area is usually far away. When choppers appear, they're almost always medical helicopters on a rescue mission, not on the attack. The bombers that came to dominate U.S. strategy are virtually absent, and even their effects—the craters, the burned-over ground—are rarely seen in the thick filmic jungles. Nor is defoliation much in evidence, although stripped ground appears in *Casualties of War* as a metaphor for the emotional wasteland of the soldiers themselves. The bombing that was so shocking a metaphoric instance of U.S. aggression in *Apocalypse Now*, whose effects pervaded *The Killing Fields* (about the Cambodian war and its aftermath), appears briefly—for instance, in a scene in *Good Morning, Vietnam* when a village is obliterated—or is only a forlorn reference by soldiers trapped on the ground, calling for air support. Once again, an air sequence in *Full Metal Jacket* is an exception, and a clue to the film's self-awareness. And so, of course, aviator heroes are hard to find in the noble-grunt films. *Top Gun* (1986), the major air-war film of the same period in movie history, takes place not over Vietnam but over the Middle East. In *Bat 21* (1988), one film that does feature airmen, the flier falls to earth to become an instant grunt and victim of fire from both sides.

These underdog warriors fight most of all for basic humanity, responsibility, integrity within a mad situation. Chris in *Platoon* is a voice of individual conscience. The conflict over Chris—or Ishmael, the observer, as Stone calls him—forces him to grow up and "shed the innocence and accept the evil the Homeric gods had thrown out into the world. To be both good and evil" (Stone 1987, 9). Patrick Duncan called *84 Charlie MoPic* a film to "make sense out of a vision of personal responsibility sustained by people who have never been trained to do anything but survive" (in Jaehne 1989, 12). The NCOs of *Gardens of Stone* spend the movie grappling with the contradictions between what they know to be true ("there is no front in Vietnam") and what they are ordered to believe. *Casualties of War* spins on the individual moral decisions of the squad in "a twisted, upside-down world in which the normal things you can believe in didn't seem to apply anymore," according to De Palma in press materials.

## Staying Human

In the struggle to remain human when your bosses aren't, cynicism is a protective device, as is irony; both mask well-armed idealism and willful innocence. The *Off Limits* detectives are modern incarnations of Raymond Chandler's last good man in a sick world, and if *Full Metal Jacket*'s Joker makes sick jokes and wears a peace symbol on his helmet, it's in the service of maintaining sanity. *Hamburger Hill*'s grunts, initially divided by race and class, have a constant and common refrain, unifying them while separating them from the higher-ups: "It don't mean nothin'" (also a common refrain during the war itself).

But the cost of such personal strategies is high. That is the central theme of *China Beach*, which builds its drama on each wounded soul's lonely alienation. Central character McMurphy, a nice girl from Kansas, has seen so much tragedy that she can't remember how to feel; she is in constant peril of "going robot." Like the heroes of the noble-grunt movie, she and the other characters exist in isolation, clutching in the air for lost community. They are innocents damaged by experience, remaining innocent by conscience, although they may, at times, be guilty by circumstance.

The noble grunts are often children (as were the real grunts of the war, whose average age was nineteen), and their vision of the world reflects it. They are often, in fact, abandoned children, with bad or absent fathers (Barnes in *Platoon*, the self-deluded drill sergeant in *Full Metal Jacket*, the dead father of *Gardens of Stone*'s orphan, and the untrustworthy officers of many such films). Their youth culture, whose rock music pervades these sound tracks, promises a substitute web of relationships for those of family and community. That is the bright hope of deejay Cronauer's musical taste, and it is a promise made wistful in the nonstop sound track to *Dear America*. *Full Metal Jacket* milks musical communitarianism for fierce irony, as the troops tromp back to base singing the Mickey Mouse Club song.

Locked into the hermetic universe of Nam, these grunts have a nostalgia for home. "Home" in these films is the cuddly image of Chris's grandmother, to whom he writes in *Platoon*, or the scenes bathed in golden light of *Gardens of Stone*, or the Mom and Pop and Sis to whom the child-soldiers wrote in *Dear America*, or the Christian, midwestern town and family of *Casualties of War*'s Eriksson. It's rarely the riven civilian world in which the antiwar movement energized popular debate over the meaning of the war. About as close as you get is a scene in *Gardens of Stone*, where a cartoonish antiwar protester, one of Vice President Spiro Agnew's arrogant "effete snobs," insults one of the NCOs.

Most of these films, of course, take place far from protest demonstrations back in America. But they are also insulated from the sentiment that did exist within the armed forces themselves, especially among African American troops; there was resistance to officers, including fragging; and there were even ad hoc truces between U.S. and Vietnamese soldiers in the field. The ranks of Vietnam Veterans Against the War were filled with grunts who had been politicized in Vietnam. Even the documentary *Dear America* gives nary a hint of that side of the war. The freewheeling Cronauer's resistance in *Good Morning, Vietnam* is typically countercultural, a protest against being stuffy and old-fashioned and liking the wrong kind of music.

The roiling social conflict that the war provoked is refracted indirectly in these films. What these good soldiers suffer is abandonment by authority, answered by ending support and solidarity with each other. That is Elias's promise to Chris and the other dope-smoking buddies of *Platoon*. The black pilot tells the downed colonel in *Bat 21*, suddenly stricken with conscience, "I don't know you, Bat 21, but you don't sound like a killer. I'm sure you couldn't stop it from happening. The important thing is to put it behind you." The found buddies of *84 Charlie MoPic* cross racial and regional lines (although the cracker sternly lectures the lieutenant about how it'll be different back home), as do the buddies of *Hamburger Hill*. As that film's producer, Marcia Nasatir, put it in press materials, "Making this movie allowed us to recognize the courage and heroism of the young men who were there and who fought for each other." And that is the recognition that kept *Tour of Duty* and *China Beach* going week after week.

The problem of maintaining one's humanity, in these war films, is linked to asserting masculinity. These soldiers have been betrayed not only by their superiors but by macho warrior values that prohibit emotional expression. The contradictions they are crucified on come out in *Casualties of War*'s misogyny-on-parade atrocity sequence; in the woman-hating murders of *Off Limits*; in the contrasting characters of Barnes and Elias in *Platoon*; in Cronauer's impish refusal to be a grown-up, a man, in *Good Morning, Vietnam*. The tough-guys-do-cry stance, the pathos of boy-man protagonists, the brave refusal to give in to despair so typical of this subgenre—all bespeak an awareness of the end of good-soldier macho imagery.

Some say these films are recovering the masculine ethos by the back door, while others hope that they reflect expanded gender definitions in the culture. The "tormented libidinal economy" of this era's Vietnam films, as critic Jim Hoberman calls it, may speak as well to a wider uneasiness in the national mood, for both men and women (Hoberman 1987, 1989; Comber and O'Brien 1988; Jeffords 1989). The heroic, sometimes tragic John Wayne–type character in war films was also an emblem of a righteous, sacrificing America on the world stage. Audiences can empathize with the grunts' struggle to find footing on uncertain emotional as well as physical terrain. They, too, are confronted with a chaotic and uncooperative world, terrorized by large consequences of individual responsibility, and terrifyingly lonely.

The noble-grunt movie thus joins past and present. Interestingly, most of these movies take place between 1965 and 1968, thus creating an image of a war that ignores the origins of America's investment in Vietnam in the Kennedy era and eliminates the process of Vietnamization with which it ended. In the slice of the war they choose, the noble grunt can take center stage, as a figure who resonates with the embattled American consumer now.

If any film confronted the implications of the omissions and limitations of the noble-grunt perspective, it was *Full Metal Jacket*. But, like his work generally, it dealt with what Kubrick perceived to be killing weaknesses in the human condition: the need to create and pursue an enemy in the search for self-definition, the dangerous delusions of the idealistic and ideological. With its black humor, savage irony, and pervasive skepticism (particularly in its central character, Joker), *Full Metal Jacket* undercut the pieties of the noble-grunt film. It did not heroize its militant innocents or render sentimental the confusion of the powerless. Neither was it intended to frame or explain the particular historical process of American involvement in the Vietnam War.

Arriving in a sudden burst at the theatrical marketplace, the noble-grunt films seemed to emerge out of a long silence on the war. But, in fact, the pop-cultural landscape had been gradually changing to accommodate this new vision.

### The Death of the Good War Film

The World War II combat film—*Bataan* (1943), for instance—makes a convenient benchmark to measure shifts in pop-cultural perception leading toward the noble-grunt film (Basinger 1986). It featured a group of diverse men, symbolic of America's pluralism, whose individual heroics are dedicated to group survival, whose sacrifices are justified, and whose battles and objectives are clearly defined.

The genre died a lingering death. After World War II the U.S. armed forces never demobilized, and the Cold War replaced the hot one. The American government's geopolitical interests became global, while daily life, in an age of affluence propped up by military spending, became more and more defined by consumer choices. The kinds of wars in which the U.S. government got involved after World War II did not lend themselves easily to the conventions of the genre.

War movies refracted the changing times in many ways. Already in Samuel Fuller's *The Steel Helmet*, made in 1951 during the Korean War, the combat unit had become offbeat, the "good guys" often none too good, and the protagonist alienated. By the time of the Vietnam War, the "dirty-dozen" subgenre (Robert Aldrich made *The Dirty Dozen* in 1967), with its corrupt and unheroic characters and objectives, had become entrenched. Even war epics were affected; compare *A Bridge Too Far* (1977), chronicling a debacle, with *The Longest Day* (1962), the last of the classic World War II films. The Korea of *M*A*S*H* (1970) was, in fact, a black-comedic displacement of the ongoing conflict in Vietnam.

The Vietnam War also touched other genres, such as the Western. Arthur Penn's 1970 revisionist *Little Big Man* and Ralph Nelson's 1970 *Soldier Blue* both used Indians as metaphors for the Vietnamese, attempting to turn the genre on its head by making whites the agents of atrocity. *Soldier Blue*'s recapitulation of the Sand Creek massacre of the Cheyennes was meant to be seen as an uneasy parallel to the My Lai massacre.

Such relatively oblique social and political references were signs of the way the war did not fit traditional values and cultural images. During the war itself major studios avoided the subject, with the notable exception of *The Green Berets,* made with the bankable weight of John Wayne behind it. When that jingoistic film instantly became more of a political object than an entertainment commodity, it proved to the studios not simply that old formulas would not contain the new realities but that Vietnam was not a profitable subject for entertainment. And it was true that while American deaths were at their height, there was something indigestible about the war, its realities, atrocities, and images. The formulas of a film like *The Green Berets* had to be at war themselves with the deluge of images Americans saw on television, in photographs, and in documentaries that provided the most contentious images to emerge then or since about the war. (Recall such celebrated ones as that of a naked, napalm-burned child running down Highway 1, or that of a Vietcong being shot in the head.) Network TV and photographs made the "living-room war" a jumble of disturbing images, even if often framed by the interests of U.S. policy (Hallin 1986). Meanwhile, leftists produced films harshly critical of Vietnam; on celluloid as in life, leftists sometimes inverted the reigning clichés, identifying with Third World guerrilla fighters and demonizing political forces at home (Renov 1988).

As Nixon's Vietnamization policy and the air war proceeded, however, the war of images cooled down. Peter Davis's superb documentary *Hearts and Minds* (1974), with its searing assessment of the war as a policy debacle, fell victim to a post-Vietnamization consensus and was rarely seen, despite winning an Academy Award. Fiction films that broke through that consensus did not send studios searching for more Vietnam scripts. *The Boys in Company C* (1977), *Coming Home* (1978), *Go Tell the Spartans* (1978), and *Apocalypse Now* (1979), for instance, all tripped over cinematic conventions and popular unease with the issues of the war. For instance, Sidney Furie's *The Boys in Company C* milked the one-of-every-body platoon formula for its melodrama and created a cognitive dissonance that it never acknowledged. Ted Post's grimmer *Go Tell the Spartans*, which charts officer Burt Lancaster's discovery that the war was unwinnable, fell between camps of opinion and failed miserably at the box office (a failure deepened by the coincidence of a newspaper strike in New York with its release).

Other films groped for a way to address the political conflicts inflaming the war. *Apocalypse Now* was a self-referential epic about American solipsism, drawing on Joseph Conrad's nightmarish *Heart of Darkness.* Kurtz's pronouncement in the film, "It is impossible to describe what is necessary to those who do not know what horror is," was prophetic. The film, an enduring box office success, was admired for its spectacular production design. The film's publicity was also aided by the way its filming had duplicated, in miniature, the war itself. But it did not reshape Vietnam in popular consciousness; rather, it deepened popular confusion in its very theme. In Hal Ashby's *Coming Home,* a morality play with a political message, the veteran-victim was redeemed by taking a stand against the war, while the intransigent officer walked out to sea. The partisan message rankled, and *Coming Home* fell into the entertainment limbo reserved for Hollywood message movies.

The themes and narrative of Michael Cimino's 1978 *The Deer Hunter,* an elegy to American-white-male bonding and a eulogy for its sacrifice on the altar of Vietnam, presaged the parade of noble-grunt films, with heroes who were survivors of their own disillusionment. The film opens with holy rituals of all-American working-class life—hunting and a wedding—filtered through the golden haze of autumn. Then community is brutally shattered in the tropical hell dominated by evil North Vietnamese, whose (invented) torture tactics identify them as subhuman. *The Deer Hunter* powerfully played on aggrieved sensibilities and feelings of betrayal. But its torture sequences and the visually spectacular celebration of its protagonists tripped over conflicts still raging about the politics of the war. The publicity these "statement" films garnered, and the relative success of some of them, did not spur studio producers to search out similar projects.

### New Markets, New Dawn

For years thereafter, in fact, movie producers of the Big Chill generation avoided the subject of Vietnam. They didn't lack material. The publishing industry was creating bookshelves' worth of Generic Vietnam War Film Narrative; many of these books were optioned by independent producers. But in an industry where novelty is prized far above innovation, and where risk—even with big stars and safe subjects—is always high, this subject was declared off limits.

What finally triggered the noble-grunt subgenre was the changing economics of the film industry. The studios had long since become financial brokers rather than producers, with the trump card of distribution to play. With cable, videocassette, and changing opportunities in overseas markets, new distribution outlets opened up. Small producers, and the distribution companies that burgeoned briefly in the mideighties, seized those opportunities, and some turned to Vietnam projects that had been stalled for years. Major distributors only leaped on the bandwagon once they had proof that a Vietnam film—one cut down to a more comfortable size and rid of the contentiousness of the war itself—would sell. And *Platoon*, financed by the English company Hemdale and distributed in 1986 by minimajor Orion, sold very well.

Thematically as well as economically, the ground was being laid for the new Vietnam films in the decade preceding the noble grunt's emergence on screen. George Lucas's *Star Wars* (1977), a self-conscious epic, established the imperial hero as an underdog warrior for justice. There the good (read: American) guys were a guerrilla force against "the Empire." *Star Wars* and the ensuing films in the trilogy transported the underdog-warrior theme into space (Sobchack 1987). There, power and innocence could be conjoined easily with individual heroics, and the burden of empire could be dumped on "them," the bad guys, whoever they were. The trilogy also asserted other elements soon to become familiar in the noble-grunt film: the missing or bad father (Luke Skywalker's dad turns out to be villain Darth Vader), bungling bureaucrats, male bonding.

At the same time that Star Wars was breaking box-office records and giving back to us an "us" that could win on screen and in space, Americans on the ground were being buffeted with bad news. A nation that, with an energy shortage in 1973, had been given a taste of the end of affluence now faced international humiliation when Iranian students kidnapped U.S. embassy personnel in Teheran in 1979 and held them for more than a year. "America held hostage!" blared the television sets in millions of homes. It seemed as if the specter of Nixon's "pitiful, helpless giant" had taken on flesh. Environmental crises further ate away at the image of a nation both preeminent and righteous.

When Ronald Reagan assumed office, he seized on a reason for the precipitate decline in American prestige: "the Vietnam syndrome." More, he promised a new dawn, a morning in America. And he proceeded to conduct international affairs as if he were reading a film script, altering reality to fit needs. Nazi SS soldiers at Bitburg became "victims" as much as the concentration camp dead. The tiny island of Grenada, completing a small landing strip for tourism, became an invasion threat to the United States and in turn the object of an invasion. The rantings of the bizarre dictator Muammar al-Qaddafi became a justification for the first overt American attempt to kill the head of another country. The Nicaraguan contra forces became freedom fighters for democracy.

No matter what the outcome—even when hundreds of Marines died in a terrorist attack on a barracks in Lebanon—Reagan personally garnered support because he resolutely played the role of ordinary American, outraged and aggrieved. The decision maker, the power holder projected the attitude of a put-upon victim of decision making. It was a brilliant psychological ploy for a president who depended on popular support while exercising policies that were often unpopular and sometimes secret.

Reagan found a movie hero to match his own public persona, one to whom he proudly compared himself: Rambo. It was an interesting choice for the powerful man who played to fantasies of righteous vengeance among those who felt themselves powerless. Rambo was the perennial righteous underdog, the survivor of alienation and rejection.

Rambo—a preadolescent boy with Nautilized muscles, a wounded giant in chains, who although he breaks the chains, can never be healed—was also the figure who paved the way for public acceptance of the noble grunt. Sylvester Stallone had initially played the character in *First Blood* (1982, directed by Ted Kotcheff). John Rambo was a vet with post-Vietnam shock, who acted out the nihilistic rage of the forgotten man, among other things wasting a local police force contemptuous of war-torn vets. The first film ended downbeat, with Rambo going to prison. *Rambo*, the 1985 film directed by George Cosmatos, picked him up there, breaking rocks in a hellhole whose value for the battered and betrayed vet is that "here at least I know how I stand." And it transformed Rambo from psychotic to savior.

The plot, larded with explosive action sequences, revolves around a secret mission to find MIAs (soldiers missing in action). The choice of target is significant; the question of whether any living Americans remain in Vietnam has lingered in public consciousness as a kind of objective correlative to our lack of closure about the Vietnamized war. Rambo, too, is a symbol of the war's unresolved end. He's a ghost in the machine, like the MIAs. When his mentor Trautman warns him, "The old Vietnam is dead," he says, "I'm alive, it's still alive, ain't it?" And, indeed, Rambo gets to rerun history in this movie, which allows him to refight the war alone.

Refighting the war had been a staple of prisoner-of-war and MIA films such as *Uncommon Valor* (1983), *Missing in Action* (1984), and *Braddock: Missing in Action II* (1985). Playing successfully to audiences more interested in action than in Vietnam, they celebrated the (usually officer-status) prisoner of war. *Rambo* departed from the formula by making the action hero a rejected marginal, an outsider returning to battle. Focusing on the hero's sense of loss and his hurt at being misunderstood broadened the film's appeal from the male, action-oriented crowd to general audiences.

The character of Rambo crudely but effectively combined elements that expressed power and powerlessness, making him both victor and victim. And it helped complete the reversal that *Star Wars* had begun in space—a reversal that helped tame the war to entertainment proportions. "We" became "them," the underdogs, guerrillas, embattled victims.

Crucial to Rambo's stance as innocent betrayed is his childish character. At the outset Rambo asks Trautman, in a way that combines deference and petulance, "Sir . . . do we get to win this time?"—as if this were a children's game in which he had been cheated (as many Americans felt, by the outcome of the war). Throughout the film Rambo is the victim of repressive father figures. The bad fathers are the military and civilian bureaucrats who want to bury the POW-MIA issue. Trautman is too enmeshed in the system to protect him; he, too, falls victim to the schemes of the higher-ups. When Trautman discovers that Rambo has been betrayed again, he says of the mission, "It was a lie—just like the war."

Abandoned by corrupt or ineffectual officials, Rambo assumes the role of guerrilla fighter played the first time, and successfully, by Vietnamese. But he's a superguerrilla (part Indian, part German, he is thus part "primitive," part supercivilized). He skulks through the jungle half-naked, and his tools are a peculiar mix of high- and low-tech. He rips up scenes with submachine guns seized from his Vietnamese captors. He blows up enemies with a bow and arrow, but the arrows are tipped with explosives. And he always falls back on his lucky hunting knife. His victories in action are a boy's orgasmic fantasy of power, not just liquidating the enemy but annihilating the very landscape.

Vietnamese in this born-again war are both victims and villains. Rambo's liaison is a young girl, who falls in love with him; her dream is "Maybe go America—live the quiet life." She doesn't make it, dying in Rambo's arms. (Of course, she must die—Rambo is too much a child to be a lover.) The Vietnamese military men play a high-tech, big-operation game that evokes the U.S. war effort. Armed with sophisticated equipment, in charge of elaborate camps, they also use air power against Rambo. This is a film in which helicopters do attack—Vietnamese helicopters (one of which Rambo commandeers).

Rambo plays not just hero but a holy figure on crusade, and images conjure up that connection. For instance, we see him crucified on an electrical torture apparatus, echoing our first close-up sight of an MIA, also in a Christ-like agony. When the girl dies, Rambo holds her in a Pietà position, the image joining themes of holy suffering and righteousness.

Rambo's ultimate triumph is as much over the corrupt bureaucrats as over the Vietnamese; after returning to base with the MIAs, his last act of violence is to machine-gun the corrupt bureaucrat's equipment and threaten his life. But even in victory Rambo is condemned to obscurity; the heroic innocent remains the victim. Rambo's guerrilla war has a special poignancy because he is the unacknowledged secret defender of American values. "All I want," he tells Trautman with choked anger at the end, "all they [pointing to the rescued MIAs] want, and every other guy who came over here and spilled his guts and gave everything he had wants, is for our country to love us as much as we love it."

Rambo is the tragic image of an America wounded by circumstance.

Life has not been fair to him, or to America. The film's legacy was not so much in its muscular action sequences—although they guaranteed its enduring international success—as in the image of a vet wronged but right.

Just how well Rambo fit the times was evoked when Lieutenant Colonel Oliver North testified in Congress during the Iran-Contra scandal. His demeanor recalled the same petulant, self-righteous, hurt-little-boy attitude that Stallone expresses at the beginning of the film. Ollie North's behavior as a member of the National Security Council also had parallels with Rambo's. He, too, was a cowboy of foreign policy, having "learned" from Vietnam to do it right this time, demonstrating contempt for lines of authority in the name of patriotism.

## Learning to Live Again

The Rambo age of presidential image politics came to a end with the 1988 election. George Bush did not have the style, skill, or will to reverse, in his personal presentation, the image of power as Reagan had done so deftly. He did, however, invoke the specter of Vietnam in his inaugural address. "That war cleaves us still," he said. "Surely the statute of limitations has been reached. . . . No great nation can long afford to be sundered by a memory."

The movies, however, had already re-remembered Vietnam, in the process transforming the social cleavages to which Bush referred into smaller, far more manageable psychological ones. They had cleared the way for the next phase of reimagining the Vietnam experience on screen: the part where the vets come home. Even as Bush called for a kinder, gentler America built on local volunteerism and a rebuilding of community spirit ("a thousand points of light"), Vietnam vets in the movies had come back and were learning to live again.

For the major studios the moment of the noble-grunt film had, by 1989, passed. Few post-*Platoon* films bore out the box-office promise of *Platoon*, and of course, the genre itself was limited in its profitability. Although Lee Iacocca linked patriotism and Chrysler's new Jeep Eagle line in an ad preceding *Platoon* on videocassette, the advertising, licensing, and marketing possibilities of the noble-grunt films were clearly never going to match those of a *Star Wars* or a *Batman*.

But the process of learning to live again in the wake of the war was still a hot Hollywood subject, with such projects as Oliver Stone's *Born on the Fourth of July* and Norman Jewison's *In Country*. The unpredictable, violent psychotic vet of films like *Taxi Driver* (1976), *Tracks* (1977), *Rolling*

*Thunder* (1977), and *Who'll Stop the Rain?* (1978)—embodiments of the disjunction between national self-image and experience—had been virtually read out of movie scripts by the late eighties. That was in part because of lobbying by veterans' groups. But it was also because the violent irruption of Vietnam into the American self-image had been successfully transformed into a sturdier image of decent but powerless Americans doing their best to survive the decay of community around them.

In the later eighties, movies about returning vets did not put the issue of the vet's political judgment at the center of the story, as *Coming Home* had done so uncomfortably. Now the issue was the plight of the vet attempting, in the midst of a shattered community at home, to recover from the shattering of community in Vietnam. In films like *Heartbreak Ridge* (1986), *Distant Thunder* (1988), *Jacknife* (1989), and *In Country* (1989) the vet is the symbol of an America scrambling for its moral and psychic footing. All these films stress the pathos of the man who suffered and was scarred, who performs the heroic act of returning to life, and who calls into question the macho John Wayne image that got packed into the baggage along with the rifles in Vietnam.

In these films veterans have buried themselves for long years in grief or dull withdrawal. They are alone with memories and values that no longer fit. Clint Eastwood's *Heartbreak Ridge* presaged some of these later themes. In it hero Tom Highway—survivor of not one but two meaningless wars (Heartbreak Ridge was the Hamburger Hill of Korea)—stubbornly clings to his outdated Marine machismo as if time had stopped. In *Distant Thunder,* directed by Rick Rosenthal, the protagonist is a "bush vet" hiding out in the Northwest rain forest with other survivors. In David Jones's *Jacknife* a vet hides out in his house, drinking away his future. *In Country* features a vet who can talk only to his war buddies, taking refuge from bad dreams and bad memories in his ramshackle family home.

These vets hide from an unfriendly, unfeeling world where the rules have changed. Tom Highway pores over women's magazines to try to figure out why his wife left him and suffers lectures from younger officers who remind him that it's a time of low-intensity peace. The bush vet of *Distant Thunder* must listen to a redneck's smarmy antivet rantings. The vets of *Jacknife* live more with their flashbacks than with the trashy, complacent world of civilian consumer life. The vets of *In Country* think they're uncomfortable relics of a past no one wants to remember; proving them right, a dance honoring them draws few of the town's residents.

The therapeutic action of family and buddies helps these vets once again to love themselves. *Distant Thunder*'s bush vet, after venturing from his hideout with the aid of a friendly woman in town, gathers the courage to live again with the help of his son, who reveres him for his high school sports record and who wants to be proud of him for his war record. In *Jacknife* the vet finally comes to terms with the secret horror he's been living with—the death of his buddy, one of a trio, in combat. The other surviving member of the trio finally makes him relive the moment and thereby abandon the search for blame; in the bargain he, too, rejoins society, winning the heart of his buddy's sister. A vets' therapy group also helps the two remaining buddies face the rest of their lives. *In Country*'s vet finds closure, and the beginning of a new life, when his niece—whose father had died in Vietnam before she was born—and her grandmother persuade him to visit the Vietnam Memorial to see the names of their dead on the wall. His coming-to-terms with his past is also the beginning of a new life for his niece, who has been haunted by the mysterious past.

The earlier *Heartbreak Ridge* is not nearly so sentimental or optimistic. Of course, it came out at the emergence of the noble-grunt subgenre, when public sympathy for the vets was still in the process of becoming pop-cultural currency. As well, Clint Eastwood is a postmodern macho man, playing both to that image and against it. *Heartbreak Ridge* raises both eyebrows at its archaic hero. Tom Highway recovers his self-esteem by going to battle in Grenada, but it is a silly little exercise, and he returns home, as Eastwood later said, "a warrior without a war, without any place to go. . . . Where he goes, who knows?"

*Born on the Fourth of July* (1989), on the other hand, raised sentimentality to a battle cry of betrayal. The crippled survivor-hero (Tom Cruise as Ron Kovic) rages against his impotence, which director Oliver Stone has said symbolizes the plight of America today. It is a fate brought on by a macho Marine recruiter, a steely commander who denies him his remorse at killing Vietnamese civilians and one of his own men, and most of all by a Catholic mom who sold him on simplistic patriotism. Aided by antiwar vets, Kovic finally comes "home" when he delivers a speech at the 1976 Democratic Convention, although home will always be, for him, pathetic impotence in a wheelchair.

Whatever happens to them, these vets are survivors of a general breakdown of community. Their heroism lies in their choosing to forgive themselves, improvise a future, weather hostility from a few unfeeling civilians, and accept the acceptance of many others.

**Feeling Better**

We are on our way, in the movies, to forgiving ourselves not for anything the U.S. government and forces did in Vietnam but simply for having felt so bad for so long. It remains to be seen whether this is a cultural landscape in which, as some hope, "we can find new determination to brave the opening expanse" (Marin 1982, 562), or the platform on which new castles of nostalgic delusion will be built (Hellman 1986)—or both. Either way, it is a profoundly personal matter rather than a political or historical one, emotionally predicated on a sense of loss and propelled by a therapeutic tone of self-help.

The Vietnam movies of the later eighties expressed and helped to shape a consensus that the event was not a war but a tragedy. This tragedy was not political, and it was certainly not shared by or with the Vietnamese. It was entirely ours—the grunts of history, the innocents, the powerless ones, the "good soldiers." The enemy was not over there but above us, somewhere in the cold regions of policy and commerce, those regions beyond the control of the consumer. We have been abandoned, these films told us, and must heal ourselves. The war is over, but the damage remains. Distrust, alienation, a loss of history, and a huddled-over sense of self-protection are our legacy.

## References

Auster, A., and L. Quart. 1988. *How the War Was Remembered: Hollywood and Vietnam*. New York: Praeger.

Baritz, L. 1985. *Backfire: A History of How American Culture Led Us into Vietnam and Made Us Fight the Way We Did*. New York: William Morrow.

Basinger, J. 1986. *The World War II Combat Film: Anatomy of a Genre*. New York: Columbia University Press.

Bryan, C. 1984. "Barely Suppressed Screams: Getting a Bead on Vietnam Literature." *Harpers* (June): 67–72.

Calloway, C. 1986. "Vietnam War Literature and Film: A Bibliography of Secondary Sources." *Bulletin of Bibliography* 43 (3): 149–58.

Comber, M., and M. O'Brien. 1988. "Evading the War: The Politics of the Hollywood Vietnam Film." *History* 73 (June): 238, 248–60.

Epstein, E. 1974. *News from Nowhere: Television and the News*. New York: Random House.

Gitlin, T. 1988a. "Hip-Deep in Post-Modernism." *New York Times Book Review*, November 6, p. 1ff.

———. 1988b. *The Sixties.* New York: Bantam.

Hallin, D. 1986. *The "Uncensored War": The Media and Vietnam.* New York: Oxford University Press.

Hellman, J. 1986. *American Myth and the Legacy of Vietnam.* New York: Columbia University Press.

Hoberman, J. 1987. "Hi, Nam." *Village Voice,* December 29, p. 63.

———. 1989. "Vietnam: The Remake." In *Remaking History,* ed. B. Kruger and P. Mariani, 175–96. Seattle: Bay Press.

Jaehne, K. 1989. "Company Man." *Film Comment* (March–April): 12 ff.

Jeffords, S. 1989. *The Remasculinization of America: Gender and the Vietnam War.* Bloomington: Indiana University Press.

Marin, P. 1982. "What the Vietnam Vets Can Teach Us." *The Nation,* November 27, p. 562.

Morrison, M. 1988. "'China Beach' Salutes the Women of Vietnam." *Rolling Stone,* May 19, p. 75–79.

Renov, M. 1988. "Imaging the Other: Representations of Vietnam in '60s Political Documentary." *Afterimage* (December).

Rollins, P. 1984. "The Vietnam War: Perceptions through Literature, Film and Television." *American Quarterly* 36 (3): 419–32.

Schell, J. 1989. *Observing the Nixon Years.* New York: Pantheon.

Silverman, R. 1988. "The Art of War: Vietnam Terminal and Interminable." *Afterimage* (September): 10–12.

Sobchack, V. 1987. *Screening Space.* New York: Ungar.

Stone, O. 1987. *Platoon and Salvador: The Original Screenplays.* New York: Vintage Books.

U.S. Senate. 1980. Committee on Veterans' Affairs. *Hearings.* 96th Congress, 2d sess. February 21, March 4, May 21. Washington, D.C.: Government Printing Office.

Weber, B. 1989. "Cool Head, Hot Images." *New York Times Magazine,* May 21, p. 24 ff.

# Black

# Magic

*For several years in the 1980s, along with my weekly* In These Times *reviews I produced an occasional essay for* The Progressive, *regularly responding to Erwin Knoll's crisp but effective postcards that always said the same thing: "But what have you done for me lately?" (In our circles, guilt was the currency of choice.) In the essays, I would look for connections between the tensions in the movies and in the varied lives we were leading. This was, of course, an era before special effects had come to their pride of place in film production. "Black Magic" and "When Any Alien Looks Good" are a couple of examples, lightly edited, from that period.*

Religious practices of the African diaspora—voodoo, macumba, Santería, candomble, and many other branches of that syncretic religious expression—have become staples of movie storytelling. They have, however, along with African American contributions to American music, poetry, and other aspects of popular culture, usually been exoticized in the movies, zoned into an area where their disturbances can be about anything other than endemic racism. In David Byrne's *True Stories*, Jonathan Demme's *Something Wild*, Alan Parker's *Angel Heart*, and John Schlesinger's *The Believers*, this tradition is tweaked, reflecting not only the enduring divisions of racism but also current anxieties.

In *Something Wild* and *True Stories*, mystery in the form of black and brown folk culture expressions is called in as a kind of positive contrast, and sometime comfort, to the centerless world of commercial popular culture. Both films are self-conscious explorations of postmodernism, both as a phenomenon of the art world and as a daily experience of the taxpaying public. In *Something Wild*, yuppie Manhattanite Charlie (Jeff Daniels) encounters the riotous disorder below the neat surface of his desk in the person of Audrey (Melanie Griffith). In a world of image and artifice (the production design of the film is a moving-image testimonial to the eclectic and syncretic energy of New York artists), Audrey is the fetish master. An obsessive dresser, calculatedly individualizing borrowed "looks," she also travels with voodoo dolls and lives among icons of mystic power. She needs them, too. Fetishistic ritual is the secret to living in a world where even the most minimal family and workplace expectations are absent but where people act as if they existed. The sound track sets the pulse and tone for Demme's vision of a world run ragged by the hectic production and recycling of meaning. And African American music of course provides the rooted baseline. The sound track descends from upbeat pop to driving Afro-accented rock to ominous ostinato, surfacing into the carnal daylight of Sister Carol's full-bodied rendition of the theme song "Wild Thing." The singer is our last image in the movie, a sly suggestion of the endurance of subcultural vitality—"wild," primitive—under the shifting surface of postmodern life.

*True Stories* is far more explicit and personal a film about the puzzle of postmodernism for the artist. Byrne sets himself down, as himself, in the imaginary town of Virgil, Texas, to study the habits of hicks plugged into a national commercial culture. Distinctions between regional folk and mass culture collapse under the self-styled normalcy of the town. No matter how weird it gets—and a fashion show in which outsized people model shapeless clothing made of Astroturf, living plants, and material painted to look like bricks is pretty bizarre—the people of Virgil don't find it strange. And the unfailingly polite observer, an artist-anthropologist in the field, does not hold the locals up to ridicule, either.

But is a decentralized, virtually valueless mass-folk culture a genuine popular expression? Byrne is clearly no aficionado of the mass-culture-dupes-the-masses school, but the film is punctuated with pointed question marks, and the boldest of them comes in the shape of a reverential bow to black-and-brown music and magic. *True Stories*' only engaging tale is that of Louis (John Goodman), a hearty lonelyheart who valiantly applies the tools of electronic culture to his wife search: he lip-synchs, barhops, and places TV ads. Finally, he decides to write a song himself and perform it at the talent show. His ripely sentimental country song features the chorus, "People like us—we don't want freedom, we don't want justice. We just want someone to love." (Just try to imagine this lyric in a blues song.) It reaches out to a lonely lady who lives in bed and who finally gets out of it to respond to him.

Louis's success wasn't grounded in mainstream, lip-synching culture. He got help from two friends in less integrated subcultures. When he's in despair, his Hispanic friend Ramon (Tito Larriva) takes time out from a rip-roaring set of Tex-Mex bar-band music to give him the name of an African American practitioner of Santería (Pop Staples). The man's magical practices seem to turn Louis's luck for the better.

For Byrne and Demme, both pop artists confronting a Brave New World that they're trying to find a role for themselves in, subcultural magic is a poignant counterpoint to the quiet and noisy desperation of their subjects. Two contemporary thrillers, *Angel Heart* and *The Believers,* put on display the horror of the Other, in romantic forays into the forbidden.

*Angel Heart* by Alan Parker *(Midnight Express, Fame, Shoot the Moon),* a detective-horror meld, is an excellent example of pop thrills built on deep social prejudice. Mickey Rourke plays a '50s detective whose trademark look is anachronistic facial stubble. His name is Harry Angel, but he's no saint. Unlike his pop-cultural reference, the Raymond Chandler detective who eschewed ordinary slime work to investigate the corruption at the heart of society, Angel does take divorce cases; in fact, that's mostly all he does, and that poorly.

Then he meets Louis Cyphre (Robert DeNiro), an icon of the forces that feed on the desires of the disenfranchised. We meet Cyphre, whose overlong fingernails curl ominously around his elegant cane, above an African American prayer hall. Cyphre wants Angel to find a missing person: Johnny Favorite, a prewar jazz musician. Angel's search for that missing person sends him to New Orleans. There, a beautiful young woman, Epiphany (improbably played in what *Variety* accurately called "a Valley girl accent" by the *Cosby Show*'s Lisa Bonet) introduces him to the world of voodoo.

What Angel ultimately finds is a cut-rate version of the Faust story. Faust was attracted to worldly power. The attraction that makes you sell your soul here, though, is addiction: the drugs—whether sex, opium, or magic, and they're all related here—that are crutches to the powerless. That fascination with addiction is reflected not only in the themes of the film but in Parker's trademark style, honed by years of making commercials. The film, full of high-impact shock scenes, runs less on the narrative than on the impending sense of horror to which the ripe colors, shadows, noises, religious artifacts, and the flash-cut editing between states of consciousness drive you.

*Angel Heart*'s disturbing power prompted an X rating. The criticisms, however, focused on the sex. (A ten-second cut finally passed the film through with an R rating.) But sexual explicitness is the least of it. What is so disturbing is the pervasive sensationalizing of evil. Questions of fundamental morality—the soul is at issue here—are the grist for an orgasmic sensory revel. To sensationalize evil, *Angel Heart* reaches deep into the social subconscious. Voodoo is the vehicle through which the characters cross over the line into the forbidden. The ordinary secular world, which also happens to be white, middle class and urban, contrasts with mystery in the form of supernatural rituals of a dark-skinned underclass with rural roots.

This use of voodoo in particular is grounded in a deep working misunderstanding between religious traditions. The religious practices of the black diaspora have many expressions, but they all share at least one aspect: they are not focused, as in the Christian tradition, on salvation. They instead invoke a connection with ever-present spiritual forces, both for communion and in an instrumental way. In Christianity, tapping into the world of the spirit for tools is, categorically, witchcraft.

African American culture, in *Angel Heart*, taints Christianity with the witchery of the Other. Whether in the fundamentalist church that Louis Cyphre hovers over or in outdoor voodoo rites, ritual is ominously other—dark, powerful, and instrumental. African American music is used, in this context, as a related transcendental practice. Horror enters in when decadent whites (one, a fortuneteller, played by the anorectic-looking Charlotte Rampling) cross over color and culture lines to cut themselves in on some supernatural clout.

In the press materials, Alan Parker talks about historical research he did on "the various extreme and bizarre religious movements of the '30s and '40s, mostly born out of economic isolation, and perhaps spiritual desperation," especially in Harlem. In this time of renewed economic crisis and fundamentalism, the theme of extremist belief is appropriate. But the phenomenon is certainly not restricted to African Americans, or to traditionally oppressed cultures. A resurgent Ku Klux Klan, right-wing populism fueling rural anger, and Shirley MacLaine's pop mysticism are only three examples. *Angel Heart*'s lush diabolism resonates with all-too-timely anxieties, framing them in terms of ancient fear and attraction.

*The Believers*, a far less effective thriller, depends on the same gambits as *Angel Heart*. It pits the sunny, light-skinned, suburban world of rationality and order against the passionate thumping tribal rhythms of dark-skinned spirituality, evoked through Santería. It takes place in our very own Sin City, New York, which appears to have been taken over by an occult underworld powered by the magic of people of color. Martin Sheen plays, with his typical suffering-Christ act, a newly widowed psychotherapist who comes from Minneapolis to New York with his son. He gets caught in a web of intrigue among African American and Latino practitioners of Santería and corrupt whites who draw their power from them. Directed by John Schlesinger, once a director of ambition, it's an incoherent, murky mess of a movie; its slovenliness makes the racism inherent in its approach boldly apparent.

As in *Angel Heart*, what's so diabolical is not the Other's religious practice in itself; the Other is always presumably irrational and mysterious and gets dangerous only when in contact with Ourselves. It's the crossing over between races, classes, and cultures that poses the threat. The plot features decayed, corrupt, and rich whites who seize on the forbidden power that the Other holds and use it to build real estate empires, political clout, and fortunes. The racial hierarchy is explicit: the agents of evil are African American and African (the whole trouble started in the Sudan). The practitioners of Santería who want to channel those forces for good are Caribbean. The prime beneficiaries of evil are white, as is the potential victim, the little boy Chris (Harley Cross).

Carla Pinza, who plays the housekeeper trying to protect Chris, is herself a Santera. "It was important to me to clear up the confusion surrounding my faith," she explained in press materials. "Santería is . . . a positive force, a practical force, for helping people—physically and spiritually—through the gods." That's not what *The Believers* shows, though. It shows a Santería rooted in human sacrifice, primitive and dangerous. It shows that it's a dangerous game to get down with the underclass, where primal rhythms and primitive practices shatter cool rationality. And possibly even more than that: that the problems of corrupt power can ultimately be laid at the altar of the Santeros.

It's no news that cultures of the disenfranchised provide rich pools of exoticism and romance for pop artists. The exploiting of those pools as a vision of the Other mysteriously affecting "us," however, boldly evokes a warranted crisis of confidence in the coherence, flexibility, and renewability of a commercial popular culture that practices denial and exclusion.

# When

# Any Alien

# Looks Good

There have always been good aliens in the movies. In *The Day the Earth Stood Still,* for instance, a nice guy from outer space tries to tell us to stop the nuclear-arms race by pulling the plug on the world's power. Clammy but friendly aliens in *Cocoon* offer oldsters the ambiguous gift of eternal youth. *E.T.* imagines an alien who embodies the sense of childhood innocence that director Steven Spielberg finds betrayed in the adults of his authentically captured, suburban, plastic-wrapped worlds. That alien lets the best in white-bread land triumph at the movie's end, and the flood of licensed products in its wake kept us from asking what will happen when little Elliot grows up—presumably to be one of those men with clanking keys that he so fears. But in late 1980s science fiction movies, the aliens didn't have to be good guys anymore to look good in comparison to humans.

In *Aliens,* Sigourney Weaver as the androgynous heroine Ripley battles to protect humanity against the superparasites from outer space. She's as much at war with the Company and its legal eagle Burke as she is with the alien Supermom who has turned the nuclear-powered space colony into a hive for her young. It is Burke who wants to preserve the nuclear installation ("a substantial dollar value") and to bring back an alien (a great "bioweapon"). "I'm not sure which species is worse," Ripley cries. "You don't see them fucking each other over for a goddamned percentage!"

In the end, Ripley wins against both the Company and the aliens. But the question that pops up in the middle of the film never goes away. The society that Ripley returns to after fifty-seven years of drifting in space has only gotten worse since her days piloting a factory ship full of alienated drifters, tempering their routine with hostile remarks about their exploitation. The board-room executives are just as focused on the bottom line as those workers said they are. And the Marines who come out to save the colonists are just as alienated as the workers had been: "They aren't paying us enough for this," one groans as they pull themselves creakily out of their hyperspace tubes. At least they have the camaraderie of shared exploitation. Burke, like middle-management professionals all over our corporate landscape, buys the Company line. He really believes that what's good for the corporation's profit margin is what's good for people.

The only thing more powerful than Burke and the monster corporation he represents is the other horror that *Aliens* exploits: mother love. Once Burke has been swallowed into the pod-reproduction factory it is Ripley—a single mother protecting the adopted daughter she has found on the colony—against the Supermom from outer space. Our Mom wins, having put technology in the service of fierce maternal love. "Get away from her, *you bitch!*" she yells at the Other Mom, as she climbs into the clanking machinery the movie's men have dominated until now.

But at movie's end, the girls are heading home—home, where the board-room execs, the sullen dock workers, the muscle-bound Marines, and the Company clones are. So the challenge never ends. Unlike the megaorganism she fights, Ripley can't win by preserving the body alone. For human beings, the body social is the critical unit. What is gone from the universe the Company rules is any sense of community grander than that engendered by mindless military allegiance, any value higher than that of Company profits.

Other science fiction films also display an equally disturbing lack of faith in a human future, along with mordant criticism of commodity culture today. *Liquid Sky,* the cult favorite made by Russian émigrés and American punk artists, plunges its audience into a youth culture of sex, drugs, and death, and all of it with style. The heroine struggles for self-expression, but it's a lonely battle in her neon-lit, nihilistic world—so lonely, in fact, that the only person she can establish a relationship with is an alter ego. In the end, she welcomes the chance to submit to the UFO that zaps her into the ozone in an energy surge—and we're glad for her. There certainly is no place for her down here.

Coscriptwriter and star Ann Carlisle meant for her work to be seen as a "memorial," she told me soon after the film's first national splash:

> New Wave was a very black protest, so black that there was nothing left to talk about. It's like, the world is so full of lies we don't want to speak our own. The look was everything. I got involved in the film because so many people died, and I felt it was very sad that this whole cultural upheaval that had happened at night, a theater in life, would die—pass on once it had hit the windows at Macy's.

She wanted the heroine to stand as a critique of image freedom: "Margaret had the attributes of liberation, in the way she dresses and speaks. And she found a niche in the New Wave, but in the end she looks for a prince again—and it's a UFO. She's American, in that sense."

Floating up to the sky with the UFOs is also the solution for Otto, played by a mournful looking Emilio Estevez, who takes that way out in Alex Cox's *Repo Man*. The movie does for supermarket culture what *Liquid Sky* does for downtown New York. In this parallel universe, everything is a generic product—down to a can labeled FOOD in generic packaging. (So is it a statement that a prototypical generic pop star, Michael Nesmith of the Monkees, produced the film?)

The hero is a lost kid, an inheritor of the character played by James Dean in *Rebel without a Cause*. Like him, Otto wants to be both a kid and a man, both hip and in charge. But two generations later, the kid isn't looking for romance, just a job. The unemployment office presents him with his choices: night watchman, asbestos worker, fast-food flipper. And in this era, the parents—who in *Rebel* are anguished, if ineffectual—are not up to worrying about his situation. They are glued to the television preacher who promises them salvation. Media fundamentalism isn't enough for Otto; he is not ready for the living grave of the living room. He finally finds work repossessing cars. His boss, played by Harry Dean Stanton, goes at it with a crusader's zeal. He has a mission: rescuing consumer culture. He's the Don Quixote of Credit Worthiness.

At the same time, anonymous aliens are trying to repossess their radioactive treasure, stashed in the trunk of a 1964 Chevy Malibu. They are creepy and grasping and conscienceless. But so what? At the end, the hero sails into the sky in the Chevy, in an apotheosis as tacky as the generic culture he leaves behind. Wherever he's going, at least he will be spared the exhausted version of consumer life to which his buddies, staring up at him from the parking lot, are condemned.

Too bad he left before he could make a date with Elaine, the heroine of *Letter to Brezhnev*, made by unemployed Liverpudlian youth about the despair at the core of Maggie Thatcher's England. Elaine, played by Alexandra Pigg, is young, cute, and desperately unemployed. She falls in love with a Russian sailor and fantasizes about defection from capitalist decay. Pigg explained recently in press interviews: "From Elaine's point of view, if she could go to Russia, at least it's an adventure. If you're living in a place where there are no prospects for you, you don't see yourself as having any future."

*Uforia*, by John Binder, is built from some of the same raw materials as *Repo Man*. It's about grown-ups, but they are as lost and yearning as any teenager. It takes place in trailers and tents in the Southwest, where the new migrant workers get tacky jobs and tacky lives and look to roving fundamentalists for tacky salvation. This offbeat film was directed by John Binder, who worked on *Marjoe*, a film about a faith healer. Again, Stanton stars. This time he's a hustler-preacher who believes his own message to the extent that it works to keep him in beer. Arlene (Cindy Williams of TV's *Laverne and Shirley*), though, is a true believer. She swallows everything she reads about UFOs in magazines at the checkout counter of the supermarket where she is a cashier. Arlene is the real miracle worker: she can take cheap lies and turn them into real inspiration. Her boyfriend (Fred Ward) and the preacher first pooh-pooh her fantasies and then exploit them, turning her sweet conviction that life does have meaning—at least in outer space—into a new hustle. Outraged, she calls the police. Guess who saves them? That's right. We leave them just as the UFOs are landing.

The link between zealotry and despair, between fundamentalist ecstasy and hopelessness in everyday life, is overt in *Uforia*. You can't help siding with Arlene against the con artists who try to capitalize on her faith. But you also can't help wishing, at movie's end, that there were some way other than up to get off the mountain on which they are perched.

The New Zealand import *The Quiet Earth*, directed by Geoff Murphy (known for his international hit *Goodbye, PorkPie*), works a different subgenre: the end-of-the-world story. An experiment has gone awry. In an electrical blitz, everyone on Earth is zapped out of existence, it seems, except for one of the engineers (Bruno Lawrence) who worked on the doom project. He assuages his guilt by overindulging in now-plentiful consumer pleasures. But somehow, they don't satisfy.

Soon, he has collected a couple of companions—a young white woman (Alison Routledge) and a Maori (Peter Smith). Ancient patterns of jealousy and control surface. They manage to pull together to try to save the

Earth from final destruction, and it almost works. But not quite. In the last scene, our hero wakes up to a vision of another planet. It's a beautiful vision, even a lyrical vision. Also a lonely one, capping the sense of doom for the engineer-dominated society that infuses *The Quiet Earth.*

In the madly inventive *Brazil,* Terry Gilliam imagines a *1984* organized by a combination of the telephone company, the Pentagon, and the Social Security Administration. The System doesn't work, but it makes sense of a sort—a totalitarian sort. The hero escapes, but to inner, not outer, space. Caught inexorably by the oppressive political machine, he fantasizes about disappearing with his girlfriend over the horizon into a bucolic never-never land free of hardware and blisses out as torturers go to work on what's left of his body.

What was driving these movie heroes into outer space with the aliens, forcing them into the arms of the transcendent unknown was the seamless exhaustion staring out at them from supermarket shelves, unemployment offices, and the gateways to trailer courts. It was the uninviting prospect of pledging their allegiance to systems that only work with a deathly logic. It was the grim suspicion that if there are ways out of how we are now, they do not lie in our power to come up with answers. At the same time that teenage movies portrayed a world in which it was impossible to imagine being a grown-up and liking it, these science fiction films abandoned the utopian thread on which our modern morality plays have been hung.

The heroes and heroines of these movies were courageous enough to be wistful—for meaning, location, belief, love. They looked to the sky, hopefully, with just the attitude that fed an array of New Age and born-again religious movements.

# Part II.  Communication and the Public Interest

# The What and How

# of Public Broadcasting

*In a country where commercial radio and television function as our virtual shopping mall of culture, public broadcasting is often expected to be everything else—school, day-care center, town hall of the air. But it's an institution with its own history, structure, and constraints, and you can't usefully celebrate or denounce it without understanding it. I wrote this as a primer, to ground discussion of its present, promise, and future.*

Big Bird. Garrison Keillor. Bill Moyers. *Car Talk*. *All Things Considered*. *The Civil War. Eyes on the Prize. This American Life.* The Watergate and Iran-Contra hearings, gavel to gavel.

These and other remarkable, diverse expressions of American culture have been brought to us by one of the most peculiar creatures in electronic media, public broadcasting. At its best, public broadcasting has been the place on the airwaves that provides programming that advertisers wouldn't pay for—like educational programming for kids, long-form documentaries on social issues, artistic experiments with the medium, and critical analysis of the rich and powerful (including major media). It represents images and the views of groups not normally heard from in commercial media, such as seniors, regional cultures, and ethnic, cultural, and gender minorities. It has been a site for technical innovation.

Closed captioning started with public TV, and both public radio and TV were pioneers in the use of satellite technology. And it has been a place where public affairs, debates, and controversy can be aired and even, occasionally, launch community action.

Public broadcasting has had a disproportionate weight in American culture, despite the fact that it is perpetually embattled. It is constantly attacked by both right (in publications such as *COMINT* and the *Accuracy in Media Newsletter*) and left (by organizations such as Fairness and Accuracy in Reporting and as summarized in Hoynes 1994). Politicians find it an easy target of ridicule and outrage. And it is largely ignored, on any given day, by most of the listening and viewing audience.

Still, it has been dubbed "a barker channel for the culture." Its significance has to do with its unique position on the media landscape, as a service that is neither governmental nor commercial. Public broadcasting is that rare place on the air where commercial interests do not necessarily tailor the programming (although they often do indirectly, anyway). It is a place where public concerns can sometimes (although not necessarily) be raised. It therefore has unique credibility among American media and unique possibilities.

## Who Tunes In?

From the outset, public broadcasting has mostly defined its relationship with the public as serving an audience. It has assumed the challenge foisted on it to compete with commercial services for attention. Its audience is relatively educated and influential, though overall demographics show a rough equivalence with the American population as a whole.

Public radio has a large and diverse audience, but not as large or diverse as the population at large. National Public Radio, the largest public radio entity that keeps audience figures, reaches about one in eleven radio listeners older than twelve years old each week, and it has an average-quarter-hour (AQH) rating of 0.5. This compares with, for example, a weekly AQH of 0.8 for the commercial network CBS stations (which typically broadcast adult-oriented public affairs programming), putting public radio's audience in the same ballpark with some commercial services. Listeners, more of them men than women, are considerably more highly educated and affluent than the population at large, and also more rural, the core audience being thirty-five to fifty-four years old (Montgomery 1998; NPR 1998).

Public television has a prime-time rating overall that averages 2.2 (that is, 2.2 percent of homes with television, tuned in for fifteen minutes or more), a rating consistent over the past decade. Children's programming pulls household ratings that range from 0.3 *(Where in the World Is Carmen Sandiego?)* to 1.6 *(Sesame Street)*. Public TV's audience is far below that of commercial broadcast TV, where prime-time audiences start above 10.0 and a children's cartoon show (often also viewed by adults) might garner a 5. But the majority of the American public tunes in for at least fifteen minutes each week. Public TV's demographics vary according to the program. Public TV's children's programs draw disproportionate numbers of poor and ethnic-minority families, while adult, prime-time audiences overrepresent white, educated, and male viewers. Viewers older than fifty make up 47 percent of the prime-time audience, while only 27 percent of the general population is in that age range (PBS 1998).

Public broadcasting's core upscale audience has been cultivated over time, and it is both an advantage—it is an audience with clout—and a curse. Whenever politicians decide to cut public broadcasting's funds, they claim it serves an elite that could pay for it in the private sector. (No private service, however, has volunteered to take on public broadcasting's array of programming, and furthermore, although its demographics "skew" upward, they still include vast numbers of the nonelite, who usually receive it over the air.)

Elite or representative, what public broadcasting's audience is first of all is an audience, and not—with occasional exceptions—an active public. It has, however, the potential to act like one, which it regularly does at times of life-and-death crisis for the service.

### History

U.S. public broadcasting is unusual, compared with other systems internationally (Garnham 1986; Rowland 1976, 1986; Etzioni-Halevy 1987; Blumler and Nossiter 1991; Blumler 1992; Foster 1992; Avery 1993; Hoynes 1994). European public service broadcasting—the major alternative model—was usually established early on as a government program that either dominated or monopolized the national spectrum. These broadcasting services have usually assumed the role of both informer and entertainer of their audience. The promotion of civic values and political and social debate has always been an active goal. In practice, *public service* has, as in the United States, been defined in many ways, but some typical strategies have been to provide news reporting, opportunities for disenfranchised groups to air views, children's programming, public debate, and documentaries.

In the United States, by contrast, public broadcasting has always been a small, niche service (Rowland 1991, 1993). In fact, it was created as an afterthought. Legislators, helped along by corporate lobbyists, between 1927 and 1934 decided the shape of U.S. electronic media for the next fifty-two years (McChesney 1993). In the United States, commercial enterprises were given permission, through licenses, to use designated zones of the frequencies, used for broadcasting, or spectrum, for profit by selling advertising time. Other interests—labor unions, religious organizations, educators, private foundations—had warned that such commercial use would eliminate community and educational use of the spectrum. And indeed, despite industry promises, within months after the passage of the Communications Act of 1934, programming time by and for these noncommercial constituencies simply dried up. In 1938, a small part of the FM spectrum—then pioneer territory and generally regarded as worthless—was reserved for educational broadcasters, as a sop to the most well-organized of the losers. Later, in 1952, educational TV got the same kind of deal—reserved spectrum, mostly in the UFH band. It was then regarded as vastly inferior spectrum, because it was much harder to tune in to than VHF, where almost all commercial channels were placed.

Airspace—spectrum—without resources was not much of an opportunity. Many of the available channels stayed dark, and those that attempted to broadcast—usually through a school or university—often carried dull, cheap programs, perhaps talking heads in a classroom (Witherspoon and Kovitz 1989).

Then came the Public Broadcasting Act of 1967, which turned U.S. public broadcasting into a national phenomenon for the first time. It came about partly because after World War II (which had proven the power of mass media to manipulate masses), major U.S. foundations such as Ford and Carnegie committed themselves to funding electronic media as a vehicle for greater social justice (Carnegie Commission 1967; Ford Foundation 1976; Baughman 1985). President Johnson's then-aide Bill Moyers presented a proposal to Congress that became the Public Broadcasting Act of 1967.

But the law did not create a strong public broadcasting system. In fact, driven by conservative fears of a liberal broadcasting service and commercial fears of rivals, Congress deliberately created a decentralized service that was anything but a system. Under the circumstances, it is an impressive testimonial that the service has managed to achieve a national presence and to respond to public needs in any measure at all.

## Public Broadcasting's Structure

The core institution of public broadcasting is the station, operating through a nonprofit entity, usually a university or nonprofit community organization, but possibly a local or state government or even a religious group. It is run by its board, sometimes with advice (but no authority) from a community advisory board. A minority of stations, mostly radio, are run by community groups formed for that purpose. "Community broadcasting," which grew from a movement in the late '60s for grass-roots media, usually has an alternative cast and often has wildly eclectic programming reflecting the interests of various constituent groups.

About 15 percent of all radio stations in the United States are non-commercial—about 1,860 FM stations (*Broadcasting & Cable Yearbook* 1998). But only about 700 are "public radio" for the purpose of qualifying for federal support, and they reach about 86 percent of the American population with formats that range from classical music to jazz to long-form public affairs. (The rest are small, student-run, or religious, usually evangelical Christian stations.) Big cities might receive four or five public radio signals. But public radio also serves small communities and rural areas that no commercial signal reaches, such as Indian reservations and remote parts of Alaska (NPR 1993, 1998).

There are approximately 365 public television stations, out of a total of around 1,550 TV stations, given to about 180 licensees (meaning that some licensees have more than one station, often within a state network). Around 240 of public TV stations, about two-thirds, transmit in the weaker-signal UHF frequency—a distinct disadvantage since 40 percent of Americans still get UHF signals over the air instead of by cable. Still, almost all U.S. television viewers have access to at least one public television signal, even when they do not get a commercial signal (CPB 1997; *Broadcasting & Cable Yearbook* 1998).

This broad coverage means that public radio and TV form the largest potential broadcast networks in the United States. However, the stations rarely act in any kind of unison. In fact, they are fiercely independent, not just from each other but even from citizens who want to participate in decision making. They get together with each other and with corporations to produce or distribute programming or offer other services (for instance, locator services or commercial data transmission, on unused parts of a station's spectrum), but only with great difficulty do they make united decisions.

This tendency is further exacerbated by the fact that there are several kinds of stations, each with its own interests. In radio, some seventy "flagship" stations—the leaders of state and regional public broadcasting networks—tend to dominate both production and policy. Public TV is much more polarized. A few powerful program-producing stations are extremely important in setting program agendas. A handful of stable local stations engage in community programming and perhaps some enterpreneurial activities (distribution, programming, community outreach). A much larger number of small stations produce no programming and simply retransmit packaged programming. In fact, the big three stations—in New York, Boston, and Los Angeles—produce around 60 percent of the programming for all public stations. In most large markets there are several stations, some of which may duplicate most of the major programming coming from prime-time distributor PBS. In twenty-two states, TV stations are united into state networks, permitting group purchases and planning, but not necessarily promoting independent and local programming.

This decentralized structure explains several things about U.S. public broadcasting: the difficulty of initiating national projects, for instance; the many-faceted image of public broadcasting; and the uneven distribution of resources among stations. One chronic debate within public broadcasting serves as an example of the dominance of local interests in the service as a whole. Many TV stations in large cities duplicate program services, leading some planners to argue that the number of stations—each of which duplicates sizable basic expenses such as light bills, executive salaries, and rent—should be reduced for efficiency's sake. But no station is likely to volunteer to liquidate itself, and no one else can. At the same time, the decentralization makes it difficult to challenge those who argue for eliminating stations, which would destroy the potential inherent in a local broadcasting resource for the community.

There are also powerful national organizations within public broadcasting, each with its own unique interests, limitations, and shaping force on the service. The Corporation for Public Broadcasting (CPB) is a nongovernment entity with a politically appointed and balanced (along partisan lines) board, funded solely by federal tax dollars. It supports public radio and television stations with grants to improve equipment and services, research and policy development, and since 1980 with limited programming funds (Lashley 1992). The CPB has become a relatively large bureaucracy, with very limited powers. Its board has at times become highly polarized on political lines, and the ensuing fights have encouraged the organization to become extremely cautious, often avoiding risk taking in either promoting station activities or programming.

Because the CPB is the organization that receives federal funds, it is also a lightning rod for congressional attacks on public broadcasting. Over the years, Congress has removed much of CPB's decision-making power, forcing it to act as a simple funnel for tax dollars, although CPB continues to be responsible, in one sense, for public broadcasting as a national phenomenon.

In spite of attempts by Congress to prevent a national network, public broadcasting does use programming services that establish a national schedule of sorts. Since the 1970s National Public Radio (NPR) has provided, from its base in Washington, D.C., a morning and evening news service to its member stations. Since the mid-1980s, a regional service—Minnesota Public Radio, now Public Radio International (PRI)—has become a major rival to NPR for member dues. In television, the Public Broadcasting Service was created in 1969, with the help of the CPB and member stations, as a subscription service for programming for public stations (Avery and Pepper 1976; Pepper 1979). Thus, stations could get the benefits of quality programming—far too expensive to produce locally—without violating the law that banned CPB from distributing programs.

These distribution services (there are other, smaller, and regional ones as well) are perhaps synonymous with public broadcasting for most listeners and viewers, but in fact they are private services that depend on the dues of their member stations for support. They do, however, have a major role in determining what viewers and listeners receive, because most high-quality programming depends on national distribution to cover costs. Because they depend on station dues, these services all strive to provide programming that will be popular, bring in upscale viewers and listeners, win critical approval, avoid political ire, and encourage donations and corporate support. While each has specific programs and projects that demonstrate social and public priorities, each also must meet the demands of the broadcast marketplace.

The question of production opens other areas of contest over the notion of the public. Public broadcasting offers, in theory, a place for perspectives and groups that are either uninteresting or unpalatable to commercial broadcasting to be heard. But how to get such perspectives before viewers and listeners is a hotly debated question. Many independent producers argue that public broadcasting ought to be more open to independent productions and to a wider range of styles and expressions than it is. Broadcasters often claim that they must meet audience expectations of quality and objectivity, and that independent productions often do not attain that standard.

In fact, the great majority of production is either done within particular stations or groups of stations, or by production houses and individuals with close, long-standing relationships with public broadcasters. Public radio stations, on far smaller budgets and with much lower production-quality demands than television, typically produce half (49 percent over-all) of their own programming (occasionally with independents), the greater proportion in daytime hours. Other programs, either individual-ly or as part of a package, are sold to stations by NPR, PRI, or public radio stations, which produce them individually or in partnership or even di-rectly with freelancers (Collins 1993; CPB 1997).

Public TV produces far less local programming—and far less of it is public affairs programming—than in radio; CPB estimates, in fact, that only 4 percent of all public TV programming is local (1997). It also uses even fewer truly independent productions. Stations and PBS depend heavily on programming by the big three stations, and on a few produc-tion houses—notably, the Children's Television Workshop for children's programming. Public TV used to carry far more foreign programs, espe-cially from Britain, than it does today; cable services pay better, and buy those programs first.

Complaints from independents over the years, expressed most clearly by the Association of Independent Video and Filmmakers from 1978 for-ward, became a major conflict throughout the 1980s, resulting in the for-mation of the Independent Television Service (see "Public Television and the Public Sphere").

### Financing

The financing of public broadcasting in the United States is as complex as its structure. Each of the three major sources of funding—government, viewers, and corporate donors—comes with its own set of constraints.

Tax dollars—state, local, and federal (the last only 15 percent)—account for almost half of the nearly $2 billion annual pie for public broadcasting. Even so, the American taxpayer pays only about $1.30 a year in tax contributions for all public TV and radio services—far lower than in most other countries where public service broadcasting exists. For instance, in Britain government funding comes to $45 a person, and Japanese government funds average $40 a person. In the United States the federal portion has steadily dropped as a proportion of the whole over the past two decades, leaving stations ever more dependent on local and state revenues—which, unfortunately, are even more at risk than federal funds (CPB 1997; Lashley 1992). Tax money is largely used to pay for infrastructure and technical improvement costs, investments that are extremely difficult to fund-raise for.

Public broadcasting's large dependence on taxpayer dollars—appropriated every three years—also means that it is very vulnerable to political attack. Such attacks have been unremitting and have made station managers and bureaucrats gun-shy. At the federal level, picking on public broadcasting has become part of the Republican agenda. This tendency started early, with President Nixon, the first president to experience the newborn service (see "Public Television and the Public Sphere"), and has continued. When the Republicans won the majority of both the House of Representatives and the Senate in 1994, a long-smoldering conservative hostility toward public broadcasting resurfaced with a vengeance. Significantly, massive response from concerned voters who were viewers— many also Republican—was important in checking the effort.

Viewer dollars, about 22 percent of the budget, constitute the single largest source of funding for public broadcasting (CPB 1997). (Although tax dollars form a larger total figure, they come from at least five different kinds of taxpayer-funded organizations, each with its own funding logic.) Although listeners and viewers are sometimes led to believe that their donations contribute to purchasing popular programs like *Sesame Street*, viewer dollars can and usually are poured into general funds. Only about one in ten viewers and listeners actually donates, and the percentage does not seem to be growing. Viewers and listeners who are most likely to donate are typically culturally and politically cautious. This tends to skew programming decisions toward the bland and genteel (*Lawrence Welk, Championship Ballroom Dancing, The Three Tenors*)— what the great historian of broadcasting, Erik Barnouw, calls "the safely splendid" (1993), especially in television, where viewers tune in for a program rather than a format, as in radio. It also means dedicating perhaps 10 percent or more of a station's production resources to pledge weeks.

The "safely splendid" programming mode fits the interests of public broadcasting's third funding source—corporations—very well. Corporations provide about 15 percent of public television's funding (CPB 1997), but unlike other sources, they pay to associate their name with specific programs or to participate in joint ventures.

Corporations find public broadcasting's audiences very appealing. Upscale demographics typically resist advertising. Reaching them through brought-to-you-by announcements is one form of what corporations call "ambush marketing"—sneaking up on the kind of people, usually better off and influential, who are suspicious of advertising. Corporate underwriting inevitably changes priorities, to include the interests of the corporation. For instance, a four-part program funded by Northwest Airlines, which has Asian routes, on how to do business in Asia takes up production time and airtime that a station might otherwise allocate to, say, a local public affairs program or a documentary on a controversial topic. Furthermore, corporations have no interest in programming that risks losing the upscale audience or that generates controversy.

More far-reaching still are the implications of corporate partnerships, in all of public television's efforts to discover ways to be self-supporting. For instance, in 1994 then-dominant cable company TCI purchased a major interest in the *MacNeil-Lehrer NewsHour* (later, the *NewsHour with Jim Lehrer*); the nightly public affairs program has now become in part a commercial venture, answerable to the needs of a major industry player. Similarly, in 1997 public television negotiated a piece of the product licensing profits for the popular television show for under-two-year-olds *Teletubbies*; the decision was widely taken as an indication that future programming decisions would be affected by related licensing opportunities.

Public broadcasters thus must beg for dollars and favors equally—but with different consequences—from individual viewers, corporations, and the government. Inevitably, it is uncomfortably close to the priorities of both government and corporations, in spite of its name. The public, in any real sense, is rarely invoked by executives and programmers, except during pledge week. However, at the same time, public broadcasting's diverse funding structure, combined with its claims of excellence, makes it a surprisingly resilient punching bag as an institution, able to resist pressure and absorb losses and attacks from any one side, including that of the public.

### Looking to the Future

As public broadcasting enters the twenty-first century, it faces challenges that are political, technological, and financial (Twentieth Century Fund 1993).

Politically, public broadcasting is ideologically in disfavor internationally (Rowland and Tracey 1990). Politicians worldwide, in an era of deregulation and privatization, are defunding public broadcasting services. Since the U.S. service has ample experience with begging from and cooperating with the private sector, this is not as dramatic a challenge as it is, say, in Europe. But political battles still absorb a large amount of time and effort, and each one seems to erode ground.

Some within public broadcasting believe that the secret to continued government funds is to both further develop and highlight public broadcasting's instructional role, and to stress its capacity to be a here-now version of the much-vaunted National Information Infrastructure. This effort would emphasize public broadcasting's least visible aspect: its work with educational institutions and its programs for learning outside these institutions.

CPB and PBS officials have challenged broadcasters and legislators alike to consider public television, for instance, as a community public information resource—a virtual public library. Public television exists in almost every community and thus has the potential to be a link between schools and providers of distance learning of all kinds. This approach could turn into an advantage the existence of hundreds of local stations that produce very little local programming. It would exploit taxpayer-funded satellite technology. PBS has already made major investments in instructional and educational programming, including distance learning, and has deepened its existing relationships with public schools by offering some of its programming material to teachers free of copyright restriction (Jensen 1994; Twentieth Century Fund 1993). This vision of the role of public television, however, is ahead of that of most station managers.

This attempt to capitalize on emerging technological possibilities as communications markets converge elsewhere well reflects the rapidly changing telecommunications marketplace. Cable's entry changed public television's programming options by offering better prices for popular programming such as the so-called Britcoms and nature documentaries. The proliferation of independent television and the success of the VCR also forced public TV to compete with evermore video options. Digitization challenges both radio and TV. Public radio faces the challenge of digital audio broadcasting, which promises (or threatens) to bring vastly more choice but to eliminate local presence. Public TV must find funds to invest in digital technology for its stations, in order to hold on to new spectrum given to broadcasters for digital television. It must also find uses for new channel capacity that will both be justifiable to Congress, which will foot some of the bill, and have a money-making element, in order to pay for the rest.

U.S. public broadcasting will probably become even more aggressively entrepreneurial and ratings oriented in its broadcast aspect. Public radio has increasingly become more market sensitive, with streamlined formats and greater dependence on audience research. In the 1990s, the success of *Car Talk*, a witty talk show in which two scientist-cum-car-repairman brothers answer questions about fixing cars, established a new model for winning programming, as have upscale quiz shows. While clearly offering quality listening alternatives, neither format works very well for many important community and public issues. Public TV has focused for more than a decade on core programming that would boost ratings—series (which allow for better promotion), high-profile subjects (the Civil War, baseball), and drama (*I'll Fly Away* became a PBS show for a season after it failed on commercial television). Coproductions such as the Seattle public TV station's venture with Disney to make a science program, *Bill Nye the Science Guy* (later distributed on commercial as well as public TV), were encouraged. Underwriting guidelines were relaxed to the point that it became possible to run the same message both as an advertisement on commercial TV and as an underwriting acknowledgment.

As well, broadcasters in both radio and television have launched a series of (often-failed) commercial enterprises. Among the successes are a chain of public broadcaster-related educational toy stores, a video fulfillment service for public television programs ("Call here to order a tape of the program you just saw on public TV"), and an audio fulfillment service for any music presented on public radio. Chicago public TV station WTTW has even initiated a home shopping service for upscale items its audience might be interested in.

If such enterprises succeed, how do taxpayers get paid back? If they fail, do the taxpayers pay for such gambits? How does success or failure affect a station's ability to serve interests that are not marketplace based? Will audiences remain fiercely loyal to services that look and sound more and more commercial?

Public broadcasting remains not only an important site of diversity and demonstration of public life in mass media but could become an important site of democratic behavior in the developing information infrastructure. For this to happen, its supporters need to demand that public broadcasting define and exercise a public mandate that goes beyond niche marketing to the upper middle class.

### References

Avery, R., and R. Pepper. 1976. "The Evolution of the CPB-PBS Relationship 1970–1973." *Public Telecommunications Review* 4 (5): 6–17.

Avery, R. K., ed. 1993. *Public Service Broadcasting in a Multichannel Environment: The History and Survival of an Ideal.* White Plains, N.Y.: Longman Publishing Group.

Barnouw, E. 1993. Personal communication, May 21.

Baughman, J. 1985. *Television's Guardian: The Federal Communications Commission and the Politics of Programming, 1958–67.* Knoxville: University of Tennessee Press.

Blumler, J., ed. 1992. *Television and the Public Interest: Vulnerable Values in West European Broadcasting.* London: Sage.

Blumler, J., and T. J. Nossiter, eds. 1991. *Broadcasting Finance in Transition: A Comparative Handbook.* New York: Oxford University Press.

*Broadcasting & Cable Yearbook 1998.* New York: Bowker.

Carnegie Commission on Educational Television. 1967. *Public Television: A Program for Action.* New York: Harper & Row.

Collins, M. 1993. *National Public Radio.* Washington, D.C.: Seven Locks Press.

Corporation for Public Broadcasting (CPB). 1997. *Frequently Asked Questions about Public Broadcasting.* Washington, D.C.: Author.

Etzioni-Halevy, E. 1987. *National Broadcasting under Siege: A Comparative Study of Australia, Britain, Israel, and West Germany.* New York: St. Martin's.

Ford Foundation. 1976. *Ford Foundation Activities in Noncommercial Broadcasting, 1951–1976.* New York: Ford Foundation.

Foster, R. 1992. *Public Broadcasters: Accountability and Efficiency.* Edinburgh: Edinburgh University Press.

Garnham, N. 1986. "The Media and the Public Sphere." In *Communicating Politics: Mass Communications and the Political Process,* ed. P. Golding, G. Murdock, and P. Schlesinger. New York: Holmes & Meier.

Hoynes, W. 1994. *Public Television for Sale: Media, the Market and the Public Sphere.* Boulder, Colo.: Westview.

Jensen, E. 1994. "Public TV Prepares for Image Transplant to Justify Existence." *Wall Street Journal,* January 13, p. 1ff.

Lashley, M. 1992. *Public Television: Panacea, Pork Barrel, or Public Trust?* New York: Greenwood.

McChesney, R. 1993. *Telecommunications, Mass Media, and Democracy: The Battle for the Control of U.S. Broadcasting, 1928–1935.* New York: Oxford University Press.

Mills, C. W. 1956. *The Power Elite.* New York: Oxford University Press.

Montgomery, A. 1998. Personal communication, National Public Radio strategic planning, June 5.

National Public Radio (NPR). 1993. *A Brief History of National Public Radio.* Washington, D.C.: National Public Radio.

National Public Radio, Strategic Planning and Audience Research. 1998. *Listeners by Choice.* Washington, D.C.: Author.

Public Broadcasting Service (PBS). 1998. *PBS National Audience Report.* Washington, D.C.: Author.

Pepper, R. 1979. *The Formation of the Public Broadcasting Service.* New York: Arno Press.

Rowland, W. D. Jr. 1976. "Public Involvement: The Anatomy of a Myth." In *The Future of Public Broadcasting,* ed. D. Cater and M. Nyhan, 109–39. New York: Praeger.

———. 1986. "Continuing Crisis in Public Broadcasting: A History of Disenfranchisement." *Journal of Broadcasting and Electronic Media* 30 (3): 251–74.

———. 1991. "Public Service Broadcasting: Challenges and Responses." In Blumer and Nossiter 1991, 315–34.

———. 1993. "Public Service Broadcasting in the United States: Its Mandate, Institutions and Conflicts." In Avery 1993, 157–94.

Rowland, W. D. Jr., and M. Tracey. 1990. "Worldwide Challenges to Public Broadcasting." *Journal of Communication* 40 (2): 8–27.

Twentieth Century Fund Task Force on Public Television. 1993. *Quality Time?* New York: Twentieth Century Fund Press.

Witherspoon, J., and R. Kovitz. 1989. *The History of Public Broadcasting.* Washington, D.C.: Current.

# Public Television

# and the

# Public Sphere

*For more than a decade, I covered as a reporter the struggle of independent filmmakers to establish good-faith relationships with public television. Finally, independents succeeded in getting the Independent Television Service (ITVS) created. The years of bureaucratic conflict had opened up whole philosophic swamps before me, and when I became an academic, I decided to look carefully at the question of what the term* public *really meant to different players in that conflict. I uncovered several historical layers of such struggles, each conditioning the next.*

The formation of the Independent Television Service (ITVS) showcased U.S. public television's most enduring and bedeviling question: what is public about public television? In one sense, the answer is simple: nothing in particular. Overlapping sets of private, nonprofit bureaucracies juggle broadcasting budgets. But a large chunk of the money in public television's $1 billion-plus annual budget comes from taxpayers, on the promise that public television offers something important to the body social.

The formation of ITVS, examined in historical context, permits an analysis of the fluctuating definitions of public television's role. From this perspective, it is clear that

- public television has never had an explicit mandate;

- various interest groups have exploited the resulting ambiguities;

- a public television with a unique role to play in American media must redefine itself not as primarily a broadcast service but as a service to foster and fortify, through programming, the public sphere.

## The Public and the Public Sphere

This argument depends on the concepts *public* and *public sphere*. A public shares in common the social effects of both private actions (such as pollution, crime, the consequences of rapid urban development) and governmental actions (such as war, medical research funding, and educational projects); it also shares in common an interest in addressing them in its own defense, as John Dewey and others so well articulated. A public constitutes itself, as Dewey said, in the process of communication, a process that becomes action (Dewey 1927; Mills 1956; Boyte and Evans 1986; Carey 1989, 81ff).

What a public is not, except for extremist rhetoricians, is consumers. Consumers have defensible individual and group interests, but they are not the same thing as a public. The public is also not individuals whose aggregate individual opinions add up arithmetically to public opinion. The public is a social construct and as such needs social spaces in which to exist, to learn about the public interest, to debate it, and to act. Social spaces such as town meetings, community groups, and electronic bulletin boards for virtual communities of interest are all potential vehicles for public activity through communication, insofar as they grapple with the challenges of defending the public interest.

The public sphere, as introduced seminally by Jürgen Habermas, refers to the social fabric within which those spaces are generated and maintained. It is an elusive concept, with its own contested history (Habermas 1989; Calhoun 1992; Garnham 1990; Schudson 1995; Carey 1995). Whether it even exists is in debate. It has existed; it was born with the growth of the bourgeoisie at the beginnings of the capitalist era, and doctrines of individual rights rest on it and depend on it. But has it shrunk to ineffectuality, with the growth of state bureaucracies and large economic interests? The withering of the public sphere in late capitalist society, as Habermas so provocatively sketches it, occurs with the penetration of the state broadly into social life, in conjunction with the organizing of powerful economic interests, including media (Habermas 1989,

142 ff). Is it reconstitutable as grassroots, local, and virtual communities, interest and political groups organize to defend common interests against the pressures of big government and big business? Is the bygone public sphere of bourgeois males an expandable concept for a multicultural, multiclass, even multigender society? Have mass media replaced the public with an ersatz, marketed simulacrum? Concerns about the future of a multicultural society without political avenues to exploit the benefits of cultural diversity democratically; about the power of media and of advertisers in shaping social and political life; about voter apathy and the rise of disenfranchised, impoverished subcultures all return, ultimately, to questions about the public sphere (Entman 1989; Ewen 1988; Times Mirror Center 1990).

What is not in debate is that without a public, there is no real democracy. Economic and governmental interests do not necessarily act in the public interest; they act in their own interests. And without a separate realm of society to act, the public shrinks down to isolated individuals. The public sphere is, willy-nilly, a political sphere—it is about the people discovering their public aspects, and finding political mechanisms to resolve them. That is not to say that the public sphere is only about political issues, or that cultural expression is not important. Rather, cultural expression in its vast diversity is always, in the words of James Carey, a prime site of "social conflict over the real" (1989, 87). So social scientists, humanists, and social and political activists all have a fascination with the public sphere.

Mass media can foster the communication essential to formation of a public sphere. Mostly in the United States they do not, since mostly they are corporate entities governed by the profit motive and functioning largely to deliver eyeballs to advertisers. But public media could be different. They could have a central mandate to foster a viable, vital public sphere. Their knowledge brokers would assume the challenge of decentering the focus of mass media toward the public. But mostly they do not. The reason is not hard to find: an already disorganized and weak public loses out to vested interests.

This is what has happened time and again to public television, a rare noncorporate and nongovernmental site on the media landscape, and that is why the foundation of the ITVS is such a remarkable event. At its best, it reminds us of what public television could be and perhaps even must be to survive. With its drawbacks, it shows the enduring limitations of U.S. public television.

ITVS was created by Congress in 1988, as a separate production entity under the Corporation for Public Broadcasting (CPB). With a three-year annual budget of $6 million plus promotional monies, the service was "to expand the diversity and innovativeness of programming available to public broadcasting." The law also mandated an increase in funds for consortia of minority producers, and report language required CPB to focus its resources generally on "unserved and underserved audiences" (Public Telecommunications Act of 1988; U.S. Congress 1988). However, no new money was allocated.

Congress, strongly pressured by independent producers angry at public television's slighting of their work, thus demonstrated its frustration at public television's public service record. It also replicated traditional organizational problems—by putting CPB in charge of the ITVS, by making the ITVS an ancillary service to what was already an ancillary service, and by perpetuating public television's financial agony.

But it did signal well the fact that public television today has a crisis of mission. Its mandate was never made explicit, and permanent endowed funding was never provided. Its loose federation of 365 local stations (held by universities, schools, municipal or state entities, or community boards) shares some common resources through the federally created but nongovernmental organization CPB; their membership organization the Public Broadcasting Service (PBS), which offers program packages; and through other regional and national program services. It claims a small percentage of the viewing audience, and even that figure is boosted by a few shows such as *Sesame Street*. Commercial competitors are chiseling away at public television's market niche—for instance, Discovery Channel's nature programming, Arts and Entertainment's culture programming, Bravo's international films, C-SPAN's political coverage, CNN's news. As broadcasting's grip on the televisual marketplace is challenged, public television also confronts technological challenges.

Money problems haunt the service and have pushed public television ever further toward prioritizing consumers, not a public; toward valuing funders, not expanded constituencies; and away from programming that might not appeal to large numbers or to the service's core membership (Aufderheide 1990). Public television has accommodated competitive forces, including a proposed cable–public television programing alliance and a reorganization that will create a national schedule on the model of commercial networks. (The network concept—once a dread specter to politicians who feared public television would become a liberal preserve— now goes uncontested, and no wonder, given the lack of a demanding public constituency.)

But money is a symptom of a deeper problem, that of mission. The public television bureaucracy today—and it is a formidable one—is committed to a broadcasting service, not to a public project executed through broadcasting. Its aspirations are more similar to those of, say, commercial stations and programmers (find a large audience, a hit show) than they are to the ideal of using mass communication as a tool of public life. And that is not surprising, given the striking absence from its origins of a public mandate.

Of course, public television would not have a crisis at all if it were simply content to become a nicer version of commercial broadcasting. And however content some of its bureaucrats may be with that goal, other forces inside and outside the service militate against it. Indeed, the perceived need for society to have something beyond commercial media pervades its uneven history.

Concern for the perceived weakness of the public sphere, cast in terms of preoccupation about breakdown of community and active citizenship, infused debate at public television's creation, as educational television. The Ford Foundation's lavish backing of television, first commercial and then educational, between 1952 and 1977, was grounded in the belief that "more effective use of mass media" might address "the high degree of public apathy prevailing in this country" and "the lack in the lives of many persons of a realistic and meaningful sense of values" (Ford Foundation n.d. [1976], 2). The 1965 Carnegie Commission on Educational Television (Witherspoon and Kovitz, 1989, 8 ff; Carnegie Commission 1967, chap. 2) asserted the need for a service beyond instructional television for a politically, culturally diverse nation in danger of fragmentation. It claimed that a "Public Television" could "help us see America whole, in all its diversity" and "help us know what it is to be many in one, to have growing maturity in our sense of ourselves as a people" (92–93). Report language in the Public Broadcasting Act of 1967 also argued the necessity of such a service for a healthy citizenry, menaced by the decline of localism and the rise of mass media itself:

> Who can estimate the value to a democracy of a citizenry that is kept fully and fairly informed as to the important issues of our times and whose children have access to programs which make learning a pleasure? The town meeting may have disappeared, but nevertheless the success of our democratic institutions still depends ultimately upon the informed judgments of the citizens of our cities, towns, and local communities. . . . Expensive and complex technology is outstripping

the ability of local communities to adequately serve the educational needs of their citizens. (U.S. Congress 1967, 10–11)

However, the practice of public television shows a variety of other objectives and working definitions of *the public*, none legally explicit and some competing with each other. Is public television merely a specific instance of "the public interest," which all broadcasters pledge to serve? Is it enough that it merely be noncommercial and educational, as opposed to corporate or governmental? Is it to aid the democratic process of information getting and receiving, or to deliver the cultural cream? Or to make public the voices of the underrepresented minorities of a pluralist society? Is it to be "quality" television or, instead, "anti-television"?

Confusion and opportunism in these debates have thrived on the unarticulated assumption of the public sphere. The perennial assumption of a viable public, which could and would hold this service accountable, has coexisted with a sense of public television's potential to reinvigorate a fragmented, inarticulate society, leaving the service a fertile field for competing interests that invoke the public interest. Public television has not defined coherently who or where the public is, as an entity separate from individual consumers and citizens. And so it also has not defined how it should mediate that role (Avery and Pepper 1980; Garnham 1986, 48).

### Backstopping Commercial Television

These problems go back to public television's origins as educational television. U.S. public television arose, unlike most other state-supported television systems (Etzioni-Halevy 1987), as a rump feature of broadcasting, a creation of the interests of educational broadcasters and institutions. As such, it grew up as a gap filler that has increasingly become a subcategory of the commercial marketplace.

The need for a public television was not even envisioned in founding broadcast legislation, which instead mandated a vague public service mandate for all broadcasters (Barnouw 1975, chap. 2; Gibson 1977, chaps. 1, 2; Krasnow and Longley 1978, 15–17). Legislators' belief in an elision between the commercial marketplace and the marketplace of ideas (Kahn 1988; Schwarzlose 1989) presumed an active public that comparison-shops for facts and ideas, unaffected by the ideological shaping of choices by the largest marketplace forces.

But the public interest as what is common, or available to all, failed the market test and proved the validity of complaints by hopeful institutional educational licensees who were languishing in the marketplace. They progressively won legal protection for their own stations and interests (Gibson 1977, 16, 49; U.S. FCC 1951); their interests were not necessarily reflective of public interests. Federally protected broadcasting was limited to instructional programming that could be conceived as pre- or non-political (not mobilizing the public as a public but instead educating individuals for their individual betterment) and controlled by large institutions, some owned by the state or local government. Even community licensees were a late addition to public broadcasting, following the 1949 founding of community-based public radio. No wonder that commercial broadcasters helped out with used equipment and occasional donations; the noncommercial licensees harmlessly held down space that otherwise would go to competitors. And no wonder that noncommercial television had a pale presence (Carnegie Commission 1967, 227–34).

## Imagining a Public Television

The notion of a service that would be more than safely instructional, which began in the mid-1960s, was precipitated by roiling changes in the wider society and the consolidation of national networks that eroded television's vaunted localism (Powledge 1972). Educational broadcasters, the Ford Foundation, an advocate at the FCC, and a president who perceived the government's job as enhancing the quality of life joined in launching the Carnegie Commission on Educational Television (Baughman 1985, chap. 10).

The Carnegie Commission's report, issued in 1967, expanded the definition of public broadcasting, while preserving its ancillary nature. It defined the new concept of public television, as contrasted with instructional television, as "all that is of human interest and importance which is not *at the moment appropriate or available* for support by advertising" (1967, 1; emphasis added). Imagining a service free of commercial restraints, the authors said, "We seek for the citizen *freedom to view*, to see programs that the present system, *by its incompleteness,* denies him" (99; emphasis added).

Thus, the commission kept the focus on programming as a passive activity for viewers, not on a mandate to fortify the public sphere through the public's organizing, making, and viewing (as a social project) television. It also preserved the assumption that the commercial marketplace occasionally fails, rather than assuming that the market shapes the context of information reception and therefore the marketplace of ideas as well.

The commission's vision of a public television also entailed a view of a more vital public through better television. The vision of a service that, in the words of one supporter, would "aim at filling, not gaps in the commercial media, but gaps in people's lives" (Blakely 1971, 37) posited a need for not only a better television but a better public. This notion could easily transmute into elitism, especially in a society divided by racial, class, and gender conflict.

The authors were aware of this danger, as well as the danger of government control. They proposed a substantial, permanent government endowment for a national, nongovernmental service and for support of local stations. Its accountability would be secured by a national board composed, eventually, of elected and appointed officials and by active involvement of citizens at the local level. The commission further asserted that a public television must at base be a local service:

> To be truly local, a station must arise out of a sense of need within a community, must have roots in the community, and must be under community control. It is not the physical location of studio and transmitter that is significant but the degree to which the station identifies itself with the people it seeks to serve. (Carnegie Commission 1967, 34)

Local programming would thus become a forum for debate and controversy within a community, especially for groups "that may otherwise be unheard" (92). This commitment to localism, as an avenue to social regeneration, was also why it proposed decentralized interconnection to avoid a "fourth network," prey to a media elite (Pepper 1979, 52–58).

A utopian vision of television as a social unifier and spiritual uplifter informed the report. That utopianism, which typically confuses social with technical processes, has a long legacy, with its origins in a union between technological determinism and a faith in progress (Carey 1989, 113–41; Mander 1988). The commission once again evoked the hope that a mass medium could play a unifying role. Its optimism was phrased most eloquently in a letter to the commission by author E. B. White:

> Noncommercial television should address itself to the ideal of excellence, not the idea of acceptability—which is what keeps commercial television from climbing the staircase. I think television should be the visual counterpart of the literary essay, should arouse our dreams, satisfy our hunger for beauty, take us on journeys, enable us to participate in events, present great drama and music, explore the sea and the sky and the woods and the hills. It should be our Lyceum, our Chautauqua,

our Minsky's, and our Camelot. It should restate and clarify the social
dilemma and the political pickle. (In Carnegie Commission 1967, 13)

White's definition of *excellence* was vigorously diverse, not only mixing
highbrow and populist images but also imagining the service as an electronic public space. However, it also presumed a public that would seize
on and lay claim to such a service, a public that was (whether it knew it
or not) hungry for excellence, not mere acceptability. But a television
service that programmed for such a public without building a base of
public participation would inevitably fall outside existing expectations
for television. Only a television that confronted that mandate in its very
processes (organizing a public—not an audience—simultaneously with
its programming) could truly be, to choose White's most public example,
a Chautauqua.

The commission's vision was never tested, because public television
was created in 1967 without adequate annual funding and without an
endowment; with only political appointees on CPB's national board;
without mandatory community participation in local boards; and with
built-in institutional tensions, especially over interconnection. The law
never defined *public*, except as "noncommercial." It failed to answer the
question of responsibility for television officials' mediation of a public
role (as opposed to its fiscal responsibility to Congress), except negative-
ly, by removal of power and money from centralized entities. In fact, the
law's rapid passage was grounded in the fact that, as one critic noted, it
"poses no threat to the status quo" (Les Brown, cited in Pepper 1979, 59).

Various interests actively opposed a service that might have a powerful
social impact, testifying indirectly to the encroachment of economic and
governmental forces on the realm of the public sphere. Not only did industry oppose a powerful alternative (Gibson 1977, 128), but legislators
feared a new outlet for a liberal media elite, as conservatives signaled
when they worried that a national body, CPB, might become the "high
mogul of a new nationwide network." They perceived the danger of elitism as a political threat:

It will be the highbrow answer to mundane commercialism. . . . It will
be a force for social good (as Mr. [Fred] Friendly [Edward R. Murrow's
producer and major supporter of public television] and his fellow
enthusiasts see the social good). It will bite at the broad problems of
national policy and make timid men (such as Presidents, Governors
and legislators) cringe. It could, and in the opinion of some witnesses,
should and will crusade.

We know that we are not alone in feeling some misgivings about creating a mechanism for the kind of broadcasting which might result from ambitions such as these. (U.S. Congress 1967, 59–60)

Even President Johnson, the bill's strongest supporter, evoked this concern when signing it. Praising its potential to "make our nation a replica of the old Greek marketplace, where public affairs took place in view of all the citizens," he also said, "in weak or even in irresponsible hands, it could generate controversy without understanding; it could mislead as well as teach; it could appeal to passions rather than reason" without "enlightened leadership" (in Macy 1974, 29). Just what "enlightened leadership" was would be left to political infighting.

### Incursions on Public Television

Public television post-1967 has suffered dramatically from incursions from both government and economic interests, and it has been hamstrung by its vague mandate, its self-identification as another broadcast service, and its inability to marshal public support. Both the Nixonian attack on public television between 1969 and 1974 (Stone 1985) and the advancing role of corporate funding illustrate these opportunistic incursions.

Nixon's attack on public broadcasting was targeted at public affairs. His perception of public television programs as flagrantly antiadministration and elitist—he fingered programs produced by national, New York–based producers, critical of the status quo and especially of his own programs and allies—was not entirely unfounded, either. Such programs were also indirect evidence of disproportionate foundation funding to the Middle Atlantic states, especially New York, in the period 1967–73 (Lashner 1976, 537; Rowland 1986, 257–59), funding that reinforced an image of Eastern-oriented public affairs. He got support from some public television station bureaucrats, distrustful of the Eastern establishment and fighting internal political battles (Avery and Pepper 1976, 13–15).

Administration staff memos betray a canny understanding of public television's limitations as a public medium. The public participated only as viewers, and they were relatively few, as advisor Clay Whitehead told Nixon (NAEB n.d. 75). A memo drafted by then–White House counsel Antonin Scalia demonstrated an understanding of the power of organized interest groups, industry, and competing political forces. It also succinctly demonstrated that public television's most well-identified and supported programs were prepolitical:

An attempt to cut back public broadcasting as a whole would be doomed to failure because of the strong support that medium receives, not only from education interests, minority groups and liberals, but also from Congressmen whose districts contain stations which contribute to local education. . . . In view of the widespread support for many aspects of public broadcasting outside of public affairs programing, such as *Sesame Street, Forsyte Saga,* high school equivalency programs, etc., we think it would be unwise to attempt an across-the-board cut in CPB funding. . . . Any significant effort to reduce CPB effort of public affairs programing would run into resistance from commercial broadcasters who would just as soon leave this to public television and would raise a hue and cry about government control, etc. (In NAEB n.d., 34–35)

The failure of a frontal attack to destroy public television had little to do with public mobilization. It had partly to do with conflicts within the Nixon staff, and with some members of Congress (Stone 1985, 305–6). Resistance also came from the American Civil Liberties Union, the National Association of Educational Broadcasters (NAEB), some members of Congress, and the elite press (NAEB n.d., 59–65; Carnegie Commission on the Future of Public Broadcasting 1979, 43–46). Viewers also protested; the proposed canceling of *Washington Week in Review* drew fifteen thousand complaints, which resulted in reinstatement of the program. As well, memberships increased unprecedently and soared when public television nationally aired the Watergate hearings (Stone 1985, 242). However, public support was largely limited to consumer protest and action. Public television officials never even tried to politically mobilize broad public support (Rowland 1976).

Nixon eventually succeeded in politicizing the CPB board, eliminating endowment plans, reducing foundation funding, and siphoning more federal funds off to local stations—which, as he had hoped, were less critical of the status quo than Eastern producers were. The affair made public television's leadership more cautious and reinforced the service's image as providing primarily genteel cultural programming—the kind that Nixon thought safe. And this left the service open to the Reagan administration's later claims, under a deregulatory ideology that rejected information subsidy wholesale, that it merely provided a cultural welfare program for the overeducated (Rowland 1986, 265–69).

The Reagan administration called for public television's total defunding. Its argument was put forward in a statement by the Office of Management and Budget:

The prime beneficiaries of a public broadcasting station are its listeners and viewers. Any benefit which non-listeners and non-viewers receive from the Corporation for Public Broadcasting (CPB) is purely conjectural and more than likely nonexistent. Thus, there is no overriding national justification for the funding of CPB. Moreover, the audience of CPB-supported stations tend to be wealthier and more educated than the general populace; they certainly possess the personal resources to support such stations and they should do so, if they want to enjoy the benefits of public broadcasting. Taxpayers as a whole should not be compelled to subsidize entertainment for a select few. (U.S. Office of Management and Budget 1981, 344)

The Reagan administration also did not wholly succeed, but federal funding was reduced substantially and programming zeroed in on what the CPB TV Program Fund's then-head, Lewis Freedman, frankly called "middle class programming," in order to attract more paying members (in Aufderheide 1984, 34).

Corporate encroachment has also eroded public television's potential to become an electronic public space. It has contributed to purveying a notion of excellence that conforms to what Habermas calls the "pseudo-public or sham-private world of culture consumption" (Habermas 1989, 177). Corporations use public television for "ambush marketing," or influencing upscale consumers who are suspicious of advertising through what Erik Barnouw so neatly dubbed the "safely splendid." Corporate underwriting—which plays an agenda-setting role because its dollars go directly to programming, unlike most other contributions—understandably eschews contentious public affairs (Aufderheide 1980, 1984, 1988) and has reinforced a trend away from local input and influence. Accounting for only 3.3 percent of PBS programming in 1973 (Roman 1980, 151), it now composes more than 16 percent of public television's budget.

Herb Schmertz, long Mobil Oil's marketing wizard, has eloquently described the advantages of public television to reach a "public" that means, for him, demographic marketing segments: "When we give certain publics a reason to identify with the projects and causes that we have chosen to support, they will translate that identification into a preference for doing business with us." It worked with *Masterpiece Theatre*, for which Schmertz himself selected the programs. The high-toned series left viewers feeling "enriched and ennobled," and surveys showed that Mobil had become "the thinking man's gasoline" (Schmertz 1986, 210–25).

Ironically, corporate funding has had a backlash effect. As public television has become increasingly strapped for funds, corporations have also more boldly promoted their own agendas—for instance, a host of business-backed programs aimed a small investors. This has jeopardized funding by large donors, particularly oil companies, which value a distanced cultural look; and PBS has had to reinforce mildly its underwriting standards. Furthermore, public television's upscale audience segment increasingly finds the "safely splendid" on alternative services. Thus, corporate funding contributes to public television's growing irrelevance.

### Conflict over the Real

Public television nonetheless has been, in small measure, a site of open social conflict over the real. It has prudently maintained demonstration projects in its publicness, which serve it well when accounting to Congress, especially where such projects do not openly raise contentious political issues—for instance, such programs for children as *Sesame Street* and *Reading Rainbow*. It has showcased work impossible to imagine in its scope on commercial media, such as *Eyes on the Prize,* a revisionist look at the civil rights era; and *The Civil War,* which used innovative formal strategies and approached a well-worked area of American history with little-used material and some new insights.

Many producers seek out the service for a chance to do something they cannot achieve in commercial television. Those whose perspectives are marginalized in the mainstream media, including organized labor, public interest groups such as the Center for Defense Information, and less frequently the organized right-wing, sometimes seek it out. It has been a site of intense debate over the responsibility of its public affairs programming, from its *Vietnam* series to *Days of Rage,* a program on the *intifada* (Abramson, Arterton, and Orren 1988, 133–34; Gottlieb 1990; Bullert 1997).

Those who find their opinions or worldviews excluded from commercial media argue, in effect, that they legitimate its claim both to be public and noncommercial, and that its top priority should therefore be their perspectives. They implicitly posit (like the most optimistic of public television advocates before them) a unitary public sphere, which their viewpoints enrich. Their demands range from the brokers serving as traffic cops for viewpoints, to new leadership, to protected space for marginalized groups.

However, they also petition a service that depends on the largesse of the powerful, and that has little flexibility. Furthermore, they do so in an atmosphere in which the notion of a "public culture" itself is embattled

(Rowland and Tracey 1990; Price 1995). Showcasing their perspectives may be seen (and is, by many public television bureaucrats) merely as servicing a small minority. Such criticisms may even be borne out, since public television operates within the universe of entertainment television, catering to demographics.

## The Public as the Underserved

This linking of the underserved and the public interest has most boldly surfaced in a special interest group: independent producers, who want public television's production resources and airtime. Mainstream media regularly slight their work for various reasons: minority, female, gender, or disabled status; regional isolation; lack of professional training; a style that reflects a subculture; experimental approaches to the form; or interest in subjects that often fall outside the purview of commercial media (e.g., criticism of nuclear power; labor history and struggles; criticism of conglomerate media). By the fact of being "independents"—divorced from institutional interests—they lay claim in the aggregate to representing the public interest. Independent producers are a rare example, in the history of public television, of a voluntary association that coalesced around an issue self-defined as a public concern (Boyte 1992), demanding eventually not only access but control. Their struggle to create ITVS first legitimized their own rhetoric and then extended it into the concept of television as a public space.

ITVS was the result of a decade-long political battle in which the vagueness of the service's mandate was spotlighted. In the campaign that resulted in the 1988 Act (U.S. Congress 1988a, 1988b), independent producers, led by a national organization (the National Coalition of Independent Public Broadcasting Producers, which heavily used the resources of the five-thousand-member Association of Independent Film and Videomakers), based their case on a definition of the public that echoed the 1967 Carnegie Commission report.

They claimed to represent elements of the public disenfranchised in commercial media and whose voices are significant when heard on public television, not only to themselves but to a wider social whole. They then argued that public television had flouted the 1978 requirement of Congress that a substantial portion of its funding go to independent producers, as well as exercising bad-faith conduct in peer panels and a slighting of minority production (Association of California Independent Public Television Producers, n.d.).

Producers argued their case on the basis of their function in a democratic society. If public television prioritized programming outside the habits of its central demographics, it might establish a more active relationship not only with the minorities most directly concerned but with a broader citizenry. Pamela Yates, whose documentaries included one on human rights in Guatemala and another on the resurgence of the Ku Klux Klan, argued,

> As the money dwindles and public access diminishes for independents, who will believe in the young, the minorities, the up and coming filmmakers with fresh ideas who may never get a chance to produce their first project? What effect will this exclusion have on the future of Public Broadcasting's ability to respond to a democratic society and not just the consumer market?
>
> Innovation and diversity in programming will guarantee that the full spectrum of voices and opinions are heard and seen on public television. Independent producers who are passionately concerned with their subjects, not their ratings, will insure that this diversity exists. While independents may be small in absolute numbers the idea and subject matters which their films touch on affect the vast majority of Americans. (Yates 1988, 6)

Yates thus envisioned a general receptivity to issues that may touch on "the vast majority of Americans" but that they have not had the opportunity to know about.

The independents charged that television was a battle over "the real," and that all cultural expression carries within it an ideological framework. The independents, many of whom were also community organizers or political activists on particular issues, were staking a claim to redefining reality for a wider society. For them, cultural programming was as much at stake as public affairs. African American producer Marlon Riggs argued that public broadcasting had made its lowest priority "emerging independent producers, producers of color, producers with voices and visions that risk upsetting the status quo, that challenge not only what public television says but *how* it says it" (Riggs 1987, 2). He assumed that perspectives that questioned consensus were not only an addition but a challenge to received wisdom, and a potential source of conflict.

This was a battle not merely about access or inclusion of minority views, charged one of the lead organizers, Lawrence Daressa, but about a new definition of public television's function. He imagined the future service as "anti-television," forcing viewers into an active consideration of the terms of their lives and forcing independents to think more creatively.

He therefore saw the ITVS as "a political organization, not in the liberal-conservative sense but in terms of making a strong case for a radically new kind of media" (Aufderheide 1989b).

The public interest rhetoric of the independents was important. Their success, however, was largely attributable to canny strategic alliances, which also indirectly demonstrated the lack of a broad appetite in television viewing for diversity—and the social challenge it implied—in the wider society. They were most successful mobilizing organized arts groups, and in manipulating existing entrenched interests. The campaign, targeting Congress only after fruitless negotiations with CPB, drew in diverse arts organizations, both national and regional, mobilized through both the national and local offices. Journalists already disillusioned with public television were fed information, especially during CPB's twentieth anniversary year; assessments of its achievements were damning. The campaign also strategically exposed to Congress public television's unwillingness or inability to mobilize public support.

Finally, it demonstrated a savvy awareness of political realities. For instance, organizers played on a building hostility in Congress over the Reagan administration's attacks on public television; on legislators' eagerness to cater to rising numbers of minorities in their districts with small but highly visible allocations; and on legislators' willingness to listen to celebrity entertainers who are good fund-raisers (Aufderheide 1989a; Ivers 1989; Sapadin 1990; "From Boston to Honolulu" 1988).

The victory precipitated the conflict over publicness into different arenas and challenged the simple equation of the marginalized with the public. Independent producers themselves began to differ about how to mete out these new resources. Some independents challenged ITVS's right to coordinate and produce, rather than simply being a broker for independent productions. Others argued that ITVS bureaucrats had a responsibility to create a service, fearing otherwise it would become the thrift shop of public television. Public television's lack of accountability to an organized public became part of this debate, as did the claim by some independents to represent the public in their work. Meanwhile, institutional pressures hobbled the nascent service. CPB resisted the funds transfer for two years, pending contractual safeguards.

If ITVS survived these founding crises, it would then face the hurdle of convincing station managers—still not accountable to a diverse community board, and not required to accept its work—to broadcast programs. At its best, ITVS would be the rump end of rump-end services; it would be a laboratory for what all of public television, in the eyes of some of its supporters, should be doing.

Even in this small laboratory, there was a shift from public television's traditional approach in the planning process alone. As ITVS addressed its mandate, it grappled with the question of its own publicness, effectively reenvisioning television as a project to organize the public sphere. Board and staff discussed ways to make the service interactive with, in the first instance, producers themselves (e.g., by holding conferences, establishing a database of proposals, establishing a workshop format). They discussed how to challenge people to organize themselves both as viewers and producers (e.g., using call-in shows to link viewers with related organizations; creating shows that require locally produced components; airing live teleconference programs; producing in conjunction with grassroots organizations). They solicited suggestions for programming that challenges viewers to see television itself as a cultural artifact.

### Envisioning a "Public" Public Television

The creation of ITVS has reshaped familiar debates about public television. The arguments leading to its creation informed recent remarks of ITVS board member Lawrence Daressa on what a "public public television" might look like:

> Public television . . . would foreground the audience rather than its own programming; it would place the audience *in* the picture not *in front* of it. . . . Instead of presenting the world to its audience ready-made, it would invite the audience to remake its world. . . .
>
> Public television should . . . deliberately integrate itself into larger social contexts—family, civic organizations, ethnic group, city, nation. Public television should not stage media events so much as community events, at times when people could congregate via television to explore shared concerns . . . in cooperation with various civic organizations. . . .
>
> Public television . . . should consist of an ensemble of parallel programming strands [resembling] a collection of mini-cable services, video magazines or broadcast workshops—a Democracy Channel. Each workshop could develop an electronic forum for new "virtual communities" of youth, gays, Spanish speakers. . . .
>
> Public television should be heterogeneous, even contradictory. It should deliberately mix points of view and artistic approaches . . . invite the discontinuities, the ruptures, which provide the space in which democratic debate and personal growth can occur, the fissures

in the status quo which show that we can invent a future different from the past.

Such a "prismatic" public television would deliberately undermine the autocracy of the image over the viewer, would give visibility back to the viewer in the dark. It would emphasize that what we see is not as important as how we see it . . . it would position the viewer in the center of a matrix of arguments about how to construct social reality. . . .

A democratic television would make society itself a subject of discussion; it would "textualize" culture, everyday life, into language which can be continuously read and rewritten. The public sphere is society's laboratory for itself, a school for the free development of sociability, for the evolution of Aristotle's "political animal." (Daressa 1990)

That vision is unlikely to capture the balkanized public television bureaucracies that have gambled on a national prime-time schedule and shrunk local public affairs programming. Whether the pilot projects of ITVS alone can mobilize a public is also a slim, if nobly taken, chance. But without such a vision, public television remains condemned to the fate of nicer television in a marketplace that does not much prize niceness, unprotected in risk taking by governments confronting cutbacks.

A truly public television would have to become an institution whose first job is not to make programs, whether safely splendid or utterly outrageous, but to fortify the public sphere. Assuming this challenge would mean forsaking the traditional role of broadcaster, to become an organizer of electronic public space. It would foreground the struggle to establish relationships among people whose differences are deep, with the goal of finding common ground to articulate and address issues that pertain to the common good. That organizing would be built into all processes of production and distribution. It would require a financial base protected from corporate pressures and government censorship, and an explicit mandate. That way, the measure of success would be the level of active citizenship, not membership contributions or ratings. Public television might incur the wrath of commercial media, especially if it promotes media literacy, but it will not have to compete with them.

It is not surprising, given the history of public television in the United States, that the service has so often fallen short of its most idealist visionaries' goals. More surprising is that the service has so often been the site of social contest over the real. Educational organizations, public interest groups, independent producers, and voices marginalized from other media have capitalized on conflicts within the state and the service to reinforce its distinctiveness. The frailty of those forces is related not only to large institutional interests but to the frailty of a broader public. That is perhaps the most compelling reason for public television to carve out a space within the public sphere.

## References

Abramson, J., F. Arterton, and G. Orren. 1988. *The Electronic Commonwealth: The Impact of the New Media Technologies on Democratic Politics*. New York: Basic Books.

Association of California Independent Public Television Producers. n.d. (1988). *Corporation for Public Broadcasting Funding of Independent Production FY 1982 through FY 1987—Preliminary Findings*. San Francisco: ACIPTP (630 Natoma St., San Francisco, CA 94103).

Aufderheide, P. 1980. "The Selling of the Audience and the Buying of the Sponsor." *In These Times*, June 4–17, pp. 18–19.

———. 1984. "TV Worth Paying For?" *The Progressive* (May): 33–36.

———. 1988. "The Corporatization of Public TV." *Union* (Service Employees International Union, Washington, D.C.) (October–November): 11–13.

———. 1989a. "The Final Word." *Cineaste* 17 (1): 48.

———. 1989b. "Toward Anti-Television: The Independent Production Service and the Future of Public Broadcasting." *Afterimage* 16 (8): 4–5.

———. 1990. "Public TV Tunes out the Big Picture." *In These Times*, July 4–17, pp. 19–21.

Avery, R., and R. Pepper. 1976. "The Evolution of the CPB-PBS Relationship 1970–1973." *Public Telecommunications Review* 4 (5): 6–17.

———. 1980. "An Institutional History of Public Broadcasting." *Journal of Communication* 30 (3): 126–38.

Barnouw, E. 1975. *Tube of Plenty: The Evolution of American Television*. New York: Oxford University Press.

Baughman, J. 1985. *Television's Guardian: The Federal Communications Commission and the Politics of Programming, 1958–67*. Knoxville: University of Tennessee Press.

Blakely, R. 1971. *The People's Instrument: A Philosophy of Programming for Public Television*. Washington, D.C.: Public Affairs Press.

Boyte, H. 1992. "The Pragmatic Ends of Popular Politics." In Calhoun 1992.

Boyte, H., and S. Evans. 1986. *Free Spaces: The Sources of Democratic Change in America*. New York: Harper and Row.

Bullert, B. 1997. *Public Television: Politics and the Battle over Documentary Film*. New Brunswick, N.J.: Rutgers University Press.

Calhoun, C., ed. 1992. *Habermas and the Public Sphere.* Cambridge: MIT Press.

Carnegie Commission on Educational Television. 1967. *Public Television: A Program for Action.* New York: Harper and Row.

Carnegie Commission on the Future of Public Broadcasting. 1979. *A Public Trust.* New York: Bantam.

Carey, J. 1989. *Communications as Culture: Essays on Media and Society.* Boston: Unwin Hyman.

———. 1995. "The Press, Public Opinion, and Public Discourse." In *Public Opinion and the Communication of Consent,* ed. Theodore L. Glasser and Charles T. Salmon, 373–402. New York: Guilford.

Daressa, L. 1990. "Does the Public Have a Future in Public Television?" Presented to the Center for Communications colloquium, New York, December 14.

Dewey, J. 1927. *The Public and Its Problems.* Athens, Ohio: Swallow Press (reprinted 1983).

Entman, R. 1989. *Democracy without Citizens: Media and the Decay of American Politics.* New York: Oxford University Press.

Etzioni-Halevy, E. 1987. *National Broadcasting under Siege: A Comparative Study of Australia, Britain, Israel, and West Germany.* New York: St. Martin's.

Ewen, S. 1988. *All Consuming Images: The Politics of Style in Contemporary Culture.* New York: Basic Books.

Ford Foundation. n.d. (1976). *Ford Foundation Activities in Noncommercial Broadcasting, 1951–1976.* New York: Ford Foundation.

"From Boston to Honolulu: Organizing for the National Independent Program Service." 1988. *The Independent* (October): 23–27.

Garnham, N. 1986. "The Media and the Public Sphere." In *Communicating Politics: Mass Communications and the Political Process,* ed. P. Golding, G. Murdock, and P. Schlesinger, 37–53. New York: Holmes and Meier.

———. 1990. *Capitalism and Communication: Global Culture and the Economics of Information.* London: Sage.

Gibson, G. H. 1977. *Public Broadcasting: The Role of the Federal Government, 1912–1976.* New York: Praeger.

Habermas, J. 1989. *The Structural Transformation of the Public Sphere: An Inquiry into a Category of Bourgeois Society,* trans. Thomas Burger. Cambridge: MIT Press.

Ivers, S. 1989. "Congress, the Corporation for Public Broadcasting, and Independent Producers: Agenda Setting and Policy Making in Public Television." Presented to the Broadcasting Education Association Annual Convention, Las Vegas, April.

Kahn, P. 1988. "Media Competition in the Marketplace of Ideas." *Syracuse Law Review* 39: 737–94.

Krasnow, E. G., and L. D. Longley. 1978. *The Politics of Broadcast Regulation,* 2nd ed. New York: St. Martin's.

Lashner, M. 1976. "The Role of Foundations in Public Broadcasting. Part I: Development and Trends." *Journal of Broadcasting* 20 (4): 529–47.

Macy, J. W. Jr. 1974. *To Irrigate a Wasteland.* Berkeley and Los Angeles: University of California Press.

Mander, M. 1988. "Utopian Dimensions in the Public Debate on Broadcasting in the Twenties." *Journal of Communication Inquiry* 12 (2): 71–88.

Mills, C. W. 1956. *The Power Elite.* New York: Oxford University Press.

National Association of Educational Broadcasters. n.d. (1979). *The Nixon Administration Public Broadcasting Papers 1969–1974.* Washington, D.C.: NAEB.

Pepper, R. 1979. *The Formation of the Public Broadcasting Service.* New York: Arno Press.

Powledge, F. 1972. *Public Television: A Question of Survival.* Washington, D.C.: Public Affairs Press.

Price, M. 1995. *Television, the Public Sphere, and National Identity.* New York: Oxford University Press.

Public Telecommunications Act of 1988. 1988. *Congressional Record—House,* H 10477, October 19.

Riggs, M. 1987. Testimony before the U.S. Senate, Subcommittee on Communications, March 15.

Roman, J. 1980. "Programming for Public Television." *Journal of Communication* 30 (3): 150–56.

Rowland, W. D. Jr. 1976. "Public Involvement: The Anatomy of a Myth." In *The Future of Public Broadcasting,* ed. D. Cater and M. Nyhan, 109–39. New York: Praeger.

———. 1986. "Continuing Crisis in Public Broadcasting: A History of Disenfranchisement." *Journal of Broadcasting and Electronic Media* 30 (3): 251–74.

Rowland, W. D. Jr., and M. Tracey. 1990. "Worldwide Challenges to Public Broadcasting." *Journal of Communication* 40 (2): 8–27.

Sapadin, L. 1990. President, Association of Independent Film and Videomakers. Telephone interview, July 15.

Schmertz, H., and W. Novak. 1986. *Goodbye to the Low Profile: The Art of Creative Confrontation.* Boston: Little, Brown.

Schudson, M. 1995. "Was There Ever a Public Sphere?" In *The Power of News,* ed. M. Schudson, 189–203. Cambridge: Harvard University Press.

Schwarzlose, R. A. 1989. "The Marketplace of Ideas: A Measure of Free Expression." *Journalism Monographs* (occasional publication of Association for Education in Journalism and Mass Communication): 1–41.

Stone, D. 1985. *Nixon and the Politics of Public Television.* New York: Garland
   Publishing.
Times Mirror Center for the People and the Press. 1990. *The Age of Indifference:*
   *A Study of Young Americans and How They View the News.* Washington, D.C.:
   Times Mirror Center for the People and the Press.
U.S. Congress. 1967. First Session. House of Representatives. Report No. 572.
   Public Broadcasting Act of 1967. August 21. Public Law 90-129, 81 stat. 365.
U.S. Congress. 1988a. House of Representatives. Committee on Energy and
   Commerce. 100th Congress, 2d Session. *Public Telecommunications Act of*
   *1988. Report 100-825, August 5.* Washington, D.C.: Government Printing
   Office.
U.S. Congress. 1988b. Senate. Committee on Commerce, Science and Trans-
   portation. *Public Telecommunications Act of 1988. Report 100-144, August 2.*
   Washington, D.C.: Government Printing Office.
U.S. Federal Communications Commission. 1951. Third Notice of Proposed
   Rulemaking on Television Assignments, 16 FR 3072, 3079, March 22.
U.S. Office of Management and Budget. 1981. *The FY 1982 Budget Revisions:*
   *Corporation for Public Broadcasting* (Washington, D.C.: OMB), 344–45.
Witherspoon, J., and R. Kovitz. 1989. *The History of Public Broadcasting,*
   ed. J. J. Yore and R. Barbieri. Washington, D.C.: *Current* (newspaper).
Yates, Pamela. 1988. Testimony before the Subcommittee on Telecommunications
   and Finance Committee on Energy and Commerce, U.S. House of Represen-
   tatives, March 10.

# Access Cable TV

# as Electronic

# Public Space

*This article started out as a briefing paper for friends in the public interest community working on the bill that eventually became the 1992 Cable Act (and was then incorporated into the Communications Act of 1934 as an amendment). Our question then, as it has been since, is what would be a useful way to define the public interest as communications systems grow and change. As the 1992 act was being shaped, conservatives pressed hard the argument that less regulation meant more benefits to the public. Consumer advocates pushed for price regulation, supporting a broad public outrage at deregulated prices and poor quality. I argued the need to consider as well the need for public spaces and public behaviors. This version of the article was published in the* Journal of Communication *and was used in a lawsuit ensuing from the act (see "Access Cable in Action"). The issues endure, since cable has continued to operate with monopoly power, and since public cultures continue to need nourishment.*

As a regulated telecommunications service, cable TV has been under scrutiny for its service to *the public interest*—a central term in U.S. communications policy (Aufderheide 1999). Perhaps the most high-profile public interest issue in cable service has been rates, an issue that reflects both consumer concern and its monopoly clout. I would like to propose that the public interest can be served not only by regulatory mechanisms that check market power and enhance diversity in the commercial market-place, but also by mechanisms that guarantee and protect electronic spaces—channels, centers, services—exclusively for public activity. This is because the public interest is broader than that of consumers, or even protection of the individual speaker; the public has its own interests, separate from those of government or business.

## Cable TV Today

Cable is now the primary delivery medium for television in a majority of American homes. Currently, almost all American television homes can receive cable, and more than 66 percent of those homes do receive it (U.S. FCC 1998). Cable has become an essential information service for the majority of Americans, and for many has always been so. The cable industry argues that cable is not nearly as important as it appears, because consumers have alternatives (newspapers, videocassettes, broadcast, theaters) to the various elements of its communications package. But this ignores questions of accessibility, comparative cost, and consumer habits. In rural Madelia, Minnesota, cable brings in the only clear signals. Cable is also a virtual necessity in Manhattan, where dense building placement means poor reception. And in Laredo, Texas, where 94 percent of the population speaks Spanish as the language of the home and one in four speaks no English, Spanish-language programming appears only on cable (U.S. Senate 1990a, 52).

Historically, cable policy has been hammered out among a handful of special interests, all of whom have invoked the public interest. The Cable Communications Policy Act of 1984 was passed with a minimum of public participation. This law, a hasty resolution to a three-year argument between the largest cable operators and the municipalities that control franchises, created a national cable policy for the first time. The law attempted to encourage the growth of cable, partly "to assure that cable communications provide, and are encouraged to provide, the widest possible diversity of information sources and services to the public" (U.S. Congress 1984). It also attempted to balance the concerns of the major parties, for example, the cablers' desire for minimal regulation and the cities' desire for accountability (Meyerson 1985).

The cable industry did grow dramatically once the law went into effect. Viewership grew rapidly, and prices skyrocketed. Even the law's modest public interest provisions—for example, leased access and public access—were poorly enforced, sometimes leaving those who wished to gain access to the cable systems worse off than before (Lampert, Cate, and Lloyd 1991; U.S. Senate 1990a). Consumers' outrage over prices and services, and municipalities' indignation over contracts violated, triggered passage of the 1992 Cable Act, which among other things required cable rates to be more closely regulated and required cable operators to carry broadcast signals on a third of their capacity. The cable industry conducted a high-visibility public relations campaign to blame industry problems on government regulators, while also lobbying Congress on the rewrite of the Communications Act, which eventually became the Telecommunications Act of 1996. In that process, cable industry leaders represented themselves as the nation's only business ready to compete with the telephone companies, if properly favored. Once so favored, with (among other things) deregulation of most cable rates, cable and phone companies regrouped and opted not to compete, at least in the short term (Aufderheide 1999).

The virtual absence of a public voice on cable policy, if typical, may be related to the fact that policy has not encouraged the use of mass communication, including cable, for explicitly civic activity. One important yet neglected vehicle for such stimulation is access cable.

### The Public Sphere and the First Amendment

The public sphere, a social realm distinct from both representative government and economic interest (see "Public Television and the Public Sphere"), is barely recognized as such in common parlance in the United States. *Public* is commonly a simple synonym for *consumers* or *demographic set*. While public spaces are regularly carved out with ingenuity and against the odds by citizens across the nation, they are rarely noticed in national media. Even more rarely are they identified as examples of activity in the public interest, as well as of their particular issue (e.g., school reform, toxic waste dumps). Typically such groups and movements lack access to media, particularly on their own terms.

Communication is central to political life in a democratic nation, as John Dewey made clear long ago. When members of the public have resources to raise issues of public concern, debate them among themselves, and develop ways to act on them, telecommunication becomes one tool in the public's organizing of itself. The First Amendment is important, not merely because it guarantees free speech to individuals but because by doing so it is a tool in defense of the public sphere, protecting the right of the citizenry to "understand the issues which bear upon our common life" (Meiklejohn 1948, 89). Ruling in the context of broadcasting, the Supreme Court has said that the ultimate objective of the

First Amendment is to create a well-informed electorate, and that the public's rights are paramount over all (*Red Lion Broadcasting Co. v. FCC* 1969; reinforced in *Metro Broadcasting Inc. v. FCC* 1990).

Concern for the quality of public life has marked other judicial decisions, such as the Supreme Court's ruling supporting free and open airing of contemporary issues so that "government may be responsive to the will of the people and that changes may be obtained by lawful means" (*Stromberg v. California* 1931). It is the basis for Judge Learned Hand's celebrated statement that the First Amendment "presupposes that right conclusions are more likely to be gathered out of a multitude of tongues, than through any kind of authoritative selection. To many this is, and always will be, folly; but we have staked upon it our all" (*U.S. v. Associated Press* 1943). "A multitude of tongues" has a social utility; it is not a good in itself. What is involved is not mere data delivery, but a process in which many are involved as producers and presenters as well as receivers.

This concept has been given a shorthand definition as diversity of sources, a long-standing measure of the First Amendment in communications policy (Melody 1990a, b). Diversity's primary value is to offer ranges of viewpoints and sources on problems affecting the public sphere. In recent years, the notion that the marketplace of ideas is well served in the commercial marketplace without regulatory protection for such diversity has become popular. However, a public without a thriving marketplace of ideas may not be educated to demand it either (Entman and Wildman 1990, 36–37).

### Advertisers and Eyeballs

Cable is hardly a thriving marketplace of ideas. There have been, historically, harsh limitations on the current cable industry's ability to provide diversity of sources and viewpoints on issues of public concern, much less to be a service that fortifies civic activism. Those limitations lie in the conditions of commercial television programming, whatever the delivery vehicle, as well as the current structure of the cable industry.

Cable was once trumpeted as the "technology of abundance," a medium so expansive that no social engineering would be needed for a multitude of tongues to flourish. But this turned out to be another instance in a long-standing tradition of blind optimism in technologies to bring about social change (Streeter 1987; Winston 1986; Le Duc 1987; Sinel et al. 1990). Although cable has ushered in new formats, from CNN to Nickelodeon to Court TV, the unforgiving logic of commercial production has shaped them all, and ownership has increasingly centralized in a few hands. C-SPAN, funded by voluntary contributions of the cable industry as a noncommercial project (and as a kind of insurance policy with legislators), says nothing about the capacity of the television marketplace to function in the public interest.

Most television programming, including cable programming, is supported by advertising. Programming is designed to attract the audience for the advertising; the public interest may lie in the opposite direction, and the public as a concept is virtually erased in favor of the consumer—who is often referred to as "the public" nonetheless. The most vulnerable members of the public—the young—have been long slighted. Even with the stimulus of legislation mandating children's programming, educational programming for children is still mostly dependent on the slim resources of public television. An issue of great public importance that commercial television never frankly addresses is its own social effect. Bill Moyers's TV series *The Public Mind*, which did address this issue, was on public television and was not even carried by all public stations.

Cable's increased channel capacity does not miraculously create new opportunities for public participation in this technology, nor even for greater diversity of sources (Le Duc 1987; Winston 1990). Eyeballs and dollars set a low ceiling even on experimentation within commercial priorities. Television viewing overall has increased only by minutes a day since the wide distribution of cable, and this fact affects the available universe of advertising. While the high costs of production are lowering, as the networks brainstorm cost-cutting measures including "reality" programming, such as *Cops*, this merely reflects that the total amount of production dollars is being spread ever more thinly. Compression technologies, multiplying the possible channels, and digital set-top boxes that promise vastly expanded options, threaten to spread the viewers out even further, to many programmers' dismay.

Producers know that new technologies do not bring new creative options, new voices, new viewpoints. One study surveying 150 television producers on the options for creativity in the "new television marketplace" found several biases pushing programming away from creativity, including bottom-line strategies, and horizontal and vertical integration (Blumler and Spicer 1990).

## Cable's Control

Cable's industry structure has historically discouraged diversity of sources and perspectives, and leaves virtually no opening for use of the system as a public space. The simple fact that one operator controls all the channels—

a practice that cable industry leaders have zealously guarded, whatever the technical possibilities—concentrates decision making. That tendency has been greatly increased by waves of centralization and vertical integration (U.S. House of Representatives 1990; U.S. FCC 1998). As the Supreme Court has recognized, concentration of ownership militates against diversity in principle: "The greater the number of owners in a market, the greater the possibility of achieving diversity of program and service viewpoints" (*FCC v. National Citizens Committee for Broadcasting* 1978). In 1984, the top four companies controlled 28 to 29 percent of the national market (U.S. FCC, 1990a, app. G: 3; U.S. NTIA 1988, 555). As the cable law went into effect, mergers and takeovers flourished; the selling price of cable systems tripled in the 1980s (U.S. Senate 1990b, 10). By 1991, four companies controlled, at a conservative estimate, 47 percent of all cable subscribers—a national figure that grossly underestimates often total regional control (U.S. FCC 1990a, app. G: 1; U.S. FCC 1990b, 15–16). By 1998, the top four controlled 62 percent of subscribers (U.S. FCC 1998, E-5). A single multiple system operator (MSO), by a decision to carry or not to carry a service, can decide its fate. To add to the problem, the large MSOs have steadily bought equity in program services (U.S. FCC 1990a, app. G: 4, 6–9; Davis 1990, 38; U.S. FCC 1998, 89ff), with Tele-Communications Inc. (TCI) and Time Warner leading the industry with a combined investment in 45 percent of all national cable programming services and similar holdings in cable programming networks. The industry practice has become general, with the eight largest MSOs holding interests in all the sixty-eight vertically integrated services. Moreover, throughout most of the 1990s, most of the largest cable interests developed joint strategies, for instance, through participation as board members of Ted Turner's cable operations and through complex programming partnerships.

The result is impressive market power, as the FCC, the General Accounting Office, local officials, and Congress have all admitted (U.S. FCC 1990a, para. 13.4ff, par. 69; U.S. GAO 1990; U.S. Senate 1990b, 9; "Why Viewers" 1990, B1; U.S. FCC 1998). It is evident from pricing to quality of service to availability of C-SPAN and other programming to availability of new services.

Historically, cable MSOs have militated against programming diversity, even within the limits of what advertisers want and what viewers find entertaining. Cable companies favor programs they own, and they also discourage new, competing programming. They required legislation to force them to carry all local broadcast signals, on up to a third of their capacity, to permit programmers to sell programming on the open market, and to permit programmers to lease available space on their systems at reasonable rates. New technologies and a changed policy platform, in the Telecommunications Act of 1996, did not create a friendlier, more accessible market for independent programmers, and prices of cable service continued to rise.

Cable television service offers a highly constrained range of programming to American viewers. Even if it were a more vigorous programming marketplace, however, the available programming would still be subject to the eyeballs-and-advertisers limitations. People would be able to see what would attract a demographic slice of American consumers interesting to advertisers.

## Electronic Public Spaces

If electronic media policy is to fortify the public sphere, members of the public must be able to use this resource as a public space and in support of other public spaces. The success of this use of the medium would not be measured in commercial criteria, but on its ability to promote relationships within its communities of reference, on issues of public concern. Numbers would be less important than contributing to the perpetual process of constructing a public.

One of many potential resources already exists—public, educational, and governmental access channels. They exist thanks largely to grassroots activism resulting in local regulation, and a since-revoked 1972 FCC rule requiring access channels (Engelman 1990, 1996). Such channels—especially public access—have long been portrayed as electronic soapboxes, where the goal is simple provision of a space in which to speak. The 1984 act continued this tradition, describing public access as

> the video equivalent of the speaker's soap box or the electronic parallel
> to the printed leaflet. They provide groups and individuals who gener-
> ally have not had access to the electronic media with the opportunity
> to become sources of information in the marketplace of ideas. (House
> report, cited in Meyerson 1985, 569)

But what if everybody can speak but nobody cares? The real value of such services has been and must be in helping to build social relationships within which such speech would be meaningful—constructing that "marketplace of ideas." Such a service needs to be seen and used not as a pathetic, homemade version of entertainment, but as an arm of community self-structuring.

Access programs often have been, in the words of one tired access director, "programmed to fail." This is less remarkable than the fact that they exist at all. Only canny, ceaseless, locality-by-locality citizen activism wrested access centers and channels in the franchise process in the first place, and all such victories are temporary. The 1984 act sabotaged some of those victories. It had capped localities' franchise fees and required them to be unrestricted. It did not require access channels. Points of confusion in the law—particularly the definition of *service*—as well as restrictions on renewal procedures, among others, made it easy for cable operators to pay more attention to their bottom line and for franchisers to pay more attention to road paving than to cable access (Meyerson 1990; Ingraham 1990; Brenner, Price, and Meyerson 1990, sec. 6.04[3][c], 6.04[4]). The 1992 act not only did nothing to remedy these weaknesses but further crippled the service by permitting operators to censor controversial programming (see "Access Cable in Action"). Reversing that decision required extended legal action. In the 1996 act, access cable was given a curt nod, by requiring competitors to cable systems in any community to carry the equivalent of the cable operator's access obligations, but no other provisions for access cable were made. In fact, proposals in earlier drafts of the legislation for nonprofit set-asides were struck (Aufderheide 1999).

Even under starvation conditions, access has carved out a significant role in the minority of communities where it exists. Currently only 18 percent of systems have public access; 15 percent have educational access, and 13 percent have governmental access (*Television and Cable Factbook* 1998, F1). An abundance of local programming is produced in some two thousand centers—about ten thousand hours a week (Ingraham 1990), far outstripping commercial production. The Hometown USA Video Festival, showcasing local origination and PEG (public, educational, and governmental) channel production, annually attracts thousands of entries from dozens of states.

These channels are often perceived to be valued community resources, using traditional measures. One multisite study shows that 47 percent of viewers watch community channels, a quarter of them at least three times in two weeks; 46 percent say it was "somewhat" to "very" important in deciding to subscribe to or remain with cable (Jamison 1990). Another study, commissioned by the cable access center Access Sacramento, showed that two-thirds of cable subscribers who knew about the channel watched it (Access Sacramento 1991). Access centers provide resources and services typically valued at many times what they cost. Access Sacramento, for instance, estimates a community value of its equipment, training, and consultation at $4.5 million, ten times its budget (Access Sacramento 1990), an estimate corroborated by the experience of access cable in Nashville and Tucson.

But the most useful measure is not, and should not be, numbers of viewers or positive poll results, but the ability of access to make a difference in community life. Access cable should not function like American public television does. Public television offers a more substantial, thoughtful, challenging, or uplifting individual viewing experience than a commercial channel. Access needs to be a site for communication among members of the public as the public, about issues of public importance.

Beyond a basic technical level of quality, the entertainment value of such programming comes far secondary to its value as a piece of a larger civic project, whether it is citizen input into actions the local city council is making, or discussions of school reform, or a labor union's donation of services to low-income residents, or the viewpoints of physically challenged people on issues affecting them, or the showcasing of minority culture, such as youth music. This is because viewers are not watching it as individual consumers, but as citizens who are formulating a response. In each case, the program—unlike a commercial broadcast or cable service—is not the end point, but only one of the means toward the continuing process of building community ties.

In small and incremental ways, the access cable channel acts as a public space, strengthening the public sphere. In Tampa, Florida, for instance, public access cable provided the primary informational vehicle for citizens concerned about a county tax that was inadequately justified; major local media, whose directors shared the interests of politicians, had failed to raise accountability issues. The tax was defeated in a record voter turnout. In the area's educational cable access system, airing school board meetings has resulted in vastly increased public contact with school board members. And a children's summer reading program in which libraries, schools, and the access center worked together resulted in the committee members, officers of thirteen different institutions, finding other common interests.

Access does not need to win popularity contests to play a useful role in the community. It is not surprising if people do not watch most of the time. (Indeed, given the treatment access gets by cable operators, it is a kind of miracle that viewers find the channel at all.) It is indicative of its peculiar function that people find the channel of unique value when they do use it.

Different kinds of access are used for very different purposes. Government and educational channels may feature such programming as the city council meeting, the school board meeting, the local high school's basketball game, religious programming, or rummage-sale announcements on a community billboard. Some colleges have sponsored oral history sessions that illuminate immigrant history (Agosta et al. 1990; Nicholson 1990).

Public access channels, run on a first-come-first-serve basis, are responsible for much of access cable's negative image, and some of its most improbable successes. There is often a strong element of the personalist and quixotic in the programming, and public access channels have sometimes been a source of scandal and legal controversy, for instance when the Ku Klux Klan started circulating national programs for local viewing (Shapiro 1990, 409f; Brenner, Price, and Meyerson 1990, sec. 604[7]). Less reported is that often the Klan issue spurred civil liberties and ethnic minorities organizations to use the service for their own local needs; and these groups have continued to use the service. Voluntary associations, for instance, the Humane Society's adopt-a-pet program in Fayetteville, Arkansas, and a musical education series sponsored by the Los Angeles Jazz Society (Nicholson 1990), also use public access. In a some places—for instance, New York City, where Paper Tiger Television regularly produces sharply critical programs on the media; or Austin, Texas, home of one of access cable's oldest talk shows—public access has become an established alternative voice in public affairs. Public access is host to viewpoints as diverse as those of leftist critics of the Gulf War (in Deep Dish TV's national series) and those of conservative Rep. Newt Gingrich (R-GA), who hosts half-hour shows produced by the Washington, D.C.-based American Citizens' Television (ACTV).

Thus access has a history of fulfilling a role of community service and has been recognized in law as performing a useful First Amendment function. Access cable could, in every locality, provide an unduplicated, local public forum for public issues.

Cable operators and municipalities alike have found access cable to be a thorn in their sides (Ingraham 1990). In municipalities such as Pittsburgh, Milwaukee, and Portland (Oregon), cable companies immediately rescinded or renegotiated franchise terms regarding cable access, once the act went into effect. Even when access was established or reestablished, the cost was often significant. For instance, in Austin, Texas, the Time-owned company only two weeks after deregulation went into effect announced that it could not afford to meet its franchise obligations—

especially its $400,000-a-year funds for access television and the provision of eight channels. It took eleven months of civic organizing and city council pressure, and some $800,000, to restore the provisions.

In localities beset with fiscal crisis—a widespread problem, since in the 1980s many costs of government were shifted downward—revenues once designated to access have gone into general revenues. For instance, when Nashville found itself in a budget crisis in 1988, a program by a gay and lesbian alliance on public access triggered a city council debate. The cable company, a Viacom operator, supported city council members trying to rechannel access funds into general operating funds. The upshot was near-total defunding of the access center. In Eugene, Oregon, and Wyoming, Michigan, among others, municipalities have drastically cut or eliminated access budgets in favor of other city projects.[1]

## What It Would Take

Local citizen activism has kept access cable alive, but its limits, in a situation where national cable policy shapes the economic environment, are clear. Consistent, federal-level reservation and subsidy would be needed to create the opportunity for creative experiments in public spaces on cable TV. Reservation of channel capacity would need to be accompanied by adequate funding—for facilities, professional production assistance, a local public production fund, and promotion—through the franchise and through annual franchise fees.

Centers should universally have funding for professional staff, which would not mitigate the value of access cable as a public space. There is no need to fetishize the amateur and the homemade; professional craftsmanship can improve the functioning of a public forum and enliven the public sphere as much as it can the realm of commerce. Professionals' tasks, however, would be as facilitators of communication rather than promoters of expression for its own sake.

National public cable channel capacity, with protected funds to avoid both censorship and the distortions of corporate underwriting, could further broaden the public forum. C-SPAN's admirable record, and that of a foundation-funded regional public affairs channel focusing on the state legislature (CAL-SPAN: The California Channel) might serve as prototypes for such an effort (Westen and Givens 1989). The service would not, however, have to be limited to legislative or judicial issues. Nor would it be beholden to the whims of the cable industry as C-SPAN is. This service would differ from public television—another valuable service—not only in its subject matter but in its primary mandate to respond to the moment, a flexibility that public television does not exercise except in extremity.

Such national channel capacity would boldly raise the perennial problem of who should broker information and how, a problem that in itself could become another opportunity for civic organizing and creative rethinking of how television is and can be used. Without doubt, it too would require professional staff, with rules and structures guiding their work. For instance, users might have to meet a minimum standard of organization; public interests least likely to be served in the commercial marketplace might be prioritized. Arenas of concern such as educational and health policy, multicultural questions, environmental and workplace issues, and the arenas of public discourse themselves (e.g., events of public interest groups) could be the basis for ongoing electronic workshops.

Another resource for such a reinvigorated public interest could be a national video production fund, with its products available for distribution through all televisual vehicles, including cable, broadcast television, and videocassette. Such a fund could be paid for in a variety of ways, such as spectrum fees, revenues from profits from sales of broadcast stations and cable systems, and charges on videocassettes, VCRs, and satellite dishes. Its goal too would be to promote citizen organizing; some of the early projects of Britain's Channel 4, particularly its workshops and special programming sections, could provide useful models. The funds could be allocated to community organizations of all kinds, rather than to media organizations.

### That's All Very Well, But . . .

Would protection for access channels and other public spaces even survive the cable companies' claim to First Amendment priority? Operators have made vigorous, and largely but not wholly successful, arguments for the primacy of their First Amendment rights over cable access (Shapiro 1990). And commercial media lay a legitimate claim to First Amendment rights, one recognized extensively in law since the mid-1970s (Robinowitz 1990, 313, n. 29). However, First Amendment rights are not absolute, or the special preserve of economic as opposed to public interests; and there is powerful precedent for the democratic state structurally promoting the public's right to speak (Holmes 1990, 55). In many of their aspects cable operators are not speakers or even editors (Brenner 1988, 329ff). Policy mandating access centers certainly would not abridge "expression that the First Amendment was meant to protect" (*First National Bank of Boston v. Bellotti* 1978) but, rather, the opposite, and furthermore withstand constitutional scrutiny (Meyerson 1981, 33–59). Congress has also found that leased and PEG access regulation meets First Amendment and constitutional standards (U.S. Senate 1990b, 46; U.S. House of Representatives 1990, 35).

Is it reasonable to assume, though, that people want to "make their own media," when the record shows so decisively that people prefer to pay someone to make it for them? No, and that argument is not made here. For entertainment, most people do and will choose high-quality product paid for mostly by their purchase of advertisers' products. Parents of junior high school football stars will find school sports carried on an educational access channel more interesting than the top-rated sitcom or even the NBA, of course, but most people will select commercial alternatives. Indeed, that is why it is important not to abandon that arena to the iron grip of a few MSOs.

But people using cable as a public space are using it to communicate with others about particular issues and projects of public interest. Whatever the level of their involvement, they perceive it and use it—as producers, viewers, or organizers of viewers—not as a consumer experience but as a participatory step in a relationship that is not, typically, either electronic or commercial.

Is access cable part of a dinosaur technological model, in a world in which consumers increasingly can obtain audiovisual services from satellite providers or even from phone companies? Is it unfair to cable operators to saddle them with electronic public spaces that others either do not have to or cannot provide? These are issues, in fact, not of technology but of political and social will. It is perfectly possible to level the policy playing fields, once committed to public spaces. Direct broadcast satellite (DBS) providers do, in theory, have public set-aside obligations (see "The Missing Space on Satellite TV"), and it is possible to imagine comparable obligations in other technologies.

If the public needs such spaces, why not simply pay for access on an open market, and fund the program through general tax revenues? This is indeed one plausible approach to the project of reserving public spaces, but it would confront immediately the fact that the markets for electronic space in telecommunications policy are profoundly distorted, because of both existing policy and market dominance.

Why should we assume a demand for something that's been around so long to so little effect? This question builds on the negative image of access cable, which like all stereotypes has an origin in some kind of truth. A variety of answers, substantiated above, address different facets of that negative image. One is that some programming, primarily in public access, has indeed been trivial, self-indulgent, and derivative, and that those uses often reflect an interpretation of access that sees the First Amendment as an end rather than a means to democratic vitality. More important is the gross underfunding of access cable, its abandonment by legislators and regulators, and the unrelenting attacks by cablers and cities on centers; in that light, much more shocking is that access centers survive anywhere. It is particularly impressive that access channels have been able to do as much as they have with so little professional staff. Finally, access, lacking as public television did until 1967 a national substructure, is still in its prehistory.

But can we afford to have such ambitious programs? One answer is to ask, can we afford not to? Less rhetorically, this is a question that needs as yet ungathered data. Cable and other mass media interests would probably make a substantial contribution to the costs. Operators have powerful arguments against any of these proposals, and they all hinge on the inability to afford them—an argument unprovable without accounting evidence. So telecommunications media, especially cable MSOs and broadcast stations, should open their books for the public record.

Finally, are access and other mechanisms to promote the use of the medium as a public space cost-effective? This is a wildly speculative area of economics because it deals with externalities such as the health of a democratic polity. In the absence of social cost-benefit studies—an area begging for more economic research—one can make some basic points. The technological level of equipment and expertise needed to do so is comparatively low; the price of even lavish subsidies cannot compare with even a small road-paving job; and the benefits are widespread and incremental. Civic life is a cultural process that must be nurtured. Television, and increasingly cable television, has a central role in American consumer habits, and it has unique capacities to transmit complex, multisensory messages. Why should that capacity be used exclusively to sell things and not to develop civic projects?

## Notes

Research for this project was partly funded by the Donald McGannon Research Center at Fordham University.

1. Interviews with the following people between September 1990 and August 1991 informed the analysis of access cable: Andrew Blau, then-

communications policy analyst, United Church of Christ Office of Communication, New York; Alan Bushong, executive director, Capital Community TV, Salem, Oregon; Gerry Field, executive director, Somerville Community Access Television, Somerville, Massachusetts; Ann Flynn, Tampa Educational Cable Consortium; Nicholas Miller, lawyer, Miller and Holbrooke, Washington, D.C.; Elliott Mitchell, ex-executive director, Nashville Community Access TV; Randy Van Dalsen, Access Sacramento.

## References

Access Sacramento. 1990. *Access Sacramento Annual Report: 1990, The Year in Review.* Sacramento, Calif.: Coloma Community Center.

Access Sacramento. 1991. *1991 Audience Survey Findings Report.* Sacramento, Calif.: Coloma Community Center.

Agosta, D., C. Rogoff, and A. Norman. 1990. *The PARTICIPATE Study: A Case Study of Public Access Cable Television in New York State.* New York: Alternative Media Information Center (121 Fulton St., 5th flr, NY, NY 10038).

Aufderheide, P. 1999. *Communications Policy and the Public Interest.* New York: Guilford Press.

Blumler, J. G., and C. Spicer. 1990. "Prospects for Creativity in the New Television Marketplace: Evidence from Program-Makers." *Journal of Communication* 40: 78–101.

Brenner, D. 1988. "Cable Television and the Freedom of Expression." *Duke Law Journal* (April/June): 329–88.

Brenner, D., M. Price, and M. Meyerson. 1990. *Cable Television and Other Nonbroadcast Video: Law and Policy.* New York: Clark Boardman.

Davis, L. J. 1990. "Television's Real-Life Cable Baron." *New York Times Magazine* (Part 2: The Business World), December 2, 16 ff.

Engelman, R. 1990. *The Origins of Public Access Cable Television.* Journalism Monographs (Association for Education in Journalism and Mass Communication, 1621 College St., University of South Carolina, Columbia, SC 29208-0251), (October): no. 123.

———. 1996. *Public Radio and Television in America.* Thousand Oaks, Calif.: Sage.

Entman, R. M., and S. Wildman. 1990. "Toward a New Analytical Framework for Media Policy: Reconciling Economic and Non-Economic Perspectives on the Marketplace for Ideas." Presented at the Annual Telecommunications Policy Research Conference, Airlie, Va., October 1–2.

*FCC v. National Citizens Committee for Broadcasting.* 1978. 436 U.S. 775, 795.

*First National Bank of Boston v. Bellotti.* 1978. 435 U.S. 765, 776.

Hauser, G. A. 1987. "Features of the Public Sphere." *Critical Studies in Mass Communication* 4: 437–41.

Holmes, S. 1990. "Liberalism and Free Speech." In *Democracy and the Mass Media*, ed. J. Lichtenberg. New York: Cambridge University Press.

Ingraham, S. B. 1990. On behalf of the National Federation of Local Cable Programmers. Testimony before the U.S. House of Representatives Subcommittee on Telecommunications and Finance of the Committee on Energy and Commerce, May 16.

Jamison, F. R. 1990. *Community Programming Viewership Study Composite Profile*. Kalamazoo: Western Michigan University Media Services Department.

Lampert, D., F. H. Cate, and F. W. Lloyd. 1991. *Cable Television Leased Access*. Washington, D.C.: Annenberg Washington Program.

Le Duc, D. 1987. *Beyond Broadcasting: Patterns in Policy and Law*. New York: Longman.

Meiklejohn, A. 1948. *Free Speech and Its Relation to Self-Government*. New York: Harper & Bros.

Melody, W. H. 1990a. "The Information in I.T.: Where Lies the Public Interest?" *Intermedia* (London) 18 (June–July): 10–18.

———. 1990b. "Communication Policy in the Global Information Economy: Whither the Public Interest?" In *Public Communication: The New Imperatives*, ed. M. Ferguson. London: Sage Publications.

*Metro Broadcasting Inc. v. FCC*. 1990. 110 S. Ct. 2997.

Meyerson, M. I. 1981. "The First Amendment and the Cable Operator: An Unprotective Shield against Public Access Requirements." *Comm/Ent* 4: 1–66.

———. 1985. "The Cable Communications Policy Act of 1984: A Balancing Act on the Coaxial Wires." *Georgia Law Review* 19: 543–622.

———. 1990. "Amending the Oversight: Legislative Drafting and the Cable Act." *Cardozo Arts and Entertainment Law Journal* 8: 233–55.

Nicholson, M. 1990. *Cable Access: A Community Communications Resource for Nonprofits*. (Benton Foundation Bulletin 3). Washington, D.C.: Benton Foundation (1710 Rhode Island Ave., NW, 4th Floor, Washington, D.C. 20036).

*Red Lion Broadcasting Co. v. FCC*. 1969. 395 U.S., 367.

Robinowitz, S. 1990. "Cable Television: Proposals for Reregulation and the First Amendment." *Cardozo Arts and Entertainment Law Journal* 8: 309–35.

Shapiro, G. H. 1990. "Litigation Concerning Challenges to the Franchise Process, Programming and Access Channel Requirements, and Franchise Fees." In *Cable Television Law 1990: Revisiting the Cable Act, Volume 1*, ed. F. Lloyd. Washington, D.C.: Practising Law Institute.

Sinel, N. M., et al. 1990. "Current Issues in Cable Television: A Re-Balancing to

Protect the Consumer." *Cardozo Arts and Entertainment Law Journal* 8: 387–432.

Streeter, T. 1987. "The Cable Fable Revisited: Discourse, Policy and the Making of Cable Television." *Critical Studies in Mass Communication* 4: 174–200.

*Stromberg v. California.* 1931. 283 U.S. 359, 369.

*Television and Cable Factbook.* 1998. Washington, D.C.: Warren.

*U.S. v. Associated Press.* 1943. 52 F. Supp. 362, 372 (S.D. N.Y.)

U.S. Congress. 1984. Cable Communications Policy Act of 1984. Sect. 601[4]. 47 U.S.C. Sec. 532[4].

U.S. Federal Communications Commission. 1990a. "In the Matter of Competition, Rate Deregulation, and the Commission's Policies Relating to the Provision of Cable Television Service." MM Docket No. 89-600, FCC 90–276, July 31.

U.S. Federal Communications Commission. 1990b. "Reexamination of the Effective Competition Standard for the Regulation of Cable Television Basic Service Rates." MM Docket No. 90–4, FCC 90-412, December 31. Further Notice of Proposed Rule Making.

U.S. Federal Communications Commission. 1998. "Fourth Annual Report: In the Matter of Annual Assessment of the Status of Competition in Markets for the Delivery of Video Programming." CS Docket No. 97-141, January 13.

U.S. General Accounting Office. 1990. "Telecommunications: Follow-Up National Survey of Cable Television Rates and Services." GAO/RCED-90-199. Report to the Chairman, Subcommittee on Telecommunications and Finance, Committee on Energy and Commerce, House of Representatives, June 13.

U.S. House of Representatives. 1990. *Cable Television Consumer Protection and Competition Act of 1990.* House Report, H.R. 5267. Report 101–682, 101st Congress, 2d Session.

U.S. National Telecommunications Information Administration (NTIA). 1988. *NTIA Telecom 2000.* Washington, D.C.: Government Printing Office.

U.S. Senate. 1990a. *Competitive Problems in the Cable Television Industry: Hearing before the Subcommittee on Antitrust, Monopolies and Business Rights of the Committee on the Judiciary.* United States Senate, 101st Cong., 1st Session, April 12. Washington, D.C.: Government Printing Office.

U.S. Senate 1990b. *Cable Television Consumer Protection Act of 1990: Report on S. 1880.* Report 101-381, 101st Congress, 2d Session.

"Why Viewers Would Like to Zap Their Cable Firms." 1990. *Wall Street Journal,* March 19, B1.

Westen, T., and B. Givens. 1989. *A New Public Affairs Television Network for the State: The California Channel.* Los Angeles: Center for Responsive Government.

Winston, B. 1986. *Misunderstanding Media.* Cambridge: Harvard University Press.

———. 1990. "Rejecting the Jehovah's Witness Gambit." *Intermedia* 18 (November–December): 21–25.

# Access Cable

# in Action

*Access cable is easy to make fun of, and even easier to ignore. So when access cable centers across the country were threatened with extinction because of a clause in the 1992 Cable Act, no one knew exactly what was at stake in this decentralized and slighted medium. I did a survey to collect some information that lawyers fighting the clause could use; the Supreme Court finally decided the clause was unconstitutional. I reworked the original affidavit for publication, to expand the audience for the argument.*

What difference does it make in a community to have access cable programming? A national survey of controversial programming on access cable in 1992 suggests that such programming provides a valuable service for immediate communities of reference but also expands the public sphere by increasing public discussion, debate, and awareness of community issues and cultural realities.

## Access Cable as a Public Space

Access cable—the channels variously known as public, educational, and governmental (or PEG) and offered as part of basic cable wherever they have been called for in franchises—is that rare site on cable where public interest comes before profit. It is also fiercely embattled and widely disrespected.

Cable companies and local governments have often found access cable, especially public access, exasperating and even infuriating. On such channels appear usually inoffensive items such as community news bulletin boards, junior high school sports, city council and board of education meetings, and senior citizens' workshops. As well, because of public access' wide open, first-come-first-serve policies and its uniqueness as a free and profitless entry point to television, what also sometimes appears there is the dissenting opinion, the deliberately outrageous youthful statement, the talk show that escalates into a free-for-all, nagging critiques of public officials—programming virtually guaranteed to irritate someone. And yet the programming that authorities and some consumers find most obnoxious might turn out, at least at times, to be a unique service to the public sphere.

Public access television, imagined by Congress as "the video equivalent of the speaker's soap box or the electronic parallel to the printed leaflet" (U.S. House 1984, 21–22), has a unique function on television, which usually is one of the most tightly guarded gates in mass media. It has been celebrated as a First Amendment victory because of its accessibility alone. But to become socially significant, its open access needs to result not merely in the service's being a catch-all, a kind of garbage can, for leftover opinions and rejected behaviors in the society.

"Public access brings private citizens into public life," one scholar involved with the service argues (Devine 1992, 9). At its best, public access can create new and expand existing venues for public discussion uncontrolled by government and not conditioned by commercial messages. It can act as an electronic public space, contributing to the elaboration of the public sphere, an arena outside economic and governmental institutions and structures where a polity can form and establish priorities and procedures for managing public resources and problems.

No one, including its strongest supporters, believes that public access universally exemplifies that ideal, and some argue that access center directors need to reenvision themselves explicitly as providers of public space rather than as brokers, facilitators, or retailers of individual opinion (Blau 1992). Occasional flurries of publicity for access—whether publicizing a *Wayne's World* image of the service or that offered by Ku Klux Klan programming occasionally carried there—seem inevitably to embarrass its advocates. Cable access, in short, lives out the tensions between individual and community that infuse discussion of free expression.

One place to assess the utility of public access cable is therefore at what some might consider its most embarrassing, the programming most likely to trigger concern or complaint on the part of the cable operator. This is programming also likely to trigger an operator's interference, under the new legislation.

## Method

This study explores the social function of public access, as seen in programming that could be seen as controversial. Such programming provides an indication, among other things, of how public access works as an electronic public space.

Eighty-one access centers were surveyed in November and December 1992, in conjunction with research conducted for the Alliance for Community Media's intervention in a Federal Communications Commission rule making that interpreted operator control over programming (U.S. FCC, 1992, 1992b, 1992c). (See appendix for details of the lawsuit and specifics of the survey.) Access directors were asked to identify programming that was or might be construed to be controversial, and also to describe current gatekeeping arrangements and relationships with the cable company. They were also asked to speculate on the effect of operators' having more control over programming.

Some thirty-one access directors—chosen through their participation in the Alliance for Community Media, which represents the interests of cable access—were interviewed by telephone. Most (twenty) headed independent nonprofit entities; the rest were functionaries of local government (nine) or the cable company (two). The majority (twenty-one) came from smaller communities, while ten worked in major cities or state capitals. The sample was regionally diverse, with thirteen from the East, seven from the Midwest, three from the South, and eight from the West.

A mail survey, sent to some two hundred access directors on the mailing list of the Alliance for Community Media, then asked the same questions. Among the fifty respondents, thirty-four headed nonprofit entities. Seven centers were run by the city, and four by the cable company (six were some combination, usually city-run nonprofits). Thirty-nine were from smaller communities; eleven were from major cities or state capitals. Twenty-two came from the East, fifteen from the Midwest, three from the South, and ten from the West.

### Programming That Tests the Limits

Access directors argue that successfully executed programming, particularly programming that wins a regular time slot, is evidence of more than an individual opinion and reflects a concern somewhere in that community. They gauge this concern in part through enthusiasm for program production and in part through responses to programming. "If it has an audience," said director Deb Vinsel in Olympia, Washington, "it's part of your community, even if you wish it were not."

Such programming is here analyzed in two categories, taped and live programming, because each type creates different opportunities for raising issues, discussion, and debate, and so fostering the public sphere.

### Taped Programming

Taped programming, which often includes some "imported" shows (made elsewhere but sponsored locally), demonstrates a conscientious investment of time and energy on the part of people eager to communicate their views, either with peers or beyond their immediate circle. The airing of these provides an otherwise inaccessible platform for sometimes unpopular views.

The examples that access directors offered, when asked to consider prerecorded programming that a cautious programmer might reject for fear of being interpreted as containing "obscene material, sexually explicit conduct, or material soliciting or promoting unlawful conduct" provide a sample of expression that goes past the idiosyncratic into the social. The most importance categories include sex education, public affairs, and cultural minorities.

Sex education, and particularly AIDS education, was a frequent item mentioned by access directors; it was both popular and controversial. Such programming was often, though not necessarily, an indication of the self-awareness and public self-identification of a gay and lesbian community. Furthermore, it was an instance of introducing a hitherto unknown or forbidden item of knowledge—transmission of AIDS—into public discourse. Series such as Fairfax (Virginia) Cable Access Corporation's *Gay Fairfax*, Grand Rapids (Michigan) Community Media Center's *The Lambda Report*, Tucson (Arizona) Community Cable Corporation's *Empty Closet* all touch on AIDS education. Single programs such as Cambridge (Massachusetts) Community TV's *Truth or Consequences: A Guide to Safe Sex at MIT*; *AIDS*, a documentary cablecast at Spring Point Community Television Center in South Portland (Maine); and an AIDS prevention special involving role playing at Kalamazoo (Michigan) Community Access Center frankly confront an emerging health menace with approaches that may offend some.

Imported public affairs programs trigger complaints but also enhance the range of debate, according to center directors. Several centers reported that the talk show *Alternative Views,* produced through the Austin, Texas, access center but distributed where the program finds a local sponsor, often draws criticism for its leftist perspective. It offers a clear example of the long-standing goal of "diverse and antagonistic sources" (*Associated Press v. U.S.* 1945) in a democratic society's media, however, and furthermore demonstrates resonance cross-regionally by its acceptance in very different localities. Similarly, the regular programming of Deep Dish TV, which anthologizes local access programming and packages it around themes ranging from agriculture to AIDS to border cultures, has been a source of contention in some communities, where access center directors nonetheless see it as offering an important alternative perspective and an opportunity to see what other localities are producing.

The Left has no special purchase on unpopular but vocal minority opinion. Several access centers (Forest Park, Ohio; Fort Wayne, Indiana; Sacramento, California; Kalamazoo, Michigan; Portland, Oregon; Dayton, Ohio; South Portland, Maine; Portland, Maine) reported either local or imported programs opposing abortion, some by Operation Rescue. These tapes typically encourage blocking of access to abortion clinics and/or include graphic, possibly offensive images.

Access cable is sometimes a major site of electoral controversy, which otherwise, in an era in which the Fairness Doctrine has been suspended, can be left without a televisual battlefield. In Oregon during election season 1992, Ballot Measure 9, which would have criminalized some homosexual behavior, was hotly debated on access cable. Oregon access center directors in Portland and Salem both reported extensive use, both in live and taped programs, of access by opposing sides. Both sides incorporated material that might have been perceived as sexually explicit.

Another topical instance was the Gulf War, where access cable provided a rare site of dissent, including a series of programs by Deep Dish TV. This programming was typically controversial. For instance, in Winsted, Connecticut, the Mad River TV access service weathered demands to remove anti–Gulf War programming while it was being cablecast. A production group in Portland, Oregon, the Flying Focus Video Collective, has taken controversial stands on issues ranging from the Gulf War to local environmental issues.

Thus, on electoral and topical political issues, access cable seems to serve as a kind of televisual op-ed page, where clashing opinions can be aired and where a public forum can be created—registered not least in the hot contest over the right of dissenting groups to cablecast their views, and the eager pursuit of reply time by opposing sides.

Cultural minorities create a communications space for themselves on cable access, by producing and cablecasting programs of primary interest to their constituencies—otherwise neglected in mass media. For instance, young people are catered to as individual consumers of media and the products they tout but are rarely given their own forum in the media. Young people eagerly use access cable both to speak to their own peers and to speak about an experience underrepresented in mainstream media.

A program wildly popular with teenagers, *Silly Goose,* was for a season a weekly comedy program in at least arguable and certainly adolescent taste in Defiance, Ohio. (Director Norm Compton recalled one episode that featured the theme of running with scissors.) Other regular local programs in that area that promoted youth culture on access were *Musical Mayhem,* featuring music videos, and *Hard Hits,* a rap show produced by a young African American man. Similarly, in Olympia, Washington, a youth-oriented music video program, *Mosher's Mayhem,* accounts for both a passionate teen audience and also the bulk of the occasional complaints to the service. In Grand Rapids, Michigan, *Blackwatch* focuses on the language and images of inner city youth. Public access in Malden, Massachusetts, has weathered controversy over youthful productions marked by vulgar language.

In each case, the programs were supported by young people and denounced by others, usually for bad taste. In these cases, public access provided a venue for a self-described cultural minority to assert the existence of its reality and values to itself and the wider community, to challenge and be challenged.

### Live Programming

Live programming makes cable an interactive experience, cultivating on-air discussion and debate, and most centers surveyed offer it. It also defines and shapes audiences. In interviews, access directors often singled out live programming as of particular interest to their communities. They highlighted several kinds of programming, demonstrating the role of access cable as a public space: sexual and health education; topical call-in; and minority cultures.

Sexual and health education is an area where live programming draws an engaged, often young audience, for whom this may be the first opportunity to perceive these issues as legitimate objects of public discussion.

In Chicago, *AIDS Call-In Live* is the only regularly scheduled TV program offering AIDS education, according to director Barbara Popovic (Popovic 1992). Various area organizations are showcased, each focusing on its own agenda and issues.

Two such groups, the Westside Association for Community Action and the Howard Brown Memorial Clinic, aspire to reach minority youth and find that four-fifths of their phone calls are from African Americans, most of them teenagers. Typical of the kind of interchange was the phone call of one seventeen-year-old girl who wanted to know how to respond to a boyfriend who assured her they need not use condoms because he was "loyal" to her. The conversation was frank and colloquial on both sides, while also giving the girl much-needed information. As well, on air, speakers hold up items such as condoms and dental dams and explain their use. Organizations also achieve other goals with such participation. For instance, Chicago House wanted more volunteers and found that their volunteer base grew 10 to 15 percent, with a marked increase in minority volunteers, after participating in *AIDS Call-in Live*. The Portland, Oregon, *AIDS Forum Live* has a similar format.

Other health programs similarly frame sexual and health issues as ones of public information and discussion, sometimes quixotically. On public access cable in Austin, a program called *Midnight Whispers* frankly encourages viewers to call in to share their sexual fantasies, so that an on-air nurse can respond to them and discuss safe sex practices. Some programming uses demonstrations or images that may offend. A Tucson program, *Bridges,* by and for the disabled, has featured AIDS education involving anatomical models. In Sacramento, the monthly *Health in America* program on alternative and holistic health options, has featured graphic images of women with mastectomies and damaged breast implants.

Topical call-in more traditionally—and sometimes in a more volatile way—raises public issues for community debate. In Sacramento within hours of the Rodney King verdict a special edition of the weekly *Live Wire* community call-in program was airing, with scores of viewers, most apparently African American, responding to a host known in the community for his success in working with alienated youth. The staff found that the discussion was less raw than expected.

Programs such as Fort Wayne's program *Speak Out* and Tucson's *You're the Expert* touch on controversial local issues ranging from street signs to police behavior, without any way of predicting how callers might behave. NDC Community TV in West St. Paul, Minnesota, aired a series *Facts Not Friends* around 1992 electoral politics, which the access director saw as expanding the debate. In South Portland, a call-in show debated U.S. policy during the Gulf War; some callers suggested illegal actions as protest.

Minority cultures have an opportunity on cable both to build community and to reach out beyond what may be a misunderstood community to a wider public. The Fort Wayne program *Coalition for Unlearning Racism,* a live twice-a-month program, deals with topics on which, as access manager Rick Hayes puts it, "people are already irate," and has been the site of heated, wide-ranging discussion about racism. Also on the same system is a program *Message to the Black Man,* a black nationalist program that purveys a distinctly minoritarian view in the area and is, apparently, a unique resource for those who support its perspective.

As with recorded programming, teenagers make extensive use of this rare public forum for them. In Tucson, they produce a live program called *The Forbidden Zone,* in which they talk in the slang and curse-laden jargon of their peers, involving sexually explicit language and sometimes addressing illegal activities such as drug use. Cable TV North Central in White Bear Lake, Minnesota, hosts a teen talk show with the sometimes vulgar language typical of that subculture. This kind of programming easily raises eyebrows. For instance, the live teen show *Active Butch/Pensive Willy* in Newton Highlands, Massachusetts, has with its raw language in call-ins roused the ire of a board member. Nonetheless, it also evidences the importance of that venue for the young people themselves.

### Prescreening and Banning Programming

How do access centers handle conflicts over programming? Until now, most public access centers have functioned primarily as sites of technical assistance for whoever wants to use the service, on a first-come-first-serve basis; this is the strict construction of access in the 1984 act. Thus, many access centers surveyed do not prescreen at all; in a minority of centers surveyed, ten to eighteen hours a week of prescreening is built into the work schedule (e.g., Prince George's Community Television, Landover, Maryland; Pittsburgh Community Television, Pittsburgh, Pennsylvania). Many access centers have guidelines prohibiting obscene and commercial material and require producers to read guidelines and certify that they abide by them.

Public access directors do become adepts at dealing with complaints from viewers, and from city and cable officials. But rarely, according to these interviews, had complaints resulted in prohibition of programming, and then only after it had already run at least once.

Several reported incidents of attempted programming intervention point up the importance of an independent public forum on controversial political issues. A Cincinnati channel accepted a tape from one political party in 1991 local elections; the other party promptly obtained a restraining order, although it had the right to air a program and, furthermore, center staff had volunteered to help produce one. Ultimately, the complaining party lost in court, and the tape was aired. In the small town of Defiance, Ohio, several years ago town officials attempted—also unsuccessfully—to block a program criticizing the town's plan to privatize emergency medical services. In Marshall, Minnesota, the city council tried to block a tape of a demonstration against ordinances and owners of a mobile home park but was eventually dissuaded by the access director's First Amendment arguments.

Other reported cases usually involve questions of taste and decency. For instance, in Columbus, Ohio, in September 1992 the city, which controls transmission from the independent nonprofit center, responded to complaints about frontal nudity in a program on gays and AIDS by dropping the program after it had run. Upon legal consultation, however, the city reversed its decision because the program could not be considered pornography.

In Sacramento, a similar incident appears part of a larger struggle between the center, the city, and the cable company. The cable company representative seized on a viewer complaint about a videoplay, *Dinosaurs,* and eagerly argued for shutting down the independently run center to the city, which allocates its funds. Written and produced by a young local man, the play involved scenes of nudity and sexual aggression as part of the author's social critique. (The center's attorney advised the center the piece was not obscene.) Center director Ron Cooper recalls that the local cable operator, long a grudging supporter of the service, had warned him that he would "shut [them] down" and that he had the approval of the multisystem owner to take the case to court.

### Expanding Speech

Access center directors confront controversy by encouraging more speech, not only by allowing all voices a hearing but also by encouraging complainants to make use of training and production assistance, and by explaining the philosophy of the access center. This process appears to expand the opportunity for speech, not only for producers but for viewers, who may call in.

Officials' calls for banning sometimes result in reasoned accommodation such as guidelines devised by aldermanic and cable boards, given directly to producers. Sometimes, attempts to ban programming can act as a powerful threat. When a program by and for teenagers, *Streetwatch,* ran on Columbus Community Cable Access several years ago and frank sexual language offended city officials enough to pull the program from rotation briefly, the board was badly shaken. "When government taps you on the shoulder and tries to crush it at the same time, you take notice," recalled center director Carl Kucharski. He noted that several board members, whose corporations did business with the city, felt particularly vulnerable to official discontent. The board contemplated over a period of months ways to prescreen programming but could not find a workable arrangement. It returned eventually to its open access policy.

But often the solution to a piece of unpopular speech is bringing the offended parties into the debate, thus carving out new public ground. At Malden Access TV, director Rika Welsh recalled a program made by local youths in summer of 1992 with "what was to my taste and probably yours an excessive amount of profanity." After the program, the center scheduled a two-hour call-in, which was vigorously used. For Welsh, "That's what public access is all about—creating that public space. It allows the community to speak to issues; it's not just about the programming itself."

At Waycross Community TV in Forest Park, Ohio, director Greg Vawter pointed to response to a racial hate text message posted on a nearby suburban system. Several of his access center's board members composed and aired passionate arguments against intolerance, part of a community-wide electronic conversation. Director Rick Hayes of the Fort Wayne library system's public access channel noted that a well-established twice-weekly program, *Coalition for Unlearning Racism,* supported by the local NAACP and Urban League among others, began as a response to the possibility of carrying the Ku Klux Klan's *Race and Reason* (which never did run). Making the program also brought together nine groups that hitherto had not worked jointly.

But what about people who do not choose to enter into that public space? The 1984 Cable Act requires the operator to provide lockboxes, or the consumer option of blocking the channel entirely. This option would appear, from this survey, to be widely available. In the thirty-one interviews conducted, all but one person, who did not know, said the system had the capacity. In two cases, directors interviewed said that the company either appeared unwilling to block the channel or simply did not make public the ability to do so. In the fifty written surveys, thirty-eight reported lockboxes available, although one said that they were not available for public access (a violation of the law), and two said they did not know.

Access directors have evolved a variety of mechanisms to deal with First Amendment rights conflicts, which appear to have worked fairly well. The process has renewed their commitment to public access as a public space, open even to repugnant speech but using it as an indication of unrepresented opinion and an opportunity to spur discussion.

## Conclusion

Public access cable, seen through the atypical angle of its most controversial programming, demonstrates its unique role in electronic media, as a local community television service open to all. The programming produced by various community interests with minimal access to mainstream media showcases concerns of a subculture to itself in the language of that subculture, whether through public affairs or dramatic work or music video. This is apparent in programs by, for instance, African Americans, gays and lesbians, and young people.

As well, public access acts as a place where citizens can and do not only hear about issues of public concern but participate in the creation of that debate, whether through making programming or through the debates both on and off the cable service precipitated by the expanding of the arena for speech.

## Appendix

The 1992 Cable Act included a clause that would let cable operators—who must by law otherwise stay out of access program decisions—ban indecent or obscene material, or "material soliciting or promoting unlawful conduct." Most access providers felt that cablers, who have often found access a thorn in the side, would use this clause to meddle with and possibly even shut down access centers. Petitioners led by the impressive, dedicated pro bono lawyers for the Alliance for Community Media (ACM) asked for a suspension, or stay, of the rules, and won that stay, while a lawsuit against the Federal Communications Commission went forward. The firm of Shea and Gardner, where Michael Greenberger, David Bono, and Michael Isenman led the legal team, could undertake the work specifically because they had no conflicting interests in the area. As a result, they also lacked basic information on the nature of access cable. James Horwood of the firm of Spiegel and McDermott and an ACM board member, aided by Joseph Van Eaton of Miller and Holbrooke, who have guided ACM's legal work over the years, consulted with the Shea and Gardner team. I volunteered to conduct this survey, in which I asked access center directors specifically what kinds of programming, and by implication what kinds of public service and public debate, were actually in practice and at stake. My original report, from which this is derived, was filed as an affidavit in the access centers' brief.

On November 23, 1993, a panel of the only three Democratic judges in what was then an appeals court of ten decided the case (*Alliance for Community Media et al. v. FCC* 1993) in favor of access centers. The court found that the clause effectively makes the government a censor, because the government strongly encourages a private actor to do so, and so is unconstitutional. Because of appeals claims by the FCC and the Department of Justice, the case eventually went to the Supreme Court, where two cases were considered jointly (*Denver Area Educational Tele-Communications Consortium, Inc., et al. v. FCC* 1995; *Alliance for Community Media et al. v. FCC* 1995). The justices concurred with the lower court that the clause was unconstitutional because it was "not appropriately tailored to achieve the basic, legitimate objective of protecting children from exposure to 'patently offensive' material."

The following access directors, in alphabetical order, were interviewed by telephone: Sam Behrend, Tucson (Arizona) Community Cable Corporation (November 13, 1992); Rick Bell, Tampa (Florida) Cable TV (November 13, 1992); Joan Burke, Community Access Center (Kalamazoo, Michigan) (November 13, 1992); Alan Bushong, Capital Community TV (Salem, Oregon) (November 13, 1992); Mary Bennin Cardona, Glenview (Illinois) Television (November 13, 1992); Norm Compton, Defiance (Ohio) Community TV (November 17, 1992); Paul Congo, Austin (Texas) Community TV (October 27, 1992); Ron Cooper, Access Sacramento (California) (November 13, 1992); Neal Gosman, Cable Access St. Paul (Minnesota) (October 23, 1992); Patricia Havlik, Intercommunity Cable Regulatory Commission (Cincinnati, Ohio) (November 13, 1992); Rick Hayes, All County Public Library Public Access (Fort Wayne, Indiana) (November 13, 1992); Irwin Hipsman, Cambridge (Massachusetts) Community TV (October 28, 1992); Dirk Koning, Grand Rapids (Michigan) Community Media Center (October 27, 1992); Carl Kucharski, Columbus (Ohio) Community Cable Access (October 22, 1992); Myra Lenburg, Amherst (Massachusetts) Community TV (November 20, 1992); Deb Luppold, Portland (Oregon) Cable Access TV (November 16, 1992); John Madding, Wadsworth (Ohio) Community TV (November 17, 1992); Paula Manley, Tualatin

Valley (Oregon) Community Access (October 27, 1992); Fernando Moreno, City County Access TV (Albuquerque, New Mexico) (October 27, 1992); Jeff Neidert, City of Brunswick, Ohio (November 18, 1992); Abigail Norman, Somerville (Massachusetts) Community Access TV (October 23, 1992); Barbara Popovic, Chicago Access Corporation (October 23, 1992); Tony Riddle, Minneapolis TV Network (October 23, 1992); Alex Quinn, Manhattan Neighborhood Network (October 23, 1992); Nantz Rickard, DC Public Access Corporation (Washington, D.C.) (October 28, 1992); Suzanne Silverthorn, Vail (Colorado) Valley Community TV (November 13, 1992); Fred Thomas, Fairfax (Virginia) Cable Access Corporation (October 27, 1992); Greg Vawter, Waycross Community TV (Forest Park, Ohio) (November 13, 1992); Deb Vinsel, Thurston Community TV (Olympia, Washington) (November 20, 1992); David Vogel, Community TV of Knoxville (Tennessee) (October 27, 1992); Rika Welsh, Malden (Massachusetts) Access TV (October 28, 1992).

Surveys were sent out on November 16, 1992. Those received by December 23 are alphabetized by town, township, or county of origin: AACAT, Ann Arbor, Michigan; Arlington Community TV, Arlington, Virginia; Baltimore Cable Access Corporation; Bellevue Community Television, Bellevue, Nebraska; Bethel Park Public Access TV, Bethel Park, Pennsylvania; Cincinnati Community Video; Anderson Community Television (Anderson Township), Cincinnati, Ohio; Davis Community TV, Davis, California; DATV, Dayton, Ohio; Denver Community TV; Access 4, Fayetteville, Arkansas; WFRN, Ferndale, Michigan; Fitchburg Access TV, Fitchburg, Massachusetts; College Cable Access Center, Fort Wayne, Indiana; Public Access Corporation, Great Neck, New York; MCTV Gresham, Gresham, Oregon; HCTV, Holland, Michigan; Public Access TV, Vision 26, Iowa City; Prince George's Community Television, Landover, Maryland; CTV 20, Londonderry, New Hampshire; PAC 8, Los Alamos, New Mexico; Suburban Community Channels, Maplewood, Minnesota; Studio 8, Community Access TV, Marshall, Minnesota; Nashoba Cable Community TV, Nashoba, Massachusetts; Medfield Cable 8, Medfield, Massachusetts; Medway Cable Access Corporation, Medway, Massachusetts; Mountain View Community TV, Mountain View, California; Middlebury Community TV, Middlebury, Vermont; Monrovia City Hall (KGEM), Monrovia, California; Newton Cable, Newton Highland, Massachusetts; Mid-Peninsula Access Corporation, Palo Alto, California; Pittsburgh Community Television; Portland Community Access Center, Portland, Maine; Sierra Nevada Community Access TV, Reno, Nevada; Montgomery Community TV, Rockville, Maryland;

RCTV, Rye, New York; Community Access TV of Salina, Salina, Kansas; Saratoga Community Access TV, Saratoga, California; Viacom Community TV, Seattle, Washington; NDC-TV, St. Paul, Minnesota; SPTV, South Portland, Maine; Montague Community TV, Turners Falls, Massachusetts; Wakefield Community Access TV, Wakefield, Massachusetts; Westbrook Cable Channel, Westbrook, Maine; Cable TV North Central, White Bear Lake, Minnesota; Windsor, Connecticut; Wilmington Community TV, Wilmington, Massachusetts; Mad River TV, Winsted, Connecticut; Winthrop Community Access TV, Winthrop, Massachusetts; Yakima Community TV, Yakima, Washington.

Access directors were asked these questions:

1. Do you or anyone else prescreen programming on public access for content or for technical reasons? If so, how does this affect programming, especially live programming? How much staff time does it take?

2. Does your system have the capacity to block channels or programs, or provide lockboxes?

3. Has anyone ever prohibited—or attempted to prohibit—someone from running a program on public access? What happened?

4. How much staff time do you think would it take to prescreen programming on public access? What impact would it have on the budget? Would programming be delayed?

5. Do you have live programming now on public access? (Please give an example.) How do you think it would be affected if you were legally responsible for the programming, as you might become under some interpretations of the 1992 cable act?

6. If up till now you *had* been legally responsible for the programming on public access, is there a program(s) you might have considered *not* carrying, whether because of your own or board or city or cable company concern? Issues include sexual content, nudity, language or because it promotes unlawful conduct—for instance, gambling, civil disobedience, anti-abortion actions. (Could you include the title, a brief description, if possible when it was carried, and tell us briefly why you might not carry it.)

7. Has the cable operator issued any new rules or procedures as a result of the 1992 Act?

## Note

The Freedom Forum and the School of Communication at American University both provided resources to conduct this research. The author gratefully acknowledges the assistance of Tamar Rotem in administering the written survey.

## References

*Alliance for Community Media et al. v. FCC.* 1993. D.C. Circuit, 93–1169.

*Alliance for Community Media et al. v. FCC.* 1995. 95–227.

*Associated Press v. U.S.* 1945. 326 U.S. 1, 20.

Blau, A. 1992. "The Promise of Public Access." *The Independent* (April): 22–26.

*Denver Area Educational Tele-Communications Consortium Inc. et al. v. FCC.* 1995. 95–124.

Devine, R. H. 1992. "The Future of a Public." *Community Television Review* 15 (6): 8–9.

Popovic, B. 1992. Personal correspondence, October 26.

U.S. House of Representatives. 1984. *The Cable Communications Policy Act of 1984.* Report 98–934.

U.S. Federal Communications Commission. 1992a. "In the Matter of Implementation of Section 10 of the Cable Consumer Protection and Competition Act of 1992." MM Docket No. 92-258, Notice of Proposed Rule Making, November 5.

U.S. Federal Communications Commission. 1992b. "In the Matter of Implementation of Section 10 of the Cable Consumer Protection and Competition Act of 1992." MM Docket No. 92-258, Joint Comments of the Alliance for Community Media, the Alliance for Communications Democracy, the American Civil Liberties Union, and People for the American Way, December 7.

U.S. Federal Communications Commission. 1992c. "In the Matter of Implementation of Section 10 of the Cable Consumer Protection and Competition Act of 1992." MM Docket No. 92-258, Joint Reply Comments of the Alliance for Community Media, the Alliance for Communications Democracy, the American Civil Liberties Union, and People for the American Way, December 21.

# The Missing Space

# on Satellite TV

*When the FCC opened up a public discussion in 1997 of how to use reserved space on satellite TV, I wanted to find out who wanted to come to the party. It shouldn't have been a surprise. I also wanted to find out why, even after the pro-competitive Telecommunications Act of 1996, "scarcity" was still a living concept in communications policy. That shouldn't have been a surprise either.*

The multichanneling of television has been marked by utopian and dystopian rhetoric and battles over public interest obligations, competing First Amendment rights, and ownership. Channels have multiplied, in fact, without much changing the nature or weight of public interest obligations of providers. A certain kind of abundance has flourished, without affecting another kind of scarcity.

Direct broadcast satellite (DBS) again expands the number of channels available in American homes and again raises basic questions of how such abundance can benefit the democratic society into which it beams its offerings. The debate that occurred in 1997 over how to define DBS's public interest obligations put into sharp relief the weaknesses of existing policy defining the public interest in mass media, and also revealed the weaknesses of existing stakeholder organizations.

154

## The Public Interest in Mass Media

Since the prototype of telecommunications legislation was passed in 1927, the public interest in U.S. mass media has been a term of art, anchored to an acceptance of monopoly power and its consequences. The public interest in electronic media developed as a corollary of the creation of monopoly spectrum holders. The 1934 Communications Act (47 U.S.C.) was part of a larger process of institutionalizing "corporate liberalism." The creation of monopolies, cartels, and sectors typified by substantial market power was seen as having powerful benefits, most especially a stable marketplace, properly regulated by government (Douglas 1987; Horwitz 1988; Streeter 1996). Spectrum licensees exclusively controlled a communications resource and operated oligopolistically at best. As programming networks and syndication services developed, these also operated oligopolistically. Their market strength also brought economic power to the sector.

The term *the public interest* originally linked broad commercial appeal and the public good. In 1925, then–Secretary of Commerce Herbert Hoover argued that commercial owners of radio channels should provide a "public benefit," meaning services available to "the great body of the listening public," with regulation to be designed as the activity evolved, to protect "the public interest" (Robinson 1989, 9; Rowland 1997, 367, 371–79). The FCC contrasted broadly entertaining programming to special-interest moneymaking schemes, for instance, the on-air broadcasts of a doctor who prescribed over the air, with prescriptions filled only by participating pharmacies, and also against highly partisan or propagandistic owner/operators (Wollenberg 1989). Guiding the evolution of the public interest concept in mass media was the notion of scarcity—that broadcasters were monopoly editors over spectrum that was both owned by the American people and not sufficient for all the potential and desiring voices to be heard.

Partly in response to the powerful centralization of electronic media around national networks and partly in response to consumer and social issue organizations (Montgomery 1989), public interest regulations were designed to tailor and shape the marketplace designed and now maintained by regulation. Some were structural, for instance, cross-ownership and concentration of ownership limitations. Some were explicitly editorial, especially in the 1960s and early 1970s as television's cultural power grew—for example, electoral rules and guidelines encouraging some public affairs programming. As well, electronic spaces protected from commercial entertainment priorities—public radio and TV—were established, implicitly acknowledging the limitations of the commercial model but operating within its terms. These three approaches to the public interest all operated within an architecture created in the 1920s. The government, by allocating spectrum for specific uses, by opting to lease uses rather than to issue specific property rights, and by defining the public as a commercial consuming audience, created the conditions for a booming national economic sector, and for a powerful cultural force. The public interest became contested terrain by virtue of the success and power of electronic media.

## Deregulation and the Television of Abundance

From 1970 forward, as Robert Horwitz elegantly charts (1988), there was a dramatic, societywide shift in the notion of what role regulation, and even government, should play. Nurturing and regulating key industries were superseded by the goal of encouraging competition to meet emerging consumer needs. The FCC and its policies came to look old-fashioned.

Electronic media regulation was challenged by regulators, government lawyers, ideologues, and politicians. The scarcity doctrine, the pinion of public interest regulation, came under attack, because roughly comparable alternatives (cable, videocassette, a greater number of independent stations) now existed. Critics attacked the notion of spectrum monopoly as an artifact of a mutually convenient and rewarding relationship between big broadcasters who wanted a protected environment and politicians who wanted control over spectrum (Krattenmaker and Powe 1994). From the late 1970s forward, the FCC began weakening the public trusteeship obligations of broadcasters. Mark Fowler, head of the Reagan-era FCC, with his chief aide Daniel Brenner, boldly asserted, "Communications policy should be directed toward maximizing the services the public desires. . . . The public's interest, then, defines the public interest" (Fowler and Brenner 1982, 207). Meanwhile, a private satellite business emerged from the shadow of government, in the process making cable television a national business, by providing relatively cheap interconnection. By 1984 cable was no longer a booster service for broadcasting. It had become a lightly regulated, booming business.

In 1996, an omnibus overhaul of the 1934 Act (Aufderheide, 1999) codified the equation of the public interest with a competitive environment for telecommunications, in its crisp Title IV. This title asserted that the public interest could be neatly associated with a competitive environment. It still, however, was not extended to mass media,where monopoly licenses were still given.

## DBS and the Return to Scarcity

The DBS proceeding began in a consumer backlash to media deregulation. Rising prices and poor service after the 1984 Cable Act had provoked consumers and consumer organizations such as the Consumer Federation of America to pressure for a return to more traditional regulation. The 1992 Cable Television Consumer Protection Act, incorporated into the Communications Act, contained a clause (47 U.S.C. 335) intended to impose traditional public interest obligations and to reserve space for noncommercial programming and programmers on incipient new competing multichannel video services: direct broadcast satellite. In 1992 there was only one DBS provider, and spectrum allocations had just begun. Public television entities; consumer groups such as the Consumer Federation of America; and advocacy and nonprofit organizations, including the policy advocacy group the Center for Media Education and public interest law firms Media Access Project and Institute for Public Representation—all pushed to insert specific public interest obligations.

The law held DBS providers to two specific kinds of public interest obligations. Section 25(a) of the act required the FCC to design rules for public interest requirements on DBS providers. At a minimum, Congress demanded that DBS providers, like broadcasters, be forced to make time available cheaply to federal-level electoral candidates. It also required the FCC to consider how the congressional goal of localism in mass media could be promoted in this medium (quite a challenge, since by definition, DBS is not a local service, and the signal often may even be national in reach). These rules affect programming decisions of DBS providers and of the programmers to which they rent space. Section 25(b) requires a DBS provider to "reserve a portion of its channel capacity, equal to not less than 4 percent nor more than 7 percent, exclusively for noncommercial programming of an educational or informational nature." A DBS provider was to meet these requirements "by making channel capacity available to national educational programming suppliers" at special low rates to be determined by the FCC.

Time Warner and other media companies immediately challenged the public interest provisions in court, in a complex, omnibus suit that broadly attacked the 1992 Cable Act. The lawsuit charged, among other things, that the provisions were unconstitutional because they violated the First Amendment rights of DBS providers. In March 1993, the FCC, observing the timetable established in the law, initiated a proceeding to implement the provisions, opening a docket that became MM Docket No. 93-25 (U.S. FCC 1993). But on September 16, 1993, the U.S. District Court for the District of Columbia ruled that the provision was unconstitutional (*Daniels Cablevision, Inc. v. U.S.* 1993). Action stopped.

The lawsuit on appeal became an urgent issue for a variety of public interest organizations; it was seen as a watershed moment for public interest obligations of electronic media. The amicus brief filed by the Center for Media Education and the Consumer Federation of America, for instance, argued that DBS's public interest obligation "clearly enhances rather than abridges freedom of speech protected by the First Amendment, and should be upheld" (*Time Warner et al. v. FCC* 1993; and consolidated cases, Brief for Amicus Curiae CME/CFA, 9).

The provision was reinstated by an appeals court decision of the Time Warner suit that reversed the first court's decision (*Time Warner Entertainment Co., L.P. v. FCC* 1996). Responding to the FCC's appeal of the earlier decision, the court made a decisive, clear, and articulate ruling. It endorsed the notion that scarcity continues to exist, despite new multichannel technologies, and despite new competition. Citing the critical cases on the issue, all footballs in the ideological debate over scarcity— Red Lion (*Red Lion Broadcasting Co., Inc. v. FCC* 1969), DNC (*Columbia Broadcasting System, Inc. v. Democratic National Committee* 1973), NCCB (*FCC v. National Citizens Committee for Broadcasting* 1978)—it reiterated their validity for the current day.

It said that, just as *Red Lion* had said that broadcast spectrum was scarce in a way print was not, so was the spectrum DBS uses. Just as *DNC* held that listener and viewer rights were paramount, so were they in the DBS medium. This was because, as *NCCB* had itself reiterated from an earlier case, the First Amendment's goal is not merely the right of anyone to say anything, but "the widest possible dissemination of information from diverse and antagonistic sources." That is, the point of regulation that limits the First Amendment rights of media corporations is to foster democratic discourse and decision making. The decision asserts that because electronic mass media continue to exert monopoly control of spectrum space that many more people want than can use, traditional public interest regulation continues to be a legitimate use of the power of government.

The decision specifically recognized the history of legal decisions affirming that, as legislative language for the 1967 Public Broadcasting Act said, "the economic realities of commercial broadcasting do not permit widespread commercial production and distribution of educational and cultural programs which do not have a mass audience appeal" (U.S. H.R. Rep. No. 572 1967). The public interest provisions for DBS, the decision said, was simply "a new application of a well-settled government policy of ensuring public access to noncommercial programming" (976). Finally, the decision noted that the law does not specify exactly what kind of programming should be reserved, and that its function is to increase, not limit, speech.

This decision powerfully challenged the notion that the basic structure of mass media, affecting its social role, had changed or would change soon with a multichannel environment and with competition. It portrayed DBS as just more television, still charged with public obligations because it continued to operate under the old, top-down, mass media paradigm. It also reinforced the notion that such obligations continued to express appropriately the public interest. Under this logic, to fulfill their obligations, DBS providers should create an environment where "the widest possible dissemination of information from diverse and antagonistic sources" could take place.

Thus, the law still asserts that scarcity continues to exist. It is, however, a fragile conclusion. After the appeals court ruling, Time Warner asked the full court to reconsider its decision. The ensuing vote to rehear the case was 5-4, not enough to win a rehearing but enough to signal continuing contention about the issue. The majority of judges would have liked to revisit the *Red Lion* rationale.

## The Challenge of Occupying New Spaces

The rule making that was triggered by the appeals court ruling offered the first major platform for discussion of the public interest in mass media after the passage of the Telecommunications Act of 1996. In a Notice of Proposed Rule Making initiated January 31, 1997, the Federal Communications Commission reopened its process of taking comments before decision making. In this round, the pool of participants was the same kind and size as previously.

On the commercial side, there were:

- DBS providers and trade associations (nine comments, five reply comments);

- cable operators, programmers, and trade associations (five comments, five reply comments); and

- commercial programmers (three comments, three reply comments).

On the noncommercial side were:

- universities and public television entities (both were included in legislative language in the designation "national educational programming suppliers") (four comments, two reply comments);

- noncommercial programmers, including a consortium of universities planning distance learning (three comments, two reply comments);

- the national cable access association, Alliance for Community Media (one comment, one reply comment); and

- public interest, issue-based, and minority organizations, including two loose and overlapping coalitions of public interest, nonprofit, and minority interest ranging from the National Association of Elementary School Principals to the American Psychological Association to the Association of Independent Video and Filmmakers (three comments, four reply comments).

Several others submitted short comments or letters addressing specific concerns, for example, Morality in Media's concern that indecency provisions be applied to DBS programming.[1] These organizations generally took the same positions they had taken four years earlier. Positions clearly reflected, as the process is designed to do, stakeholder self-interest.

The DBS providers vigorously attempted to diminish their obligations in both 25(a) and 25(b). They argued that a new business (despite the fact that four commercial services were now in business) should not be burdened with obligations. Regarding 25(a), they argued that DBS providers should only have to make room for presidential campaign ads, since Senate and House campaigns were not of national interest. They should not have to offer other public interest programming, such as children's, civic, or educational programming.

Regarding 25(b), most providers did not want to establish separate space. They should, they argued, be permitted to aggregate all the minutes of qualifying programming from all video services to make up the set-aside, which should be 4 percent, not 7. They should be able to count toward their obligations any good deeds they were now doing, and they should be able to use commercial services whose content might not be frivolous, such as Discovery, WAM!, or in the case of a rural cooperative using DBS transmission, Channel Earth. Channel Earth is a commercial channel that provides "live and late-breaking agricultural news, weather and livestock and commodity market information" (National Rural

Telecommunications Cooperative, Reply, 6). The cooperative argued that the commercial channel should qualify for the noncommercial set-aside because it "mixes information, educational and entertainment programming of particular interest to rural America" (7).

DBS providers were centrally concerned about editorial control. They suggested the creation of an organization to be dominated by DBS interests that would certify appropriate programming. They were also concerned about cost of access to any set-aside channel space. They wanted to calculate the discount rate stipulated by Congress to include many basic and infrastructure costs.

Cable operators and associations, competitors with DBS (at least for now), generally demanded that the FCC apply any public interest obligations they had (e.g., must-carry, leased access, rate regulation) to DBS. Commercial programmers argued that commercial programming should both fill the public interest obligations and be permitted on the set-aside, if such programming was truly educational and informational. They pointed out, among other things, that public television regularly worked with commercial entities, including many of the program producers for the service.

Noncommercial interests shared certain positions: DBS was now a viable competitive business, not a nascent one; it should be expected to devote 7 percent of the space to a set-aside; it should not have editorial control or create an accrediting board; capacity should be calculated in terms of megabits or total capacity, not merely the part devoted to video; the price for set-aside rates should be an incremental rate, not one that builds in infrastructure or promotion or other costs. Those who addressed the responsibility of DBS operators on electoral issues under 25(a) declared that operators had a legal obligation to carry any federal candidates who demanded space. Only the Alliance for Community Media addressed the issue of localism, projecting the possibility in the future of spot beams to target localities and regions.

Public television, universities, and public access organizations—institutions that already developed educational or informational programming—argued that the best interpretation of the obligations would be to extend the model that each worked on. Public television argued that the set-aside pertained only to the entities mentioned in the legislative language: public television stations; national public telecommunications entities (including, for them, public television–related organizations such as Public Broadcasting Service, which is actually a member organization of stations that provides core programming to its members); and institutions of higher learning. One entity such as PBS, public TV argued, ought to be able to occupy the entire set-aside, while public TV still ought to be able to enter into business ventures with commercial entities and even rent commercial space on DBS.

Universities, most visibly through a consortium-in-formation calling itself Research TV composed of large public and prestigious private universities, proposed that the full 7 percent should be divided equally among the three kinds of entities designated in the law. A third would then go to accredited educational institutions; they proposed that K–12 schools, research universities, and postsecondary institutions should all have equal access. An educationally based, cable access–style body could adjudicate use if there were conflicts. The hastily assembled consortium did not claim to have programming but suggested the service could be used to release research information, and also to showcase events such as examples drawn from recent university efforts: a seminar on teens, drugs, and pregnancy; a symposium on space technology; a seminar on biotechnology business opportunities (Research TV, Comments, 5). The consortium's filing identified two uses: "information access for professionals," and "public first-hand access to the most up-to-date information" (6). *Public* in this case simply meant audience members with particular needs, for example, diabetes patients.

Children's Television Workshop (CTW), the leading producer of quality children's educational programming, had long sought a larger window on television. It was frustrated by public television's small demographics, and equally by network TV's low tolerance for research budgets and for educational content (ABC's casual treatment of CTW's short-lived network series *Cro* had been chastening). Several attempts to launch an educational children's cable channel, under various models, had failed for lack of capitalization; it was then in discussion with Fox about trading equity investment for programming on Fox's newly acquired Family Channel (Ross 1997). The DBS set-aside, if CTW could qualify, would solve the problem of access, but only if CTW, a small, lucrative, but expensive operation, could make it pay. As CTW said in its comments, "While qualifying to supply programming for the reserved DBS capacity, [CTW] would find it difficult to do so given DBS' currently limited nationwide subscriber volume, absent the ability to include commercial matter within the setaside programming" (CTW, Comments, 6). So it proposed that in 25(a), DBS providers be required to make 3 percent of its capacity educational and informational children's programming. Whatever part of this programming was produced by noncommercial entities could count toward the set-aside (from 4 to 7 percent). The CTW proposal also suggested that the noncommercial set-aside providers be permitted joint ventures with commercial partners, and that on a section of the set-aside, qualifying users be permitted limited commercial matter. This would address, CTW said, the widespread concern of DBS providers that low-quality material would be used to fill the noncommercial space.

The Center for Media Education and some twenty-one other organizations (nine of which participated because of an interest in children or to safeguard specific media agendas, e.g., the hearing impaired) developed an argument focused on children, through the law clinic Institute for Public Representation. Concerning itself only with 25(a) and not the set-aside, and building narrowly on success, it demanded that DBS providers be held to the same standard as broadcasters were in the 1990 Children's Television Act.

The Alliance for Community Media, a membership organization of cable access organizations, focused on 25(b), filing in combination with the National Association of Telecommunications Officers and Advisors (NATOA). The Alliance and NATOA claimed to represent "the interests of religious, community, educational, charitable, and other non-commercial, non-profit institutions who utilize PEG [public, educational, and governmental] access centers and facilities . . . and participate in an ever-growing 'electronic town hall,'" as well as those who believe "that the tremendous resources of the Information Age should be made available to 'at-risk' communities" (Alliance/NATOA, Comments, 2). The filers saw the potential of the noncommercial set-aside as a chance for DBS subscribers

> to see varieties of programming that encompass the range of human experience, but which generally are not seen because they lack commercial viability. Such programming includes not only distance-learning and public affairs programming, but also the performing arts, regional affairs, programming by and about minority and at-risk populations (programming by and about ethnic groups, religious organizations, women, the disabled, social service agencies, etc.). (10)

The filers proposed to use the cable public access model, with a programming body administered by a national board of directors largely drawn from the nonprofit world. This body would be run, and promote and fund programming with monies generated, by an up-to-5-percent cut of DBS profits. Tacitly addressing widespread doubt that local PEG access programming was a model for national-level programming, the filers stressed the importance of distance learning as a core programming activity, along with event programming and a special role for public television programming, which in their scheme would be permitted a greater-than-10-percent share of time on the reserved space.

The group of clients assembled by the public interest legal firm Media Access Project, led by the Denver Area Educational Telecommunications Consortium (DAETC, a nonprofit producer and distributor of independent video) dealt with both parts of the requirement. Besides DAETC, potential producers also included the independent video and film producers' association, a public access cable center, a consortium of land grant colleges with distance learning programs, and the National Federation of Community Broadcasters, a public radio organization.

The DAETC filing called under 25(a) for DBS providers to be required to provide civic, children's educational and informational, and/or fine arts programming. To fill the 4 to 7 percent of capacity set aside for noncommercial use, DAETC strongly resisted the notion that commercial programmers could be used and suggested that any noncommercial programmer (such as PBS) should only have one channel.

DAETC's vision was similar to that of Alliance/NATOA. Nonprofit institutions could use the set-aside

> for distance learning, low cost internet access, community radio, and video programming that otherwise would only be viewed on PEG access channels in a handful of communities . . . [while section 25a, under DBS' public interest responsibilities, could provide a] secure home for C-SPAN, which has become the mistreated stepchild of the cable industry, or by providing several channels of children's educational and informational programming. Candidates for President could receive cross country access for their messages in one shot. (DAETC, Comments, 3)

Confronting the question of resources for production, DAETC suggested that DBS providers should subsidize production for the set-aside space. If they do not, it said, then the space between 4 and 7 percent could be used for material that was "80 percent noncommercial" (a figure borrowed from the amount of advertising permitted on broadcast children's programs), with some of the profits from that sector returning to the noncommercial programming carried on the reserved spectrum up to 4 percent. Monies would be paid directly to a nonprofit programming consortium, free from DBS editorial control (DAETC, Comments, 15, 19).

## Implications

The challenges of interpretation posed by the two aspects of Section 25 were different in kind. Debate over the meaning of 25(a) operated within a well-established set of regulatory expectations for commercial television. It called on DBS operators or their renters to make space for political candidates and to address the weaknesses of the marketplace for vulnerable constituencies, especially children. Noncommercial stakeholders wanted DBS providers to assume more editorial responsibility for civic, educational, and children's programming, and DBS operators wanted to minimize it.

The question of 25(b) posed a far greater challenge, inviting commenters to imagine electronic space that does not now exist and propose uses for it. The set-aside discussion was a greater test of the vigor of the public interest concept today.

One of the salient features of the DBS set-aside discussion was its narrowness. It did not generate much enthusiasm, either in the general public, or in more immediately affected constituencies. In spite of the fact that this was new televisual space opened up for public life, national newspapers merely mentioned it in passing, and it was nearly invisible on electronic media. Several newspaper and magazine editors that I contacted simply found the story lackluster. The narrow stakeholder participation would seem to prove them right.

The proceeding did not take place in obscurity or without warning. Individuals and organizations had months and even years to work out their interest in the proceedings and were given ample warning by the FCC through familiar channels. Once the proceeding became a reality, Gigi Sohn of the Media Access Project (MAP) prepared an action alert distributed by way of the Internet. Meetings among stakeholders were held, some to brainstorm potential entities that might be able to contribute to diversity of expression and representation through the set-aside. The MAP press release, aimed at the community of independent film and video producers, said in part,

> Without the active participation of independent producers and the education community, the FCC will be far less disposed toward creating a substantive access policy that, from the outset, will guarantee low-cost access to DBS service as it becomes a competitive means of program distribution to cable and broadcast television. Activism is particularly important given the skepticism of some policy-makers that the public interest programming set-aside will be no more than simply another

outlet for . . . the Public Broadcasting Service. This misperception must
be strenuously rebutted by the independent creative community and
educators. (Media Access Project n.d. [1997])

But aside from public television and universities involved in distance
learning, there were no viable institutional volunteers for that space.
Major unions and religious organizations, among others, made no direct
claims on the space. The only substantial nonprofit producer, Children's
Television Workshop, explicitly charged that a set-aside without a profit-
making mechanism or subsidy was unviable. Public television interests
argued strenuously that corporate alliances should not affect its status as
a noncommercial provider. A few months later, PBS and four of the
largest (and program-producing) public TV stations formed the PBS
Sponsorship Group to solicit corporate sponsorship in a coordinated
way, marking increased commercialization (Farhi 1997).

Other production-related organizations may become important players in the future but are not in a position to use the space immediately.
The Association of Independent Film and Video, a member organization
of producers, does not have distribution or programming mechanisms,
nor does the National Federation of Community Broadcasters, representing small community public radio stations. The Alliance for Community Media, now a small membership organization of embattled local
production centers, would require an infusion of resources. Research TV
is still an organization in formation.

The entities that even in theory could use that space had, significantly,
decades of public subsidy behind them. Public television's core structure
of stations depends on local, state, and federal tax money for nearly half
of its revenues and pass them on to services such as PBS. Universities
both private and public depend on a variety of public subsidies; the lead
participants in this discussion were land grant and state universities
whose primary revenues come from public funding. Nonprofit programmers such as CTW directly and indirectly benefit from both structures.

Entities that could not themselves use the space but that supported a
vigorous interpretation of the public interest divided into two camps.
One, through the Center for Media Education, chose not to address the
set-aside at all. The DAETC and the Alliance/NATOA coalitions both assumed the further challenge of imagining the reserve space. These proposals did not restrict suggestions to programming but extended to services and practices occurring in a protected space, where noncommercial
behaviors and relationships might be nurtured. Both grounded their

proposals in the potential of distance learning, a service for which there are today both providers and audiences.

That imaginative stretch toward public space was the exception rather than the rule. The discussion largely focused on the availability and quality of consumer programming, a point that loomed large in the FCC's informal discussions with interested parties (Chiara 1997). Programming was largely discussed within a commercial, entertainment-oriented context, which made it easy for DBS providers and commercial programmers to argue that high-quality commercial programs should count toward the obligation. Noncommercial commenters with the exception of DAETC and Alliance/NATOA did not, by and large, challenge this vision.

Nonprofit organizations mostly supported major parts of each other's proposals, with the exception of public television (which resisted any limitation on a single user of the reserved space). But one of the more visible potential occupiers of noncommercial space—one invoked in many comments—was silent on the issue: C-SPAN, after public TV, perhaps the most well-known example of public space on television. C-SPAN carries activities on the floor of Congress and covers policy issues broadly in the off-hours. A creature of the cable industry, C-SPAN is supported by voluntary industry contributions and carried as an act of good will by operators (Aufderheide 1997). Since the 1992 cable legislation, C-SPAN carriage has suffered gravely. Both from pragmatism and principle, in this case the organization chose caution. Its counsel, Bruce Collins, explained that since its patrons' interests were multiple—some of the cable owners, particularly the behemoth TCI, had DBS holdings, and most DBS operators are contributing to C-SPAN and using its programs—it chose to keep a low profile (Collins 1997). In a two-paragraph filing, C-SPAN notified the FCC it was entering the discussion only because it had been mentioned by so many others:

> We have never sought a governmental preference or advantage of any kind, preferring instead to succeed or fail in a fair and competitive programming marketplace. . . . we urge the Commission as it grapples with these issues to exercise its authority in a competitively neutral manner such that regulatory parity is the result for similarly-situated multi-channel video providers. (National Cable Satellite Corporation [C-SPAN], Reply Comments, 2)

C-SPAN thus actively rejected a reserved-space model, although it was one of the most well-developed examples of noncommercial, national public service. C-SPAN head Brian Lamb has often recognized the importance of separate spaces. As he explained the distinctiveness of C-SPAN to interviewers from *Broadcasting and Cable*, "When you get up every day and you don't have to make a profit, and you just have to meet your mission statement, you react differently than if you have to deliver eyeballs to advertisers" (West and Brown 1997, 71–72). But C-SPAN remains a private service, subject to the vagaries of private indulgence.

Although the appeals court decision eloquently argued the need for a noncommercial space that could operate as a marketplace not of products but of ideas, not under the mandate of profit but of public deliberation, the DBS set-aside discussion demonstrated that this space, at least electronically, is thinly populated and impoverished both financially and imaginatively. Where there are oases, they are fed with public and private subsidies—although the subsidies have usually been doled out without a commitment to a vigorous noncommercial space or set of relationships. Excepting children, commenters had difficulty invoking noncommercial constituencies—either producers or audiences—and to articulate what was at stake in the inhabiting of reserved space. The most immediate and largest available institution to use this space, public television, has demonstrated with painful consistency over the past few years a complacency with the vision of programming within a commercial context (Hoynes 1994; Engelman 1996). The courts seem more eager to refer to a marketplace of ideas than policy makers or cable operators seem eager to build one.

## The FCC Finally Rules

In November 1998, more than six years after Congress had established public interest obligations for DBS providers, the FCC finally issued its ruling (U.S. FCC 1998). The ruling struck a middle ground between demands of DBS operators and public interest commenters. On 25(a), the FCC simply required DBS operators to allow all candidates for federal office access to their systems, whether on a designated channel or elsewhere throughout the program offerings. It declined to require a minimum of children's programming, as it did the cable industry's request to saddle DBS with its own public interest requirements.

On 25(b), the FCC required the minimum channel space, 4 percent, but included all video channels, including barker channels (promotional and menu channels), in the count. It required DBS operators to use distinct and consistent channels, rather than sprinkling noncommercial programming throughout the day. (It thus rejected Children's Television Workshop's proposal to count programming on the commercial side toward the noncommercial 4 percent.) It did permit DBS operators to select the channels, although not without vigorous discussion and, ultimately, dissent among the commissioners. The FCC report and order also limited each program provider to one channel, relieving other program providers of the fear that public television would take the entire space. It permitted joint projects between noncommercial and commercial entities on the reserved space, as long as the project stayed educational and noncommercial, with no advertising.

Within the limits of the law it had been given to interpret, and the precedents already set, the FCC created some new spaces for noncommercial use. They would be hedged about by a DBS operator's decision to carry or not to carry, but by the end of the report and order, there existed a new window for a variety of noncommercial programmers and programs to reach national television audiences. There was, of course, no provision to support such programs financially, and could not have been, since it was not stipulated in law.

## Challenges

Current policy is extremely mild-mannered encouragement to the project of fomenting a marketplace of ideas. The challenge facing civic activists with DBS will be to stake a claim to the putatively public elements of the service, and to design and distinguish such use, not merely as good-for-you programming, and not as television that merely speaks to individuals as consumers, but to members of a multifaceted public. But it is not clear from the commenting process that there is a producing and distributing community beyond the limited world of public TV with such a vision for its use, or a set of organized interests in civil society that will commit to such a vision. It also seems patently clear from related policy skirmishes—for instance, over federal funding for the National Endowment for the Arts, for the Department of Commerce's grants for demonstration projects in public networking, and for public television— that federal government has little enthusiasm for fueling experiments in public electronic spaces.

The DBS set-aside debate thus demonstrates the consequences of an extended impoverishment of the concept of the public interest in electronic media. The conduct of commercial media demonstrates vividly, at least to appeals court judges, the need for noncommercial spaces, programs, habits, and expectations. At the same time, the culture constructed around commercial television marginalizes, even shrivels, alternatives. A strong governmental role to reallocate resources, of the kind occasionally played throughout the nation's history—in postal subsidies, in the creation of public broadcasting, in the creation of the Internet—appears essential to any viable project. Otherwise, the noncommercial set-aside is likely to confirm smug expectations that any alternative to commercial television is indeed not "what the public is interested in."

## Note

1. The Federal Communications Commission maintains an electronic database listing all filers in a docket at its Washington, D.C., offices, where hard copy comments are on file. Increasingly, commenters are filing electronically, but at the time this docket was active, most still filed hard copy, and access to these was either slow or expensive. Although I consulted these records, in most cases I used private resources. Andrew Jay Schwartzman, Gigi Sohn, and Joseph Paykel of the Media Access Project, one of the public interest filers, were kind enough to share their own copies of many of the comments, which facilitated the research considerably. Several other filers also graciously sent me their copies. At the FCC, Rosalie Chiara was gracious and helpful in providing updates and clarifications. In referring to this docket, I refer to the filer, the Comments or the Reply Comments ("Reply"), and the page number.

## References

Aufderheide, P. 1997. "Cable: C-SPAN's fight for respect." *Columbia Journalism Review* (July–August): 13–14.

———. 1999. *Communications Policy and the Public Interest: The Telecommunications Act of 1996.* New York: Guilford Press.

Chiara, Rosalie (Mass Media Bureau, FCC, lawyer). 1997. Personal communication, September 26.

Collins, Bruce (C-SPAN lawyer). 1997. Personal communication, May 8.

*Columbia Broadcasting System, Inc. v. Democratic National Committee.* 1973. 412 U.S. 94, S. Ct. 2080, 36 L. Ed. 2d 772.

*Daniels Cablevision, Inc. v. U.S.* 1993. 835 F. Supp. 1 (D.D.C.).

Douglas, S. 1987. *Inventing American Broadcasting, 1899–1922.* Baltimore: Johns Hopkins University Press.

Engelman, R. 1996. *Public Radio and Television in America: A Political History.* Thousand Oaks, Calif.: Sage.

Farhi, P. 1997. "Seeking a Word from Their Sponsors." *WashTech, Washington Post,* August 11, p. 17 ff.

FCC v. National Citizens Committee for Broadcasting. 1978. 436 U.S. 775, S. Ct. 2096, 56 L. Ed. 697.

Fowler, M., and D. Brenner. 1982. "A Marketplace Approach to Broadcast Regulation." *Texas Law Review* 60: 207–57.

Horwitz, R. 1988. *The Irony of Regulatory Reform.* New York: Oxford University Press.

Hoynes, W. 1994. *Public Television for Sale: Media, the Market, and the Public Sphere.* Boulder, Colo.: Westview.

Krattenmaker, T., and L. Powe, Jr. 1994. *Regulating Broadcast Programming.* London and Washington, D.C.: MIT Press and American Enterprise Institute Press.

Media Access Project. n.d. (1997). "Availability of Guaranteed, Low-Cost Programming Distribution for Independent Producers and Educators via Direct Broadcast Satellite at Risk." Unpublished manuscript.

Montgomery, K. 1989. *Target: Primetime.* New York: Oxford University Press.

Red Lion Broadcasting Co., Inc. v. FCC. 1969. 395 U.S. 367 S. Ct. 1794, 23 L. Ed. 2d 371.

Robinson, G. 1989. "The Federal Communications Act: An Essay on Origins and Regulatory Purpose." In *A Legislative History of the Communications Act of 1934,* ed. M. D. Paglin, 3–24. New York: Oxford University Press.

Ross, C. 1997. Fox Eyes Linkup with CTW to Boost Its Kids Offerings." *Advertising Age,* August 11, p. 2.

Rowland, W. 1997. "The Meaning of 'the Public Interest' in Communications Policy. Part II: Its Implementation in Early Broadcast Law and Regulation." *Communication Law and Policy* 2 (4): 363–96.

Streeter, T. 1996. *Selling the Air.* Chicago: University of Chicago Press.

Time Warner Entertainment Co., L.P. v. FCC. 1996. 93 F. 3d 957 (D.C. Cir.).

Time Warner et al. v. FCC. 1993. No. 93–5349.

U.S. Federal Communications Commission. 1993. MM Docket no. 93-25. "In the Matter of Implementation of Section 25 of the Cable Television Consumer Protection and Competition Act of 1992: Direct Broadcast Satellite Public Service Obligations. Notice of Proposed Rule Making." *Federal Communications Commission Record* 8 (5): 1589–99.

U.S. FCC. 1998. "In the Matter of Implementation of Section 25 of the Cable Television Consumer Protection and Competition Act of 1992: Direct Broadcast Satellite Public Service Obligations: Report and Order." November 25. *Http://www/fcc/gov/Bureaus/Mass_Media/Orders/1998/fcc98307.text* (accessed February 16, 1999).

U.S. H.R. Rep. No. 572. 1967. 90th Congress, 1st Sess. 10–11. Cited in 93 F. 3d 957, 976 (D.C. Cir. 1996).

West, D., and S. Brown. 1997. "America's Town Crier." *Broadcasting & Cable,* July 21, p. 70–74.

Wollenberg, J. R. 1989. "The FCC as Arbiter of 'the Public Interest, Convenience and Necessity.'" In *A Legislative History of the Communications Act of 1934,* ed. M. D. Paglin, 61–78. New York: Oxford University Press.

# After the

# Fairness

# Doctrine

*This piece started out as a research project to measure the effects of removing the Fairness Doctrine. The doctrine was a small piece of policy, but it became a football in the ideological warfare in '80s electronic media policy and was finally suspended in 1987. The study I did in 1991 was released in several versions, and as a* Journal of Communication *article became a staple item in policy debates over the doctrine's reinstatement. The entire universe of news has changed since this article was written—Matt Drudge, MSNBC, everybody's .com, and a host of local round-the-clock cable channels surfaced—but some of the issues addressed by the Fairness Doctrine policy unfortunately endure. There still appear to be powerful market constraints on balanced reporting of local controversial issues, and few venues where people are treated like citizens instead of news tasters.*

During a heated election, the California liquor lobby launched a well-heeled broadcast advertising campaign to fight a California ballot proposition calling for higher liquor taxes. Stations eagerly took the ads; then proposition supporters began to demand that the stations offer the other side of the story. The liquor lobby's advertising firm quickly dispatched a letter advising the stations that if the other side were aired, the ads would be withdrawn (Heuton 1990).

At the same time, a political commercial was offered to television stations in major markets. As the voice-over warned, "Your tax dollars are putting America in the red—the red of El Salvador," blood began to drip over the image of a check being written for $4 million. The ad was rejected at a rate of 3 to 1, and most major markets did not air it. As WJLA-TV in Washington, D.C., explained, "we do not air material which is intended to inflame or incite unreasoned public response rather than reasoned debate." The same station had accepted a wide array of emotion-laden negative campaign ads in 1988 (Nixon 1990).

Then came the prospect of the Gulf War, and with it an organization of passionately pacific military families. The Military Families Support Network tried to buy time for a thirty-second commercial pleading for a peaceful resolution—a point of view the organization found missing in a plethora of talk shows on the brewing conflict. In prime area Washington, D.C., network-owned stations and Cable News Network all turned down the ad; two of those stations had run spots supporting administration policy (Kurtz 1990).

These incidents, in different ways, comment on a modest piece of broadcast regulation known as the Fairness Doctrine (Rowan 1984). The doctrine from 1959 to 1987 had mandated broadcasters to air controversy and air it fairly. The Federal Communications Commission (FCC) suspended the doctrine in 1987. Its corollaries pertaining to electoral issues are still in force, although many broadcasters don't know it until public interest groups remind them, as they did in California. The liquor lobby's letter boldly shows what happens in an unregulated marketplace to controversial electoral debate. The Salvador and pro-peace ads also reveal the marketplace at work, with stations refusing to run an ad that carries a descant message on a controversial issue.

The irony is that during the years when the Fairness Doctrine was enforced, broadcasters widely claimed that the doctrine itself kept them from carrying such advocacy advertising because of the "chilling effect"—the fear that they would be penalized by the FCC as a result of frivolous or contentious pressure after airing a controversial ad. But even without the doctrine, many broadcasters still find advocacy ads a bad business proposition.

Do we still need a Fairness Doctrine? Democrats in Congress thought so, once the Republican-led FCC suspended its major provisions in defiance of the original mandate by Congress. The 100th Congress passed legislation reinstating it, although it was vetoed by then-President Reagan. In the 101st Congress, legislation failed to pass but supporters continue to promote it. During the Gulf War the proposal was revived again. "Every day the airwaves are filled with the voices of those who believe that we should go to war," said Senate Commerce Committee Chairman Ernest Hollings (D-SC). "However, there are members of the viewing public who feel that there is not sufficient coverage of the views of those opposed to war.... they should have some recourse to ensue that all viewpoints are heard. Without the fairness doctrine, they have no recourse" (in *Communications Daily* 1991).

The doctrine was a permanent site of controversy over the very principle of public interest regulation. Public interest regulation is grounded in the notion that broadcasters hold in trust a scarce public resource and must perform some public service in exchange for profiting from it. Opponents of continued public interest regulation, who took up the Fairness Doctrine as the wedge in their campaign, argued that the growing number of stations, cable TV, and videocassettes render irrelevant the argument that there is scarcity, and that the doctrine now violates the First Amendment. Proponents argued that since broadcasting is, from its origins, a public trust, the term needs enforceable measures of public service and responsibility, of which the Fairness Doctrine is one.

The Fairness Doctrine debate also raises the question of whether public interest regulation is effective. Broadcasters argue that the doctrine merely restates what good journalists do anyway, and that the negative effects of enforcement—the dreaded "chilling effect"—outweigh its usefulness. Proponents claim that the doctrine has a history of mild and flexible enforcement and only mandates balanced controversial coverage without specifying content. Broadcasters avoid controversy, they charge, because it is less lucrative than other formats.

Arguments are one thing, actions another. Looking at how broadcasters handle controversy in the absence of the doctrine puts their arguments about the supposed chilling effect—the major evidence that the rule was counterproductive—in perspective. In fact, relaxation of the rule has not enhanced controversy, either according to a survey of broadcast stations with a record of protest over the chilling effect or according to groups on record as lauding it.

Of course, the suspension of the Fairness Doctrine was not the only influence on coverage of controversial issues. Deregulation has powerfully affected the marketplace for controversial coverage. Under the Reagan-era FCC, license periods for radio and TV were extended; commercial time limits and regulations regarding children's television were abolished; guidelines for the amount of news and public affairs coverage and the requirement to keep program logs open to the public were lifted.

Lifting the rule requiring stations to be owned for three years before being sold created a boom market in broadcast stations, raising prices and debt loads dramatically (Fowler and Brenner 1982; Porter 1986).

Prime targets for budget cuts were news, public affairs, community affairs, and editorials at stations and networks. Studies by the Radio-Television News Directors Association (RTNDA) in the wake of the suspension of the doctrine showed cuts in news staffs and airtime, for both radio and television (*RTNDA Communicator* 1987, 1988). "Shortchanging the Viewers," a study by the Nader group Essential Information, found that while total news programming had increased since 1975, local public affairs programming had decreased, perhaps by 39 percent, since 1979. (Its assessment probably overestimated current public affairs coverage, since the study was forced, in the absence of regulation requiring open books or relevant FCC studies to match previous ones, to rely on *TV Guide* listings.) Why? A CBS affiliate public affairs director in North Carolina explained it to Essential Information: "You can sell commercials on an hour of *Lifestyles of the Rich and Famous* a whole lot better than an hour of a public affairs show" (in Donahue 1989).

New business in infomercials, for such items as weight-loss and get-rich-quick schemes, also cut into time for controversy and public service announcements (PSAs). And PSAs, which had been one way a station could meet its affirmative obligation to air controversy, began changing, some toward a safely consensual tone and others in the direction of a form of station promotion (Bollier 1989). San Francisco's Public Media Center (PMC) head Herbert Chao Gunther said, "These days, we tell groups it doesn't make sense even to make PSAs, unless the issue is pablum."

How significant was the Fairness Doctrine in affecting broadcasters' decisions regarding controversial programming? Measuring the effect of the doctrine's suspension takes us back to 1984, when the FCC opened an inquiry, launching it with a sharply ideological edge. In fact, its notice of inquiry announced that the FCC's own preliminary analysis (in 1981) showed "continued adherence to the doctrine might be contrary to the public interest and constitutional principles" (U.S. FCC 1984).

The notice drew a wide range of responses, the majority of which supported the doctrine. Most of those opposed were broadcast interests. Supporters were public interest groups and nonprofits ranging from the National Rifle Association to the National Coalition for Handgun Control; mainstream religious organizations; partisan political organizations such as the Democratic National Committee; and corporate voices such as Mobil Oil and the Glass Packaging Institute.

Although the hardest case against the doctrine was the so-called chilling effect, the actual case evidence that broadcasters produced was sparse and repetitive. A study included in comments from the National Association for Broadcasting (NAB) summarized most of the examples cited by others. In the NAB's study, broadcasters proved that dealing with public responsiveness to controversial programming could be time-consuming, and that offering response time (one of several options, under the doctrine, for a broadcaster to provide balance) could impinge on editorial control.  ·

But broadcasters' complaints inadvertently reflected an endemic problem with controversy in commercial broadcasting, with or without the doctrine. Most people rarely have an informed opinion on a controversial issue of public importance, especially until it has been widely aired in the mass media. Those who do, however, usually are intensely invested in their viewpoint. Sound marketplace logic argues for airing programming of greatest appeal to the greatest numbers. That's why marketplace-corrective regulation on controversial programming had so long been considered important.

Broadcasters also demonstrated the pull of the marketplace when they dealt with issue advertising. They claimed that the Fairness Doctrine inhibited them from freely airing issue-oriented advertising, by raising the specter of giving away free airtime. Broadcaster resistance, however, was not necessarily driven by the doctrine. For instance, Mobil offered to pay for response time in order to get its ads on the air (thus undercutting the station's motive to reject it under the doctrine), and broadcasters still refused. They also rejected ads about the national debt sponsored by businessman Peter Grace without calling the Fairness Doctrine into play.

Public interest groups ranging from Common Cause to the National Rifle Association, on the other hand, showed in inquiry filings that the Fairness Doctrine had been a unique tool to widen debate, particularly when issue advertising—which opened the door for demanding airtime for other views—was aired. The National Rifle Association declared that "broadcasters' willingness or unwillingness to address the pending ballot issues was strongly affected by the dictates of the fairness doctrine and its ancillary doctrines, rules and policies." Mobil Oil criticized the frailty of the doctrine but said it "is certainly better than nothing." The Public Media Center compiled a record of some twenty examples of successful citizen pressure on broadcasters to widen debate, mostly on ballot issues (which still fall under regulation) and most often in response to issue advertising.

In the end, and to nobody's surprise, the FCC came down on the side of the broadcasters, a judgment that appeared to an angry majority group in Congress to be a partisan reading of the evidence.

If the FCC was right, then one might expect broadcasters liberated from this regulatory burden—especially broadcasters vocal in the inquiry—to air controversy previously "chilled." But by and large, this is not what happened, at least in a sample of broadcast stations whose experience was used by the NAB in the FCC inquiry. (For specifics on methodology, see the appendix.)

That sample included seventeen broadcasters, all station managers or news directors, in all of the fourteen broadcasting stations—including AM, FM, and TV stations in large, medium, and small markets—cited in the NAB's 1985 filing. (The filing contained forty-five examples, but some comments were anonymous, others were hearsay, or comments by ex-network officials or general statements by network broadcasters.) All but one station was under continuous ownership since the original complaint documented by the NAB, and that station (KOLN-TV, Lincoln, Nebraska) had vigorously pursued community ascertainment. Although in some cases the original complainant had left the station—seven respondents were the original complainant; six had worked with the complainant; and four were their immediate successors—all the interviewees had continuous experience in broadcasting (most at the same place) within the past four years. These broadcasters were asked if they could provide a single example of controversial programming aired since the doctrine's suspension that they would have avoided before; if they had personally found the doctrine to have a chilling effect; and what each station's current policy on issue advertising was.

All but one could not cite a single example of controversial programming they would have been unable or unwilling to do before. Fourteen said that they had not personally found the doctrine to have a chilling effect; one abstained, and another said he thought "we might have been a little more cautious" under the doctrine but couldn't demonstrate how.

The lone broadcaster who cited an example of newly available controversial programming was J. T. Whitlock, president and general manager of Lebanon-Springfield Broadcasting in Lebanon, Kentucky. He had said his station avoided editorializing on an unspecified "very unhealthy situation" because "I simply could not afford to put my stockholders in the position of having to spend huge sums of money to prove we were right." Since the 1987 FCC decision, he now said, an open-mike program on one of his radio stations was able to address the resignation of Lebanon's mayor: "Before the end of the Fairness Doctrine, I would not have run this, even though it was in the public interest."

Whitlock also noted, however, that his disagreement was never with the doctrine itself but with "the general public's perception of their rights and our obligations." His listening public now knows that the doctrine is no longer enforced, because "we've seen to it that they knew it—we gave plenty of news coverage" to the FCC's decision: "Now John Q. Public says, 'There's no point in harassing this poor broadcaster anymore because there's nothing we can do to him.'"

Even broadcasters who couldn't point to any change in their programming didn't necessarily like it. Ed Hinshaw, manager of public affairs at WTMJ-AM in Milwaukee, Wisconsin, had cited a Fairness Doctrine complaint filed by the Milwaukee mayor after three local stations broadcast critical editorials. He now said that programming had not changed, but "we do have less concern now that we'll have to pay money for the kind of frivolous complaint we suffered in that case." Some said measuring change might be impossible because most broadcasters wouldn't want to admit they hadn't covered controversy at a time when the doctrine mandated it. "Nobody wants to stand up and say, 'I didn't want to cover this issue because I was afraid someone would complain,'" said Charleston, West Virginia, WSAZ-TV executive news editor and past chairman of RTNDA Bob Brenner. Two broadcasters suggested potential congressional action may make broadcasters wary.

Nor does the lack of change in their programming make most of these broadcasters any fonder of the doctrine in retrospect. As Paul Davis at WGN-TV in Chicago put it, "We've always done controversial programming. Now we know we're on the merits of our own integrity, and not on government hindsight." They objected to keeping records showing that they had been balanced, mostly because it was another chore they saw as unnecessary, and they occasionally cited the potential financial costs of the doctrine.

But whether they liked the doctrine or not, most of these broadcasters denied they had personally suffered the chilling effect. Typical was the comment of Bonneville International's Don Gale in Salt Lake City: "The Fairness Doctrine never inhibited us from any subject." Dean Mell, news director at KHQ in Spokane, Washington, had filed a statement during 1983 legislative debate, saying that the many FCC documents interpreting the doctrine were "self-defeating because they may inhibit me from vigorous journalism"; he also cited the costs to a competing station that suffered a license challenge. "I can't tell any difference in the newscasts [since suspension], but then we never shied away from controversy," Mell now said. At WCCO-AM, Minneapolis, which had weathered protests by environmental groups after carrying a utility company's issue advertising, current news director Bill Polish, who came from long experience at KCBS in San Francisco, said, "In a philosophical sense I applaud the demise because my newspaper brethren don't have to deal with it, but I personally have never felt the chilling effect."

A few even supported the doctrine. "It was a fine doctrine and document and served us well," said news director Bob Warfield at Detroit's WDIV-TV: "Some people maybe used to hide behind it when it was in force, and may be hiding now, not to do what is responsible." John Nackley of KIUP-AM and KRSJ-FM in Durango, Colorado, still acts as if the doctrine were still in effect. A sixteen-year veteran there, he had taken over the general manager position from Karen Maas, who had told the NAB the "Fairness Doctrine causes them to 'think twice.'" But Nackley said, "It does not hinder me, and didn't before, from airing controversial programs. . . . The laws are made for those who can't abide by the law, although this is a great profession."

Decisions that these stations once attributed to the doctrine now are justified by marketplace logic. For instance, KSL-AM in Salt Lake City, according to Don Gale in the NAB study, had decided against guest editorials because, with the Fairness Doctrine, they would "lose control." But Bonneville's stations do not now air guest editorials, said Gale, because they would still lose control: "We would have an endless debate. . . . the same problem persists." Raymond Saadi of KTIV-TV in Houma, Louisiana, who had complained about having to honor demands for airtime when he carried Ronald Reagan's syndicated radio show, says that the station does not now carry such syndicated programs, "because we don't want to defend anyone else's views, someone who is so far removed from us that we don't know who they are."

At WINZ-AM (Miami, Florida) general manager Tim Williams succeeded a general manager who launched an antiutility rate-hike petition drive that resulted in a Fairness challenge. The station would not attempt such a petition drive now, he said: "We were out of sync with the natural process [of decision making]." He called the drive an "ill-thought-out" strategy. Community affairs programming is directed now toward locally oriented community events and local organizations that appeal to the classic rock station's twenty-five-to-forty-year-old audience.

Station carriage of advocacy advertising also follows marketplace logic. Current policies vary widely but haven't changed since August

1987. Ed Hinshaw noted, "Originally we didn't [carry issue advertising], because of the Fairness Doctrine implications, but we've maintained the policy because we genuinely don't believe that public policy should be decided by the largest wallet." Other stations accept issue advertising on a case-by-case basis and assume that response time may be necessary, no longer for legal reasons but for the station's community image.

Broadcasters' own experiences thus cast grave doubt on the existence of the Fairness Doctrine's "chilling effect." But a prevalent resentment at government and public intervention in their programming power is also evident. J. T. Whitlock's remark—"Now John Q. Public says, 'There's no point in harassing this poor broadcaster anymore because there's nothing we can do to him'"—is particularly revealing in its antagonistic portrayal of the public.

If broadcasters can't demonstrate the good news for expanded coverage of controversial issues post-1987, public interest groups can't find it either. At Public Media Center, which long used the Fairness Doctrine aggressively, director Gunther has lost a key tool for gaining airtime. For instance, his client Planned Parenthood had won response time to Right to Life spots at a 1:4 ratio when the doctrine was in effect; since 1987, stations had refused the Right to Life Committee airtime. Networks have also refused Planned Parenthood AIDS education spots that mention condoms. When People for the American Way (PFAW) attempted to place an advocacy ad against the nomination of Judge Robert Bork for the Supreme Court in autumn 1987, most stations and all the networks refused to carry it, which was PFAW's experience under the doctrine as well for controversial ads.

The notion that it is hard to place advocacy ads is not the preserve of liberal and left-of-center groups. At the National Rifle Association, state and local legislative director Richard Gardner said, "[Broadcasters'] prejudices are still very apparent. It wasn't really the Fairness Doctrine that affected their decisions—they just used it as an excuse." Phyllis Schlafly's Eagle Forum group opposed a child-care bill in Congress in 1989. "Over the ten-year period of the Equal Rights Amendment," Schlafly said, "we got about one-twentieth of the total time devoted to the subject, in my informed estimate. But that one-twentieth is more than we are getting on the child-care issue now." Absent the doctrine, Schlafly argued that her group's viewpoint was shut out.

The general lack of change in coverage of controversial issues since the doctrine's suspension blunts the argument that the doctrine inhibited it in the first place. But can its absence reduce such coverage? The boldest evidence is in electoral issues, where the doctrine was not lifted in 1987.

A study of 1988 electoral issue coverage reinforces the example of the California liquor-tax proposition. U.S. Public Interest Research Group (PIRG) and Safe Energy Communication Council surveyed 432 stations that accepted advocacy ads on ballot issues. Thirty-one percent didn't know the doctrine was still in force on ballot issues. Of that group, 44 percent refused to present alternate views once informed of their obligation. By contrast, nearly all—98 percent—of the stations that did know the law agreed to present opposing points of view, almost all on first contact. In other words, the doctrine made a crucial difference in broadcasters' decisions to air more than one side of a controversial issue during elections in 1988 (U.S. PIRG 1988).

Many broadcast journalists resent the idea that they need to be told how to do a professional job, and some resent the special burdens of their public trustee function. But the industry continues to be pushed by market pressures away from the standards that journalists may prize. In fact, the very journalists who so resent the doctrine may ultimately need public interest regulation and the modest requirements of the Fairness Doctrine in order to pursue controversy according to professional standards.

## Appendix

The study located stations cited in the National Association of Broadcaster's filing in the FCC Fairness Inquiry (U.S. FCC 1984) and included in Appendix D, "Examples of the 'Chilling Effect' of the Fairness Doctrine," prepared by Whitney Strickland. Interviewed were Paul Davis, WGN-TV, Chicago, news director, an NAB complainant; Ed Hinshaw, public affairs manager, WTMJ-AM, Milwaukee, an NAB complainant; Dean Mell, news director, KHQ AM-FM-TV, Spokane, Washington, an NAB complainant; Rich Cowan, community affairs director, also at KHQ, a colleague of Mell; John Denney, news director, KOLN-TV, Lincoln, Nebraska, successor to an NAB complainant; Jim Kokesh, general manager, KHAS-AM, Hastings, Nebraska, a colleague and successor to an NAB complainant; Bob Warfield, vice president for news and director of broadcast operations, WDIV-TV, Detroit, and an ex-colleague of an NAB complainant; J. T. Whitlock, president and general manager, WLBN-AM, WLSK-FM, Lebanon, Kentucky, an NAB complainant; Don Gale, vice president for news and public affairs, Bonneville International at KSL-AM, Salt Lake City, an NAB complainant; John Morris, general manager of WHWH-AM,

Princeton, New Jersey, and of WPST-FM, Trenton, NJ, an ex-colleague of an NAB complainant; Curtis Beckmann, ex-WCCO-AM news director and now head of Radio City News, Minneapolis; Bill Polish, news director, WCCO-AM, Minneapolis, successor to Beckmann; Raymond Saadi, general manager, KTIV-AM, KHOM-FM, Houma, Louisiana, an NAB complainant; John Nackley, general manager, KIUP-AM, KRSJ-FM, Durango, Colorado, a successor to an NAB complainant; William Cummings, news director, WSAZ-TV, Huntington, West Virginia, a successor to an NAB complainant; Bob Brenner, executive news director, WSAZ-TV, Charleston, West Virginia, ex-colleague of an NAB complainant; Tim Williams, general manager, WINZ-AM, WZTA-FM, Miami, Florida, successor to an NAB complainant.

## Note

This research was supported by a grant from the Donald McGannon Communication Research Center at Fordham University.

## References

Bollier, D. 1989. "Raise the Halo High: Public Service TV Has Plenty of Clout, but Too Often Important Social Issues Are Glossed Over." *Channels* (April): 32–38.

*Communications Daily.* 1991. "Gulf War Controversy." *Communications Daily,* January 15.

Donahue, J. 1989. "Shortchanging the Viewers: Broadcasters' Neglect of Public Interest Programming." Washington, D.C.: Essential Information.

Fowler, M., and D. Brenner. 1982. "A Marketplace Approach to Broadcast Deregulation." *Texas Law Review* 60: 207–57.

Heuton, C. 1990. "California Could Be Dry State for Alcohol Ads." *Channels,* October 8, p. 4.

Kurtz, H. 1990. "Anti-War Ad Shot Down." *Washington Post,* January 12, *Style,* p. 1.

Nixon, W. 1990. "An 'On-the-Air' War over El Salvador." *In These Times,* October 17–23, p. 21.

Porter, R. 1986. "Memorandum to Jerald N. Fritz, Chief of Staff, Re: Sales of Broadcast Stations Held for Three Years or More." Washington, D.C.: Federal Communications Commission. July 23.

Rowan, F. 1984. *Broadcast Fairness: Doctrine, Practice, Prospects.* New York: Longman.

*RTNDA Communicator.* 1987. "Deregulation Felt Mainly in Large-Market Radio and Independent TV." *RTNDA Communicator* (April).

————. 1988. "News Staffs Change Little in Radio, Take Cuts in Major-Market TV." *RTNDA Communicator* (March).

U.S. FCC. 1984. "Inquiry into Section 73.1910 of the Commission's Rules and Regulations concerning the General Fairness Doctrine Obligations of Broadcast Licensees." Adopted April 11, 1984, Released May 8, 1984. Gen. Docket No. 84-282, pp. 1–2. Washington, D.C.: Author.

U.S. Public Interest Research Group (PIRG) and the Safe Energy Communication Council. 1988. "Widespread Confusion: Why Congress Must Codify the Fairness Doctrine." Washington, D.C.: Authors.

# Journalism and

# Public Life

# Seen through

# the "Net"

*When old-media professionals began to notice the big changes stirring with networking, around 1995, anxiety levels were high. But I thought I could see some strong continuities with trends that had shaped my understanding of my beat from the beginning.*

How will online journalism affect public life in a pluralistic, democratic nation? Will we see enterprising citizens exploiting their newly found "infowealth" to make decisions, and searching out electronic allies to form grassroots coalitions that open up the corridors of power to the people's voice? Or does the do-it-yourself model of "infoharvesting" foreshadow a world in which consumers are pegged into ever tighter market niches, one in which they seek out only other like-minded souls and fall victim to con games that take advantage of their accessibility on the Net?

The very way the question is posed bespeaks our national love affair with technological determinism (Iacono and Kling 1995). We love to believe that new technologies will magically transform our societies, whether for better or for worse (Smith and Marx 1994; Huber 1994). In 1944, *Scientific American* foresaw that television "offers the soundest basis for world peace that has yet been presented. Peace must be created on the bulwark of understanding. International television will knit together the peoples of the world in bonds of mutual respect; its possibilities are vast indeed" ("Fifty Years Ago Today" 1994).

But possibility and probability are not always closely related. Our technology evolves within our existing social and economic and political contexts. So if we want to speculate about the relationship of niche marketing of information to public life, we do not need to wait until people can call up their own, do-it-yourself newspapers on magic screens, or until they entrust their personal intelligent agents to stock their own customized Net niches. We can look at the world we live in today, and ask ourselves what the quality of our public life and our democratic practices are now. If we like them now, we'll love them online.

Yes, online journalism inevitably restructures relationships, redefining who is a client and what is a product. And yes, there are undoubtedly enormous changes up ahead. But they will result not from the power of new technologies in themselves but from their deployment within well-entrenched economic and cultural patterns. Therefore, the problems and opportunities of tomorrow will bear at least a family relationship to the problems and opportunities of today.

The challenge for journalists who confront the challenge of electronically restructured market and social relationships is one that ought to sound familiar. It is the challenge of participating in and fomenting democracy in an increasingly globalized and image-oriented commercial culture. It is also, in service of that goal, the sculpting of professional standards that insist on the journalist as a creator and defender of democratic public space.

### Optimism, Paranoia, and Anxiety

Journalists already feel acutely the social weight of rapid changes in technology. Scenarios range from the utopian to the paranoid. The 1994 Neiman Conference, "Can Journalists Shape the New Technologies?" (Kovach 1994), deftly and authoritatively showcased the turmoil in the field.

News professionals have, of course, immediate and parochial anxieties. Journalists—who have barely won their professional status—are now threatened by the idea that their gatekeeping function may be preempted by readers and viewers. Ed Fouhy, director of the Pew Center for Civic Journalism and the organizer of 1992 presidential debates in which candidates spoke directly with audiences as if they were talk-show hosts, notes, "The journalistic model is top-down, and the whole lesson of what we're seeing now, made possible by technology, is that the 'gatekeeper' function is being tremendously weakened" (Fouhy 1994).

But there are larger and more serious issues involved than turf guarding, most centrally the future of journalism's historical mandate. Journalists and scholars of media see an ongoing and accelerating shift in the social role of journalism, which has been to provide to communities a public space—a virtual meeting place, with a common body of daily knowledge for the citizenry (Rosen 1992). Giving ground on this claim means, for journalists, acceding to the role of publisher's pawn or adman's tout. It certainly furthers the transformation of the citizen into an infoconsumer. That infoconsumer is, according to some analysts, not the choice-empowered individual of advertising fame, but an artifact of the desires of large corporate and bureaucratic systems, which pursue the unwary credit card holder for their own ends (Schiller 1989; Gandy 1993).

In one sense, the infofuture of finely sliced and diced demographics is now. For the elite that now has access to the World Wide Web, electronic services that shop for interests and audiences have debuted and get more elaborate daily with the introduction of the programming language Java, which allows users to download not just data but whole miniapplications. Less fancy marketing and promotional services are multiplying throughout the Net. But that should not be surprising. In other senses as well, the future is now.

### Information Age, Marketing Age

The problem of creating and maintaining public space in a commercially oriented democracy is not new or emerging, any more than is the division between information haves and have-nots. The balkanization of the American public into demographic nuggets organized by zip code or car preference, the erosion of media space for noncommercial and public uses, and the segregation of the infohaves and have-nots on the basis of creditworthiness are well-entrenched processes and have reshaped the texture of American culture.

An *Advertising Age* ad demonstrates succinctly the social deployment of emerging technology. Accompanying a picture of a smiley face on a computer screen, the copy reads:

> You're not falling for this, are you? The cute little screen icons. The flashy graphics of online services. Magazines and newspapers getting on the Net to snag new readers. Those sleek, ultra-designed laptops. The "Information Age," is it? That's funny. It looks like . . . sounds

like . . . tastes like . . . marketing. And you should know. That's what you do. In fact, you've had this sussed out for a while now, haven't you? It's like TV in the '40s, like radio in the '20s; another really good way to sell stuff. . . .

After all, the Information Age is really the Marketing Age. Which is why you should be in Ad Age.

Of course, it's not just that simple. Every medium presents new marketing challenges, as a public relations executive recently noted (Ellis n.d. [1995]). Nonetheless, the new possibilities this PR pro finds in the Net sound distinctly like refinements on existing techniques: cultivate people with an interest in common, and attract users to your location with something compelling.

If *Advertising Age*'s ad is right, then we have been living in the Information Age for some time now. The most powerful revenue-generating mechanism in U.S. mass media is advertising, which shapes entire industries (Bogart 1991; Gomery 1993) and the nature of their editorial products. Of course, advertisers sometimes directly jump the imaginary firewall between the editorial and business sides of mass media; this is widely regarded as bad behavior. But far more profoundly, they shape the very structure of the business, whether in electronic media or in magazines (Collins 1992; Bagdikian 1987). They reward the efficient harvesting of particular demographic segments.

And so two media trends have resulted. Editorial content, inevitably and increasingly, seduces rather than informs, encouraging the restless fun seeking that is also its major challenge. *Clutter, info-overload, zapping—* they are all buzzwords that point to the uncommitted, dislocated consumer. Second, media products and services harvest ever more precisely sculpted audiences, selecting exactly those whom advertisers want to reach with minimal waste—*waste* being nonconsumers.

Neither trend has been hospitable to a journalistic mandate. What *Rolling Stone* dubs the "New News"—the putatively more egalitarian combination of talk shows, tabloid media, calls-ins, and ads that have changed the face of electoral reporting—devolves from fundamental changes in the way big media do business (Taylor 1992). Forums in most mass media that might offer a range of opinions about public affairs and an opportunity for public discussion are few and diminishing. In magazines, the "dinosaur" general weeklies are on the ropes; *Harper's* has to be bolstered by foundation funding; public television is perpetually embattled and ever more commercial; all politically partisan publications, from left to right, are subsidized. The magazines that do well, like *Women and Guns* (a runaway success story among niche-market magazines), discover new "taste publics" rather than providing new public platforms.

Broadcast television's small space for news and public affairs steers away from investigative and beat reporting, and toward entertainment and titillation. The local evening news has long since opted above all for consumer-friendliness, captured in the term that TV anchor Fred Graham gave an acid edge—"happy talk" (Graham 1990). Daytime is wall-to-walled with tabloid TV (Ricki Lake, Jerry Springer, and their kinder, gentler cousins such as *J & I*), where the otherwise invisible lower class becomes a freak show scantily disguised as a discussion of important social issues (transvestism, anorexia, parental neglect). The night schedule is larded with "reality" programming such as *Cops, Hard Copy,* and their descendents, which make class contempt a kind of blood sport and further erode a sense of virtual place by destabilizing the very meaning of appearances (Nichols 1994; Fiske and Glynn 1995). The subjects and the packaging of scandal, notoriously controversial as boundary-crossing phenomena in popular culture, may shift and change with pressure, but the sale of packaged emotion is a constant (Spain 1996).

Commercial radio's talk shows mostly masquerade as opinion and debate, instead selling the smugness of conviction and the self-righteousness of self-assertion. Rush Limbaugh only accepts calls from abject fans, or "dittoheads." But there are a lot of places to stop on the dial. Once there, listeners are likely to hear what they already agree with. It is interesting that bad-attitude male personalities like Don Imus (who describes himself as a "person who is basically pretty immature") and that master of profitably bad taste, Howard Stern, draw huge audiences. They sell, with their behavior, the thrill of being antisocial with impunity. They thumb their noses at the very concept of playing a public role.

The niche marketing of America is already a fact, in media as elsewhere. It also has produced a host of infoproducts and services—catalogs, for instance, and print, audio, and video newsletters—tailored to the instrumental needs of a particular virtual community, whether of paleobotanists or trolley car enthusiasts. These services produce entire new minimarkets, a fact not lost on new-era marketers. Nor are new communications technologies likely to shift the trend. The Net is now being envisioned as a place where content of all kinds becomes the bait to establish ongoing relationships with consumers. "The challenge for advertisers is to make sure that their advertising messages are inextricable from the content that surrounds them," writes computer guru Esther Dyson (1995, 182).

Daily life is already mass-mediated to an unprecedented degree. Commercial mass media appear to roam ceaselessly for new frontiers; CNN's Travel Channel in airports and the proposal for television screens (to allow personalized instant replays) on each seat of Washington D.C.'s new sports stadium are two examples. While "choice" is endlessly celebrated, it is consumer choice—its parameters preselected by marketers—that is delivered. The niche marketing of news, for example, is exemplified by the focus of MTV news on bulletins about the touring schedules of the hottest musical groups.

The proliferation of "infotainment" and of highly targeted information is not merely an economic fact but a cultural reality. There is, manifestly, a broad appetite for information that caters to lifestyle, hobby, and entertainment concerns. This is one indication of the way in which daily life has become a never-ending process of making consumer choices about relationships and activities that define social location (Aufderheide 1986; Giddens 1991; Phelan 1995). Concepts of community and social identity appear to be shifting, in a commercially oriented, increasingly globalized mass culture (Lash and Urry 1994, 31–59; Harvey 1990, 284–323). Participation in civic and voluntary associations continues to decline, as it has over the past two decades. Cynicism about traditional, institutional politics is at an all-time high. So is fascination with issues of social identity—Afrocentrism, political correctness controversies, multiculturalism debates, controversy over lurid and violent content in media, and emerging rights movements such as disability rights and proliferating gender rights, for example. These shifts inevitably affect what is meant by politics and by public life.

### Journalism and Public Life in the Marketing Age

Media now and increasingly cater to demographic clusters that are appetizing to advertisers or to highly defined interest groups, not to physical communities or to publics in the sense that Jürgen Habermas (1989) or John Dewey (1983) might have meant. While espousing very different arguments about the revitalization of civic life, both philosophers argue that publics are self-constituted, autonomous social groups, which can independently address the implications and consequences of other networks of power on the quality of shared daily life. In order for publics to act as publics, people have to see themselves as part of that larger whole, that autonomous social creation. By contrast, people organized into demographic clusters do not necessarily see themselves as part of the same universe as someone from a different cluster, even though both may face the same challenges from, say, a proposed development down the road. Indeed, individuals may themselves perform as different selves in the many different contexts through which they navigate and within which they unceasingly position themselves.

Daily newspapers, which typically live on very local advertising and sales, historically have had a structure distinct from other mass media. They have offered a product pitched at an entire physical community, providing not just information about but a forum within communities that are larger, denser, and more complex than any individual's ability to experience directly. But newspaper publishers have noted with alarm a steady shrinkage in advertising parallel with a decline in readership, focused particularly on younger people, who don't seem to be returning as they age (Ungaro 1991; Denton and Kurtz 1993). Perceptive newspaper editors have noted that this decline appears related to changing conceptions among readers of what they need to know to make it through their days, what they think are significant relationships in their lives, and what kind of role they see themselves playing in their world. Many of the communities that are intensely real to people now are virtual, and many of those communities are formed around consumer decision making.

One contingent of newspaper executives has struggled to redefine the newspaper's mix of information to be more entertaining and demographically targeted. Another and much smaller contingent has grappled with the challenge of using the newspaper's resources to create public spaces in community life, by sponsoring events, involving readers in political process, and even organizing long-term urban planning projects (Rosen 1992; Austin 1994).

These concerns among newspaper publishers and editors—for their survival, as communications services dependent on a multilayered concept of community—are not driven primarily by technology. They are affected by cultural movements that were already vividly apparent decades before, shaping a commercial culture of consumption (Sussman 1984, e.g., 211–29; Lears 1994; Frank 1997). Their implications for democratic life have been discussed widely (e.g., Postman 1985; Bagdikian 1987; Abramson, Arterton, and Orren 1988; Entman 1989; Harvey 1990; Dionne 1991; Bennett 1992; Jacobson and Mazur 1995), from voting to community organization to attitudes toward politicians and public life.

Newspaper editors are thus on the front lines of journalists' struggle with changing definitions of what is public and what is community.

## Megamedia and the Journalistic Mandate

Content creation, manipulation, and tailoring to minidemographics are critical to the development of widely popular new electronic services. The much-touted consumer choice depends heavily on having something to choose from. In response to the challenges of a rapidly changing media marketplace, the largest communications firms have chosen the strategy of centralization and vertical integration. Starting in the late 1970s, deregulatory fervor, combined with technological innovation, dismantled long-standing industry arrangements (Horwitz 1989). The phone company became a set of businesses hungry to enter the television programming and data delivery businesses; cable TV companies became rivals for basic phone service; several new television networks emerged (most importantly Fox); broadcasters began to lust after pager service business; Hollywood studios became part of international conglomerate deal making. Vertical integration and cross-ownership became the rule among the largest industry players (Bagdikian 1987; Miller 1996, 144–51). Newspaper-chain owners such as Gannett, Cox, Tribune, and Hearst also racked up purchases of broadcast stations and magazines and put in motion plans to cross-market their digitized product across media. Computer companies have become partners with phone companies and movie studios to produce both distribution systems and content. Phone companies in particular have become the newest, biggest, and most ambitious aspirants to total communications provision and service (Miller 1996, 147), to the title of megamedia (Maney 1995).

If content and conduit are now inextricable, the importance of content remains central. The linking of content and distribution has driven both mergers and alliances recently. Several large multinational corporations—News Corp., Time Warner, Sony, Viacom, Disney/ABC-Capital Cities—have pioneered centralized culture brokering. Their interests in civic and public life have been as minimal as the profits in those areas. Sites of public-space journalism such as broadcast news and upscale book publishing have been made into profit centers, drastically reshifting priorities and shrinking their public mandate (Auletta 1991).

The lords of these domains have not been shy to exert their influence throughout their organizations. For instance, the trade paper of the movie business, *Variety*, discovered a trend in recent scandals involving the industry. Authors who wrote about entertainment-industry subjects or people involved with their publishers' corporation have repeatedly found their book deals dropped ("Conglom Fever" 1993). *TV Guide* is notorious for showcasing Fox productions (which its publisher, Rupert Murdoch, also owns). The flamboyant Ted Turner has treated his news service, CNN, as a platform for his personal opinions (Goldberg and Goldberg 1995, 288ff). NBC, owned by General Electric, was caught slanting news about GE's shabby defense-contracting practices (Collins 1992, 28). When Disney bought ABC-Capital Cities, it promptly dumped the editor of ABC-owned *Los Angeles Magazine*, Robert Sam Anson, who was writing a Hollywood book on Disney head Michael Eisner (Lieberman 1996). As vertical integration has proceeded, each of the networks has made it common practice to feature stories about its own film and television productions on its own news programs.

It is now possible for a national politician to normalize the all-too-prevalent practice of shaping editorial product around corporate agendas publicly, without reproof. Speaker of the House Newt Gingrich, speaking to a reporter for the trade magazine *Broadcasting & Cable*, said with apparent indignation in 1995:

> The business side of the broadcast industry ought to educate the editorial writing side of the broadcast industry. I mean, I went into a major cable company that owns a daily newspaper and the newspaper's editorial page is attacking the very position of the cable company. I think the managers ought to sit down in a room with their writers and talk through market economics. ("Soundbite" 1995)

Just as important as—perhaps even more important than—the eroding line between business and journalistic priorities is the nature of the business. Vertically integrated infocompanies—companies with theme parks to fill and TV series to develop and lunch-box licensing to reap—benefit from cross-marketing strategies that begin with conceptualizing the product. Each item gets weighed according to its marketing potential. When *USA Today* reporter David Lieberman interviewed Michael Eisner on the occasion of the Disney/ABC-Capital Cities merger, Eisner enthusiastically celebrated the value of ABC news shows as "healthy, adolescent brands" (Lieberman 1996).

The megamonoliths that now dominate the media landscape have the same objectives for online services as they do for the rest of their operations: maximum profits. For instance, Rupert Murdoch aspires to online gaming, based on newspaper data, such as stock market information. Home shopping and video-on-demand are other hot prospects within megamedia. The information generated by journalists is part of a package of resources and assets.

Many see the blossoming of the decentralized Net, and the emerging software that allows for creation of virtual publishing, as a way around corporate control of culture. Leaving aside fond fantasies of future technologies, this hope needs to be tempered by experience. Established Net information services so far suggest the powerful role of brand-name information and of corporate alliance, and a reinforcement of the have/have-not gap. For example, as Net scholar Rob Kling points out (1995), customers using high-priced data retrieval services on Dialog or low-priced ones on Compuserve or America Online are not going to discover any of the small opinion magazines that now occupy boutique positions in publishing. Rather, they encounter the major, mainstream news sources—wire services, elite newspapers, mass distribution magazines. He also cites hand-in-glove arrangements, such as the magazine *Wired's* running of a highly favorable article on America Online, which carries the magazine online.

Vertical integration in the area of corporate information production has the power to shape fundamentally the uses of new communications technologies. It permits what professional journalists see as corruption and abuse to be built into the very creation of projects. It erodes the ideological space for journalism's public mandate, judging all information and communication by its ability to contribute to corporate synergy. The process will accelerate further. The Telecommunications Act of 1996 endorsed vertical integration in media industries on a record scale—a phenomenon that can only partly be explained by millions of dollars in campaign and political contributions by the megamedia (Auletta 1995). At the same time, legislators (backed by powerful industry lobbyists) decisively rejected provisions for nonprofit access, as well as funds for educational and other nonprofit experimentation with electronic infonetworking—ways to reduce the gap between infohaves and have-nots and help make communications networks accessible to the entire society (Miller 1996, 129–31ff).

Perhaps the most significant aspect of the creation of these megamedia in the late 1980s and 1990s has been the muffled quality of public debate about their consequences. Structural critique—analysis of ownership and influence—has largely issued from the powerless left press. Mainstream debate, including in Congress, has focused on the familiar terrain of sex and violence in particular products, a discussion focusing on the values issues that are one hallmark of lifestyle politics.

The market convergence going on in media industries today, boldly manifested by the aggressive vertical integration of the largest companies, accompanies technological convergence. But the relationship between market and technical convergence is a complicated one, driven by the passions of the powerful to get and maintain position. Therefore, the social effects of online journalism will also reflect that intertwining of socioeconomic and technological realities.

## Technologies of Abundance

Experience with earlier technologies can also be some guide here. The most recent claim of consumer sovereignty and social revolution on a technological basis was cable, the "technology of abundance" (Shenk 1995; Streeter 1987). Pundits waxed eloquent about its possibilities: "The educational and social impact of cable technology is likely to be greater than that of any other forseeable advance in telecommunications technology" (Gillespie 1975, 1). With so many channels, cable companies could easily relinquish some to the public, where access services might "revolutionize the communication patterns of service organizations, consumer groups, and political parties, and could provide an entirely new forum for neighborhood dialogue and artistic expression" (3).

But cable companies were permitted to build their business on a broadcasters/editor model, not on a common carrier model. They constructed networks that centralized control. At the moment, consumers of cable have an abundance of choices among remarkably similar kinds of products, many of them strikingly, ambitiously vulgar. In perhaps a quarter of the cable systems in the nation, viewers have the opportunity to be producers at public access studios—most of them woefully underfunded. But many citizens do not avail themselves of that opportunity, except when access center directors act as community organizers. In that case, it is not the technological innovation in itself that makes the difference, but the fact that it is deployed as part of an agenda to shift power relationships (see "Access Cable in Action").

Tomorrow's communications networks could and still might look something like today's phone systems—that is, equally accessible at any point in the system, whether a teenager's bedroom or the phone company's office. If, however, tomorrow's news shoppers use a service that is organized more like today's cable—powerful output from a centralized source, limited feedback from customers—they are nothing more than audiences, albeit ever more finely sliced ones.

We already know which model megamedia prefers, as they explore the uncharted new world of competitive telecommunications: cable TV (Miller 1996, 148 ff). Its abundance of choice lies principally with the owners, not the consumers, of media and communications services. Mega-media owners have perked up their ears at a new media category created by the Telecommunications Act: an Open Video System. A cable TV operation, whether run by a newspaper, a cable company, a phone company, or some hybrid, would be free of cable regulation if two-thirds of its service were open to any comers. This system design offers owners a hefty chunk of customers' choices, without requiring that viable competition for that "open" part of the system even has to exist.

As well, we know the general preferences of industry leaders in terms of open technology, which would allow linking of networks and thus widespread citizen access to information. The lust of major corporations such as AT&T and Microsoft for proprietary technology—which would limit openness—is an indication of their ceaseless search for control of the market. So is the recent case of Austin, Texas, where the city government has proposed building an open, broadband communications network. Southwestern Bell and infoconglom Time Warner's cable subsidiary in Austin have both vigorously opposed the service, on which they could rent space. They prefer to own systems they control, systems that almost assuredly will not be fully interactive (Chapman 1995). Phone companies have been disappointed with their demonstration projects in interactivity, which has led to exploring more centralized, less open, but cheaper systems.

Online journalistic services could enhance the efficiency, elegance, and utility of all kinds of information for an already niche-marketed society. But they will not necessarily fuel the radical vision of technological utopians such as the Tofflers and George Gilder, who imagine electronic networking as the "knitting together" of the "diverse communities of tomorrow, facilitating the creation of 'electronic neighborhoods' bound together not by geography but by shared interests" (*Cyberspace and the American Dream* 1994, 6).

Even before online virtuality, marketers had pioneered the cultivation of diverse virtual communities of interest, using technologies as old-fashioned as the postal service (for direct mail and newsletters) and the telephone. And they have aggressively shaped the culture of American virtual communities, so that shared interests tend to run along the lines that marketers encourage. It is easy to imagine the role of online journalism in fomenting this existing trend. It is much harder to imagine how journalism in an electronic age can cultivate a sense of community, of shared problems, of the need for knowledge, of respect for and curiosity about difference.

## Journalism and the Electronic Public Sphere

Journalists who prize the social role of journalism in a democracy and within a pluralistic culture have plenty of work to do, as we hurtle into the twenty-first century. But the challenge of new technologies, and in particular networked communication, is only one piece of a much larger puzzle. The larger question is the fostering and reproduction of democratic culture in the Age of Marketing. The awareness of some newspaper editors and publishers that the very notion of public life is at stake is a healthy beginning, one of many possible ones.

The rapid changes in journalism do put into focus some basic questions of professional behavior, as Jay Rosen has argued so eloquently (Rosen 1992, 1996). Journalists need to grasp the significance of their own profession, a significance that only becomes more important as information becomes a malleable piece of recombinant commercial culture. They need to put onto their own news agendas—their own sets of curiosities—the very structure of the information and communication industries. Then they can fight to create places and ways to incite public discussion of public television, or set-asides for nonprofit use of bandwidth, or cable access, or access to communications for schools and hospitals and libraries for what they are—struggles over the raw materials of our communications systems and the vehicles for an electronic-era culture.

Journalists also need to act as empathetic but not sycophantic ethnographers of cultural pluralism and daily democracy. The values and lifestyle controversies of today are not frivolous. They are genuine manifestations of majestic pressures on individuals in highly fluid cultures. Feature writing and lifestyle issues have become front-page material for legitimate reasons as well as because of consumer-centered marketing strategies.

And finally, journalists need to see themselves as the facilitators of responsible public discussion, not the guardians of public knowledge. They need to be the people who help us to make the connections between pieces of information that we are too busy or harried or ignorant to make for ourselves. Whether they do that by hyperlink or snail mail doesn't change the basic task, which does not get any easier with new technologies but just might be done creatively and well with them.

## References

Abramson, J. B., F. C. Arterton, and G. R. Orren. 1988. *The Electronic Commonwealth: The Impact of New Media Technologies on Democratic Politics.* New York: Basic Books.

Aufderheide, P. 1986. "The Look of the Sound: MTV." In *Watching Television*, ed. T. Gitlin, 111–35. New York: Pantheon.

Auletta, K. 1991. *Three Blind Mice: How the TV Networks Lost Their Way.* New York: Random House.

Austin, L. 1994. "Public Life and the Press: A Progress Report." Unpublished manuscript. New York Project on Public Life and the Press, Department of Journalism, New York University.

Bagdikian, B. 1987. *The Media Monopoly,* 2d ed. Boston: Beacon Press.

Bennett, W. L. 1992. *The Governing Crisis.* New York: St. Martin's.

Bogart, L. 1991. "The American Media System and Its Commercial Culture." *Media Studies Journal*: 13–34.

Chapman, G. 1995. Op-ed, *Los Angeles Times,* November 30. (Accessed on November 30, 1995, via chapman@mail.utexas.edu.)

Collins, R. K. L. 1992. *Dictating Content? How Advertising Pressure Can Corrupt a Free Press.* Washington, D.C.: Center for the Study of Commercialism.

"Conglom Fever Plagues Book Biz." 1993. *Variety,* October 11, p. 10.

*Cyberspace and the American Dream: A Magna Carta for the Knowledge Age.* 1994. Washington, D.C.: Progress and Freedom Foundation.

Denton, F., and H. Kurtz. 1993. *Reinventing the Newspaper.* New York: Twentieth Century Fund.

Dewey, J. 1983 [1927]. *The Public and Its Problems.* Athens, Ohio: Swallow Press.

Dionne, E. J. 1991. *Why Americans Hate Politics.* New York: Simon & Schuster.

Dyson, E. 1995. "Intellectual Value." *Wired* 3.07 (July): 135 ff.

Ellis, L. n.d. (1995). "Communicating in Chaos: Corporate Presence in the Online World." New York: Fleishman-Hillard (public relations firm).

Entman, R. 1989. *Democracy without Citizens: Media and the Decay of American Politics.* New York: Oxford University Press.

"Fifty Years Ago Today." 1994. *Scientific American* (June).

Fiske, J., and K. Glynn. 1995. "Trials of the Post-Modern." *Cultural Studies* 9 (3): 505–21.

Fouhy, E. 1994. Personal communication, July 22.

Frank, T. 1997. *The Conquest of Cool: Business Culture, Counterculture, and the Rise of Hip Consumerism.* Chicago: University of Chicago Press.

Gandy, O. 1993. *The Panoptic Sort: A Political Economy of Personal Information.* Boulder, Colo.: Westview Press, 1993.

Giddens, A. 1991. *Modernity and Self-Identity: Self and Society in the Late Modern Age.* Stanford, Calif.: Stanford University Press.

Gillespie, G. 1975. *Public Access Cable Television in the United States and Canada.* New York: Praeger.

Goldberg, R., and G. J. Goldberg. 1995. *Citizen Turner: The Wild Rise of an American Tycoon.* New York: Harcourt Brace.

Gomery, D. 1993. "Who Owns the Media?" In *Media Economics: Theory and Practice,* ed. A. Alexander, J. Owers, and R. Carveth, 47–70. Hillsdale, N.J.: Lawrence Erlbaum Associates.

Graham, F. 1990. *Happy Talk: Confessions of a TV Newsman.* New York: Norton.

Habermas, J. 1989 [1962]. *The Structural Transformation of the Public Sphere: An Inquiry into a Category of Bourgeois Society,* trans. Thomas Burger. Cambridge: MIT Press.

Harvey, D. 1990. *The Condition of Postmodernity.* Cambridge, Mass.: Blackwell.

Horwitz, R. B. 1989. *The Irony of Regulatory Reform: The Deregulation of American Telecommunications.* New York: Oxford University Press.

Huber, P. 1994. *Orwell's Revenge: The 1984 Palimpsest.* New York: Free Press.

Iacono, S., and R. Kling. 1995. "Computerization Movements and Tales of Technological Utopianism." In *Computerization and Controversy: Value Conflicts and Social Choices,* 2d ed., ed. R. Kling. New York: Academic Press.

Kling, R. 1995. "Boutique and Mass Media Markets, Intermediation, and the Costs of On-Line Services." *Communication Review* (forthcoming). (Accessed on March 12, 1996, via http://www.ics.uci.edu/~kling.)

Kovach, B., ed. 1994. "Can Journalists Shape the New Technologies? Toward a New Journalists' Agenda: Responding to Emerging Technological and Economic Realities—a Neiman Conference." *Neiman Reports* 48 (2): 3–73.

Jacobson, M. F., and L. A. Mazur. 1995. *Marketing Madness: A Survival Guide for a Consumer Society.* Boulder, Colo.: Westview Press.

Lash, S., and J. Urry. 1994. *Economies of Signs and Space.* Thousand Oaks, Calif.: Sage.

Lears, J. 1994. *Fables of Abundance: A Cultural History of Advertising in America.* New York: Basic.

Lieberman, D. 1996. Talk presented as the Carlos McClatchy Lecture on Media and Journalism, Stanford University, February 12.

Maney, K. 1995. *Megamedia Shakeout: The Inside Story of the Leaders and the Losers in the Exploding Communications Industry.* New York: John Wiley & Sons.

Miller, S. 1996. *Civilizing Cyberspace: Policy, Power, and the Information Super-highway.* Reading, Mass.: Addison-Wesley.

Phelan, J. 1995. *People like You: Casting for the Multicultural Market.* Donald McGannon Communication Research Center, Critical Studies Paper no. 1. New York: Fordham University.

Nichols, B. 1994. "At the Limits of Reality (TV)." In his *Blurred Boundaries:*

*Questions of Meaning in Contemporary Culture.* Bloomington: Indiana University Press.

Postman, N. 1985. *Amusing Ourselves to Death: Public Discourse in the Age of Show Business.* New York: Viking.

Rosen, J. 1992. "Forming and Informing the Public." *Kettering Review* (Winter): 60–70.

———. 1996. *Getting the Connections Right.* New York: Twentieth Century Fund.

Schiller, H. I. 1989. *Culture, Inc.: The Corporate Takeover of Public Expression.* New York: Oxford University Press.

Shenk, J. 1995. "The Robber Barons of the Information Highway." *Washington Monthly* 27 (6): 17–22.

Smith, M. R., and L. Marx., eds. 1994. *Does Technology Drive History? The Dilemma of Technological Determinism.* Cambridge: MIT Press.

"Soundbite." 1995. *Columbia Journalism Review* (May/June): 22.

Spain, W. 1996. "Talk Shows Heed Loud Dissension from New Voices." *Advertising Age,* January 15, p. 28.

Streeter, T. 1987. "The Cable Fable Revisited: Discourse, Policy, and the Making of Cable Television." *Critical Studies in Mass Communication* 4: 174–200.

Sussman, W. 1984. *Culture as History: The Transformation of American Society in the 20th Century.* New York: Pantheon.

Taylor, P. 1992. "Political Coverage in the 1990s: Teaching the Old News New Tricks." In *The New News v. the Old News: The Press and Politics in the 1990s,* ed. J. Rosen, 37–69. New York: Twentieth Century Fund.

Ungaro, J. 1991. "Newspapers I: First the Bad News." *Media Studies Journal*: 101–14.

# Beyond Apocalypse

# and Utopia

# in Cyberspace

*By 1997, assessments of the impact of networking on society and, especially, media, reflected all the anxiety, fear, and bedazzlement in the society about technology in general. Meanwhile, people who had their eye on policy could see that we were involved in a social process, in which political actions were powerful. Thanks to my friends André Schiffrin at the New Press and Todd Gitlin at New York University, I got a chance to make my case for a socially and historically rooted take on cyberreality.*

This is a time of great ideological peaks and valleys. One day the *Nation* tells you with grim foreboding that about seven people will have a stranglehold on your mind from now on, and in fact probably have since last week. The next day *Wired* tells you that the Net is unbounded, beyond government censorship, beyond every possible, silly, old-fashioned, tired, old-media kind of paradigm.

This flip-flop between apocalypse and utopia can make you giddy or drive you to curmudgeonly despair. Unfortunately, either pose at this moment is an expensive indulgence. We are, inexorably if ungracefully, lurching away from an era of discrete media—print, film, electronic media—and into an era of communications networks. What had been media are becoming applications, content, and appliances on a communications-transportation infrastructure—an infrastructure that may someday be as pervasive and essential to myriad small acts of our daily lives as it will be invisible.

New paradigms, new possibilities, new realities. One of those realities is not so new, though: the fact that telecommunications provision is an essential part of our daily lives and, as such, a social resource.

As a social resource, it might serve to promote and expand public spaces. This is a concept that involves both reservation of space and creation of content, and it has a long and illustrious history in this country. Technopundits are reviving it, telling us we need to understand and use the potential of our emerging communications architecture to restore civil connection (Bollier 1996; Rifkin 1995; Sclove 1995).

But to think at all about the notion of public interest in a networked era, we need to start by turning down the noise from all the doomsaying and cyberbabble out there. As a first step, let's dispense with a crippling misapprehension: that the major players—the phone companies, the entertainment companies, the cable and satellite and publishing companies— have any idea what they're doing as they face this paradigm shift. It's not an enviable position, being the chief operating officer of a large telephone company, or an electronics company, or a broadcaster or a publisher these days. These guys can no longer even be sure what business they're in. They're scared to change, and scared not to. It's really no wonder that the stink of fear pervades the industry, that strategies to stave off competition are the most popular, and that Wall Street is jittery toward players it has traditionally seen as the safest of bets.

At this moment of great anxiety, reality is very virtual indeed, and alarmists and enthusiasts of all kinds have great sway. They have purveyed, over the past couple of years, propositions that are like mirror images of each other, and that, added together, paralyze movement toward defining and deploying the public interest in telecommunications.

## Monopoly and Competition

While apocalyptics decry the rise of unregulated monopoly, utopians celebrate the imminent arrival of free-for-all competition. Both visions can easily be tempered by reality.

The Telecommunications Act of 1996 finally makes legal what has become technically possible: competition in areas that traditionally were considered natural monopolies, such as telephony and cable. There is much to admire in this model. Real competition could bring down prices, spur innovation, expand the market, and relieve regulators and watchdog groups of the painful process of regulating monopolies by rate of return on profit. But theory and reality are far apart in an industry where any competition must be contrived, managed, and monitored (Vietor 1994).

Competition in any case is a largely unwelcome opportunity for the largest industry players. They have been driven both to accept and to design a competitive future, because of potentially profit-sapping encroachments and competition. But let's not forget that it took two decades to write and pass this law precisely because incumbents had such a built-up interest in old-fashioned monopoly and market power.

We can certainly dispense with utopian dreams of rampant and spontaneous competition, at least for the short and middle term. There was very little head-to-head competition evident in the first year after the act, although lucrative niche markets were flourishing, and remarkably little convergence except on the financial side. The largest incumbent players were bulking up against potential competition.

On the other hand, outright, unregulated monopoly in converged businesses is also unlikely. The law still frowns on monopoly, and big industry players like to use the law when they're threatened. This is, after all, how Rupert Murdoch finds himself complaining to the courts about those suddenly evil monopolists Time Warner, when he's trying to get his Fox News channel on their cable services. It was advertisers, fearful of higher rates, who pushed the Department of Justice to ban radio merges that would create more than 40 or 50 percent (depending on the place) of the local market. There are also hulking forces on the landscape kicking down the doors of old monopolists, and eager to use policy to that end. Long-distance and local phone companies have freely used monopoly charges against each other. Finally, abuse of monopoly power leads to consumer revolt and the prospect of government intervention. That's a messy process without any promise that the cure won't be worse than the disease, but it is another check on the power of monopoly.

The big, however, are getting bigger and the small are getting squeezed, as Douglas Gomery regularly reports in his columns in *American Journalism Review*. Small cable owners are declining, pressed by their direct broadcast satellite (DBS) competitors. Mom-and-pop radio stations are becoming history. In enhanced network services like Internet provision, the name of the game is to launch and sell out. The 1996 telecommunications reform law permitted such unprecedented cross-ownership and concentration of ownership that in broadcasting alone the deal making reached $25-plus billion, triple the previous record of the year before. In these deals, the already big got much bigger.

That kind of consolidation looks good to some of the most eager advocates of competition because they think this new competitive environment will be a "dance of the giants," with room made for little guys in the niches and boutiques at the edges. They need a few more giants to make this kind of competition work. Permitting concentration of megamedia power is one way of growing competitors for the phone companies, and for other global media companies. But megacorporations may very well decline to compete with their megasiblings, or may find themselves in unexpected alliances with them.

Our middle-range communications future will probably be one of a rather small number of huge, complex corporations, wielding international clout and making alliances of convenience with each other. Think of it as chaos theory meets oligopoly. This makes a powerful case for the continued role of regulation in maintaining and managing competition. Or, as Eli Noam, a noted savant in this area, has said in many settings, "The price of liberalization is eternal vigilance."

### Freedom of Expression

A second set of extremist visions has to do with freedom of expression in this new environment. The doomsayers somberly predict the stamping-out of alternative voices, while on the other side people can only see a thousand electronic mailing lists blossoming.

As an editor for a small, stubborn, pathetically underfunded alternative voice—the newspaper *In These Times*—I have to say that the range of voices is a real but not new problem. It is, in fact, a variety of problems, some of which are grave without being easy to find clear villains for, like the evolution of consumer appetite for infotainment. Certainly, we have more consumer options than in the past, even if most of those options are junk. Only recently there was much less information choice—three television networks provided isomorphic versions of the news; small-town newspapers whose editors were often hand-in-glove with local politicians ran local infoautarchies; the book publishing universe didn't extend twenty-five miles outside New York City.

Of course, more stuff is not the same thing as stuff from many different sources. Consolidation certainly doesn't seem to be doing much for the quality and diversity of news—one time-honored measure of public service and the platforming of public issues in communications. In radio and TV, local news is already too rare a phenomenon, and mergers in broadcasting mean even more business for cheap syndication services like Metro Networks and Shadow Broadcast Services, which provide the illusion of local reporting. Job opportunities for journalists are actually shrinking as mergers precipitate downsizing. The instant that Time Warner merged with Turner, one thousand jobs disappeared. Synergies within may not correlate with quality. CNN hopes to expand its TV coverage by reusing *Time* reporting; but insiders at *Time* say making magazine research hostage to TV development schedules has contorted priorities and held up release of topical information.

Meanwhile, media consolidation has accelerated a disturbing trend. The cable public affairs service C-SPAN—which started as the cable industry's present to Congress for pro-cable 1984 legislation and since has become a round-the-clock civics lesson for millions—shrunk or disappeared for more than five million cable households over the past four years. Cable companies increasingly find they'd rather sell the space, for excellent prices, to channels offered by rising conglomerates like News Corp. and Time Warner. And they no longer feel like they need to kiss Congress good-night.

As well, we know our media magnates are not shy to throw their weight around in editorial meetings. Both Rupert Murdoch (who contributed $1 million to the California Republican Party in fall 1996) and John Malone have been proud to say publicly that they intend to promote conservative political views in media they control. It also is only common sense that offending one's employer is bad business; ABC's progressive radio talk show host Jim Hightower, whose show was summarily canceled, may have simply pulled low ratings, but it probably didn't help that after Disney bought ABC he said things like, "Now I work for a rodent." This problem of gatekeepers' manipulation is also familiar—we have only to revisit the lives of William Randolph Hearst or Philip Graham—and one with imperfect solutions. But the scale is unprecedented. We are reminded, in the showdown between Disney and the Chinese government in late 1996 over the making of a film about Tibet, that global companies have not only global impact but global sensitivities.

The issue of information integrity when it's an element in corporate synergy or partnering is a perennial problem that has, with the 1996 act, attained breathtaking new dimensions. Recent items in *Columbia Journalism Review*'s Synergy Watch column include an advertisers' breakfast hosted by the *New Yorker* celebrating both an upcoming issue and a book published by another arm of its corporate parent; a canny insertion of Rupert Murdoch's Sky News service into the Rupert-owned Fox movie *Independence Day*; and electronic city guides run by software companies, potentially sapping newspapers' advertising strength. The potential for crossover marketing, and shaping of infoagendas, is mind-boggling.

As long as we have gatekeepers—and they're not going away, since gatekeeping is where the money is—we continue to have very old-fashioned issues about informing the public, which return us to considerations of policy. Consider the Time Warner–Turner merger. The Department of Justice required the merged company to carry at least one other twenty-four-hour-news channel, so that the company couldn't exclude everything but CNN. That was clear evidence of the kind of regulatory micromanagement we'll probably see more of as merged companies develop.

As for a thousand electronic mailing lists blooming, this is the kind of technologically utopian argument that works better if you're not on a lot of mailing lists already. Of course, distributed networks potentially change the economics of information access. But many factors—the cost of access, the reluctance of media corporations to surrender control over content, and the bedeviling problem of getting an audience—hobble that potential. And even if thousands of infoboutiques bloom, what does that mean for shared understanding, for cultural evolution? Today's reality is markedly experimental, and too many changes need to occur to make any sensible predictions about media in a distributed environment.

Changing paradigms will not change, in other words, very familiar issues relating to gatekeeping. If we pretend we can dispense with policy controls on monopoly, or can shrug off broad (if inchoate) public and parental concern over content control, we will only return to those questions in a more highly charged atmosphere later.

### Access

While pessimists foresee the gap between info haves and have-nots growing, optimists foresee everyone benefiting from cheaper distribution of information.

Inequality is an issue in any infrastructure; technologies will have whatever effect society and government allows them to have, and inequality by and large needs redress by redistribution. The 1996 telecommunications law recognizes this in small ways, with provisions for a special small business fund, educational technology fund, and low rates for schools, libraries, and health care facilities. As usual, what this means in real life will have everything to do how much public scrutiny and pressure is on the regulatory process. It will be fatally easy to reinforce existing inequalities (Wresch 1996). Furthermore, as new and different fault lines will develop, citizens of entire states, not to mention nations, may suddenly be redistricted into the have-not category, as a result of new decisions about censorship, competition, or pricing.

As for seeing information get cheaper, that too depends on calculated political decisions. That is exactly what the phone companies are fighting about, when they argue about how much it should cost for another company to hook up to their services and compete with them. (They would like the price to be very high, which would put a serious crimp in any price competition.) That is why the Disney corporate lawyers are leaders in a campaign to extend copyright protection to current holders, which would protect their investment in The Mouse and further keep use of other decades-old material costly for everyone.

But just to look at the kinds of savings you can get today, consider that sometimes cost saving is just cost shifting. You know this if you ever had to print out a document you downloaded. That is a fact Congress understood all too well when our legislators cut appropriations in 1996 for hard copy of basic governmental documents to the depository libraries nationwide, in favor of electronic versions—trusting that costs of accessing and printing will be borne by locals.

These and other information-equality issues are tracked by the several public-interest-oriented organizations, including Media Access Project, Digital Future Coalition, and the American Library Association. But they're too often ignored in mainstream journalism. Journalists in turn complain that their editors say the subject is too dense. Some conclusions, though, are easy to draw. Cost, as we learned in the breakup of AT&T, will be a direct result of policy decisions that go in tandem with other policy decisions about social inequity and about what constitutes the public domain. And that argues for better, deeper journalistic coverage of the nexus between government regulation and industry structure. This, of course, is exactly what one doesn't expect to see on *Entertainment Tonight*, and it's a little hard to imagine an editor employed in megamedia seizing on the opportunity without pressure. The valiant boutique-information providers of journalism magazines, Internet newsletters, and action alerts need alliances with other citizen voices to provide that pressure.

## Deregulation

Has policy become an outmoded tool for citizen activists? Deregulation has cut the public out of decision making, says one side. Don't worry, says the other, regulators were part of the problem, and we're better off without them. Both sides indulge in illusions about the magnitude of

deregulation, when the real issue is understanding how regulatory paradigms are changing.

If communications has been deregulated, somebody should tell the
Federal Communications Commission (FCC) lawyers who have been
sleeping on their couches since February 1996, when the new telecommunications act was passed. True, the new law basically equates competition with the public interest and says that the FCC should abandon any
regulation that impedes competition. At the same time, the FCC is in
charge of maintaining many of the old rules—rules, for instance, that require broadcasters to provide low-cost airtime to electoral candidates,
and to air three hours of children's TV a day. Those old-fashioned rules
are there and still enforced largely because of pressure by feisty public
interest groups such as Media Access Project and the Center for Media
Education. These groups recognize that many aspects of our communications structure continue to be old-fashioned, and any public benefits of
the emerging regime entirely unproven.

The notion of the public interest is thus still alive, and being redefined
in ongoing policy. The FCC is tackling it on issues ranging from providing for universal telephone service to spectrum auctions to the use of
noncommercial reserved space on DBS services. The policy process there
is open to public comment, as it is at state Public Service and Public
Utilities Commissions, where the future of telephony is being hammered
out, and where the Consumer Federation of America and the American
Association of Retired Persons have been active for years.

Indeed, the new communications era of networking, as evidenced by
the Internet, seems only to have generated new flowchartsful of policy-
body acronyms, most of them international. And the challenges of digital
transmission to copyright are further proliferating international policy-
making bodies.

The challenge facing those concerned with social equity is thus twofold:
to understand the fast-changing road map of policy choices and to offer
proposals that can open opportunities and close resource gaps.

### Yesterday, Tomorrow, and Today

The giddiness and panic that afflict this field generally also affect any
timetable for public action. Apocalyptics think we have to act yesterday,
and utopians think we don't have to do anything right now. These may be
the most dangerous misconceptions now plaguing discussion. But what
is it exactly that Gramscian "optimists of the will" can or should do today?

An always useful thing is to launch and keep open discussion about what is at stake as we design our communications infrastructure. Of course, this is not one issue, but like any infrastructural architecture, a phenomenon that touches many different groups differently. Intellectual property, privacy, open government, educational applications, prices, among many others, attract their own constituencies, even as they affect common values and goals, as computer policy expert Steven Miller elegantly maps in terms of recent legislation (1996).

One anchor for our thought is the notion of the public sphere as a place where a democratic culture happens. We can ask how communications networks can encourage an active civil society. We have examples in front of us daily. Public broadcasting and access cable programming (see "The What and How of Public Broadcasting" and "Access Cable in Action") are two distinct stories of the significance of even small public spaces.

As a nation, we have made a sizable investment in public culture through communications policy in the past. In 1792, Congress decided to free the postal system from its time-honored role as a revenue-raiser (John 1995). Instead, Congress decided to give postal routes and post offices to any community that requested them, even if it wasn't cost effective. Legislators, of course, promptly lavished them on constituents, rapidly extending the service to the frontier. The act also subsidized the cheap distribution of newspapers to readers and the exchange of newspapers among printers, by overpricing letter rates.

That made news a cheap, widely available commodity in the new nation. Congress knew what it was doing. The point was to foster civic knowledge about other parts of a widely dispersed nation, and a sense of participation in nationhood. This was a costly decision. By 1832, newspapers made up 95 percent of postal weight, but at most only 15 percent of revenue. But the policy was so broadly popular, with merchants, printers, and citizens alike, that it quickly established itself as accepted practice.

The notion of reserved space or reserved spectrum has been poohpoohed by utopians as an old-fashioned and outdated concept. But I think it still has a lot to recommend it, partly because our telecom paradigm is still pretty old-fashioned and top-down, and partly because it seems to be an important feature of stimulating or zoning services such that cultures can grow. Certainly, the notion of some kind of reserved spectrum, which also has been called "public rights of way on the information superhighway," has been much discussed, and there are legal precedents for building it into the new paradigm (See "The Missing Space on Satellite TV"). Our three-decade tradition of funding arts and humanities expression at the local, state, and federal level also should not be ignored. Despite continuous and sometimes-rabid conservative efforts to destroy the National Endowment for the Arts and National Endowment for the Humanities, the organizations survive because of the way in which such expression feeds highly valued noncommercial relationships and public behaviors.

We have living precedents for the creation of public space. In the past, content creation was a critical part of the process, and it will be in any future that has public domains in it. We must, therefore, ask of our communications future more than simple access to cheap services that allow privacy. We need to carve out distinctive space for public life. To do that, we need to point to concrete projects so that people who are not already in on the story can imagine this. As well, we need some way of participating in policy making to make sure we get it.

What public spaces will look like fifteen years from now will depend to some extent on the shape of the industry, but it will also depend on what people demand from both industry and government. This is a good moment to pursue experiments in electronic public culture that can provoke both ideas and demands. The flourishing of Freenets, those low- or no-cost computer networks available to local citizens, dozens of which now exist across the country, is one early example, as are efforts by access cable centers to become communications nodes (Schuler 1996). At the Corporation for Public Broadcasting there are people who imagine public broadcasting as your local electronic public library of the future. They are funding demonstration projects in "civic networking." Back in more traditional public broadcasting, you can find an impressive example of community building with media in the work of P.O.V., the documentary series that conceives of documentaries as platforms for discussions, debate, and action, and as signals and generators of new nodes of public life. At the Department of Commerce, a small, perpetually endangered, but productive little program called TIIAP funds around $14 million of experiments in public networking. Projects ranging from language training in Native American school systems to telemedicine for people in the rural Southwest to areawide community development planning to jobs training for poor kids in the city—all have taken off with TIIAP funds, which challenge nonprofit organizations to team up together. And the Benton Foundation, an operating foundation dedicated to promoting nonprofit uses of new technologies, has not only established some demonstration projects in electronic public space but launched discussion platforms. Its Internet site, like that of the Media Access Project, links to those of scores of other nonprofit organizations.

These demonstration projects are only some among many. We need both to celebrate them and to learn what they do and do not do well. It's hard at this moment even to figure out what's being done. That's why a project like FARNET's database is important. FARNET, or the Federation of American Research Networks (it grew out of NSFNet, an early provider of Internet hookup) is building a database of digital networks that deliver local public services.

As we start to assemble a bigger picture, we need to develop critical insight based on that experience, to find out what electronic public space means and can mean. And if history is any guide, a lot of our pioneering efforts will demonstrate what doesn't work.

### In the Zone of Real Life

Policy, that big-footed presence of government, will not disappear with megamedia. On the contrary, it will become an ever more potent tool for better and worse, in a highly volatile atmosphere. As the big-money players already know, the United States has the most open policy process in the world (although that's not saying much). But in order to participate, at a minimum you do have to be informed. Fortunately, an impressive amount of effort and wit are going into citizen education about telecommunications, among just the kinds of organizations that Tocqueville so long ago found quaint and admirable among us: voluntary associations. These are organizations that analyze issues and mobilize constituencies for defense of the public interest, variously defined, in communications—organizations whose interests range from the price of broadband lines to children's media to intellectual property rights. Their challenge is to at once understand, translate for, and work with other organizations in civil society the issues at stake in telecommunications, as is the mandate of the budding organization NetAction.

This is a time of tremendous creativity and tremendous frustration, which under cultivation and with a little bit of luck could turn into new possibilities. That, however, will all happen in history, that zone of real life between the all-too-prevalent discourses of apocalypse and utopia.

### Note

Conversations with Andrew Blau, Mary Ellen Burns, Lisa Baumgartner, Larry Daressa, Douglas Gomery, Richard John, David Lieberman, Mark McCarthy, Andy Schwartzman, Steve Schwartzman, and Gigi Sohn were particularly helpful in shaping my understanding.

## References

Bollier, D. 1996. "Reinventing Democratic Culture in an Age of Electronic Networks." Report to the John D. and Catherine T. MacArthur Foundation. (Available at www.netaction.org.)

John, R. 1995. *Spreading the News.* Cambridge, Mass.: Harvard University Press.

Miller, S. 1996. *Civilizing Cyberspace.* New York: ACM Press.

Rifkin, J. 1995. *The End of Work.* New York: Tarcher/Putnam.

Schuler, D. 1996. *New Community Networks.* Reading, Mass.: Addison-Wesley.

Sclove, R. 1995. *Democracy and Technology.* New York: Guilford.

Vietor, R. 1994. *Contrived Competition: Regulation and Deregulation in America.* Cambridge, Mass.: Harvard University Press.

Wresch, W. 1996. *Disconnected: Haves and Have-Nots in the Information Age.* New Brunswick, N.J.: Rutgers University Press.

# Part III. Independent and International Media

# Camcorder

# Confessions

*When I began reporting, television production was a tightly centralized and highly lucrative medium. By the 1990s, camcorders had become part of the equipment families hefted into the car on the weekend, and anybody could make a movie— although not anyone could yet see it, and most wouldn't want to. When we can all make our own television, we face new challenges—what stories to tell, and who to tell them to. This article was one version of several in which I explored, partly with time purchased with a John Simon Guggenheim Fellowship, what kinds of do-it-yourself television people were making, for whom, and why.*

First-person video storytelling, fueled more every year by the flood of camcorders into the marketplace, is beginning to emerge as its own genre somewhere in between the essay, reporting, and the well-told tale. It is marked not only by the first-person voice in testimonial, but also by the bringing of the viewer into the world of the storyteller's experience. It typically does not make a direct argument, but an implicit request for the viewer to recognize the reality of the speaker, and to incorporate that reality into his or her view of the world. Such work, whose compelling quality is the drama of its storytelling, crosses the makeshift line between journalism/public affairs and culture/art/fiction. It stands both as symptom of and response to the challenge of social location in a postmodern society.

The first-person documentaries that have established a trend over the past few years can be grouped into three types: the confessional video, a first-person diary or meditation, drawing on a long history of independent and art film; collaborative efforts between artists and otherwise disenfranchised voices, drawing on a long history of social activism through documentary; and first-person or op-ed style journalism, which through the portability and quality of small-format brings to video the well-established (and often left-wing or socially activist) print genre of first-person reporting and opinion.

Intensely personal, even autobiographical, film and video essays have come to dominate the programming and distribution agendas of organizations once established as feisty bastions of left-wing perspectives. In its tenth anniversary year, the public TV series *P.O.V.*, established by left-wing film advocate Marc Weiss to feature partisan filmmaking, showcased two memoir films: Alan Berliner's *Nobody's Business,* the third in his trilogy of family history, and Judith Helfand's *A Healthy Baby Girl,* the filmmaker's recounting of the cost of cancer related to DES, a pregnancy drug, in her and her family's life. The Independent Television Service (ITVS), the product of a decade of struggle by the same kind of filmmaker that Weiss fought for, saw the category of personal or diary proposal rise to become the largest single category by 1993, or a sixth of the total (Mousley 1994), with the trend continuing until subjective filmmaking became a prize-winning, dominant category of ITVS production.

This kind of film and videomaking has already established some familiar, even celebrated titles. African American Marlon Riggs's video poem on his coming-to-terms with his homosexuality, *Tongues Untied,* came to public awareness when controversy erupted over *P.O.V.*'s slating of the film nationwide (Aufderheide 1994). Ross McElwee's journal portraits of self-discovery and questing, culminating in *Time Indefinite,* have become cult films for aspiring filmmakers searching for a voice both tentative and assertive.

But there are a wealth of other recent examples, many of them showcased on public television. From *P.O.V.*, there are Janice Tanaka's *Who's Gonna Pay for These Donuts, Anyway?*, in which a long-delayed reunion with her father is also a rediscovery of the World War II internment of Japanese Americans as family history; Barbara Bader's *Beautiful Piggies,* about her eating disorder and family life; Peter Friedman's *Silverlake Life,* the diary chronicle of a gay couple dying of AIDS; Allie Light's *Dialogues with Madwomen,* portraits of several women who survived mental illness; and Deborah Hoffman's *Complaints of a Dutiful Daughter,* which tracks the evolution of her relationship with her mother as the mother slips into Alzheimer's. From the investigative journalism series *Frontline,* there is Marco Williams's *In Search of Our Fathers,* about the African American family through his own father. The video-art series *Alive TV* has aired, among others, Mark Pellington's *Father's Daze,* a meditation on his relationship with his father, who now has Alzheimer's. ITVS has funded and promoted personal works such as Ellen Spiro's *Greetings from Out Here* (a diary film of a road trip in which Spiro, a lesbian, visits gays and lesbians living in Southern communities), and Billy Golfus and David Simpson's *When Billy Broke His Head . . . and Other Tales of Wonder* (in which Golfus, who suffered brain damage in a motorcycle accident, struggles to find ways to rejoin society).

The makers of these first-person films, mostly middle-class professional filmmakers, go on journeys of discovery, often triggered by medical crisis—AIDS, Alzheimer's, brain damage, bulimia, mental illness—or by a family crisis. Accidents of fate or birth trigger an exploration of social identity, as a way of making meaning from events. The camera becomes not just a recorder but an assistant in the construction of reality. Ross McElwee says, and he claims it is only partly in jest, in *Sherman's March,* "It seems I'm filming my life in order to have a life to film" (in Lucia 1993, 37).

Another kind of first-person documentary is made by people who are rarely seen on television, and who do not by themselves have the skill or resources to tell their own stories. For instance, *Boston Globe* journalist John Koch worked with seven sets of local teenagers to make an hour-long, seven-part tape reflecting their daily lives, *In Our Own Words* (shown simultaneously on three TV stations, one of them public, in the area). The eight-part, four-hour ITVS series *The Ride* involved seven teenagers from all over the country, who traveled to several states and interviewed other teenagers about their lives; they worked with an executive producer, trainers, and editors. Veteran filmmaker Ilan Ziv has worked with nonfilmmakers in the Middle East (*Palestinian Diaries;* *Family Scenes, Stones and M16s* [Jewish settler diaries]) and, along with Peter Kinoy, with at-risk American teenagers (*Teen Dreams*). Filmmakers Ahrin Mishan and Nick Rothenberg lived with Vietnamese immigrant teenager Ricky Phan, a gang member, for two years before composing his first-person story, *Bui Doi Life like Dust.*

As well, some journalists have found first-person storytelling a uniquely compelling way to communicate other realities. Danny Schechter and Rory O'Connor, coproducers of *South Africa Now* and a new human rights series, *Rights and Wrongs,* have often used partisan correspondents and first-person, grassroots storytelling. Their compilation of works by the Sarajevo film collective SAGA, *Sarajevo Ground Zero,* featuring what they called "first-person perspectives of people under attack," won film festival awards and aired on cable channel Cinemax (after PBS, obviously uncomfortable with personal journalism, passed on it).

First-person journalism on video has, in fact, long been a marginal but significant part of commercial television news. Independents such as Jon Alpert and Alan and Susan Raymond have staked a claim for the legitimacy of first-person journalism, and *Nightline* has featured the diary work of freelance journalist David Turecamo.

This trend toward subjective, personal essay–style documentary is also marked internationally. Britain's BBC, as part of its community outreach programs, in 1990 began a series, *Video Diary,* featuring a different person's story each week. (Storytellers tape their own work but work closely with BBC producers.) The show has become so popular that *Teenage Diaries* was inaugurated in 1992. The BBC also has run a regular, weekly short news feature self-chronicling daily life on one street in Sarajevo, as one way of reporting on the war in Bosnia.

A confessional and meditative style has also crossed borders (see "Memory and History in Sub-Saharan African Cinema"). Films out of the African cultural diaspora, such as Guinean David Achkar's *Allah Tantou,* about his quest for an understanding of his diplomat father's life and death; Raoul Peck's *Lumumba: Death of a Prophet,* in which his own childhood memories and home movies are interwoven with the early history of national Congo/Zaire; and Ngozi Onwurah's *Body Beautiful,* about her own self-image as seen through the life of her white mother— all confront controversial issues through personal experience.

There appears to be a growing appetite for experimenting with first-person documentary, as evidenced by attendance at weekend workshops hosted by the American Documentary, which produces *P.O.V.,* for aspiring personal filmmakers, in 1994–1995. Hundreds of applications flooded in for the fifteen to twenty places available for each of five workshops in different cities in 1994, associated with the launch of a new series, *E.C.U.* (for "extreme close-up").

Workshop discussions helped to illuminate the reasons why so many are turning to first-person video. Hopeful filmmakers said they wanted to make their films for two related reasons. One was to assert their own place in the world and chronicle their discovery of that place. One applicant aptly quoted an independent filmmaker, Kit Carson, who in the fictionalized narrative *David Holtzman's Diary* says: "Godard once said that film is truth twenty-four times a second, so I thought that if I filmed my life, I might be able to understand it." They often wanted to make stories about their own families, exploring relationships through rupture (witness story ideas about a lesbian's father, who is a right-wing activist; a Jewish family divided by religious belief; a mentally ill father or mother). They often saw the camera as an ally that would permit them to ask questions they otherwise could not ask.

Another way of saying what they were doing was to give social context to individual experience. Whether it was a daughter following her mother through the first year of retirement, a wife facing widowhood, a neighbor tracing community relationships through a yard sale, a Latino tracing three generations of searching for the American dream, an African American woman charting repressed anger in the workplace, or a father chronicling life with a Down's syndrome child, they wanted to make connections with smaller and larger publics. One filmmaker called it "bearing witness," while another called it countering "disorted and sensationalistic" media images. Several said they wanted to show the human face of an issue such as AIDS or aging or youth violence.

These kinds of subjective documentary consciously aim to expand the range of voices represented in mass media. Each also experiments with expanding ways in which voices are heard, characters are represented, and social issues are phrased. In this, they follow in a long, if tangled, tradition of personal documentary.

## Personal and Social

The personal documentary has tangled roots in several traditions. Disenfranchised social groups and their supporters have long used documentary to communicate directly their point of view to a broader audience—often with a pointed political objective. This was the premise of the Challenge for Change project, in which Canada's National Film Board gradually evolved a collaborative production process between filmmakers and social actors and activists (Engelman 1996, chap. 7; Henaut 1991). The power of documentary to promote social justice has been the premise of several groups that work in video with teens or disenfranchised groups, such as Educational Video Center in New York and PRIDE in Philadelphia. The same premise fueled the social issue documentary movement of the 1970s, with its oral histories of the American Left such as *With Babies and Banners* (1977) and *Union Maids* (1976). It has also been part of the rhetoric of cable access television.

The evolving tradition of cinema verité has also focused on the subjective expression of social issues. The very different works of Fred Wiseman, the Maysles brothers, and Kartemquin Films (Nichols 1991, 38 ff) has brought the powers of close observations to social institutions and processes. Most recently, Kartemquin's widely praised feature *Hoop Dreams*, partly funded by public television, uses the intimate daily life of two families to tell a saga of doomed pursuit of the American dream.

In the 1970s, experimental film artists—Ed Pincus, Jonas Mekas, Alfred Guzetti, Robert Frank, Curt McDowell, Jeff Kreines, George Kuchar—used diary and confessional film as oblique social commentary (McDonald 1988; Ruoff 1992, 295). At the same time, feminist and gay rights filmmakers—Su Friedrich, Vanalyne Green, Maxi Cohen, Ellen Spiro, Amalie Rothschild, Claudia Weill, Michelle Citron, to name a few—used diary and confessional films to express their conviction that the personal was political (Tamblyn 1990; Lane 1993; Juhasz 1994; Nichols 1991, 238).

The subjective documentaries that have surfaced on screen, primarily on public television, thus come out of a socially critical documentary history. The creation of ITVS, a haven for such work, resulted from political pressure to expand the range of expression on public television (see "Public Television and the Public Sphere").

The highly personal work at the cutting edge of documentary also parallels other trends in the arts, which equally reflect the entangling of personal and social. Over the past three decades, in literature, personal narratives that cross genre lines, such as *The Autobiography of Malcolm X*, have changed the face of publishing; memoirs now dot the best-seller lists. In journalism, the New Journalism has now become the old guard. In anthropology, subjective and reflexive ethnography has superseded the self-assured case study, while in literary studies deconstruction has destabilized the traditional role of the author (Ruby 1982, 1991). In dance, the body has become social statement, for instance, in the work of Bill T. Jones.

## Public Intimacy

The emerging genre of subjective documentary speaks, as do these other expressive movements, to much broader social trends. Their very subjectivity makes an implicit social comment, on the erosion between public and private spheres in daily life, and on the rise of identity formation as an active, self-directed process in contemporary daily life.

The restructuring of the traditionally public realm is a uniting feature in current analyses of social crisis. Historians chart the rise of new classes and of advertising as a virtual national language in tandem with the shifting boundaries between public and private (Sennett 1974; Lears 1994). Philosophers, among them Jürgen Habermas, describe the encroachment on the texture of community life by large bureaucracies and powerful corporations (Seidman 1989). Anthropologists and other humanist scholars see the never-ending search for identity as a tool to navigate the various and global landscapes of culture and power that people now inhabit simultaneously (Appadurai 1994).

In the broader social process, television has been—as Joshua Meyrowitz has argued so elegantly—an agent of the cultural destruction of older divisions between public and private life (Meyrowitz 1985). Television tears down the barriers of authority for the young, creates the illusion of intimacy, and models conversations in public (my divorce, their parents' incompetence, his impotence) that once were had only in private. It has inevitably changed what we expect to talk about and how we expect to talk about it. In particular, advertisers on commercial television have whispered consolingly and persuasively to, now, generations of viewers that they are misunderstood, neglected, put upon, and not nearly nice enough to themselves.

The pervasiveness of this kind of message, for writer Charles Baxter, is evident in what he calls "dysfunctional narratives" in mass media (1994). He argues that American storytelling—not just on television but in literature and politics—over the past two decades has been marked by what he calls the "Romance of Victimization." This mapping of "the psychic landscape of trauma and paralysis," he writes, runs parallel to "a political culture of disavowals." Confusion and powerlessness, exacerbated by advertisers' unceasing exhortation to happiness, drive speakers to a frenzy of easy blame, confession, and exculpation. A prime example, for him, of fractured narrative is the tabloid talk show. It is easy to see this fractured narrative in media performances in which media figures from rappers to Rush Limbaugh declare themselves misunderstood, neglected victims.

This logic can also be extended to "reality" TV shows. On shows like *Cops* and *Emergency 911*, fiction and reporting are deliberately blurred in ways that play on the widely felt disjuncture between personal experience and public or official "truth" (Fiske and Glynn 1995), a game that reduces social significance to gee-whiz amazement (Nichols 1994, 43–62). In this case, the spectator becomes one of the victims of narratives without heroes or resolution.

The process that started, with manifest good intentions, with *Donahue* in the 1970s by the 1990s had turned into the gleeful sleaze of *Ricki,*

*Leeza, Maury Povich, Jenny Jones,* and *Jerry Springer.* This was, of course, not simply a result of cultural trends. Deregulation beginning in the late 1970s fostered economic conditions that vastly increased programmers' appetite for cheap-to-produce shows; but among the most successful were those exploiting the theme of victimization and catering to aleatory cynicism. In them, television's virtual public space is ironized, and intimate life made a passing spectacle.

In this light, subjective documentary comes to look like both a symptom of breakdown of the boundary between private and public, and an opportunity to launch public discussion about the terms of social identity and public life. Certainly, that is what producers see themselves trying to do, in different ways. Peter Kinoy, coproducer of *Teen Dreams,* said he worked with a Harlem high school student, a Latino gang member in Philadelphia, and teen runaways in Los Angeles because "the more authentic voice you can have in this electronic meeting place of the TV, the more you begin to break down the monopolization of presentation of life at the end of the 20th century." He argues, "I don't think discussion can be there if there isn't a way for all different segments of the population to have an open voice" (1994). Ilan Ziv, who sees the subjective documentaries he has produced as one important element in a daily news diet, says, "The idea is to give the camera to people who are creating reality, and then to see how this reality takes shape through their eyes." That lived perspective, he argues, helps viewers "to connect and learn how to care" (Ziv 1994).

Some programmers have seen subjective documentaries explicitly as opportunities to expand public life, by which they mean open presentation and exchange of perspectives. For them, personal documentaries in the proper context create what *Alive TV*'s Neil Sieling calls "an alternative public space" (1995) and what *P.O.V.* codirector Ellen Schneider calls a "public sphere" (1994). The programmers' job is to shape the context so that the documentaries can be seen as more than idiosyncratic and self-indulgent expression. For instance, *P.O.V.* contacts organizations with an affinity to the issue before a program airs and coordinates activities; provides on-line forums following the airdate; and encourages viewers to send in cassettes recording their own reaction and commentary (aired in a following episode).

## Quest for Narrative

Personal documentary testifies, one way or another, to a broadly felt quest for narratives that escape commercial formula. This is the flip side of widespread public cynicism about journalists, TV news, and reality shows as biased, sensationalistic, or exploitative. Both reactions justifiably reflect a cruel divorce between viewers' lived experience and the structures of media power. Tentative though the expression of the social location of the hyperindividual may be in these works, it merits consideration precisely because the artists are struggling to find a public language for today's and tomorrow's virtual communities.

The work of taking the evolving form of confessional video and framing it as a truly public intervention ultimately lies with programmers, not producers. Aspiring programmers face an impressive challenge in finding a fit between producers and viewers. This is a challenge at several levels: finding and encouraging producers; shaping the narrative; finding the televisual venue; establishing credibility with viewers; creating formats that foster interactivity. Not the least of the problems within each of these levels is establishing the legitimacy among one's own colleagues of this kind of material as a contribution to public dialogue about our common culture.

And finally, the road to hell is already well paved with good intentions, as Phil Donahue is here to testify. It is very easy to package pain, to make vulnerability into victimhood, and to mock the hapless in the name of raising important social issues. It is easy in a different way to sneer at the sensationalists and the vendors of vulnerability, and to blame the public for its disinterest in public affairs. Meanwhile, the challenge of naming and discussing the terms of our ever-more-fluid culture is real. In sometimes clumsy, sometimes creative ways, camcorder storytellers address that challenge, as do journalists and programmers who see themselves as architects of virtual public spaces.

## References

Appadurai, A. 1994. "Disjuncture and Difference in the Global Cultural Economy." In *Colonial Discourse and Post-Colonial Theory*, ed. P. Williams and L. Chrisman, 324–39. New York: Columbia University Press.

Aufderheide, P. 1994. "Controversy and the Newspaper's Public: The Case of *Tongues Untied*." *Journalism Quarterly* 71 (3): 499–508.

Baxter, Charles. 1994. "Dysfunctional Narratives or 'Mistakes Were Made.'" *Ploughshares* (Fall): 67–82.

Engelman, R. 1996. *Public Radio and Television in America: A Political History*. Thousand Oaks, Calif.: Sage.

Fiske, J., and K. Glynn. 1995. "Trials of the Postmodern." *Cultural Studies* 9 (3): 505–21.

Henaut, D. 1991. "Video Stories from the Dawn of Time." *Visual Anthropology Review* 7 (2): 85–101.

Juhasz, A. 1994. "Our Auto-Bodies, Ourselves: Representing Real Women in Feminist Video." *Afterimage* (February): 10–14.

Kinoy, P. 1994. Personal correspondence, July 26.

Lane, J. 1993. "Notes on Theory and the Autobiographical Documentary Film in America." *Wide Angle* 15 (3): 21–36.

Lears, J. 1994. *Fables of Abundance: A Cultural History of Advertising in America.* New York: Basic.

Lucia, C. 1993. "When the Personal Becomes Political: An Interview with Ross McElwee." *Cineaste* 20 (2): 32–37.

McDonald, S. 1988. *A Critical Cinema: Interviews with Independent Filmmakers.* Berkeley and Los Angeles: University of California Press.

Meyrowitz, J. 1985. *No Sense of Place.* New York: Oxford University Press.

Mousley, S. 1994. Personal correspondence, June 27.

Nichols, B. 1991. *Representing Reality.* Bloomington: Indiana University Press.

———. 1994. *Blurred Boundaries.* Bloomington: Indiana University Press.

Ruby, J. 1982. "Ethnography as Trompe L'oeil: Film and Anthropology." In *A Crack in the Mirror: Reflexive Perspectives in Anthropology,* ed. J. Ruby. Philadelphia: University of Pennsylvania Press.

———. 1991. "Speaking for, Speaking about, Speaking with or Speaking Alongside: An Anthropological and Documentary Dilemma." *Visual Anthropology Review* 7 (2): 50–67.

Ruoff, J. K. 1992. "Home Movies of the Avant-Garde." In *To Free the Cinema: Jonas Mekas and the New York Underground,* ed. D. E. James. Princeton, N.J.: Princeton University Press.

Schneider, E. 1994. Personal correspondence, October 22.

———. 1995. "'E.C.U.': Home for Video Diarists." *Current* 14 (March 6): 4.

Seidman, S., ed. 1989. *Jürgen Habermas on Society and Politics: A Reader.* Boston: Beacon Press.

Sennett, R. 1974. *The Fall of Public Man.* New York: Norton.

Sieling, N. 1995. Personal correspondence, February 14.

Tamblyn, C. 1990. "Significant Others: Social Documentary as Personal Portraiture in Women's Video of the 1980s." In *Illuminating Video: An Essential Guide to Video Art,* ed. D. Hall and S. J. Fifer. New York: Farrar, Straus & Giroux.

Ziv, Ilan. 1994. Personal correspondence, July 26.

# The Social-Issue

# Documentary Redux

*One of the more offbeat of the film festivals that have proliferated in recent years is run by the Council on Foundations, the leading trade association for the field. It showcases films and videos supported by member foundations and so is a great place to look for high-quality, social-issue productions. Curating this festival was, for me, like being thrown into the briar patch. I wrote a version of the following article for* The Chronicle of Higher Education, *after the 1998 festival.*

Just when it seemed like we were on the verge of zapping ourselves into a multichanneled stupor, the social issue documentary is making a comeback.

In the 1960s and 1970s, documentaries rode a wave of social action into theaters, television screens, even awards ceremonies. The Maysles brothers on Bible salesmen and on the Rolling Stones, Fred Wiseman's dour but penetrating views of institutions ranging from high schools to police to hospitals, *The War at Home*'s chronicle of the anti-Vietnam War movement, *With Babies and Banners*' feminist look back at courageous women strikers, Barbara Kopple's Academy Award–winning *Harlan County, U.S.A.*—these were more than movies. They were events, ways both to record history and to make it happen. They asked questions and started conversations.

With the rise of the VCR and the cineplexing of America, what wasn't cineplexable lost its little market niche. There were, of course, heroic exceptions, like the work of the brilliant filmic philosopher Errol Morris (*The Thin Blue Line* and *Fast, Cheap and Out of Control*), and the sardonic stabs at corporate America that Michael Moore takes in movies like *Roger and Me* and *The Big One*. But times were changing. The educational market—a social documentarian's bread and butter—was collapsing with falling prices for videocassettes, which usually couldn't cover an independent project's costs. Documentary became a booming production area for product-hungry multichannel TV, but celebrities, sharks, Nazis, and how-tos were far preferred to the unglamourous and often expensive social project. Furthermore, and maybe more important, the transformation or collapse of social movements sapped the audience base for social-issue docs. They became unfashionable.

And that's a death knell in this culture. We're used to turning to the screens of our lives for entertainment, not thought. It's not hard to figure out how diversion got to be the measure of all audiovisual expression in this screen-happy society. Our hugely successful commercial entertainment business—if you want to know what I mean by *hugely*, consider that entertainment products are edging out aerospace as America's number-one export—as part of its mission has to let us know how central, compelling, and really really fun it is. That's called marketing. The marketers worship fun. They're terrified of not-fun. They know fun as the new sacred monster of our culture.

Under the daily onslaught of their salesmanship, it becomes very easy to believe that anything that doesn't end up on national television, anything that doesn't have a frisson of celebrity or the sensational, can't really be significant. Or alternatively, that anything inserted into the language and flow of mainstream commercial entertainment must be engulfed by it. You can even, depending on how you handle the nonstop deluge of infotainment in your life, become convinced that the serious work of life is accomplished out of the glare of the spotlight, thank you, and that the wise simply avert their eyes from the many idiot boxes of our lives.

Meanwhile, the fabric of our culture is being woven with the stuff of communications media, as our newspapers, newsletters, magazines, radios, televisions, movie theaters, and phone and computer networks construct our understanding of the world and our place in it. To put it another way, media are the battleground on which combatants fight to define common sense. When the great American communications theorist James Carey said, "Reality is, above all, a scarce resource," he was explaining why the work of making media is always and inevitably about power (1989, 87). It is part of the never-ending contest to control meaning. People who make social-issue films and videos understand this simple but not obvious truth. They want to redraw the landscapes of possibility inside people's heads, to change reality as we experience it.

The marketplace, quite understandably, doesn't provide very well for projects like that. And so producers often depend on grants from foundations to get their work done. As the curator of the film and video festival of the Council on Foundations, one of the events at the trade association annual conference, I look for films that use film and video creatively to address a foundation's funding concerns—which can range from gun violence to arts education to breast cancer to parenting. Curating this festival has convinced me that there is renewed energy in such film and video production, fueled in part by foundation objectives, by new technologies, and by social concern that is more diffused than in the past but widespread. And the festival has also let me see exactly how the new social-issue documentaries do what they do.

These are documentaries that often don't even aspire to compete with popcorn stuff. Indeed, they might never even be broadcast, and yet they may be highly effective. They are typically planned as part of a larger strategy. And their aesthetic choices are designed with that in mind. Consider Judith Helfand's *A Healthy Baby Girl*, which got a national audience last year on the public TV series *P.O.V.* Helfand, a trained filmmaker, made this film as a low-tech, almost amateur video journal. At the age of twenty-five, she was diagnosed with cervical cancer—news she had dreaded since learning that her mother Florence had been prescribed diethylstilbestrol (DES) while pregnant. She decided to chronicle her and her family's confrontation with the surgery, its aftermath, and the ongoing terror and guilt the cancer triggered.

The camera follows Helfand, sometimes unsteadily, from the postoperative recovery room to lawyers' offices, DES victims' organizations, a family reunion for a nephew's bris (circumcision), and frequently to her parents' kitchen table. At one crisis moment, her mother breaks down and flees the room. The screen goes dark, but a mobile microphone picks up her distraught conversation with her daughter. The next day, we learn, Florence Helfand agrees to go on taking family trauma to the wide screen.

"We've learned as a family that the camera is our friend," says Helfand. "The camera is a moral conscience, a reminder, a witness for history that we are not alone." The raw intimacy of the journal format, then, becomes a very public rebuke to the drug manufacturers, whose cold calculations wrought havoc on generations unborn.

Helfand's homemade style was also designed to trigger the sense that it could happen to you, and that you can do something about it. Visitors to the film's Web site (hosted by its primary funder, public TV's Independent Television Service) have left touching and terrifying testimonials. Several women wrote to say they got a checkup after seeing the film—and at least one got a DES-related cancer diagnosis. With help from *P.O.V.*, which invests heftily in specialized outreach, Helfand found Jewish, environmental, and women's health organizations receptive to the film. At the Sundance Film Festival, local environmental activists used the film's toxic exposure theme to connect with their protests over nearby chemical weapons incinerators, gaining wide publicity.

By contrast, there's the stealth public health video, *Following ER*. A two-minute video segment on bulimia, it looks exactly like the local TV news, and it's supposed to. The Kaiser Family Foundation, working with The Johns Hopkins School of Public Health, where the idea for *Following ER* originated, with an NBC-affiliated TV station in Baltimore, is making dozens of video news releases—VNRs, for short—on public health issues ranging from immunization to domestic violence to the sexually transmitted disease chlamydia to the nationwide problem of uninsured children. Each little news bite picks up a subject dealt with in that evening's episode of the vastly popular NBC drama *ER* and is aired on dozens of NBC local news shows.

Kaiser is after the largest audience you can get in mass media: broadcast audiences watching prime-time, network television. To do that, the foundation had not only to appeal to viewers but to TV's gatekeepers. The VNR strategy was their tool. Station managers liked it because broadcasters today are nervous about declining ratings. They are eager both to wring profits out of every part of their operations and to attract and keep viewers. This segment promotes an NBC program and is offered free, and customizable, to NBC affiliates. For a video project like this, stylistic anonymity is success.

*With Liberty and Justice for All* rocked immigration law without ever being shown in theaters or on television. Made by veteran documentarian Barbara Kopple (whose most recent work is *Wild Man Blues*), it's a three-hankie-weeper-cum-legal-briefing, in twenty-five short minutes. The Alliance for Justice hired Kopple to make the film as a centerpiece event for its 1997 First Monday conference. The alliance hosts this event annually at law schools around the country on the first Monday in October (which marks the opening of the Supreme Court session), to encourage budding lawyers to work with public interest advocacy organizations.

Intercut with lawyer interviews are the stories of two victims of poorly designed changes in immigration law. One of them, Jesus Collado, is a legal immigrant from the Dominican Republic. He had married in the United States and raised a family. Returning from visiting relatives on the island, he was summarily imprisoned because changes in the law had made him eligible for deportation. Kopple crisply brings viewers up close to the horror of this fact for his family. His wife and children, including a daughter recovering from life-threatening injuries from a car accident, visit him in prison. They try to sing "Happy Birthday" through the microphone and the plate glass, but the stifled sobs make it hard to carry a tune.

Knowing the emotional clout of the film, the Alliance for Justice partnered with 250 organizations that could take action and arranged for extensive press, permitting media outlets to use clips. The New York ABC station, for instance, ran two minutes from it, as did *Dateline NBC*. Within weeks, Jesus Collado and others being held under a mandatory detention clause of the new law were freed while their deportation proceedings continue.

Other documentaries in the 1998 festival also matched their stylistic choices carefully with their mission. *Holding Ground* chronicles the rebirth of a neighborhood as a result of community organizing. Its step-by-step, grassroots history goes along with a step-by-step printed guide to community organizing. It has been used in low-income housing projects across the country and even been seen in Siberia, as part of a U.S. AID-funded program to promote civic life. The verité style of *Take this Heart*, an alternately inspiring and heartbreaking feature-length journey through a year in the life of a remarkable foster mother, is intended to make viewers feel they've walked in the shoes of a foster parent—and might be able to again. The talking heads of low-budget oral histories like *In Search of Common Ground*, a project of the D.C. Humanities Council, become the presences of elders on local cable access and public TV stations. The elegant feminine imagery and high production values of *Rachel's Daughters*, a film in which breast cancer survivors themselves investigate the causes of the disease, are appropriate to its venue on HBO, where it attracted more than two million viewers.

Films like these and dozens of other recent, carefully crafted interventions in our consciousness could change the way in which we think about documentary film. They are not only "a movie" or even "a TV show."

Many of them are only one facet of a coordinated media and data project; they come with Web sites, brochures, 800 numbers, and multiple versions for group use. They use sophisticated techniques to awaken and move people, and show a cool awareness of marketplace realities.

But in other ways and at their most interesting, the new social-issue documentaries return to the oldest promise of the form: telling the truth. Documentaries distinguish themselves not only by being about "real life," but by making the claim that a particular slice of real life is important to us, and thus by helping to shape reality. Our craving for this kind of truth telling has increased, even as marketers have capitalized on it with sensationalized, tabloid-TV. Social-issue documentaries emerge from behind the shiny surface of our daily media experience and treat us not just as passive viewers but as social actors who can affect our world.

## Reference

Carey, J. 1989. *Communication as Culture.* New York: Unwin Hyman.

# British

# Working-Class

# Films

*In the late 1990s, stalwart United Auto Workers veteran Don Stillman indepen-
dently launched a new magazine,* Working U.S.A., *to cover cultural and social issues from a labor (but not necessarily union) perspective. He asked me to become
a contributor, and this is one of the essays I wrote there on movies.*

The crisis of working-class culture has been good for the reputation, and
sometimes for the bank balance, of British cinema. In the '50s, a celebrated movement of gritty, politically engaged, direct documentary cinema,
called Free Cinema, prepared Britons and international audiences for
the '60s Angry Young Men—Tony Richardson *(Look Back in Anger, The
Loneliness of the Long Distance Runner),* John Schlesinger *(Billy Liar),*
Lindsay Anderson *(This Sporting Life),* Karel Reisz *(Saturday Night and
Sunday Morning).*

Then, the alienated, restless protagonists of social realist films chafed
and raged at postwar commercial culture and the burgeoning welfare
state. Those characters embodied an indictment of social containment
programs that simply muffle discontent, and of social structures too vast
and anonymous to make a meaningful place for ordinary people. The
films, modeled on the socially engaged tradition of Italian neorealism,
were fueled by controlled outrage.

British cinema fell into grievous financial straits in the later 1960s and 1970s. But in the 1980s, exciting small films were made chronicling the subcultures of imperial implosion, as the former colonials settled and raised new generations on the "home" island. Asian British films such as *My Beautiful Laundrette, Sammie and Rosie Get Laid,* and *Bhaji on the Beach,* and African British films such as *Passion of Remembrance, Testament,* and *Diary of a Young Soul Rebel* put British filmmaking back on the international festival map. They did so with the help of the innovative Channel 4—a private British TV channel and film production fund, created by the government in order to provide programming diversity, and subsidized with money that the government ordered to be siphoned off commercial TV profits. Before it was Thatcherized, Channel 4 managed to reinvigorate British cinema. In connection with the British Film Institute, it did not merely fund films but cultivated new talent, particularly in Britain's postcolonial communities.

The recent wave of social realist films revives Britain's national fascination with the tenor of white, working-class culture. It does so in the wake of Thatcherite social policies, grinding recession, and a relentlessly image-conscious popular media. An entire young generation from industrial regions in collapse has grown up unemployed and on the dole, and some of them, mostly guys, have become filmmakers. Welfare payments have in fact functioned as a meager stipend for artists. Indeed, in 1998 British artists were thrown into panic anew, since the Labour government of Tony Blair introduced its welfare-to-work policy. The films themselves have largely been funded through Channel 4 and its now-independent division Film Four. The operations eagerly follow the profit trails these days, though. Channel 4 has now had its subsidy funds cut off.

The trend is large enough to have minigenres. Films such as *Trainspotting, Shallow Grave,* and *Nil by Mouth* have put a peculiar, heroin-inflected fashion twist on longer social realist traditions, such as the work of master-dramatist Mike Leigh *(Naked, Secrets and Lies).* They feature youthful characters who live in a postmodern era in which unemployment, hustling, and anomie are all there is.

*TwentyFourSeven, Brassed Off,* and *The Full Monty,* by contrast, tell well-told tales of cultural collapse. They are situated in cities that once fueled the industrial revolution, with coal and steel. As hearths of the industrial economy, these cities were also centers of what became English working-class culture. It was a highly gendered world, in which men did ferociously hard physical labor and women raised families. It was rigidly class defined and hierarchical, with laborers, foremen, and bosses all knowing their place and marking it with clothing, symbols, gestures, and habits. It was parochial, religious, chauvinistic.

There was a lot to like, a lot not to like. People grew up, raised their kids, and reproduced a way of life. And now, these movies show their audiences, it is no longer possible to reproduce that culture. Each of these films has, as a central theme, the crisis of reproduction, physically and socially.

*TwentyFourSeven*, directed and cowritten by first-time young filmmaker Shane Meadows, stars the adorably squat Bob Hoskins as Darcy. A determinedly positive chap living in the midst of a housing project's profound social decay in a Midlands city, Darcy concocts a scheme to improve the lives of the town's soul-destroyed youth, who are "getting shit twenty-four-seven." With the help of local shopkeepers, including a young woman he pines for helplessly, and the local nouveau riche, he launches a boxing club. When he was a boy, working-class lads channeled their aggression into the organized and controlled mayhem of boxing, and he hopes it will work for the shuffling louts who now litter the streets, and in whom he has boundless faith. They've got a lot to be depressed about—alcoholic parents, abusive dads, drug addiction, as well as joblessness and poverty.

For a while, Darcy's relentless boosterism carries the lads past their miserable present. In one giddy sequence, the entire lot crams into a van and goes camping in Scotland, where it's starkly spectacular, and extremely damp. In one arresting sequence (the movie is filmed in black and white by celebrated cinematographer Ashley Rowe), it seems as though ancient monks are in a processional across the rune-strewn landscape. But as we slowly come in on them, it's only the lads in their ponchos, off to pee.

The tightly structured film builds to the boys' first competitive boxing match. The violence of the older working-class culture is released unpredictably, when one boy's hostile and self-hating father demeans him before his opponents. Darcy's fantasies meet reality in a way that is both shocking and heartrending. Not only dreams die.

There is a tight, short-story quality to *TwentyFourSeven*, which shares with many other British films a scriptwriting strength (Meadows coauthored with Paul Fraser). The last fifth of the movie entirely recasts what has gone before and effectively retells the story. What had seemed a rather earnest and increasingly cute little tale becomes a small but indelible tragedy, with echoes everywhere.

It's Darcy's story, and Hoskins does a terrific job, giving him first the air of a well-intentioned sap, allowing us to patronize his character just a bit, and then showing us how that very demeanor is crafted. The elegantly bleak black-and-white photography, deftly employing close-ups and subjective camera, underlines the stark quality of the narrative. Meadows, who has already made dozens of short videos, intends to go on doing social autobiography with his camcorder.

*TwentyFourSeven* has its funny moments, but it can't stake the claim that *The Full Monty* does, to make you "weep with laughter." If you just went by hype and reviews, you'd think *The Full Monty* was a winsome, lighthearted, sex farce of a film, rather than the wry, edgy, black comedy it is. Take one of the film's setup scenes: two buddies, unemployed and aimless, run into an acquaintance in a stalled car. One of them genially fixes it and then notices that the car, now running smoothly, is set up to asphyxiate the driver. Having rescued the guy, they then brainstorm ways you could commit suicide. Drowning? "Nah, I can't swim." How about being run over? You'd need a really good friend to do that. Well, they're good friends—didn't they just save his life? And so on.

This black humor is typical, and the film also has the inestimable advantage of having a sexy, or at least fleshy, central plot element. Maybe that's why *The Full Monty*, made by Peter Cattaneo for a tiny, less-than-$3-million budget, has cleared more than $150 million in cineplexes notoriously hostile to foreign fare, even before beginning to earn in its secondary lives (the video, the CD, TV, and international sales). Sadly for the Brits, most of the money isn't coming home, because Channel 4 let the film rights slip away to Rupert Murdoch. In fact, after investing in the screenplay, Channel 4 may even have lost money.

You will, despite the advertising, wait through the whole movie before getting "the full monty" (here meaning full nudity), and you'll have to settle for the view from the back. But the film's main gimmick, the male strip show, works very well to expose the way in which work and culture intertwine. It makes you think about what work is, and what happens when work is being looked at. It illuminates the connection between gender and work. *The Full Monty* may be the most interesting film about being looked at since Michael Powell's famously creepy *Peeping Tom* in the 1950s.

As the movie opens, a promotional film about the steel town of Sheffield, made in the 1960s, is running. The oily narrator touts the fat-and-happy quality of the booming city. But that was then. The only guys in the factory now are there trying to steal a leftover girder, and they can't even get that right. They head next to a bar, where the famed Chippendale male strippers are dazzling the local women, including the wife of one. Dave (Mark Addy) is desolated by the sight of his wife gawking at other men, but a light bulb goes on for Gaz (Robert Carlyle).

Gaz needs to find a job, because his ex-wife is going to take full custody if he doesn't start paying his child support. But as they say while hanging out in the unemployment office, "Men are obsolete." There are no jobs, unless you count ones that the women have, like clerking and stacking. So it's less of a surprise than it should be that Gaz acts like a permanent adolescent, Dave is depressed and impotent, and that their ex-foreman Gerald (Tom Wilkinson) lives an elaborate charade in order not to confess to his wife that he's lost his job.

Well, if men are obsolete, one might embrace the alternative. Gaz leads the group in a plan to do a local version of the Chippendales. The gang is not only unpromising—*sagging, aging, clumsy* are some appropriate adjectives—but also entirely unversed in image-conscious performance. As they learn their routines, they also learn the work of self-presentation. One day, Dave casually mentions, looking at a girlie magazine, "Her tits are too big." Suddenly, the men realize that people will judge them with the same careless cruelty, which will only be what the men themselves are selling permission to do when they sell tickets. They begin grooming sessions and share weight-loss secrets. They alternately rejoice and despair, as the day approaches.

It's a brittle premise, but arch wit propels it forward and past the points at which we really ought, by rights, to suspend our disbelief. The movie teeters uneasily between humiliation and delight, as different members of the group have their own crises and threaten the show. The last shot, a freeze-frame, is exactly right. Their moment can be caught but not repeated, and it doesn't go anywhere. We're happy for those guys, and we're embarrassed for them, too. God only knows what they'll do for an encore.

*Brassed Off,* which is the film that Channel 4 backed instead of *The Full Monty,* has been a critical and, more modestly, a box office success. Another well-told tale, it is distinctive in this crop for naming its enemies: Thatcher and the Tories. Leaving nothing to chance, first-time writer-director Mark Herman begins the film with intertitles that explain key words such as the title ("pissed off"), *redundancy* ("unemployment"), and *Tory.* He ends the film with another poke in the eye to the Tories and gives his lead character a climactic speech in which he fulminates against the wanton destruction of jobs, culture, and hope.

Having framed the tale with such ruthless didacticism, Herman then goes on to spin a story that's practically soapy in its cross-generational drama, and sometimes a real sniffler. Like the workers in many towns, the coal miners of Grimley have a long-standing brass band tradition. The government has begun shutting down coal mines, and Grimly's day has come. The union is deciding whether to take the buyout offer, and management is in town to conduct its own research.

The band, however, plays on, preparing to compete in the national brass band championships under the able leadership of Danny (Pete Postlewaithe, familiar from *The Lost World* and *Amistad*, among others). He lives for his music and cultivates a quiet dignity. Not so his son Phil (Stephen Tompkinson), who is distracted by the repo men who have come to empty his house, and his sad wife's reproaches. Phil has in desperation taken up part-time work as a party clown, and he's not good at it.

When Gloria (Tara Fitzgerald) returns to Grimly with her grandfather's horn and the ability to send Grimly into the semifinals, the guys let her in, and shy but sexy Andy (Ewan McGregor) romances her. But Gloria is now working as an economic analyst for management, which sits poorly with the group, especially a dour hard-liner.

As the band is winning in the semifinals, the miners are losing the union vote. Danny collapses and goes into the hospital, stricken by a black-lung illness. Although the band serenades him in one of the real tearjerker moments of the movie (the music is actually played by a real coal-mine town band), the members know it's over. "The band's dead, just like everything else," says Andy to Gloria.

But it's not. Several plot twists later, the band makes it to the finals, and Danny, risen from his deathbed, delivers his speech: "This bloody government has systematically destroyed this industry," he says. In the process, it has also destroyed communities and the will to win, leaving "decent human beings without a hope left." Being able to "knock out a bloody tune" just isn't enough to keep their minds off the end of life as they know it.

There's more. But *Brassed Off* isn't just an overplotted and moralistic tearjerker. The characters are both conveniently stereotypic and also entirely plausible. The plotting, however efficiently mechanical, can also be insightful, milking moments for meaning and revealing the complexity of the situation. The film may make us angry about the dumping of communities and lives, but not by making us nostalgic for the good old days when people tootled their way to working-class bliss. Danny's black-lung disease isn't a product of the bad new days, but of the bad old ones. The brass band is both the opium of the people and their salvation.

And then, of course, there's the music, which can be unearthly good. It's no wonder that the movie has spurred a revival of brass bands in Britain, some of them subsidized with lottery money. It hasn't kept the Labour Party government from slashing welfare programs or closing industries, though.

It's hard enough to imagine an American movie on these themes, let alone a batch of films with this much variety, style, wit, and even humor. That may have to do with the fact that class is an open feature of British society, one within which distinctive cultural habits arise, as George Bernard Shaw so pointedly noted in *Pygmalion*. It is a submerged and messy category in the United States, where we all claim to be "middle class," and where ethnicity is a primary boundary marker. Class-based culture is most explicit in the most traditionally organized of heavy industries, although class gradations shape the many facets of American culture. Michael Moore, the self-styled image of the male working class in his recent documentary *The Big One,* is very much from Flint, Michigan, not Silicon Valley or New York. In that sense, we almost can't help bringing a false nostalgia to movies about class-based culture. It all looks so different, so unencoded, so Old World.

But the Old World is meeting the new, global-economy era in these films. They pointedly mark the passing of an era. Whether it's the elegiac tone of *TwentyFourSeven* or the jittery, manic quality of *The Full Monty* or the half-lugubrious, half-outraged *Brassed Off,* they all capture the sense of an ending. They make a good case that work organizes our lives, and that unemployment disorganizes them. They haven't got a clue, and we probably don't either, about what happens next.

# New

# Latin American

# Cinema

# Reconsidered

*The explosion of politicized Latin American cinema in the '70s, one strand of the "new cinema" movements that also rocked sub-Saharan Africa and the Arab world, had shown me how revolutionary hope had fundamentally shaped an entire generation of artists. And so it was with the sensation of being present at a slow-motion train wreck that I watched certain debates unroll in the heart of New Latin American Cinema, the Havana Film Festival, at the end of the 1980s. These debates not only exposed the stalled-out quality of an engaged artistic movement, but they implicitly called into question basic premises of the movement itself. I wrote many articles on my return from both the 1987 and 1989 festivals and eventually wrote the following essay, which was directed at people who study and teach about this enormously influential movement in Latin American cinema. Michael Renov graciously shepherded the piece into* Quarterly Review of Film and Video, *making sure that it didn't run afoul of academic convention.*

In the late 1980s, an era ended for Latin American cinema. In keeping with the vociferous and argumentative spirit of Latin intellectual culture, the crisis was on stage at the annual event that brought together filmmakers throughout the continent in those days: the International Festival of New Latin American Cinema in Havana, Cuba.

Through the charges, countercharges, laments, and wryly hopeful proposals that surfaced in formal and informal discussions there in 1987 and 1989, one could see, retrospectively, the profound importance of political mission to the cinema of the preceding decades. And one could sense the panic and anxiety facing those who knew they were losing a unifying link among themselves as artists and intellectuals. It was a mood that was echoed elsewhere at the time, especially in the societies being shaken by the end of the Soviet era. Havana, as always, lent the events a distinctive flavor.

## Cultural Nationalism

The rhetoric of cultural nationalism, strongly infused by leftist political ideologies, has shaped the history of New Latin American Cinema, which includes such internationally recognized names as Fernando Birri, Glauber Rocha, Jorge Sanjinés, and Tomás Gutiérrez Alea. This rhetoric, loosely defined, maintains that film—a mass art that needs to be popular in a ticket-selling sense—is also an art infused with a social mission. It needs to be popular in the sense of responding to and em-powering the popular culture of the ethnic group, nation, or region. The mission of the filmmaker is not only to produce an entertaining work, although engagement with the audience is important. The artist charges him- or herself with the dual task of reflecting and creating an au-tonomous culture, as part of a larger struggle to build popular participa-tion in society. This culture need not, in this formulation, be restricted to national borders but may reflect culture or class (e.g., Andean peas-ants or steelworkers).

In the '60s and '70s, with the encouragement of postrevolutionary Cuban filmmakers and arts bureaucrats, New Latin American filmmakers came to espouse rhetorically a pan–Latin American vision, grounded in an anti-imperialist stance opposed to U.S. popular culture. This rhetoric influenced in turn the conceptualizing of postwar Latin American film art internationally, among critics and scholars (Armes 1987; Burton 1986; Schumann 1987; King 1990). Although most New Latin American films were not commercial successes, and sometimes were even banned from distribution in their country of origin, the movement won such acclaim internationally that its history has often been equated with the history of serious Latin film art.

The militant rhetoric of cultural nationalism rested—indeed, still rests—on the cold ground of enduring economic reality. International distribution of U.S. product within Latin America undercuts the oppor-tunities of any Latin American film artists. The relatively low rental price of premium movies, the practice of selling rights to American films (many of them low quality) in blocks, and vociferous policies against national protection for national cinema by the powerful Motion Picture Export Association have given American films a priority position on screens. Further, this has historically depressed the prices that exhibitors will pay for film product that needs to recoup the majority of its costs from that market (Getino 1987).

Cultural nationalism was also, however, historically grounded in a political conjuncture in the mid-1960s. What had been a diverse film movement led by middle-class young men, many influenced by Italian neorealism, came to have a name and enough coherence to muster debates over its direction during the political polarization throughout Latin America of the 1960s. Film came to be seen as not simply an arm of political struggle but a central staging ground of the battle for hegemony (as well as, at times, explicitly political power).

The 1967 Festival of New Latin American Cinema at Viña del Mar, Chile, made official the launching of a new movement, one in which cultural nationalism and leftism were intertwined. From then on, New Latin American Cinema was justified rhetorically not only by an affirmative search for cultural identity and sometimes an explicit political mission, but also by a rejection of the formal language of Hollywood cinema, of the commercial cinema formulas of Latin American cinema. That rejection put a priority on the discovery of new modes of expression and production values, ones that could conduct that affirmative search without falling into the cultural ruts of the past (Fundación 1988; Chanan 1983; Burton n.d.; Solanas and Getino 1976). The Havana film festival, launched in 1979 as an annual event by the Cuban film institute, attempted both to respond to this maturing movement, and also to promote it commercially and ideologically. For years, a filmmaker anywhere in Latin America could count on being able to project a film at the festival, if he or she could get there. Sometimes Cuban planes, on continentwide pickups, could even offer transportation.

In 1987, what was for years a muttered undercurrent among many of the old guard New Cinema filmmakers, and a point of disaffection for many younger directors, became public. The need to rethink the basic terms that define New Latin American Cinema—or perhaps even to pronounce it dead and get on with something not quite yet imagined—was a theme of the annual seminar held during the Festival of New Latin American Cinema in Havana in 1987. It was a theme that developed in following years.

## Crisis in Production

The rethinking of conceptual terms accompanied several other process-es. Politically, this was a period of gradual return to democracy, through-out Latin America. Cuba, long idolized by Latin American leftists, was rocked by the USSR's perestroika but was not following its example. Declining subsidies from the Soviet Union left Cuban film producers, teachers, and bureaucrats in economic crisis. Cuba's political crisis trig-gered both harsher censorship and greater demands for openness. Else-where in Latin America, leftists floundered as the challenges shifted from resistance to dictatorship to playing a constructive role in building new democracies.

Economically, it was a time of austerity and reconsidering of the role of the state in production, including film production. Each of the three largest production centers, Argentina, Brazil, and Mexico, were hard hit. In Argentina, for instance, where the state had long issued favorable loans to filmmakers out of taxes on movie tickets, the loan money was im-pounded in the late 1980s, dramatically reducing Argentine production from forty-six films (1982) to four (1989). Mourning the loss of techni-cians in one of Latin America's most elaborate film industries, film union official Jorge Ventura told me, "Making movies is not an economic deci-sion in Latin America. It's a political decision." In Brazil, by 1989 produc-tion had fallen from a mid-1980s high of nearly a hundred films a year to twenty, and drastic deinflationary measures the following year effectively froze production. Mexico had a record-breaking 128 features in 1989, but most of them were low-budget romances and action films for a U.S. Hispanic market. New technologies, especially the VCR, were challenging filmmakers as well ("They've Got" 1990; Meyer 1990).

Desperate filmmakers turned to international coproductions, with varying success. The bastions of international financing for Latin Ameri-can film—European television channels such as France's La Sept, Britain's Channel 4, and Germany's ZDF—were in crisis themselves because of privatization, increased pressure to get advertising dollars and be self-supporting, and the economic changes brought by the process of European unification. Robert Redford's Sundance Institute created great expec-tations and provided some preproduction aid to such filmmakers as Brazilian Suzana Amaral and Argentine Eliseo Subiela, but it could not offer funding (Aufderheide 1990).

Aesthetically, the mandate to find new formal expressions weakened before audiences who could not be assumed to be engaged in resistance, much less revolution. Increasingly, these audiences were ticket-paying family members, expecting nothing more than entertainment. Partly because of the economic crisis and partly because of new video technologies, audiences were declining throughout Latin America (Getino 1989; "Brazil Film" 1990). The VCR and the satellite both made staying home— away from the dangers of street crime, and out of cinemas with poor sound and decaying facilities—an option for those affluent enough to consider viewing entertainment.

Veteran filmmakers took many different routes to reach a changing audience. A few veteran filmmakers began work in video, sometimes under contract to television companies. Brazilian Eduardo Coutinho (*Cabra Marcado para Morrer—Vinte Anos Depois,* 1984 *[Twenty Years Later]*) built on a long-standing relationship with Brazilian television to produce several socially insightful documentaries. Rafael Corkidi, a kind of Mexican John Waters, began making his cult movies on video. In some places, especially in Colombia, filmmakers abandoned cinema for television.

Psychological realism became a defensible style. The Oscar-winning *La Historia Oficial* (1984, Argentina *[The Official Story]*); *O Côr do Seu Destino* (1986, Brazil *[The Color of Destiny]*); *Morir en el Golfo* (1989, Mexico [To Die in the Gulf]); *A Faca dos Dois Gumes* (1989, Brazil [The Two-Sided Knife]); and the Puerto Rican Best Foreign Film nominee for the 1990 Academy Awards *La Historia de Santiago* (1989, Puerto Rico *[Santiago, the Story of His Life]*) all conformed to international commercial cinema conventions, while engaging in provocative, socially critical subject matter.

Some films of the late '80s aggressively maintained the tradition of engaged cultural nationalism. For instance, Bolivian Jorge Sanjinés and Beatriz Palácios' *La Nación Clandestina* (1989 [Clandestine Nation]), the story of an alienated Indian who returns home to die, is a bold metaphor for the alienation of the intellectual from the people. It was phrased in the film language for which Sanjinés has become famous, which he claims is derived from the storytelling practices of highlands Indians. Brazilian Tizuka Yamasaki's *Patriamada* (1984 [Beloved Country Brazil]), setting a soap-opera story within the historic drama of the 1984 Brazilian protest for direct elections, paid homage to postmodern celebrity. It interwove fictional characters and real-life events, using television novela stars who in fact were activists in the movement for direct elections. Mexican Paul Leduc's *Barroco* (1989, Spain/Cuba [Barroco]) attempted to meld opera and MTV in an aural, visual epic tour through Latin

American history. However, such films were atypical, and they have a difficult relationship with Latin American audiences and with international critics. In Brazil, Chile, Peru, and Ecuador among other places in Latin America, highly politicized work was now undertaken primarily in video (see "Grassroots Video in Latin America").

The Cuban government, perceiving New Latin American Cinema as a critical ideological resource, attempted to create or promote institutions that could nurture it. The Foundation for New Latin American Cinema, based in Cuba with international support, was established in 1987 to foster coproductions. The foundation's debut work was the "Dangerous Loves" series of six films—one by a Spanish director, the others by leading New Cinema directors—coproduced by TV Espanola. Each script was taken from a treatment by Gabriel García Márquez and was marked by his dark whimsy. Consistent in high production values, the films were widely uneven in artistic quality. What was distinctive about the series, in terms of New Cinema's traditional rhetoric, was that it was virtually devoid of political or even social themes.

Also launched in the same period was the School of the Three Worlds, the international film school subsidized in-kind by Cuba and based in the hamlet of San Antonio de los Baños outside Havana. The school was intended as a training ground for the New Latin American Cinema film and videomakers of the future and put together four-person production teams from Latin America, Africa, and Asia. It immediately confronted problems that ranged from the diversity of educational backgrounds of the students, to their lack of a shared ideological focus, to serious equipment and staffing problems.

### Crisis of Rhetoric

The 1987 seminar at the Havana festival, celebrating the twentieth anniversary of the 1967 film festival held in Viña del Mar, Chile provided a moment of often anguishing reflection on the direction of Latin cinema. The 1967 festival had marked the self-awareness of an international film movement then generating some of the most remarkable film work anywhere, by such internationally renowned figures as Fernando Birri, Glauber Rocha, Nelson Pereira dos Santos, Tomás Gutierrez Alea, and Humberto Solás. The festival's tone was marked by its honorary president: Che Guevara, then attempting to foment insurrection in the Bolivian highlands (seven months later he was captured and killed). The 1987 debate openly raised the question of this movement's historicity and its legacy. Had New Latin American Cinema achieved its objectives? Was it still alive?

As U.S. film theorist Julianne Burton noted in the seminar, this debate was part of a process:

> This 20-year marker has also brought us to the hour of historical re-visionism with its incitement to question accepted chronologies and catalogues of influence. All this is a natural if not inevitable part of the process of institutionalization of the New Latin American Cinema as an historical phenomenon, cultural movement, socio-political practice, and archive of visual and historical-critical artifacts. (1987, 5)

If a natural process, it was also a painful one for the veterans of the movement, whose mature work now appears jeopardized for lack of an explicitly politicized context. Perhaps most poignant was the opening statement, by the doyen of the movement, Cuban Alfredo Guevara, once head of the Cuban film institute and himself a casualty of internal politicking within the Cuban film community.

He spoke first of the vision of 1967. "We did not see any possible contradiction between art and militancy," although militancy, he said, did not mean orthodoxy. "The blood of Che made history anew, purified the word militant, and allowed New Latin American Cinema . . . to remake the sacred nexus between militancy and poetry." But it was time to ask, he said, "What have we done? What are we doing with our work?" Pointedly, he asked Cubans in particular to consider if current and future work could maintain the dialectical energy that top-down leadership *(dirigismo)* often suppressed or deformed. He called not just for celebration but a critical approach (Guevara 1988, 7–9).

Mexican filmmaker and distributor Jorge Sanchez promptly delivered just such a criticism. Sanchez was also a movement veteran and a member of the Comité de Cineastas Latinoamericanos (Committee of Latin American Filmmakers), founded in 1974 and composed of New Latin American Cinema leaders. He stood up promptly on the close of Guevara's remarks. "Alfredo, you talk of a nexus between militancy and aesthetics," he said. "But the political vanguard doesn't even exist now. Not only is it not like 1967, but there is no coherent left vision in Latin America, except in Cuba. It is a moment that is full of contradictions. What happens to that nexus then?"

Sanchez had posed the issue at the theoretical base of the movement. Guevara's response only underlined the seriousness of Sanchez's question. He began by acknowledging the comment, then simply denied the problem:

The desire for social transformation in Latin America has been convert-
ed into pure rhetoric. . . . There was a moment of unity between the individual and the nation. At Viña del Mar we discovered a great common-
ality among our attempts to express ourselves individually. Militancy
was part of the historical moment, not of a party line. You say that today
there is no political vanguard. But I think there is a filmic vanguard,
through New Latin American Cinema. An artistic vanguard can exist
even if a political vanguard cannot support it. It is a signal that a political
vanguard will emerge; they do not have to exist in perfect linkage.

This set off a heated debate about the success and legacy of New Latin
American Cinema. The debate was in part programmed, since speakers
had been selected by the festival committee to make formal presentations. It was also marked by vociferous interventions, some by those who
felt they deliberately had been excluded from the platform and some by
those who simply saw an opportunity to frontally engage debate. Each
session was well attended and eagerly followed from the floor.

Some panelists offered up optimistic, righteous platitudes about past
achievements (Littin 1988b). Others asked the group to rethink cultural
autonomy in a new era. Proposing that a pan–Latin American TV channel be set up along with a frank acknowledgment of entertainment cinema's primacy, critic Carlos Rebolledo argued passionately, "For aesthetic,
moral, and historical reasons, we cannot continue deceiving ourselves
with an alternative, sporadic, and unequally national cinema. Either we
definitively enter the world of the Spectacle, or we are stuck lagging behind in a trivial farce" (Rebolledo 1988, 78). Then there were the deliberately impious remarks of a Colombian student at the newly launched
international film school, a school that had been launched by New Latin
American Cinema veterans who hoped to grow a new generation of
filmic activists. "I don't even understand this talk of the legacy of New
Latin American Cinema," the student said from the floor. "I haven't seen
most of these films; they're not my model. My job is to figure out how to
make something that will reach people today."

While virtually no one denied that there was a crisis of mission, there
was little agreement as to where the blame lay. Sanjinés denounced filmmakers who strayed from the politically engaged art of 1967: "Many
propose or produce a sell-out cinema under the misguided justification
that the important thing is to 'occupy the screens,' as if the remedy for
prostitution were to prostitute yourself!" He called for a reinvigoration
of the original mandate of New Latin American Cinema, a mandate he

continues to observe: "To make a good Latin American cinema, as I understand it, it is not enough to know how to tell a story well in the European or American style. . . . anti-imperialism, in our cinema, will reveal itself by . . . affirming our *Cultural Identity*" (1988, 55, 60). Chilean filmmaker Miguel Littin, on the other hand, skirted the question of production and simply denounced U.S. control of film distribution, in a kind of flashback to dependency theory (1988a).

Cuban cultural ministry official and filmmaker Julio García Espinosa, author of the famed 1969 polemic "For an Imperfect Cinema" (Chanan 1983), described the divisions within the seminar participants as between the "apocalyptics" and the "integrationists." Calling in his written speech for a focus that could transcend these divisions, he celebrated "quality" and "diversity," then returned to a traditional theme: "We must defend art that is both militant and poetic, the art of those who defend the legitimate interests of their people. That is our position, and the one that comes out of Viña del Mar" (1988, 140–41). However, he also admitted, with remarkable candor, from the platform, "We've never been further away from a link to the public. We once had it, and we need to find new languages to remake it."

This problem was not simply with national Latin American audiences but also with international audiences, both within and beyond Latin America. Historically, serious Latin American cinema had faced a modest reception outside its nation of origin within Latin America. However, in the international circuit crucial for preproduction funds and for international prestige, the Latin American cinema that has received accolades has been that most closely associated with the New Cinema mandate and with a sharply social edge.

Manuel Pérez Estremera from Spain argued that a viable Latin American cinema would always be rooted in the mandate of the New Cinema. He reminded participants that "the little Latin American cinema that has been shown outside the continent has at base the dignity and humanist realism that characterized the movement from its origins. . . . With its advantages and dangers, Latin American cinema is identified with New Latin American Cinema." However, over time, "the search for a bigger public; the setting of a minimal standard for theme, narrative and production standards and the search for foreign markets" had taken Latin cinema "away from its thematic and narrative roots" (1988).

Moreover, he said, foreign commercial markets were effectively closed, both for economic reasons and because of the diversity of Hispanic cultures internationally. But for what small niche-market openings there were, he proclaimed optimistically, Latin American cinema could offer "variety, imagination, history, original and popular literary achievements, political and ethical engagement, youth, self-criticism, expressive rigor, analysis of one's own identity and low costs." Latin American cinema needed, he insisted, to stress its peculiar advantages and cultivate its own youth to express them (1988, 115, 118, 120). Thus, Pérez Estremera's remarks argued that in international venues the cultural nationalism, locally expressed, of the New Cinema was its only market edge.

In these discussions, dominated by the veterans of New Latin American Cinema, many of whom were raising painful questions of the legacy of their movement in public for the first time, there was no evidence of a reevaluation of the achievements of the early years of New Latin American Cinema. However, at screenings of the early work, informal and sometimes harsh commentaries suggested that such a reevaluation was beginning.

Perhaps the person who most succinctly, and painfully, signaled the rhetorical and ideological crisis was Mexican filmmaker Paul Leduc, noted for his *John Reed, Insurgent Mexico* and *Frida*. In a speech he labeled, tongue in check, "reactionary," and frankly called "apocalyptic," he described the vast changes in the cultural importance of film since the '60s. He attributed these partly to technology and economic crisis, partly to the falling away of filmmakers from their mission:

> The postmodern has come to our pre-modern countries, after plagues, earthquakes, dictatorships, devaluations, silicon chips, VHS, closing down of theaters, the disappearance of 16mm, lack of markets, Rambos and Rockys. . . .
>
> Poverty has grown and multiplied, and we filmmakers have acted as if it had all been a nightmare that already had passed, and we gave up caffeine and reality in the cinema because there was no longer a way to go on repeating ourselves and because everybody already knew it and besides it didn't do anybody any good to go on repeating ourselves and because although it's all true, we were distancing ourselves from everything, from reality. And so today's cinema no longer hurts, no longer speaks, no longer makes us laugh, gives us information, variety or taste. And then we are surprised that the theaters are empty. (Leduc 1988, 22–23)

He then proposed a solution of sorts:

> At the risk of seeming a demagogue, . . I believe there is one, difficult path to follow: quality, in its most complex and strict sense.

Not only the "well-done," but the search for roots, for the audacity, for the pleasure of doing it. Affirming our culture and our language. Daring the encounter with our originality—and with reality, the profound relationship with what happens to us and what entertains, afflicts or liberates us. That is what informed New Latin American Cinema when it began, and in many cases has been forgotten. . . .

Beyond individual efforts, we must stress collective efforts, especially now that we have the means—especially the International School of Film and TV, the Foundation for New Latin American Cinema, and the possibility (I would say, obligation) to form national foundations to support and demand the best from them. (24–26)

His conclusion—delivered in an epilogue not reproduced in the printed volume of seminar papers—offered a kind of desperate hope:

A certain idea of cinema, which ruled when we set out on this road, today is a dead idea and a closed road. . . . [But] the European auteur cinema . . . died with Tarkovsky. . . . The great American cinema . . . died with John Huston—because Coppola, Pollack and Jim Jarmusch are already something else. They are exceptions and before they would have been artisans, parts of a great apparatus. . . . Disposable cinema . . . is gaining ground. Television requires us to renounce too much. . . .

Yet even so, our children want to follow in our footsteps. . . .

Cinema, the cinema we always knew, is a dinosaur becoming extinct; but the lizards and salamanders that survived the catastrophe are beginning to appear. We need to see how they did it. . . . We need solidarity and collective action. . . . We must rescue from Viña del Mar the principle of organization, and of course we have to use, as are already being used, the VHS, JVC, NTSC and TBC, the satellites, the computers and cable. . . .

Dinosaur cinema is extinct.

Long live the cinema of the lizards!

Long live the salamander cinema! (Leduc 1987, 1–2)

Leduc's remarks struck a chord with many, both veterans and a younger generation, although his manifest tone of grief also irritated some. "We can be proud of what we've done," said veteran *cinema novo* (New Cinema) director Walter Lima Jr. (*Menino de Engenho*, 1965 *[Plantation Boy]*; *Chico Rei*, 1980–85 [The Little King]), whose sensual fairy tale from the Amazon, *Ele, O Boto*, 1986 (The Dolphin), opened the 1987 festival. "But I'm tired of listening to discussions that look at the present through the eyes of the past. There's only one way to the future—risk living in the present." In a less sanguine moment, however, Lima had professed himself demoralized, and cinema "impossible," because of economic conditions. When I asked him why it was more impossible now than in the grim economic conditions in which *cinema novo* flourished, he said, "Because then we still believed in alternatives. Now we no longer even have the comfort of a left ideology. We no longer have a vision."

The "cinema of the lizards" was represented at the 1987 festival by students at the international film school. Some of the students' short films attempted to use the language of MTV and expressed their desire to *épater les socialistes* (shock the socialists) with sexual themes and questions that unnerved Cuban officials, such as what Cubans thought would happen after Fidel leaves power. However, the students were also frustrated by the hard economic (and indirectly political) questions of distribution, where the problems of relationship with the audience become acute.

The 1987 seminar was a grim memorial service for an epoch, although both debate and speechmaking clearly demonstrated that the fundamental rhetoric of cultural nationalism had not been abandoned. Instead, speakers argued one way or another, it was necessary to translate that same ideology into new modes of expression and transmission.

## Recuperating a Legacy

The 1989 Havana festival provided some clues about the redefinition of Latin American cinema in a postmilitant era. For the first time at the festival that had come to be the central site of pan–Latin American film debate, the continent's commercial film history was publicly examined and even celebrated. A history that had long been made a villain in the drama of New Latin American Cinema's evolution was, in small measure, recuperated. It was now described as another, less articulated, but nonetheless authentic expression of cultural autonomy. A festival sidebar showcased films from the '30s, '40s, and '50s, when Latin American studios cranked out formula films and created stars like Dolores del Río, Maria Félix, and Niñon Sevilla; and an accompanying seminar provided a forum to recontextualize them. Among the showcased artists was Rita Montaner, the Cuban beauty who, after making several films in Cuba, continued her career in Mexico. Her films had long been shelved, although clearly not forgotten by the Cuban audiences that packed the cinema.

That era had long represented, for festival organizers and movement leaders, a cinema held ideologically and formally hostage to Hollywood. At the 1987 seminar, Julio García Espinosa had taken the trouble to remind participants:

Why did we call it *New* Latin American Cinema? We were disappointed—as the young filmmakers of today have been disappointed by us. However, we were disappointed by what the cinema of Mexico and Argentina was in the 1940s. Fundamentally, what it was doing was creating a vernacular version of the worst codes of Hollywood, and opening doors to the worst kind of pseudoculture. We had to fight with our films, not to copy the codes of that cinema. That was the cornerstone of our New Latin American Cinema—it was valid then, and I think it's valid today.

At a 1989 press conference opening the film festival, García Espinosa again warned sternly, "Let's not sink into cheap nostalgia. We must not forget why we have worked thirty years against this kind of cinema."

Cuban cinematheque director Hector García Mesa, who had wanted to do the retrospective for many years and only now had been able to launch it, and who had planned (before his January 1990 heart attack) a much bigger one for the international conference of film archivists held in Havana in April 1990, saw the retrospective as an ideological breakthrough within the often moralistic ideology of Cuba. "Perestroika happens, whether you want it to or not. It's happening all over the world, and here it started in the La Rampa Theater [where the retrospective took place]," he said privately, with comic hyperbole.

Both in press conferences and in the movie houses, nostalgia and celebrity fascination rivaled critical analysis. For instance, Ana Luisa Peluffo, hardly a grande dame—she made her reputation in cheap Mexican sex comedies of the '50s—arrived to a press conference packed with fans, some of them Cuban directors. "You were part of my adolescent fantasies!" the notorious bad-boy Cuban director Luis Felipe Bernaza blurted out. There was ample nostalgia in packed movie houses, for classics such as Mexican director Emilio Fernández's *Las Abandonadas* (1944 [The Abandoned Women]), starring Dolores del Río as the ultimate mother-whore; and the Cuban love story *Romance del Palmar* (1938 [A Rural Tale]), in which Rita Montaner leaves the farm to become a Havana nightclub singer.

The films raised again the question for filmmakers of reaching the audience, and the once-heretical notion was voiced that this language was legitimate because it was effective. "These studio films may have been trite in some ways, but they sure got people's attention, and you can't just write that off," said one student at the international film school.

At the seminar, commercial cinema was given serious historical treatment, sometimes as a recovery of a history of attempts to confront foreign cultural and economic domination. It was organized, as usual, with a series of programmed panels with formal presentations. In this seminar, in contrast to 1987, interventions were not as passionate, nor was attendance as universal, reflecting a shift toward a focus on critical perspectives of the past, rather than on discussion of an embattled present and its implications of judgment on principal speakers. Nonetheless, the discussions had implications for future trends. They pointed toward a recovery of the value of commercial cinema, resituated in terms of cultural nationalism.

Formal presentations largely evidenced a documentary sobriety, carefully justified in terms not only of historical accuracy but also in opposition to the simplistic notion that Latin commercial cinema was merely a cheap copy of Hollywood. José Agustín Mahieu (1989) presented a sober overview of Argentine commercial cinema, including much economic data on audiences, and José Martinez Suarez (1989) summarized the role of the star in the Argentine system as a strategy to compete with Hollywood. Marco Julio Liñares (1989) summarized the history of Mexican studios as a history of struggle against cultural imperialism. Seminar presenters also analyzed popular commercial films, stars, and formulas and proposed analysis in a critical theory or reception mode. For instance, Argentine critic Sylvia Oroz (1989) charted images of women in commercial Latin American cinema as reflections of the social and economic texture of the times, suggesting inter alia that even patriarchal images could be read in different and even empowering ways by particular audiences.

Cuban critic Reynaldo González offered a reassessment of the popular Latin American form of melodrama, with its origins in radio. Pointing to its vast audience and powerfully affective formulas, he noted:

> The link that the formal modes of expression had with their content and the communication they knew how to establish deserve study. Our grandparents recommended not throwing out the baby with the bathwater. And we as well are obliged to reconsider in detail this undeniable communication of filmic melodrama, this "conquest" of a language for certain specific objectives. Clearly, today we propose new contents, but have we offered new forms? . . . These celluloid tears may be hiding as well the lesson, the moral of the tale. (González 1989, 5–6)

Tomás Pérez Turrent, a scholar of Mexican cinema and scriptwriter (*Canoa* 1975 [Canoa]), pointedly put the case for reconsidering commercial cinema of the past. He summarized the troubled history of

Mexican commercial production. The success of Mexican cinema during the World War II period had to do, he said, not only with peculiar economic circumstances of the war but also because

> Mexican cinema knew how to establish and sustain a contact with its public, a popular audience that . . . wanted to see its own images with which it could identify. Here we pose a question of the search for a common identity that the Mexican cinema of those years developed, assuredly in the same way that Moliere's *bourgeois gentilhomme* spoke in prose: without knowing it, without being conscious of it. The Mexican cinema of those years established a contact with its public that it has not been able to establish since and that no "New Latin American Cinema" has achieved (and this contact has not been lost, at least in Mexico, if we note what has happened with the projection of these films of the 1930s, 1940s and 1950s on television . . .). . . . In spite of its tendency to copy and adapt Hollywood models, it created its own images, cultural archetypes and genres such as melodrama (and Mexican melodrama has nothing to do with Italian or Hollywood melodrama) or the *comedia ranchera* [Mexican cowboy films], with the result that a good part of our continent (including the Hispanic minorities of the United States) feels itself united by a common cultural bond. In Mexico the only thing that the various films of the period 1973–77 have achieved is to reconquer a broad public of the urban middle class, which it has newly lost and which no longer watches Hollywood products either.
>
> Although today's circumstances are very different from those of the 1940s and 1950s, would it not be useful to break with the negative attitudes profoundly linked with the moment of judging the "old" cinema? Would it not be productive to pause a moment to reflect and seriously study past experiences? I leave this question open. (Pérez Turrent 1989, 12–13)

Pérez Turrent's question functioned as a kind of legitimating signal, permitting acknowledgment of existing critical work and encouraging more of it. It articulated a growing trend. Critics and academics, including Pérez Turrent himself, had already begun to reconsider the pre–New Latin American Cinema legacy, and a sizable body of pre–New Latin American Cinema history existed in far-flung publishing venues throughout Latin America, in several languages. Film research in the 1990s would take it much further (Burton-Carvajál, Torres, and Miquel, 1998). U.S. academic Carl Mora had noted years before the pretensions of New Latin

American Cinema rhetoricians to eradicate the past, and the need to understand that movement's continuities with it:

> The idea that often is found in writings on the New Latin American Cinema—that militant or revolutionary filmmaking owes nothing to the commercial cinema of Mexico, Argentina, and Brazil—is belied by the frequent denunciations of this "old" cinema by proponents of the new. . . . the militant cineastes are reacting not only against all the perceived evils and injustices of their societies but also to both the Latin American and Hollywood movies they saw in their youth. The New Latin American Cinema has its inspirational roots in the commercial Latin American movie industries, especially Mexico's, even if only in rejection of the latter. (Mora 1982, 3)

That argument had finally breached the fortress of ideological correctness, the traditional Havana film festival seminar.

Latin American filmmakers entered the unforgiving, increasingly international marketplace of the 1990s without the protection of ideological mission or, in many cases, the soft cushion of subsidy. Cuban support for pan–Latin American cinema faded; the Havana festival shrunk, as did the school, and the foundation abandoned projects. The international commercial environment was not kind to sporadic, uneven, national production from any part of the globe, much less the perpetually underresourced Latin countries. The one astonishing international success story in film—the Mexican production *Like Water for Chocolate*— put a commercial gloss on the magical realist style that had been one of the experimental modes of New Latin American Cinema. Manuel Pérez Estremera's astute comments about the unique selling advantages of Latin American cinema seemed borne out.

The Havana debates of the late 1980s demonstrated not only an ideological crisis, but also—if sometimes bitterly—the importance of the sense of mission that had been at the heart of the New Latin American Cinema. Without it and the political movements within which it occurred, filmmakers found themselves either dying dinosaurs or lizards scurrying for survival.

## Note

Julianne Burton-Carvajál, Alan O'Connor, Ella Shohat, Eric Smoodin, the editors of the *Quarterly Review of Film and Video*, and the late and much missed Paul Lenti were helpful in preparing this article. Film titles are offered in their language of origin, often as entered in the Festival of New Latin American Cinema in Havana, Cuba, and so recorded in Teresa Toledo, *Diez Años del Nuevo Cine Latinoamericano* (Spain: Verdoux, S.L., Sociedad Estatal Quinto Centenário, and Cinemateca de Cuba, 1990). English translations are offered, italicized when titles are those used in U.S. distribution and not italicized when translated by the author, usually guided by translations most commonly used in international festivals.

## References

Agustín Mahieu, J. 1989. "Imagines del pasado: Panorama del cine argentino anos 30, 40 y 50" (Images of the past: A panorama of Argentine cinema of the '30s, '40s and '50s). Presented at Seminário de Cine Latinamericano, anos 30-40-50.

Armes, R. 1987. *Third World Film Making and the West.* Berkeley and Los Angeles: University of California Press.

Aufderheide, P. 1990. "Cuba's Conundrum." *In These Times,* January 10–16, p. 24.

"Brazil Film Bux Up, Tix Down." 1990. *Variety,* April 11, p. 72.

Burton, J. n.d. (1985). "Film Artisans and Film Industries in Latin America, 1956–1980: Theoretical and Critical Implications of Variations in Modes of Filmic Production and Consumption." Working Paper no. 102, The Wilson Center Latin American Program.

———. 1986. *Cinema and Social Change in Latin America: Conversations with Filmmakers.* Austin: University of Texas Press.

———. 1987. "The Next Tango in Finland: Visual Media and Models of Transculturation." Presented at the seminar El Nuevo Cine Latinoamericano en el Mundo de Hoy, Havana, December.

Burton-Carvajál, J., P. Torres, and A. Miquel, eds. 1998. *Horizontes del segundo siglo: Investigación y pedagogía del cine mexicano, latino-americano y chicano* (Horizons of the second century: Research and teaching in Mexican, Latin American, and Chicano cinema). Guadalajara and Mexico City: University of Guadalajara CIEC and Imcine.

Chanan, M., ed. 1983. *Twenty-Five Years of the New Latin American Cinema.* London: British Film Institute/Channel 4 Television.

Fundación Mexicana de Cineastas. 1988. *Hojas de cine: Testimónios y documentos del Nuevo Cine Latinoamericano,* 3 vols. (Pages from the movies: Statements and documents of the New Latin American Cinema). Mexico: Universidad Autónoma Metropolitana, Fundación Mexicana de Cineastas, Colección Cultura Universitária Serie/Ensayos.

García Espinosa, J. 1988. "El nuevo cine latinoamericano en el mundo de hoy"

(The New Latin American Cinema in today's world). In *El nuevo cine latino-americano en el mundo de hoy,* 137–43. Mexico: Universidad Nacional Autónoma de Mexico.

Getino, O. 1987. *Cine latinoamericano: Economia y nuevas technologias audio-visuales* (Latin American cinema: Economy and new audio-visual technologies). Havana, Mérida: Fundación de Nuevo Cine Latinamericano, Universidad de los Andes.

———. 1989. *Datos preliminares sobre el espacio audiovisual latinoamericano* (Preliminary conclusions on Latin American audiovisual space). Presented at Latin American Video Encounter, Cochabamba, Bolivia.

González, R. 1989. *Lágrimas de celuloide: Una nueva lectura para el melodrama cinematográfico latinoamericano* (Celluloid tears: A new reading of Latin American movie melodramas). Presented at Seminário de Cine Latin-americano, anos 30-40-50.

Guevara, A. 1988. "Reflexion nostalgica sobre el futuro" (A nostalgic reflection about the future). In *El nuevo cine latinoamericano en el mundo de hoy,* 7–9. Mexico: Universidad Nacional Autónoma de Mexico.

King, J. 1990. *Magical Reels: A History of Cinema in Latin America.* London: Verso.

Leduc, P. 1987. "Epilogo que intenta ser optimista" (An epilogue that tries to be optimistic). Unpublished manuscript.

———. 1988. "Nuevo cine latinoamericano y reconversion industrial (una tesis reaccionaria)" (New Latin American Cinema and industrial reengineering [a reactionary thesis]). In *El nuevo cine latinoamericano en el mundo de hoy,* 15–26. Mexico: Universidad Nacional Autónoma de Mexico.

Liñares, M. J. 1989. "Los estúdios charubusco e azteca, testigos de la história (en las Galapagos Darwin tuvo razon)" (The Charubusco and Azteca movie stu-dios, witnesses to history [in the Galapagos, Darwin was right]). Presented at Seminário de Cine Latinamericano, anos 30-40-50.

Littin, M. 1988a. "El cine latinoamericano y su publico" (Latin American cinema and its public). In *El nuevo cine latinoamericano en el mundo de hoy,* 41–46. Mexico: Universidad Nacional Autónoma de Mexico.

———. 1988b. "Viña del Mar 1967, Alfredo Guevara, Aldo Francia: El nuevo cine de American Latina" (Viña del Mar 1967, Alfredo Guevara, Aldo Francia: The New Latin American Cinema). In *El nuevo cine latinoamericano en el mundo de hoy,* 27–40. Mexico: Universidad Nacional Autónoma de Mexico.

Martinez Suarez, J. 1989. "Los estúdios cinematograficos argentinos y el star-system" (The Argentine film studios and the star system). Presented at Seminário de Cine Latinamericano, anos 30-40-50.

Meyer, N. E. 1990. "Dizzy Biz in Argentina: Money on a Roller-Coaster." *Variety,* April 11, p. 67.

Mora, C. 1982. *Mexican Cinema: Reflections of a Society 1896–1980.* Berkeley and Los Angeles: University of California Press.

Oroz, S. 1989. "La Mujer en el cine latinoamericano (decadas de 1930-40-50)" (Women in Latin American cinema [in the '30s, '40s and '50s]). Presented at Seminário de Cine Latinamericano, anos 30-40-50.

Pérez Estremera, M. 1988. "Una vision europea pero latina" (A European but Latin vision). In *El nuevo cine latinoamericano en el mundo de hoy,* 115–22. Mexico: Universidad Nacional Autónoma de Mexico.

Pérez Turrent, T. 1989. "Cine mexicano, público y mercados extranjeros." Presented at Seminário de Cine Latinamericano, anos 30-40-50.

Rebolledo, C. 1988. "Hacia la universalización de nuestra identidad: Tema de reflexión y de accion" (Toward the universalization of our identity: A theme for reflection and action). In *El nuevo cine latinoamericano en el mundo de hoy,* 71–79. Mexico: Universidad Nacional Autónoma de Mexico.

Sanjinés, J. 1988. "El perfil imborrable" (The unforgettable outline). In *El nuevo cine latinoamericano en el mundo de hoy,* 53–61. Mexico: Universidad Nacional Autónoma de Mexico.

Schumann, P. 1987. *História del cine latinoamericano* (History of Latin American cinema). Buenos Aires: Cine Libre/Legasa.

Solanas, F., and O. Getino. 1976. "Towards a Third Cinema." In *Movies and Methods,* ed. Bill Nichols, 44–64. Berkeley and Los Angeles: University of California Press.

"They've Got a Lotta Vid Decks in Brazil." 1990. *Variety,* April 11, p. 67.

# Grassroots Video

# in Latin America

*For years, as I followed Latin American cinema, I had seen video production developing as a cheaper alternative for filmmakers, and as a tool for organizers. When I returned to Brazil for a year on a Fulbright grant in 1995, I eagerly pursued the thread of this story, to find out how people were using new tools for social action.*

Latin American grassroots or "popular" video has been heralded for its possibilities for social mobilization and information equity, long-standing issues in development communication (Atwood and McAnany 1986; Hamelink 1983; Mowlana and Frondorf 1992). And it spread rapidly, with the rise of the VCR internationally, in the 1980s. Its use in the 1980s and 1990s suggests, however, that it played neither the liberating nor demonic role often assigned to new media technologies. It has, instead, often been a useful strategic tool, both on and off air, when used in conjunction with social organizing. Privatization and the end of welfare-state strategies, however, imperiled many of the video organizations established in the past two decades of the twentieth century.

## Growing from the Grass Roots

The boom in grassroots video in Latin America shared a much longer tradition of "alternative," usually oppositional media (Reyes Matta 1986).

Video production accompanied the rapid growth of VCR ownership, often with loosening of import rules for consumer electronics. Hundreds of centers of production bloomed, particularly in Brazil, Argentina, Peru, Mexico, Ecuador, Bolivia, Venezuela, Uruguay, Colombia, and Chile, with work ranging from union documentaries to church video newsletters and indigenous documentation of ceremonies (Ranucci 1989; Santoro 1989a, 59–94). In many countries, video organizations were associated with political or social causes, for example, feminist organizations such as CineMujer in Colombia and Lilith in Brazil (Burton and LeSage 1988). Socially conscious independents often worked in tandem with issue organizations, such as the Chilean Women for Life, family members of "disappeared" persons.

The most elaborate single institution for grassroots video in Latin America in the 1980s and early 1990s was the Brazilian organization TV dos Trabalhadores, or Workers' TV, founded by media activists Luis Fernando Santoro and Regina Festa. Created in 1986 by the powerful autoworkers' union headed by Luis Ignacio da Silva (Lula), Workers' TV produced sometimes broadcast-quality works, training tapes, documents of speeches and events, and also has an archive containing off-air and other stock footage. Its projects built on member enthusiasm. During a 1986 general strike in Brazil, the Workers' TV project suddenly found videotapes flooding in from union groups nationwide. Members had documented local strike events and hoped to see what was happening in other areas of the country. Initially surprised by the spontaneous outpouring, Workers' TV members edited the tapes into a single video. An interunion confederation then distributed it to members, circumventing commercial TV news (Santoro 1989a, 74–75).

The first developed network of video producers, the Associação Brasileiro de Video no Movimento Popular (ABVP), also began in Brazil. Founded in 1984 and including some forty groups, it was born out of the videotaping of the founding of the Central Única dos Trabalhadores (CUT, an interunion confederation opposing the state-run union system) (Santoro 1989a, 68). Other formal organizations were founded in Peru, Argentina, Bolivia, Ecuador, and Mexico, as well as informally in Chile and Uruguay. In Peru video centers grew out of long-standing educational work in video done by nongovernmental agencies in both rural and urban areas (Peirano 1985); a databank, Videored, established by the Instituto para America Latina (Thede and Ambrosi 1992, 224), was also established. Uruguayan video centers proliferated, involving members both in production and viewing. Even in countries where audiovisual production of any kind was very limited, such as Paraguay, video festivals showcasing independent video were being held by the beginning of the 1990s (Dinamarca 1991, 121–36).

Film festivals began to incorporate video—at the New Latin American Film Festival in Havana, the Guadalajara Book Fair in Mexico, the Gramado and Bahia festivals in Brazil, the Viña del Mar festival in Chile, and the Cartagena Film Festival in Colombia. Regional conferences and video festivals were held in Santiago in 1988, in Cochabamba in 1989, and in Montevideo in 1990 (Santoro 1991). Producers' networks emerged from these interchanges; indeed, some Latin American producers were incorporated into global video networks. For instance, Vidéazimut, with its head in Montréal, Canada, is a coalition of organizations from Africa, Asia, Latin America, Europe, and North America.

Institutions were crucial to this grassroots video boom. In several countries, including Brazil, Ecuador, Colombia, and Chile, the Catholic Church provided funds, in-kind resources, and spaces to show work (Santoro 1989a, 83–94). Several nations, including Chile and Brazil, mandated public channels (Dinamarca 1991, 151–53; Aufderheide 1997). Universities were also important bases. In Bolivia, for example, some universities ran television channels (Dinamarca 1991, 123–24). Film schools have also been important training sites. Many aspiring video-makers came out of the activist-oriented International School of Film and Television located in San Antonio de los Baños, Cuba, which has drawn students from throughout Latin America as well as a few from Asia and Africa. Other film schools such as the Mexican Centro de Capacitación Cinematográfica and the Guadalajara University School of Video have trained people who have returned to community and organizing settings with their skills.

International liaisons were also important in this growth (Thede and Ambrosi 1992). Nongovernmental organizations (NGOs) such as the Canadian Vidéo Tiers-monde and the Italian Centro Internazionale Crocevia shared expertise and resources. Northern NGOs concerned with social issues such as maternal health and the environment have supported video work on their causes. The Rockefeller Foundation invested in bolstering Latin American video, along with the MacArthur Foundation, throughout the 1980s and 1990s. International aid and development organizations, governmental and nongovernmental, have also invested in grassroots video.

Such video was used for practicing public speaking and other performances; documentation; documentaries; fiction; and critical viewing, or using commercially produced work to stimulate analysis of media (Santoro 1989a, 97–98). Unions and social organizations developed extensive archives of meetings, demonstrations, and other functions. The highly organized poor neighborhood of Villa El Salvador in Lima, Peru, for instance, has a historical archive on video (Roncagliolo 1992, 27).

Video built on the experience of the politicized "alternative cinema," *nuevo cine* (New Cinema), which had its heyday in the 1960s and early 1970s (see "New Latin American Cinema Reconsidered"). In Chile in the late 1970s, for instance, an underground VCR network showed banned works such as the New Cinema epic documentary of the decline and fall of the Allende government, *Battle of Chile*, by Patricio Guzmán and other works by Latin American New Cinema filmmakers, in community centers, churches, union halls, and social clubs. Gradually, news reports, documentaries, and critiques of official news circulated on underground networks, sometimes moving the equipment as well as the tapes (Guzmán 1985). That network evolved into above-ground production groups, including Teleanálisis and Proceso (Santoro 1989a, 87–88), and fostered more open communication during and after elections in 1989 (Dinamarca 1991, 137–54).

In Brazil, the independent social action video group TV Viva used video for popular education, employing "mobile cinema" strategies pioneered by New Cinema activists. TV Viva made public health documentaries such as *The Condom* and analytical documentaries such as *The Drought*, sharply critical of then-President Collor's handling of social welfare in the drought-afflicted Brazilian northeast. Members of the group, working with other social action groups or agencies, would show the tapes to groups of one hundred to two hundred people in the countryside, holding discussions afterward (Di Tella 1992, 45).

From the mid-1980s to the mid-1990s, local "street TV" like TV Viva became a feature of urban life in poor neighborhoods of several major Brazilian cities (LaSpada 1992). A small team would preproduce some materials and project these segments, along with live discussion and presentations, from trucks in central locations. Often community members were integrated into the production process, either as advisers or as producers. The goal was to stimulate public discussion and through it strengthen community life. Subjects could range from public health (AIDS, malaria, cholera, nutrition) to electoral issues (the importance of not selling your vote, ballot issues such as the creation of a historic district) to cultural performances and recipes. In Rio de Janeiro, TV Maxambombo established a routine of performing several times a month in the Rio suburbs, the notorious Baixada Fluminense. São Paulo's street program, TV Anhembi, launched in 1990. Almir Almas, who ran the São Paulo street TV program for four years, recalls audiences that numbered between one hundred and five hundred people (Almas 1995). In Santarém, in the Amazon basin, TV Mocorongo, begun in 1989, was not "street TV" but "river TV"; members of a nongovernmental organization promoting public health coordinate TV into their river circuits, providing a means of audiovisual exchange of information and perspectives between river communities (Scannavino 1995).

Similar in concept was Waiting Room TV, begun in 1994 and produced in Belo Horizonte, Brazil, and projected in several public health posts with a large turnover, thus reaching thousands of viewers per month. Evolving with local community participation, the show interspersed person-on-the-street interviews (some functioning as advertisements for services) with recipes, public health advice, and short children's programs developed by other independent producers. Community residents began to drop into the clinics just to see the latest monthly installment of this program (Ferreira 1995).

**Not Ready for Prime Time?**

Independent video has always been rare on mainstream television in Latin America, particularly for art-experimental work. Exceptions included the idiosyncratic and diverse productions of the Brazilian Olhar Electrônico (Meirelles and Tas 1988), whose members went on to work in various aspects of commercial television; rural development programs broadcast in indigenous languages in Bolivia and Peru (Roncagliolo 1992, 29); and occasional experiments on cable television, where programmers often seek out a local or regional fillip to an often largely international feed (Burton and LeSage 1988, 228).

Grassroots video, meanwhile, was typically excluded, both from nationalized and private mainstream television. Producers have had more luck launching a video on broadcast outside their own country than within it, since international broadcasting organizations such as the International Broadcasting Trust, Channel 4, and other European broadcasters have commissioned work. Such commissions also have sometimes stimulated international coproductions among Latin American videomakers, including the work of Brazilian Cecilio Neto with Chilean Pablo Basulto, giving producers national prestige (Boero 1992).

In much rarer cases, low-power or other highly local television has provided some access for grassroots producers. ECO-TV was launched by Brazilian social and environmental activists in 1991, with a prehistory dating back to 1978. In four beach communities near Rio de Janeiro with a broadcast audience of 400,000, stations authorized under a peculiar "mixed," public-private arrangement—they are basically retransmitters that are allowed to carry local programming—would share programs related to ecological issues produced at a center in Rio de Janeiro. The effort drew primary funding from the nationalized Brazilian oil company Petrobras, which maintained coastal refineries and drew constant criticism from local communities for them. The service produced a daily, half-hour news show, all done with local reporters, and a ninety-minute talk show. Video in the Villages, a Brazilian project to foment Indian cultural identity through video use, in 1995–1996 produced a monthly, one-hour broadcast program linked with the state university and aired on state educational TV, in the interior state of Mato Grosso. Produced in collaboration with Indians, starring Indians as anchors and subjects, it was called *Programa do Índio.* (Although the translation is "Indians' Program," this is a sly joke, since the term is slang for "a big drag.") The program features snappy graphics, teasers ("Identify this place"), segments that parallel mainstream programming ("Indians Who Get Things Done" takes as its model a popular news segment called "People Who Get Things Done"), cultural information, and hot debates such as ecological damage to Indian lands done by development projects (Bastos 1995).

This, however, was highly atypical. One producer drew a generally applicable distinction between "those who make TV [television] and those who make VT [videotape]" (Waismann 1988, 190), a logical distinction given the norms of the television business. Throughout Latin America, television is still highly centralized, usually private, advertiser driven, and entertainment oriented. It reaches virtually all sectors of the population, typically extending to 80 percent of urbanites (Straubhaar 1996). Its programming is anchored with the immensely popular prime-time *telenovela,* a form that straddles the miniseries and the soap opera. Brazil and Mexico export worldwide, with formats such as variety, music, talk, and comedy shows as well as *novelas.*

Electronic media, one Brazilian scholar says, "has involved the selling of the ideology of consumption for those who can afford it" (Oliveira 1991, 212). Owners and advertisers are at least as powerful as governments in setting agendas; political change has not drastically affected distribution structure or corporate goals. Brazil's TV Globo dominated the market throughout political shake-ups (Straubhaar 1989; Besas 1992) and has now transformed itself into the leading multichannel television provider as well. Even television with strong government participation, such as in Colombia, has a format whose stability derives from advertiser power (Fox and Anzola 1988). Where public or government-sponsored television is an ancillary service, it is often hostage to commercial forces, as happened in Uruguay (Faraone and Fox 1988). Many channels do not necessarily mean increased access. In the 1980s Bolivia had many, virtually unregulated commercial channels, featuring low-quality, sometimes pirated international programming (Rivadeneira Prada 1988).

Latin American television can be rich in wit, social relevance, and national cultural style. Brazilian *novelas* have dealt with bureaucratic corruption, single motherhood, and the environment; class differences are foregrounded in Mexican *novelas,* and Cuba's *novelas* are bitingly topical as well as ideologically correct. Characters, as in U.S. popular culture, are complex cultural artifacts (Mattelart and Mattelart 1990, 82–87). But there is a great gulf between TV and VT producers.

## Ideological Ambition

Grassroots video production evolved within ambitious ideological contexts. Its development, like much of the "alternative" media, was seen by many as part of the attack on transnational and elite control of information (e.g., Schwarz and Jaramillo 1986, 68; Simpson Grinberg 1986). It has also been seen optimistically, as it has in the United States (Paper Tiger 1991), as an example of technology overcoming social constraints, and often with as blind an affection for technology (Blau 1992). Chilean Hernan Dinamarca, for instance, heralds "this process that is democratizing audiovisual communications and recuperating Latin American identity through video," seeing video as "capable of showing the images of a society prohibited from recognizing itself in the electronic circus" (Dinamarca 1991, 74, 116). This focus on promotion of public life directly involves aesthetic issues, he notes, contrasting popular video with crudely commercial Brazilian TV: "The search for a popular language that is not crude, imbecile or manipulative is a very great challenge."

These perspectives partake of a long tradition, analyzed extensively by Latin American communications scholars, of alternative media jockeying for a place on the national informational agenda (Simpson Grinberg 1986). Among the unexamined assumptions that can creep into these perspectives, they note, are the notions that media messages in themselves have the power to liberate (or dupe) and that media production is by definition empowering.

Videomakers have envisioned video with a mission to construct or reconstruct civic and cultural life. In manifestos, producers described video use as "a major initiative of the democratic and participatory use of audiovisual communication" (Anonymous 1987, 1), so that "our people appear at last on the screen as the protagonists of the time in which they live and to which they aspire," as participants at a later meeting declared (Anonymous 1988). Videomakers vowed to "oppose ourselves to neo-colonialist and culture-deforming practices of transnationals . . . and to make video an arm of struggle in the improvement of the social processes that Latin America and the Caribbean are undergoing" (Anonymous 1989).

Claudio Ceccon, executive secretary of the Rio group Centro de Criação de Imagem Popular (Center for the Creation of the Popular Image), describes one of the group's efforts as an attempt to promote civil society:

> The Popular Video Project is an experiment with media usually used to reinforce oppression. Our idea is to use it to respond to questions that commercial mass media seem to be unable to address as they should, such as, Can democratic values be constructed within daily life? Can the experience of popular movements be recognized and become a model for others? (Ceccon n.d., 28)

These statements echo the long-standing rhetoric of New Latin American Cinema and speak most directly to the ambitions and mindset of politically motivated independent producers. New Cinema had upheld the social mission of art, as part of the aesthetic of colonized, neo-colonized, or oppressed peoples of the third or underdeveloped world (Rich 1991; see also "The Crisis of Latin American Cinema").

In a time of collapse of political ideologies and of economic crisis, video became, for some of the old guard of New Cinema, a new hope. Mexican filmmaker Paul Leduc called it "the cinema of the salamanders" succeeding the cinema of the "dinosaurs"—his generation. Brazilian critic Fernão Pessoa Ramos called it "the bastard relative, still not quite of a stature with its cousin," the legatee of "alternative cinema" (Pessoa Ramos 1986). Indeed, many once and future filmmakers and video artists turned to the medium, simply for its affordability (Di Tella 1992), at the same time that nonprofessionals and activists began experimenting with it.

Some video organizers, using that model, have called for government subsidy and support to independent producers, and for independent producers on behalf of silenced majorities to assume the challenge of confronting mainstream media (Santoro 1991; Festa and Santoro 1992;

Roncagliolo 1992). Speaking out of a long tradition of oppositional media, they called for video to transcend its local and grassroots objectives, and to "[conquer] the space of the mass media" (Roncagliolo 1992, 29).

In contrast (but not necessarily in opposition, in practice), others such as Valdeavellano (1989) and Cardoso (1989) argue that the strength of video is in the process, not the product, and that other measures may be more important than impact on television (Fontes 1992). Examples might be the effect on a land rights movement of training videos or documentaries; the strengthening of group solidarity from documenting group events; forging of international relationships; building of civic skills; and decentralized information networks. Some practitioners have asked how dispersed practices can evolve beyond, in the image of one Catholic church organizer, the family-photo-album-and-holiday-slide-show model (Bruce 1991, 88).

The product/process argument is ultimately one of emphasis, with both sides agreeing on the importance of popular participation in production and the utility of video to support goals such as social empowerment of the disenfranchised, diversity of information sources to strengthen democracy, and the growth of an autonomous audiovisual culture.

## Assessing the Value of Video

The history of committed cinema was cautionary for those who dreamed of making inroads into commercial television. Entertainment cinema has always vastly outsold serious filmic expressions such as those of New Cinema. While the "electronic circus" in Latin America may be as vapid and vulgar as anything on North American television, it is also often an indigenous or regional product. People who may want to be "protagonists of the time in which they live and to which they aspire" may not want to do it in prime time.

But in fact, video activists rarely competed for viewer attention with on-air entertainment programming. When they did occasionally get airtime, producers sometimes played cannily on the difference between grassroots and commercial televisual styles and purposes. The television campaign for Brazilian presidential candidate Lula in 1989, conducted under laws that mandated some broadcast time for each major candidate, exemplified the contrast between its candidate and glossier ones. In one ad, a housewife threw candidates into her shopping cart as if they were detergent, then testified from her kitchen sink that Lula worked better than the others. The ad frankly acknowledged the expectations and frameworks of commercial television (and packaged politics) and then manipulated them. Commercials like these were, apparently, an important element in a dramatic increase in voter support for Lula and for other Workers' Party candidates in the 1989 campaign (Santoro 1989b). They went hand in hand, however, with an elaborately organized face-to-face campaign (Straubhaar et al. 1991, 52).

In another Brazilian political campaign, for governor of the state of Acre, small-scale video on air leveraged large-scale political results. Workers' Party candidate Jorge Viana, with almost no public recognition, used government-reserved airtime to challenge a candidate from a right-wing party. This candidate, a rancher, with impressive support in the polls, had invested heavily in high-gloss television. Viana's low-tech ad ridiculed the rancher's grand development schemes. Piqued, the rancher began attacking Viana in his ads. The tactic boomeranged, giving Viana enough support to knock his opponent out of the election (Schwartzman 1992). In both campaigns, low-tech video made it possible to use the available time, but success was defined by the political strategizing that went into the ads' design.

Off-air grassroots video work has had a variety of uses, tied directly to social organizing. For example, during collective bargaining one Brazilian union used unedited videotapes of the bargaining process to educate tens of thousands of massed rank-and-file workers (Fontes 1992, 11). *The Triumph,* a videotape decrying rain-forest destruction made by the Mexican collective Video Servícios, was widely shown by regional environmental groups (Ranucci and Burton 1990, 200). Similarly, the tapes of the Brazilian collective Lilith circulated widely among working women's organizations and unions, with some organizations even creating video lending libraries (Burton and LeSage 1988, 229). Video newsletters have sporadically functioned in several institutional contexts.

Confidence building and community pride were other, self-defined objectives of grassroots video. In Mexico a group of poor housewives resisting evictions worked with producers from Colectivo Cine Mujer to create a short training tape, *Housewives,* in which activists role-play an eviction; they repeatedly used the tape in organizing. Some kinds of events-documentation tapes might have this signal confidence-building utility. Also in Mexico, a Oaxacan village corporately sponsored purchase of a video camera, bought with proceeds from migrant labor in the United States and mastered with the help of independent Mexican videomakers. One product is *Our Cooperative Work Project,* documenting a day of mutual labor to repair a municipal building. In their own community meetings villagers eventually used a much longer version than the ten-minute one available in the United States (Ranucci and Burton 1990). One unusual case, where the social impact was wide ranging, was *Pathway of the Souls*, made in a Bolivian village with the help of independent producers and national and international nongovernmental organizations. Bolivian villagers reenacted the theft and export of ancient weavings with ritual significance. By circumstance a human rights lawyer in the United States saw the video, which apparently was originally made to warn other villages to the possibility of theft. He alerted other professionals, and ensuing legal actions resulted in the discovery and return of some textiles, as well as in tightened U.S. customs procedures (Ranucci 1992). Lowlands Amazonian Indians (see "Making Video with Indians in Brazil") have used videotape for information sharing, organizing, creating a databank, and for building archives of traditional practices.

### The Next Challenge

In the later 1990s, with the reconstruction of relatively open political practices accomplished in many places, economic privatization and a push for internationally open markets followed in Latin America. This happened in tandem with an explosion of new options for communications technology. Cable TV, cell phones, multichannel-multipoint distribution service (MMDS), or "wireless cable," and other innovations brought new consumer choice, and the prospect of decentralizing, democratizing, and diversifying opportunities.

At the same time, however, video activists lost international foundation support and the political and moral high ground of working in "the opposition." Increasingly, their survival strategies needed to include competitive business plans. The marketplace was not forgiving to noncommercial initiatives, and newly open policy processes were also open to highly organized corporate forces.

The Brazilian case was exemplary. The government of Fernando Henrique Cardoso, which took power in January 1995, articulated and began to implement a trend toward privatization, the breakdown of old systems of entitlement, and the encouragement of civil society. As an anchor to this process, the government rigidly controlled inflation and created a strong currency. Nonprofit video producers immediately faced financial crisis, since the Plano Real dramatically reduced the buying power of foreign grants by shrinking the difference between the dollar and local currency.

At the same time, the broad coalition of forces that brought forth democracy and a new constitution fell apart. Some of the Workers' Party governments fell from power, resulting in collapse of ambitious popular video programs. A certain skepticism among international funders about the wisdom of autonomously funding media projects became general. With the departure of Luis Fernando Santoro, who became a political consultant, Workers' TV became a mere service organization for the union. Street TV operations collapsed in Recife and São Paulo. The breakup of Petrobras imperiled ECO-TV. *Programa do Índio* went into hiatus for lack of funding. The ABVP, once an organization most of whose members were representatives of institutions, became an organization largely made up of struggling individual producers. Its video rental business and production workshops failed to cover costs, and it went into hiatus in 1995.

At the same time that economically the movement was thrown into the marketplace, dramatic changes in communications policy promised new opportunities—for those who could mobilize political pressure. In 1995, the Ministry of Communication introduced, for the first time, nonpolitical criteria for electronic media licensing and regulated cable TV. It began to institute enforcement procedures for license renewal. Popular video producers applied pressure on policy makers, on the issues of community low-power TV and cable TV.

The optimistic argument that market values can invigorate public life became, by the end of the 1990s, a necessary article of faith even among grassroots, social-action video producers. For instance, after hosting a demonstration event of community TV, Julio Wainer, the organizer of the workshop and a veteran video activist and teacher, argued to the ministry:

> Community TV stations can be of fundamental importance for local development, not just in social but in economic terms. People who see themselves and recognize themselves on TV (not only on the crime news or during special election programs) have more tools with which to know and value themselves. Community TV . . . can intensify local social relationships, deepen the identity and diversity of our people, and give voice to millions of marginalized Brazilians. . . .
>
> The benefits are many, not only to the community served but also to business people who will have a chance to advertise; to the electronic equipment and maintenance industries; to communications professionals and technicians; to the public, which will have another place to meet and converse; and to students, schools, and businesses in communication, which will have a permanent laboratory. (Wainer 1995)

Unfortunately, far more powerful interests were also lobbying for the ministry's attention; commercial broadcasters succeeded, at least in the short run, in stalling out reform.

Many of the same problems afflicted activism around cable TV. Although powerful commercial interests and conflicts of interest among producers and activists resulted in a minimalist approach to access channels, the law ultimately did set aside channels for governmental, cultural, and educational use (Aufderheide 1997). Funding problems crippled many initiatives, particularly by universities, but one success story was that of TV PUC—the São Paulo Catholic University's attempt to use the educational channel set-aside. It was not, however, one with much good news for grassroots activists. Gabriel Priolli, the veteran journalist who produces the channel, considered the fact that only Brazil's elite can afford cable TV and that they zap between channels and thus adopted a high-culture talk-show format (Priolli 1995).

The democratizers who in the 1980s and 1990s turned to socially committed video faced, by the turn of the century, a grossly unequal race with corporate and political interests that also seized the opportunities offered by open political process and the open market. They also maintained an embattled but persistent vision of grassroots use of audiovisual media, a vision that is likely to be carried into an era of networked communication.

## Note

Patricia Boero, Julianne Burton, Faye Ginsburg, Douglas Gomery, Lawrence Lichty, Stephan Schwartzman, Joseph Straubhaar, and Karen Ranucci helped with information and comments on this article. The Fulbright Commission in Brazil funded visits to Rio de Janeiro, São Paulo, and Curitiba in relation to popular video.

Sources for video include Karen Ranucci, 124 Washington Place, New York, NY 10014, (212) 463-0108; Pedro Zurita, Videoteca del Sur, 512 Broadway, New York, NY 10003, (212) 334-5257; Women Make Movies, 225 Lafayette St., #206–7, New York, NY 10012, (212) 925-0606.

## References

Almas, A. 1995. Personal communication, October 20.

Anonymous. 1987. "A veinte años de Viña del Mar: Por el video y la televisión latinoamericanos" (Twenty years after Viña del Mar: For a Latin American video and television). Presented at the ninth Festival International del Nuevo Cine Latinoamericano, Havana, December.

Anonymous. 1988. "Manifiesto de Santiago" (Manifesto of Santiago). Santiago, Chile: Primer Encuentro Latinoamericano de Video.

Anonymous. 1989. "Encuentro de realizadores" (Meeting of producers). Presented at the eleventh Festival International del Nuevo Cine Latinamericano, Havana, December 12–15.

Atwood, R, and E. G. McAnany. 1986. *Communication and Latin American Society: Trends in Critical Research, 1960–1985.* Madison: University of Wisconsin Press.

Aufderheide, P. 1997. "In Search of the Civic Sector: Cable Policymaking in Brazil, 1989–1996." *Communication Law and Policy* 2 (4): 563–93.

Bastos, G. 1995. "Vincent Carelli dá voz aos índios brasileiros" (Vincent Carelli gives Indians a voice). *O Estado de São Paolo, Caderno Dois,* December 7, p. 1.

Blau, A. 1992. "The Promise of Public Access." *The Independent,* April, pp. 22–26.

Boero, P. 1992. Personal communication, September 1.

Bruce, I. 1991. "Televisión y video popular: Las otras caras del poder" (Television and popular video: The other faces of power). *CEPAE* (Dominican Republic) July–December: 80–89.

Burton, J., and J. LeSage. 1988. Broadcast Feminism in Brazil: An Interview with the Lilith Video Collective." In *Global Television,* ed. C. Schneider and B. Wallis. Cambridge: MIT Press.

Cardoso, R. 1989. "Popular Movements in the Context of the Consolidation of Democracy." Working paper #120, CEBRAP, University of São Paulo, Brazil, March.

Ceccon, C. n.d. "Uma semente em solo fértil" (A seed in fertile soil). *Proposta* 43. Rio de Janeiro: FASE, 26–31. [Author's translation.]

Di Tella, A. 1992. "Video in Latin America." *Review: Latin American Literature and Arts* 46 (Fall): 42–46.

Dinamarca, H. 1991. *El video en America Latina: Actor innovador del espácio audiovisual* (Video in Latin America: Innovative actor in audiovisual space). Santiago, Chile: ArteCien.

Faraone, R., and E. Fox. 1988. "Communication and Politics in Uruguay." In *Media and Politics in Latin America,* ed. E. Fox, 148–56. Newbury Park, Calif.: Sage.

Ferreira, C. 1995. Personal communication, December 15.

Festa, R., and L. Santoro. 1992. "New Trends in Latin America: From Video to Television." In Thede and Ambrosi 1992, 84–93.

Fontes, C. 1992. "Defining Popular Video: Emerging Strategies in Latin America and the United States." Presented at International Association for Mass Communication Research, São Paulo, Brazil, August.

Fox, E., and P. Anzola. 1988. "Politics and Regional Television in Colombia." In *Media and Politics in Latin America,* ed. E. Fox, 82–92. Newbury Park, Calif.: Sage.

Guzmán, P. 1985. "El video, formato o arma: Alternativa popular de la información audiovisual en Chile" (Video, tool or weapon: People's alternative for audiovisual information in Chile). In *Video, cultura nacional y subdesarrollo.* Mexico City: Filmoteca de la UNAM, 55–60.

Hamelink, C. 1983. *Cultural Autonomy in Global Communications: Planning National Information Policy.* New York: Longman.

LaSpada, S. 1992. "Grassroots Video and the Democratization of Communication: The Case of Brazil." Ph.D. diss., Teachers College, Columbia University.

Mattelart, M., and A. Mattelart. 1990. *The Carnival of Images: Brazilian Fiction Television.* New York: Bergin & Garvey.

Meirelles, F., and M. Tas. 1988. "Produção independente—idéias e propostas" (Independent production—ideas and proposals). In *TV ao vivo: depoimentos,* ed. C. Macedo, A. Falcão, C. J. Mendes de Almeida, 173–89. São Paulo: Brasiliense.

Mowlana, H., and M. H. Frondorf. 1992. *The Media as a Forum for Community Building.* Washington, D.C.: Paul H. Nitze School of Advanced International Studies, Johns Hopkins University.

Oliveira, O. S. 1991. "Mass Media, Culture, and Communication in Brazil: The Heritage of Dependency." In *Transnational Communications: Wiring the Third World,* ed. J. Lent and G. Sussman, 200–14). Newbury Park, Calif.: Sage.

Paper Tiger Television Collective. 1991. *ROAR: The Paper Tiger Television Guide to Media Activism.* New York: Paper Tiger Television Collective (339 Lafayette St., New York, NY 10012).

Peirano, L. 1985. *Educación y communicación popular en el Perú* (Education and popular communication in Peru). Lima: Centro de Estúdios y Promoción del Desarrollo, Instituto para America Latina.

Priolli, G. 1995. Personal communication, December 15.

Pessoa Ramos, F. 1986. "Una forma histórica de cinema alternativo e seus dilemas na atualidade" (A historical outline of alternative cinema and its dilemmas in practice). In *Vinte anos de resistencia: Alternativas da cultura no regime militar,* ed. M. A. Mello. Rio de Janeiro: Espaço e Tempo.

Ranucci, K. 1989. *Directory of Film and Video Production Resources in Latin America and the Caribbean.* New York: Foundation for Independent Video and Film.

————. 1992. Personal communication, July 23.

Ranucci, K., and J. Burton. 1990. "On the Trail of Independent Video." In *The Social Documentary in Latin America*, ed. J. Burton. Pittsburgh: University of Pittsburgh Press.

Reyes Matta, F. 1986. "Alternative Communication: Solidarity and Development in the Face of Transnational Expansion." In Atwood and McAnany 1986, 190–214.

Rich, B. R. 1991. "An/Other View of New Latin American Cinema." *Iris* 13: 5–28.

Rivadeneira Prada, R. 1988. "Bolivian Television: When Reality Surpasses Fiction." In *Media and Politics in Latin America*, ed. E. Fox, 164–70. Newbury Park, Calif.: Sage.

Roncagliolo, R. 1992. "The Growth of the Audio-Visual Imagescape in Latin America." In Thede and Ambrosi 1992, 22–30.

Santoro, L. F. 1989a. *A imagen nas mãos: O video popular no Brasil* (An image in the hands: People's video in Brazil). São Paulo: Summus.

————. 1989b. Personal communication, December 10.

————. 1991. "O Video popular no Brasil: A febre e as miragens" (Popular video in Brazil: The fever and the mirages). Unpublished manuscript.

Scannavino, C. 1995. General coordinator, ABVP and director, TV Mocorongo, personal communication, December 15.

Schwarz, C., and S. Jaramillo. 1986. "Hispanic American Critical Communication Research in its Historical Context." In Atwood and McAnany 1986, 48–77.

Schwartman, S. 1992. Personal communication, August 12.

Simpson Grinberg, M. 1986. "Trends in Alternative Communication Research in Latin America." In Atwood and McAnany 1986, 165–89.

Straubhaar, J. D. 1989. "Television and Video in the Transition from Military to Civilian Rule in Brazil." *Latin American Research Review* 24: 140–54.

————. 1996. "Radio and Television in Latin America." In *Encyclopedia of Latin American History*. New York: Charles Scribner's Sons.

Straubhaar, J. D., O. Olsen, and M. Cavallari Nunes. 1991. The Role of Television in the 1989 Brazilian Presidential Election." In *Brazil and Mexico: Contrasting Models of Media and Democratization*, ed. I. Adler et al. Providence, R.I.: Thomas J. Watkins Institute for International Studies, Brown University. Occasional paper #6.

Thede, N., A. Ambrosi. 1992. *Video the Changing World*. Montreal: Black Rose.

Valdeavellano, P. 1989. "América latina esta construyendo su propria imagen" (Latin America is constructing its own image). In *El video en la educacion popular*, ed. P. Valdeavellano, 73–130. Lima: IPAL.

Wainer, J. 1995. "A TV Comunitária de baixa potência: Recado ao Ministério das

Comunicações" (Low-power community TV: A message for the Ministry of Communications). Unpublished manuscript.

Waismann, S. 1988. "Produção independente—idéias e propostas" (Independent production—ideas and proposals). In *TV ao vivo: Depoimentos,* ed. C. Macedo, A. Falcão, C. J. Mendes de Almeida, 189–93. São Paulo: Brasiliense.

# Making Video

# with

# Brazilian Indians

*Vincent Carelli is one of our family's more extraordinary Brazilian friends and colleagues—a photographic artist, an activist for Indian rights, a teacher of video skills to Amazonian Indians. When Video DataBank (VDB) decided to distribute his videos in the United States in the mid-1990s, the distributor wanted to provide some context. VDB's Kate Horsfield asked me to explain, in an essay included with the tapes, what exactly Carelli intended and achieved with these videos, and* Visual Anthropology Review *agreed to publish a version of the article as well.*

Video is a highly prized tool for cultural renewal and communication among Brazil's indigenous groups. About 250,000 Indians—0.2 percent of Brazil's population—live dispersed among 200 societies, in which 170 languages are represented. They are scattered across vast regions of a country the size of the continental United States. They face daily challenges to physical and cultural survival and are constantly confronted—in the media as elsewhere—with images of their technological inferiority and their relative powerlessness in the society (Ricardo 1992).

The Video in the Villages project of the Centro de Trabalho Indigenista (CTI) is the major organization working with Brazilian Indians to register their image and culture on videotape. Because the project both makes videotapes and provides technical assistance to Indians to make their own, the work demonstrates the different challenges of making video about and with indigenous peoples who see an instrumental and political utility in it. This article first describes the differences between work by and about indigenous groups for three Video in the Villages videos and then discusses, with the help of an extended interview with project director Vincent Carelli (Carelli 1993), issues of power and representation that he sees arising from his work.

Three of the project's tapes—*Festa da Moça* (Girl's puberty ritual), *O Espirito da TV* (Spirit of TV), and *Pemp* (Male initiation rite)—offer useful platforms for discussion of the function of video by and about indigenous groups (Centro Ecumênico de Documentação e Informação, 1992). These particular tapes are not, and do not claim to be, films by Brazilian Indians, or even, in the first instance, for Brazilian Indians. The bulk of the organization's work is assisting Indians to produce videos that they conceive jointly with the organization, and in which they dictate the thematic and compositional choices. Video in the Villages also exhibits tapes, particularly in an extended project circulating videotapes among different groups and, now, in organizing meetings between groups that have "met" already by video. It helps build archives and videotheques and replaces moldy or damaged tapes. Its choices for video work are driven by ways in which video can foment the larger project of cultural integrity and reconstruction.

As a result of this work, Video in the Villages has extensive experience with the experimentation with video by indigenous groups. The tapes discussed here are documents recording the process. They were made by Video in the Villages members, virtually all non-Indian, principally Vincent Carelli.

They are not ethnographic videos, either. Although anthropologists have an active role in working with Indians who document their experience on video, there is no pretense of ethnographic or social scientific method. At times, the makers of these videos were excluded from discussions of the meanings of the events they filmed, and sometimes they filmed discussions in languages they did not understand. These videos have an activist, political rationale, and a familiar, didactic documentary format. They are intended to explain to as large as possible, often non-Indian audiences why video is a useful tool for Indian cultural survival. The immediate, core audience is funders, activists, and where useful, other Indian groups that want an introduction either to use of video or to the culture featured in the video. Beyond that audience is the lay public.

Perhaps this kind of work, and enthusiasm for it among anthropologists, is a mark of the continuing erosion of ethnographic film's boundary lines (Nichols 1991). It is certainly evidence of the incorporation of video into social change agendas nationally and internationally (Dowmunt 1993; LaSpada 1992; Thede and Ambrosi 1992). And it reflects a tendency in indigenous media production generally toward the use of video to reinforce or even reconstitute traditional culture in the face of a dominant, mass-mediated culture (Ginsburg 1991). In any case, the clear distinction made within the project between indigenous-directed video and promotional video by the project obviates some of the conceptual problems commonly associated with ethnographic films today (Ruby 1991).

The videos for outsiders take on a straightforward advocacy role, calculatedly deploying the images. The very otherness of much of the imagery—the dances, the feathers, the beads, the hortatory rhetoric by chiefs armed with ceremonial weapons—tends to lend the subject's credibility to the advocate. The palpable authenticity of the material easily erodes a viewer's skepticism about the videomaker's role and perspective. This is a gambit that works generally; it is equally true, for example, of a video news release featuring angry mothers in a Chicago housing project, created by the community organizing group ACORN.

It is easy to see the difference between the process of recording and making video and the tapes distributed internationally—which are only one kind of product in the process—by putting the titles in context.

### Festa da Moça

*Festa da Moça* (1987, 18 min.) was the first video made by Video in the Villages (Carelli 1988), as a result of a project with the Nambiquara of northern Mato Grosso. The Nambiquara are the remnants of a once-large group, who twenty-five years ago were nearly exterminated by the opening of a road through their land, were in some instances forcibly relocated, and whose lands were invaded and in part seized by ranchers.

Nambiquara leader Captain Pedro eagerly welcomed the Video in the Villages team and directed the filming of a puberty ritual attended by related groups. Video in the Villages staff encouraged the Nambiquara to explain on tape what they had filmed, in order to be able to show it to other groups. This process involved close analysis of the video material and discussion of traditional practice. It triggered a decision to revive a nose-piercing ritual that had been in abeyance virtually since contact; that decision-making process was also filmed and discussed. A month later, videotape of the girl's puberty ritual was shown to a different group of Nambiquara, which also discussed it extensively and critiqued it for being conducted in Brazilian clothing; the ritual was performed again, this time in a more traditional manner (Carelli 1988).

Captain Pedro has continued to work with Video in the Villages, documenting Nambiquara culture while continuing to search out pockets of uncontacted Nambiquara. He initiated and made a video about his own group's reconquest of traditional lands, which he used as an impetus to organize a meeting of Nambiquara from other villages about recovery of lost lands (Carelli 1988, 11). He has gone on to make an investigative piece of political journalism, about a massacre of an Indian group that had been covered up (Carelli 1988, 13). Video in the Villages has also traveled to several Nambiquara villages with a taped oral history of an owner of a rubber tapping operation who exploited the rivalry between the Nambiquara and a nearby group to drive Indians off the land. Villagers, both Nambiquara groups and their one-time rivals, have recalled their own version of this history and this too has been taped and discussed (Carelli 1988, 13).

*Festa da Moça* synopsizes the story of the initial ritual quickly. The tale unites Captain Pedro's concerns—publicity about Nambiquara fierceness and ability to hold on to (or even re-create) traditional culture—with Video in the Villages' objective, which is demonstrating the power of video to affect the self-image and behavior of indigenous groups. It does not pretend to explain or give all the pieces of the rituals it alludes to. It does not probe for opinions other than those of the leadership. It does not attempt to mimic the pace or the focus of the tapes documenting the rituals, made with Captain Pedro for the Nambiquara and other groups. It does claim the approval and participation of Captain Pedro as "codirector," somewhat in the style of ethnographic films made in a collaborative "third voice" (Ruby 1993, 6), although it is clear from both narration and editing structure that the Brazilian director is firmly in charge of ultimate design; and it incorporates scenes of his directing the camera. The message is clear: video can level the symbolic playing field. By making social behavior self-conscious, it can help reinvent traditional practice.

The Nambiquara experience with video was so intense that Carelli describes himself dismayed by *Festa da Moça*: "The encounter was so rich and profound and their understanding of what was possible with video was so instant; the video by contrast leaves such a pale reflection of the madness that was going on. They were moving so much faster than we ever expected."

## Pemp

*Pemp* (1988, 27 min.) was the next video, the by-product of work with the Gavião (Paracetejê). The Gavião group had been contacted in 1957 and within days began suffering from contact diseases so massively that the group was decimated and social ties broke down. The remaining members of the group were moved to a reservation under the care of the Indian agency, which proceeded to spirit away the income from the group's Brazil nut collection. Since their revolt in 1975, they have handled their own business.

The group today lives near Marabá, at the heart of industrial development (hydroelectric power, iron mining, charcoal-fired pig iron production) in the eastern Amazon. Its lands have been affected by both the dam and an industrial railroad. In both cases the group has managed to extract significant indemnification; the proceeds have gone to build a permanent village with Brazilian-style houses in a traditional circular village plan. In this process, younger generations in the fragmented community adopted many Brazilian cultural elements—soccer, television, Portuguese.

The group's leader, Kokrenum, also the last person who still knows the ancient chants, has long waged a campaign to reconstitute traditional culture. He understands commercial television well; in fact, he is a great fan of Ramboesque action dramas and even complains that U.S. films are not dubbed, since he cannot read subtitles (CTI 1993).

He instantly grasped the possibilities when, in an initial meeting with Video in the Villages, he viewed tapes of Kayapo-Xikrin rituals. Already the possessor of a video camera (but not the needed editing equipment), he seized on the chance to work in production and chose as the group's first project a male initiation rite—a choice that reflects his central concerns for cultural revitalization. He eventually convinced TV owners in the village to turn them into monitors for his cultural projects, once the group bought a VCR. The group now regularly has showings at night of its own rituals and forbids outsiders (including Video in the Villages) to record them independently. In their evening television viewing, the Gavião watch not only their own ceremonies but tapes of other groups, and showings, with help from Video in the Villages, of tapes from other groups have resulted in vigorous discussion of comparative ritual practice. Indeed, they resumed the custom of lip piercing, after watching the Nambiquaras' ritual tape, and recorded that event without CTI's help (CTI 1993, 4).

Filming the rituals created internal tension in the group, as Kokrenum debated with two other elders (all of them holding partial knowledge) how the rituals should be conducted. These debates also involved young people curious to learn. For most of such filming, Carelli and others were largely in the dark about the meaning of the rituals, or indeed the actual words of the chants, and understood Kokrenum's reluctance to share with them their meaning (Carelli 1988, 16–17).

*Pemp* uses the log-racing ritual called Pemp, a male initiation rite, as a set piece around which to demonstrate the larger Gavião project of cultural reconstitution and the utility of video in achieving that goal. Laying out Gavião history with the help of a map and historical footage, it introduces a much younger Kokrenum arguing fiercely with Indian agency FUNAI (Fundaçáo Nacional do Índia, or National Indian Foundation) representatives about its Brazil nut payments, establishing him as a political leader. Kokrenum then explains the value of video to record for posterity, saying that young people "will watch and say, 'I know how to do it.'" We see young kids watching action dramas on Brazilian TV, and we watch them being lectured on how to speak their own language while in school. The story of the Gavião struggle for indemnification is summarized, with help from Gavião and Brazilian TV images, and the recording of the Pemp ritual is alluded to.

The traditional ritual is thus placed in the context of a struggle for political, economic, and cultural space. The recording of ritual is an act that, as Kokrenum makes explicit, fosters his cultural recovery program. The tape does not delve into internal differences over interpretation of the ritual, or invidious Gavião judgments on other Indian cultures; nor does it explore reactions of other villagers. It tells a story congruent with Kokrenum's revitalization mission.

### O Espirito da TV

*O Espirito da TV* (1990, 18 min.) results from work with the Waiãpi Indians in the state of Amapá. The Waiãpi, who in Brazil number only a few hundred (more live in French Guiana), are an almost exclusively monolingual group in the Tupi linguistic family. They have resisted threats to their land from the military (to establish a national forest) and from mining interests. Their leaders have actively sought relief in state capitals and in Brasília. Their activism has given them a leadership position among Indian groups in the area (Gallois 1992; Gallois and Carelli n.d.).

The Waiãpi had had bitter experience with commercial and ethnographic film projects, which they had never seen after letting strangers into their villages. They wanted to use video as a means to assert their own version of their culture to outsiders, although their first notion of this was to make a film in which a white person would present this culture to other whites (Gallois and Carelli n.d.).

This work began with filming the Waiãpi chief Wai Wai in Brasília, on a trip to demarcate his group's land. He wanted to take the resulting videotape to each Waiãpi village to demonstrate his leadership. Video in the Villages people went along to document his use of the video, accompanied by an anthropologist who speaks the Waiãpi language, Dominique Gallois. Video in the Villages also brought along tapes and footage from other groups and TV news broadcasts about Indian issues; these tapes were shown as well. The team left a generator, recorder, TV, and blank cassettes with the Waiãpi; Chief Wai Wai built a special house near his for the equipment, where public screenings now take place, including materials Video in the Villages sends.

Growing experience with video has, according to Gallois and Carelli, enriched their political style. Their leaders have clearly borrowed some of the aggressive media strategy, sometimes playing on the exotic stereotypes of Indians and of other groups, especially the Kayapo. They have also deployed new information to political ends. Upon capturing two goldminers who had invaded the area with others, they refrained from simply killing them. Instead, they made the miners aware that they knew what had happened to Yanomami (Indians whose territory had been devastated) as a result of such invasions; they knew the standard tricks miners used to deceive Indians and apparently managed to convince them to leave the area (Gallois and Carelli n.d., 6–8). Videotaping political interventions of the chiefs has become standard practice, resulting in public analysis and discussion of issues and the chiefs' handling of them (13). Video is seen as a powerful tool to speak to whites—in specific groups and settings, for instance, the Indian agency, goldminers, the national government. It has also become part of Waiãpi strategizing in intertribal diplomacy (16). Recently, with the help of Video in the Villages, Waiãpi leader Wai Wai and a small group met face-to-face with members of the Zo'é group of Guarani speakers whose language is similar enough for mutual understanding and whom they first "met" on video. The encounter was documented in *Meeting Ancestors: The Zo'é* (1993, 21 min.).

*O Espirito da TV* charts the beginning of the Waiãpi contact with video, showing reactions to screenings of other groups' videos, chiefly presentations in Brasília and testimony. Chief Wai Wai promptly sets forth two related points of the videotape: "After I've died," he says, "my grandchildren can still see me on television. . . . Now the young can see their elders and learn from them. . . . It's good to meet others through TV." Excerpts from videotapes of other Indians' work, including the Gavião and Nambiquara, shown to the Waiãpi are matched with shots of the Waiãpi reacting (Wai Wai says of Kokrenum's denouncing of FUNAI, "They did the same thing to us!"). When the Waiãpi watch southern Guarani speakers (separated by thousands of miles) talk in a language very close to theirs, Chief Wai Wai marvels, "After a little while, we can understand them!"

The video also follows a Waiãpi event in which young men get drunk. Chief Wai Wai worries openly to the camera about the reputation of the group, and particularly about letting potential enemies know that there are moments of weakness. "When you show these pictures, tell people, 'These people are killers when they're drunk,'" he says.

Thus the tape demonstrates three related political roles for indigenous video: fostering indigenous traditions; fostering communication among Indian groups; and providing publicity to the outside world. Virtually erased from the story is Gallois, who had worked with this group for twelve years and who refused despite the urging of Carelli to appear on camera, in favor of making a video in which the only voices would be those of the Indians themselves.

## The Uses of Video

Perhaps because the work is so explicitly political and the goals instrumental, Carelli is highly articulate about the utility of video and the implications of Video in the Villages' role in shaping these ideas. Some of these ideas are addressed here.

### The Video Option

Why should indigenous groups use video at all? The equipment is expensive and subject to breakage, it requires bulky monitors to be seen, and the tapes easily break or decay. Carelli argues that the costs involved are far outweighed by the gains, which he measures by the group's ability to define and defend itself culturally and politically before the national society. He argues that seeing both oneself and related groups' culture on video has a power unique to the form and only recently accessible in terms of technology.

Video in the Villages, begun in 1987, originally posited two objectives: to "make accessible to Indians the vision, the production and the manipulation of their own image, and at the same time to see to it that these extremely isolated communities could get to know other groups, fostering comparisons of their traditions and experiences of contact with national society" (CTI 1993, 1).

Carelli himself began working with Indians in 1969 and worked within and outside of FUNAI. He entered the field with a fascination for photography, which was fueled in his position as archivist for the Indigenous Peoples of Brazil historical photographic collection at one of Brazil's largest nongovernmental organizations, the Centro Ecuménico de Documentação e Informação. He recalled being moved by the reaction of Indians when he could locate a historical photo containing pictures of their ancestors, the contact situation, or documentation of rites.

For Carelli, video's utility is measured against only one standard: whether it becomes part of the process of cultural survival. For him this is "the process of realizing the projects of the leadership for the survival of the groups, control of their territory; the process of affirmation, so young people can resolve the question of identity in a satisfactory, integrated way; the process of getting territory demarcated [legally recognizing Indian land rights]." He professes himself constantly astonished at the power of the image to communicate and inspire: "The image is beautiful, it's synoptic, it unites different aspects of life; it's not 'blah blah blah.'"

This locating of video production within a larger project of cultural revitalization is similar to use of grassroots video in other contexts, both within Brazil and elsewhere (see "Grassroots Video in Latin America"). For instance, grassroots activists in the United States claim, "The creation of video 'documents' is only part of the projects that we are discussing. . . . *group* empowerment is primary, superseding any notion that this is a reflection of a group of 'others' to the 'world,' although this may be a secondary and quite important result" (Halleck and Magnan 1993, 157).

### Video and Television

Introducing Indians to video also means introducing them to kid-vid star Xuxa, Rambo, and the sexy, gory, sentimental private worlds of Brazilian *novelas*, or soap operas. The "contamination" of traditional culture and the willy-nilly adoption of "Western" expression have long been a concern (Faris 1992) and continues to be a roiling point of debate among anthropologists and critics (Rival 1992). Indigenous Brazilian producers and leaders have not typically shown such anxieties. Anthropologist Faye Ginsburg has sensibly argued that video can work productively to foster cultural self-consciousness and strengthen interest in cultural autonomy (Ginsburg 1991), an assertion that well matches the experience of Video in the Villages.

Carelli notes that getting control of their own media image has been a constant desire of indigenous groups for as long as he has been working with them: "They are bombarded by journalists and photographers who exploited them and never even send them a copy of the photo in return." He has noted as well that video is only the latest technology that Indians have fought to get access to; Indian groups have long struggled to control the short-wave radio system installed by the government in the reserves (CTI 1993, 8). Furthermore, many Indian groups, such as the Gavião, are already being barraged by Brazilian television; some, such as the Rambo-loving Kokrenum, appear to be able to juggle the two kinds of use as adeptly as anyone.

Getting video equipment means getting access to national culture even if Indians were not plugged in before, and Indians have seized on the chance to rig antennas and receive satellite signals. Without doubt, this experience also affects their culture. For instance, one Xavante group, with the arrival of an antenna, must now decide whether and, if so, how, to control access to commercial programming.

Carelli sees a clear difference between groups that have commercial TV and those that don't. He sees it among young people, whose values tend to be more individualistic among the TV watchers, and also in film language. The TV watchers absorb the rhythm and style of commercial TV and have a better grasp of the language of outsiders. But he does not worry about his video work contributing to cultural decay:

> I think it's ridiculous to worry about this—they are in contact with everything from our culture. There is no way for them to avoid it. They watch soap operas; the Kayapo have satellite dishes; the Gavião already have thirty televisions. It has an enormous impact on young people, on their values.
>
> Our work is contrapuntal to this. They'll see Rambo no matter what we do. We don't need to patrol them. But we need to give them something to make themselves and their own culture strong in contrast to it.

This corresponds with the experience of Australian media activist Philip Batty, who argues that "resistance" to global TV "can only be accomplished in any effective way, by gaining an active if basic knowledge of television technology, and applying that knowledge in locally relevant and meaningful ways" (in Ginsburg 1993, 570).

## Video and Traditional Attitudes toward Image

What do the processes of filming and viewing their own and other Indians' cultural events mean to Indians? Carelli and others in the Video in the Villages project have found that each group incorporates and interprets the process differently. As well, familiarity with the form changes attitudes. For instance, the sacred flutes of the Enaunê-Nauê, which women may not see in real life, could be filmed and their images shown in the center of the village because they believe that the spirits that are attracted by the sound of the flutes and that can threaten the women were not present at the time of the projection.

For the Waiãpi, the image not only reproduces but materializes the vital force of the represented people and objects. For this reason, when a video was shown to a family watching its own image for the first time, it was seen as a duplication of forces, which could threaten them and which led them to paint themselves with the red vegetable dye achiote to protect themselves. The Waiãpi made it very clear that anything about shamanism must not be filmed, since it dealt with very dangerous knowledge reserved for the initiated (CTI 1993, 10).

Anthropologist Dominique Gallois also noted that the Waiãpi distinguish between symbols that do not "bear life elements of the being represented," and the likeness that photography and video bring. During some initial screenings, women were shielded from the screen by a young shaman (Gallois and Carelli n.d.). When a related group of Waiãpi from French Guiana, already familiar with photographic realism and television, came to visit and scoffed at this kind of behavior, "some Waiãpi . . . concluded that they would 'get used to' the presence of TV" (Gallois and Carelli n.d.).

The meaning of sharing one's own video record with others also varies with different groups. The Waiãpi exercise a strict principle of exchange, showing their videos only to people who they have "met" by video, while among the Xikrin and Xavante, chiefs must negotiate directly with each other over showings (CTI 1993, 14).

### Aesthetics of Indigenous Video

The stylistic and expressive options chosen in this highly visual medium, by people who do not necessarily share the aesthetic conventions of the dominant society, says as much about the dominant society's assumptions about the form as it does about the indigenous use of the medium.

The experience of Video in the Villages suggests that, as with the above issue, neat generalizations are difficult to make. Nonetheless, Carelli easily admits, "Our intervention is decisive. My presence alone is a huge influence. An indigenous person's camera begins working through a long intervention." Although he has participated in, and accompanied Indians to, events showcasing their video work, he also finds such activity problematic. He worries especially about Indians making a video career, rather than cultural renewal, their goal.

Carelli has found that the Indians he has worked with usually resist editing of the kind he uses in the center's documentaries. They prize long, uninterrupted sequences and assemblage that closely follows events. There are a variety of reasons, he believes, for these choices. As in any home movie, each element of the event is likely to be interesting to some member of the group. As well, in this region the beauty of a ceremony is often measured, at least in part, by its completeness in detail and by repetition.

Indians carefully discriminate between audiences, both as producers and viewers. As is clear in Terence Turner's work with the Kayapo, they clearly can and do learn different editing styles (Turner 1992). But in the Video in the Villages projects they have usually emphasized their most immediate audience. Carelli recalls a discussion with a young Xavante who worked with the CTI team editing images from a male initiation ritual. When asked about his target audience, he said that all of the raw material was intended for the village, while the edit was designed "for the outside public, for whites, and other Indians." The ritual involved five social groups repeating each segment, and Carelli suggested editing to allude to the repetition. But the Xavante resisted this, even for "outsiders," for fear that his own group would accuse him of not knowing how the ritual was supposed to be done or that other groups would not believe they did it correctly. "Although the video supposedly was for an outside public, in fact, he never managed, at any moment, to free himself from the inner view," noted Carelli (CTI 1993, 12).

Carelli believes that his own tapes—such as those discussed here—are essentially a different project from that of Indians making their tapes. In the latter case, he says, "We work more with the idea of just 'cleaning up' the material and making the exhibitor's work easier, grouping together the parts best liked by the local audience" (CTI 1993, 12). He also sees that Indians who have more familiarity with Brazilian and U.S. television adapt their visual styles to it, and he believes that indigenous work is evolving unpredictably.

## The Internal Politics of Video

As Terence Turner has eloquently discussed (Turner 1991) and as others practicing technical assistance in video know well, decisions about how and with whom to work involve the technicians in complicated political dynamics.

In terms of selecting sites, Video in the Villages typically works with groups with whom Carelli or others already have a relationship or have established one as a result of relationships with other groups. In a few cases, such as the Xavante, Indian groups sought out the project. Carelli limits the project's obligations, since its infrastructure is small, and he will not work with groups whose leadership is contested or whose political internal organization is not relatively stable (Carelli 1993). Carelli accepts that

> leaders perceive from the very first moment the importance of exercising their control over this image, as much at the level of internal circulation as in the projection of the group's image outside. They incorporate video into their own political and cultural projects. (CTI 1993, 13)

Since Carelli's objective is to foster cultural integrity and since he perceives strong leadership as important to that project, this is not an ideological problem for him. It does, however, pose some practical difficulties. For instance, he works and must work with the young people selected by the leadership, not necessarily those most interested or adept. He also accepts that their dream of having Indians share video knowledge throughout their community is "utopian": "The one in charge never relinquishes his privilege and doesn't cede the camera to anyone" (CTI 1993, 13). He accepts that unforeseen political consequences can occur, for instance, when the Waiãpi became fascinated with the political rhetoric of rivals to Chief Wai Wai (Gallois and Carelli n.d.).

### Indians and Mass Media

One of the most common reactions to the tapes Carelli has made to explain his work has been amazement that Indians can analyze the power of the media, want to participate in that power, and have explicit, concrete ideas about how to deploy it. This may sometimes appear quaint, crude, or touching to the viewer, for instance, when Chief Wai Wai worries about showing the group in a drunken state for fear that landowners will see that they are vulnerable. Or it may appear forthrightly practical, as when Kokrenum says of a descendant watching the tape, "He will watch and say, 'I know now how to do it.'" But there is no doubt that Indians grasp the power of representation and misrepresentation. The canny use of "savage Indian" stereotypes in the media by groups such as the Xavante and the Kayapo (imitated eagerly by Chief Wai Wai and others) highlights that awareness and indeed plays on their perception of others' naïveté. What may ultimately be most interesting about this amazement that Indians have their own analysis of media is its striking evidence of ignorance about Indian contact with mass media, which has been—as Carelli is at pains to point out—perforce a part of most of their lives.

### Revitalization and Video

The experience of Video in the Villages reminds us at every point that indigenous cultures incorporate video into complex, distinctive cultural and political patterns. Uses of video have ranged from home movies for the village to circulation of tapes between cultures to strategic use of clips in press conferences and political meetings. Styles have differed depending on a group's cultural expectations and on audiences. The tapes discussed here have documented some of the processes and results in order to demonstrate—most immediately to potential allies of CTI in the effort to maintain the project—that such video use helps indigenous peoples revitalize their traditional cultures.

### Note

Video Databank, 37 S. Wabash, Chicago IL 60603; (312) 899-5172, distributes the Video in the Villages collection.

### References

Carelli, V. 1988. "Video in the Villages: Utilization of Video-Tapes as an Instrument of Ethnic Affirmation among Brazilian Indian Groups: Un Instrument de Reaffirmation Ethnique." *CVA [Commission on Visual Anthropology] Newsletter* (May): 10–15.

———. 1993. Personal communication, July 21.

Centro Ecumênico de Documentação e Informação (CEDI). 1992. "O Índio imaginado: Mostra de filmes e vídeos sobre povos indígenas no Brasil" (The imagined Indian: An exhibit of films and videos about indigenous peoples of Brazil). São Paulo: CEDI.

Centro de Trabalho Indigenista (CTI). 1993. "Relatório MacArthur" (MacArthur Foundation project report). Programa Vozes Indígenas 1992, Projeto "Video nas Aldeias." Unpublished manuscript.

Dowmunt, T. 1993. *Channels of Resistance: Global Television and Local Enforcement.* London: British Film Institute.

Faris, J. 1992. "Anthropological Transparency: Film, Representation and Politics." In *Film as Ethnography,* ed. P. Crawford and D. Turton. Manchester, England: Manchester University Press.

Gallois, D. 1992. "Floresta nacional? Waiãpi: Trajetoria da tentativa de redução de uma area indígena" (National forest? Waiãpi: Trajectory of an attempt at reducing an indigenous area). *Povos indígenas no Brasil 1987–1990,* Serie Aconteçeu Especial 18. São Paulo: Centro Ecumênico de Documentação e Informação, 216–21.

Gallois, D., and V. Carelli. n.d. "Video in the Villages: The Waiãpi Experience." Unpublished manuscript.

Ginsburg, F. 1991. "Indigenous Media: Faustian Contract or Global Village?" *Cultural Anthropology* 6 (1): 92–112.

Ginsburg, F. 1993. "Aboriginal Media and the Australian Imaginary." *Public Culture* 5 (Spring): 557–92.

Halleck, D., and N. Magnan. 1993. "Access for Others: Alter (Native) Media Practice." *Visual Anthropology Review* 9 (1): 154–63.

LaSpada, S. 1992. "Grassroots Video and the Democratization of Communication: The Case of Brazil." Ed.D. diss., Columbia University Teachers College.

Nichols, B. 1991. "The Ethnographer's Tale. *Visual Anthropology Review* 7 (2).

Ricardo, C. A. 1992. "Organizações indígenas" (Indigenous organizations). *Povos indígenas no Brasil 1987–1990,* Serie Aconteçeu Especial 18. São Paulo: Centro Ecumênico de Documentação e Informação, 67–72.

Rival, L. 1992. "3rd RAI Film Festival: Report on the Conference and Workshops." *CVA [Commission on Visual Anthropology] Newsletter* 2: 2–6.

Ruby, J. 1991. "Speaking for, Speaking about, Speaking with, or Speaking alongside—an Anthropological and Documentary Dilemma." *Visual Anthropology Review* 7 (2).

———. 1993. "The Moral Burden of Authorship in Ethnographic Film." Presented at the Duke Documentary Conference, Society for Cinema Studies, Durham, N.C., September 10.

Thede, N., and A. Ambrosi, eds. 1992. *Video the Changing World.* Montreal: Black Rose Press.

Turner, T. 1991. "The Social Dynamics of Video Media in an Indigenous Society: The Cultural Meaning and the Personal Politics of Video-Making in Kayapo Communities." *Visual Anthropology Review* 7 (2): 68–76.

———. 1992. "Defiant Images." *Anthropology Today* 8 (6): 5–16.

# Memory and

# History in

# Sub-Saharan

# African Cinema

*I saw several of the films and met the filmmakers mentioned in this piece in one amazing week at Filmfest DC, in Washington, D.C., in 1991. There, I came to understand how the next generation of African and African-diaspora filmmakers was taking shape.* Lucien Taylor at Visual Anthropology Review *nurtured my curiosity and encouraged me to publish this article with his journal. Since then, I have had the privilege of screening* Allah Tantou *for groups of African students and faculty at American University, where it has provoked soul searching that echoes the concerns that the filmmaker raised in the following interview.*

The cinema of sub-Saharan Africa has a somber realist tradition (called by some African realism, and others social realism [Diawara 1992; Turvey 1985]), which has perhaps been its most familiar side for the film festival–going public internationally. Typical themes include colonialism, neocolonialism, political corruption, women's rights, and the tensions between country and city. Filmmakers have often spoken in a kind of "we the people" collective voice, as the storytellers of their society. That tradition has had much to do with artists' postcolonial commitment to use the form to build cultural independence, and with the practicalities of making movies in poor countries.

Work by African film and videomakers in the later 1980s and 1990s explores approaches of the next generation to the intersection of political history and personal identity in the postcolonial era. The moods of this work include a sense of loss or derailment from exile internal or external, and anger at false claims to traditional authority. This seems appropriate to a generation of filmmakers many of whom are permanently liminal characters, living between Africa and Paris, London, New York, Brussels, or Berlin.

For instance, John Akomfrah's *Testament* is a disturbing, elegant meditation in which a fictional female protagonist—Akomfrah's alter ego—returns to a country much like his native Ghana to confront the wreckage of liberatory political idealism. His later essay on popular African diasporic music's fascination with outer space and aliens, *The Last Angel of History*, takes this mood into an intergalactic realm. In a more stylistically traditional example, Senegalese Amadou Saalum Seck's *Saaraba* also features the theme of return and confrontation with ideals; a man returns to Senegal to discover that you can't go home again and tradition isn't what it was. In *Quartier Mozart*, Cameroonian first-time director (at twenty-six) Jean-Pierre Bekolo combines anger with attitude in a self-conscious youth film that skewers the hypocrisy of an older generation, manipulating traditions such as polygamy for personal indulgence.

African filmmakers are also using a form that seems to be multiplying on the international landscape with the widespread amateur and independent use of video: we might call it the memory film. Snapshots, home movies, objects, and fragments of writing—assembled collage-style—allow personal memory to comment on history and inform a meditation on the way in which we understand ourselves in the world.

This is an international phenomenon. American independent films like Rea Tajiri's *History and Memory*, about her parents' experience of Japanese internment camps, and Alan Berliner's *Intimate Stranger*, a bittersweet portrait of his Jewish Egyptian grandfather caught in political crossfire during and after World War II, are two U.S. examples of a pastiche approach to the past, both involving family members. The use of video diaries like the ones that Ademir Kenovic, in *SA-Life*, recorded to document daily life in Sarajevo and that Israeli filmmaker Ilan Ziv now contracts around the world for U.S. television; the recovery and reshaping of personal material, as Harriet Eder and Thomas Kufus did by juxtaposing six German soldiers' amateur films of World War II with interviews with them in *Mein Krieg*; and even the simulation of home-movie memories, such as U.S. video artist Su Friedrich used in *Sink or Swim* all betoken a fascination with the hidden meanings behind the seeming transparency of the image.

This approach has become a powerful tool for young filmmakers to reassess the recent African past, and their artistic role as spokespeople for the society. It is one that radically questions received wisdom and asserts the need for a vulnerable, individual voice. *Lumumba: Death of a Prophet,* by Raoul Peck, a Haitian raised in Congo, and *Allah Tantou,* by Guinean David Achkar, are both courageous, ambitious statements as intensely political as they are personal.

*Lumumba* resurrects the memory of a man whose name connoted, for a generation, integrity against the forces of neocolonialism and who is now largely forgotten by a new generation internationally. It took a consortium of television services from eight European countries to fund *Lumumba* over massive discouragement from the Zairian government of the time.

Lumumba, the first prime minister of Congo and a man who fiercely refused to bow to ex-colonialists, symbolized first the hope of independent Africa and then the tragedy of new states in crisis—as he was thrown from power and finally murdered by the corrupt-from-the-start, U.S.- and UN-backed military man Joseph Désiré Mobutu (later Mobutu Sese Seko, who renamed Congo to Zaire).

Filmmaker Raoul Peck lived in Congo/Zaire as a child shortly after Lumumba's fall because his Haitian father was hired there as an agricultural expert. In the film, Lumumba's decline and fall are intertwined with the young boy's confusions over his own status and place, and his anxieties over the fate of his own parents.

Peck re-creates a sense of loss of the smashed promise of Lumumba's Congo with fragments of newsreel footage, home movies, old photographs, and audiotape. He interviews close observers, journalists, and officials both Belgian and Congolese, who recall the crisis. Their recollections become disturbing statements about the legacy of colonialism.

These fragments never add up to a simplistic eulogy for a larger-than-life hero and cannot make up a comfortingly complete picture. They act, rather, as broken bits of memory that beg to be made sense of. The personal jostles the public, and uneasy questions of conscience surface.

Peck frames the crisis visually with images from the Congo's ex-imperial owner, Belgium—wintry streets, a museum full of stuffed African animals and glassed-in African trophies. Peck was scheduled to film in Zaire but canceled his trip when he found that Mobutu's secret police were already watching him. The absence of Zairian images speaks volumes about the Mobutu regime. Meanwhile, the Belgian material becomes a disturbing, reinforcing backdrop to the profile of Lumumba—nowhere more so than when Peck visits the Belgian graves of several Congolese who were imported for a turn-of-the-century exhibition and, as was the rule under colonialism, never allowed to return to the Congo.

Like *Lumumba*, *Allah Tantou* probes the relationship between memory and history. Guinean David Achkar's father was a dancer in the Ballets Africains during the continent-wide independence movement in the 1950s. A prominent figure in the struggle to assert African independence, he became part of the Guinean movement led by Sékou Touré, then a champion of Pan-Africanism.

Upon freedom in 1958, Marof Achkar, of Guinean and Lebanese descent, became a United Nations ambassador and moved to New York with his métis (mixed-culture) wife and family; David was born there in 1960. In 1968, Marof Achkar was recalled by the increasingly brutal Touré regime and disappeared into the notorious prison Camp Boiro. His family was exiled, unable to know his fate until many years later, after Touré's death and the institution of more open government.

*Allah Tantou* is a set of meditations on the world that David Achkar's father knew and a reimagining of the past, including his father's experience of torture. To do this, Achkar assembles a collage of provocative images and scenes. He uses his family's home movies—kids around a Christmas tree, dad in the driveway. He juxtaposes them with newsreel and film images of the public Achkar at the UN, posing with Martin Luther King Jr. and other celebrities and politicians when he chaired the UN Commission on Apartheid.

Interpolated are scenes in which an actor plays the part of the imprisoned Achkar; the scenes and voice-over narration are drawn from letters the family was given only a few years ago. Here, the self-assured and elegant character of the historical footage becomes an anguished and increasingly disoriented lonely soul, gradually growing blind but ultimately returning to a sense of pride and destiny. On the sound track, overlapping and echoing rhetorical phrases about revolution and democracy echo grandly around the actor; they are the sound of destroyed hopes.

Achkar gradually emerges both as an individual of profound integrity and as an example of a movement infused with idealism and betrayed into despair. As Lawrence Daressa of California Newsreel wrote anonymously, "The final shot of an anonymous road on a memoryless morning, a truck bouncing into the future, does not just express the irrevocable absence of his father. It denotes all the 'disappeared,' the insignificant and unsignified, the unrecorded and immemorial millions of Africans and others who have been edited out of history" (Anonymous [Daressa] n.d.).

The disparate images, sounds, objects, and fragments function not merely as documents but as evocative talismans, indeed acting as memory itself at times. Each item, each image, conditioned by others, loses its independent authority as historical proof and becomes part of a search for integrity and identity. David Achkar was looking not only for his father but for a way to follow in his footsteps, to live an independent life within a larger web of meaning.

### Interview with David Achkar

David Achkar spoke with me while attending Filmfest DC, the international film festival in Washington, D.C. on April 13, 1993. He died at the age of thirty-eight of a heart attack, in January 1998.

*How did you decide to make a film rather than working in another medium?*
I've lived in Paris for seventeen years. Over the last ten years, I've been a writer and actor for plays we put on in Paris, and as an assistant to a black film director from Martinique living in Paris. That's how I got acquainted with black filmmaking in Paris.

This film was released in France two years ago and now is starting a life here in the United States.

*Would you say the film has a theme or message?*
The question my film is addressing is, what we in Africa did with the independence that we fought for, and that brought expectations we weren't up to thirty years ago. It's also the story of a man being held, and seeing his whole political past, and trying to find out what went wrong and why.

*How has the film been received in Guinea?*
In Guinea the film is well received. There is Sékou Touré as the myth and Touré as the leader. At the time we needed strong myths, because otherwise Africa never would have liberated itself. But at the same time we have to see the reality of the failure of the system, the dysfunction, in Guinea.

There is an association, the Group of Children of the Inmates of Camp Boiro. It's four or five years old, but it's only been working for a couple of years because we had trouble finding money to start up. There are many of us; whole families were affected. We need it now because Sékou Touré's party is rising up again. We need it so people won't forget the past.

I gave the association a 35mm copy of my film. The film has been projected several times by them, and the money is used to buy basic things, even T-shirts, for the association families.

It was also shown in my village, but I don't know how it went. People who have been in Camp Boiro or who had relatives there say, "That's what it really was like." Some of them, those who had been tortured, wanted to see the torturers and the effect of torture. I didn't want to do that—it was too easy. The only way you hear that in the film is from the voices of people crying. If you understood the language, you could hear they're crying out for their mothers. Grown men, forty, fifty years old, crying out for their mother. It's stronger to put it that way than try for sentimentality.

*Do you see yourself as part of a wider movement aesthetically, a movement to use and reinterpret personal and official visual documents?*
I'm part of an international movement in the sense that a lot of people have these photographs at home, these home movies. They're always questioning these photos, and some of us use them in films. Every time you look at a picture, you have a past that comes back to you. I've seen more work like this—Raoul Peck's film *Lumumba: Death of a Prophet,* for instance. My film was done before Raoul's, and I thought it looks a lot like mine. They were programmed together at New York Film Festival, and they were clearly talking to each other, these films, and the audience was with us. These people didn't suffer in any way, but they saw their own families, and the relationships within their own families.

What a film like this says is that "history" is a collection of "little histories," *petites histoires.*

I'm a métis who doesn't have a country. I am black in Paris and white in Africa. Under these circumstances, you have to imagine even your own nostalgia. You create an image of your past that doesn't exist; you have always a compulsion to re-create things. But at the same time, the memory is still based on some real image, and that is what gives us the courage to go on.

Last time I met with artists in Dakar, where my family lives, I was fascinated because I didn't know anything about the cultural movement in Dakar. With painters and sculptors, there was something great going on there, and people were not only doing figurative art, but cubism, everything. I said in wonder, "We can do this in Africa!" I was amazed to see it—there was so much liberty in the air.

In Paris you're always living alone in your apartment; even at film festivals you barely talk about your work. It's not just me, but other métis Guineans living in France, with a will to go back to their country and analyzing the life they're living. Not just because that's their past but because that's the life they're living.

*Was it difficult working on your own father's letters and images?*
When I first went into the letters, I knew it was going to be painful, and then something happened that I'm still questioning. I unplugged something in my head. Suddenly, I was just working on documents; it was no longer my father. I was just like any scriptwriter who was saying, "This will work and this won't."

And then I made the film. I shot it with my cousin. He doesn't really look like my father—he's my mother's nephew. He didn't even see the home movies, although I asked him if he wanted to. On the set, we didn't have enough film to make mistakes, to do three or four takes. I said, "Do it the way you want to because we don't have time."

And then a year passed. At the same time I had an accident and needed an operation, and I was always postponing the operation because I had to finish the film. I felt I would only exist once I had finished the film.

Then we had a meeting with the editor and sound mixer. The sound mixer, a woman, said, "Let your mother come." (I work with a lot of women; the team was 90 percent women.) She bought a bottle of champagne. When we watched it, my mother cried a lot. She has the film and has a private projection two or three times a month. It was like therapy for her, seeing me through this, and now it's therapy for my brothers and sisters.

In making the film, I wanted to meet my father's ghost. But unfortunately, I didn't meet anything. I just had this film, the one I'm now taking from city to city. So I know my father's part of me, but I'm just doing what comes next.

*Do you find any political resistance to your film?*
I don't think I have anything to defend. In Guinea they know they can't stop me, because they will have the whole country against them. People know I'm harmless. The government paid for my plane ticket to come here; they knew it was a controversial film.

The association actually set up a screening for the officials. But no one came. The film did make some of the association members think again. The wives of those who died, all of them asked, "Why didn't we put this government on trial, sue them, do anything?"

Now Sékou Touré's party is coming back. If the government stops the democratic movement, they will have big problems. They've been postponing the democratic elections from one day to the next. We have sixty parties, and that's not good for real democracy. Everyone wants to be the chief, and no one has anything to propose.

*How did you finance the film?*
It was made in two stages. The first stage only cost $4,000. It was family money, and it took a few days. People contributed for free because I was letting them express themselves. We ended up with two hours of film. The shooting ratio was one-to-one. I kept the film in a drawer for a year, trying to raise money. I went to Amnesty [International] and they said I shouldn't have made a film about my father. I thought that was nonsense. No death is more beautiful than another.

I made the film look like a short feature and got funding from the French Minister of Cinema. And I got $30,000. They thought I was making a feature, but the script was pretty much what you have on the screen. And I got money from the French Ministry of Cooperation. Guinea wanted to back the film but didn't have any money, so the money came from France and was routed through Guinea. They gave $50,000. The whole thing came up to $80,000. There was a lot of work on the editing, and we had to blow up the 8mm.

*Do you think video is an option for this kind of production?*
Eight-millimeter works better than video. These films are thirty years old, and there's not a scratch on them. I hate video. It's easy to work in, but the image is flat, it's ugly. It has no brilliance. It's good for news, but cinema isn't news.

*What are you doing next?*
I'm working on a feature, the story of a musician, supposedly myself. I work in studios as a musician; I sing and produce records for fun. It's the story of someone who lives in Paris, is caught in a jam, and goes back to Africa, going upriver to find his mythical roots. The river is used in a semiological way; he's going up the river of his memory, to solve the problem of being considered black in France and white in Africa.

I don't want to deal with political issues. I just want to have this homeboy going to Africa. He's falling in love with a part of himself, but there's nothing to find, and that's the problem with it. I had some people tell me it's very frustrating because he doesn't find anything, and I say, "That's the frustration I live." *Allah Tantou* is frustrating, too, because the last words are, "It was on a day like this that I was shot in 1971," and then it ends.

Why do I end films like this? Maybe it's because I'm a sad person.

## Note

Most of the African films mentioned in this article are available from California Newsreel, 149 9th St., #420, San Francisco CA 94103; (415) 621-6196.

## References

Anonymous [Daressa, L.]. n.d. *Allah Tantou* (film notes). San Francisco: California Newsreel.

Diawara, M. 1992. *African Cinema: Politics and Culture.* Bloomington: Indiana University Press.

Turvey, G. 1985. "'Xala' and the Curse of Neocolonialism." *Screen* 26 (3–4): 75–88.

# Part IV. Living with the Media

# Why and How

# to Teach

# Media Literacy

*When I began teaching in a communications program, I seized on the work that brilliant teachers in K–12 education had done on media literacy. Traveling to Ontario to attend a conference that pulled together teachers and researchers from Australia, Britain, the United States, and Canada, I got a better understanding of the implications and challenges of a media literacy curriculum. And I also got teaching tools that I have never stopped adapting. This combination backgrounder/ toolkit synthesizes several of my writings on media literacy in the 1990s.*

*Media literacy* is a term that has its theoretical roots in left-leaning cultural studies. It is also the inheritor and, to some degree, synthesizer of curricular forays into the film-oriented visual literacy and critical viewing. It further works as an umbrella term for ingenious teaching practices that make students aware of the constructedness of mass media. The theory and the practice don't always meet, but the term has nonetheless generated some fascinating experiments in teaching about mass media.

Media literacy is a contentious concept from the start. If literacy is being able to read, then what needs to be "read" about the mass media? What does a literate person need to know further to be "media literate" about a newspaper or magazine? Toddlers can listen to the radio and watch TV and "read" them with sometimes disturbing ease. And if critical reading—the ability to divine construction and decipher buried codes of meaning—is at issue, then what kind of critique is the goal?

If there is any consensus about what media literacy is, it comes from the work of British, Australian, and Canadian teachers, whose formulations are captured well in the Ontario Ministry of Education's guide to media literacy. There, eight "media literacy key concepts" are spelled out, including "all media are constructions," "media have economic implications," and "media contain ideological and value messages" (Masterman 1985; Ontario Ministry of Education 1989; see below for "Key Concepts"). Unifying these concepts is the idea that all mass communication is crafted, for a purpose, and within certain cultural parameters. You cannot communicate outside ideology any more than you can write on a computer diskette without formatting. A media-literate person does not accept at face value the communication that has been naturalized with such cleverness but can recognize the constraints under which it was made ("brought to you by . . ."), perceive the social implications of the shaping of the message, and be able to manipulate—at least in theory or model—the constructing devices. Media literacy acknowledges, sometimes implicitly, that communication is a cultural artifact, not a transparent recorder of "fact," and that mass communication is shaped by powerful social and political forces.

That sounds pretty clear, and even a lot like what many teachers have been doing with "critical thinking skills" teaching for some time. Still, just below the surface media literacy as a project easily becomes confused, not only because of its political implications. It is grounded in the swamp of popular culture research.

Among the most ambitious of the intellectual projects to address popular culture is cultural studies (Grossberg, Nelson, and Treichler 1992). But it has been strongest in the leftish wing of the academy, and in other cultural sites such as museums and grassroots cultural projects. Conservatives have portrayed cultural studies as a politically dangerous project to deconstruct the canon and glorify the forces eroding consensus, but the intellectual movement has lacked a relationship with social movements that would justify conservative fears (Aufderheide 1992). From the left, Todd Gitlin has argued that cultural studies has been a resort of academics "to take the sting out of political defeat" (Gitlin 1997, 79). Academic and education critic Henry Giroux charged in a November 1990 *Afterimage* interview with David Trend (later the author of the provocative *Cultural Pedagogy* [1992]) that the movement "has no frame or political project. Cultural studies for what?" (Trend 1990, 17).

This question can be asked for media literacy as well. Why do students need to be media literate? Some teachers want to give them the tools to control their own expression, or even provide them with a job skill—a forlorn expectation for the great majority, perhaps, in mass media, where the advertiser-driven few talk to the consuming many. Some want to give them weapons against mass media's seductions, an armoring concept that pits the teachers against a pop culture envisioned as the latest Satanic lure in a puritanical high culture. Some see media literacy as a Trojan horse within which leftists can sneak in their agenda critical of a commoditized culture, a position that puts them at odds with many public school teachers. Teachers may even be caught up in sentimental, self-marginalizing solidarity with students, or a voyeuristic fascination with their separate worlds (Giroux and Simon 1989).

This problem of defining goals reflects the state of research on popular culture generally. How influential are mass media in shaping attitudes and actions? We do not have good enough answers. In the classroom, teachers often veer between moralizing and enthusing along with the students. This vacillation has something to do with class control—don't disparage the stuff they like or they won't talk about it in class—and something to do with partly digested reception theory.

Reception analysts, opposed to the old-guard Frankfurt School theorists of mass delusion, argue that different audiences "read" media very differently and that ostensibly oppressive messages may be read in empowering ways. For instance, unlike some adult critics who may see gangsta rap as reinforcing sexist and racist stereotypes, young people may find resistance to demeaning stereotypes. But then what? Audience response theory has promised to take the snobbery out of pop cultural studies, but it remains an area in need of much more concrete research. This has not impeded a flood of romantic empowerment rhetoric, postulating without substantiation pop culture as a culturally liberating force.

The very project of teaching about popular culture can be inflammatory. Parents often object when public school teachers assign prime-time television, for example. Students may resist the invasion of their cultural privacy. Conservative administrators and teachers often abhor the intrusion of "trash culture" into the school day.

For many teachers and analysts, *media* might as well be coterminous with *television*, admittedly a powerful source of information but only one of the mass media. (Radio is my personal selection for most and most unjustly neglected.) Some would like to teach media throughout the curriculum, while others want a media studies class. And some, especially television producers and distributors, use the term *media literacy* to include television about anything "educational"—gun control, family stress, teen pregnancy—rather than media about media itself. HBO's excellent half-hour shows, made with Consumers Union, *Buy Me That* and *Buy Me That Too*—about TV commercials for kids—avoid this pitfall.

These confusions might be considered part of the normal messiness of the birth of a new approach. But if media literacy is to establish itself, it must confront the issues of knowledge and power always inherent in mass media.

### Key Concepts in Media Literacy

*In the practice of teaching, I evolved my own version of some basic concepts that evolved within this movement and were passed from teacher to teacher. I built on a summary of them used in the Ontario Ministry of Education's resource guide (1989). What follows, then, is what I hand out to my students, with the reminder that it builds on working documents in the media literacy movement and the encouragement to redesign.*

We know about the world primarily from the media. But the media don't simply give us the world. They interpret reality, tailor it, perform it.

Each medium does this in different ways, and no medium is "free" of bias, or objective. It can't be, because making media involves making choices, selecting from reality the part you show or tell. Mass media carry messages, not just the obvious ones (buy this shampoo, the president made a speech) but also more subtle ones (girls with bouncy hair get boyfriends, the president is an authority to be respected).

They carry their messages differently according to their particular capacities (some media, like radio, reach a lot of people at once, while some, like newsletters, reach a small targeted audience; some media, like television, transmit images powerfully while others, like CDs, carry audio powerfully).

They also carry messages to us, shaped by their economic and political contexts. Commercial media mostly depend on advertising and can't afford to produce their product without that support. Public television needs the support of Congress and its viewers, as well as of friendly corporations.

In order to be responsible citizens, we need to be media literate. To help you engage in that process, here are eight "key concepts" of media literacy. We will be using these concepts throughout the course.

1. All media are constructions.

Media do not simply reflect reality. They present productions, which have specific purposes. The success of these productions lies in their *apparent* naturalness. They don't look like constructions. But they are, and many different constraints and decisions have gone into why they look the way they do. Often they are superbly produced, and mostly they are part and parcel of our daily lives. So we're not used to thinking about how they're made, and why they're made that way, and how that conditions what we receive as "reality." Our job is to rediscover the complexity in even very simple media texts, and in that way, to discover media as social constructions.

2. The media construct reality.

While they are constructions, media productions also construct within each of our heads a notion of the real. We each carry within us a model of reality, based on our observations and experiences. We believe that, using that model, we're capable of distinguishing truth from lies and are confident that we won't let "them" pull the wool over our eyes. But much of that model of reality comes from the media we've seen, or that other people who we take as models (our parents, our teachers) have seen. So it's not as easy as it might seem to draw the line between personal lived experience and the world of "the media." In fact, the media are constructing our sense of reality each day.

3. Audiences negotiate meaning in media.

Even though media carry messages, they aren't received by everybody in the same way. When you like a movie your roommate hated, that's pretty clear. Each of us filters meaning in media through our different experiences: our socioeconomic status, our race, cultural background, gender, whether we're tired, whether we know somebody involved in the story.

When the camcorder footage of the police beating in Los Angeles was aired, an African American living in southeast Washington, an Ohio police officer, a camcorder enthusiast took different meanings from the airing. A parent reacts to a LimpBizkit CD very differently from a teenager, and African American female teenagers react differently from Italian American male teenagers. The romance novels that look to a college professor like a retreat from feminism may be used by working-class women in the home as an important source of nurturing and reinforcement of self-esteem.

Each of us negotiates meaning in different ways. However, negotiation of meaning is not purely idiosyncratic; you can't dismiss the social importance of media simply by saying, "Well, everybody sees things differently." Meaning is negotiated by people *within their cultural contexts* because each individual exists within a social network. Meaning is something we share with other people, and the more widely it is shared, the more powerful and pervasive it is.

### 4. Media have commercial implications.

If you are going to be media literate, it's crucially important to know the economic basis of mass media production, and how that affects content, techniques, and distribution. Most media production in this country is a business, and it must make a profit. This is not a criticism. It is a fact. Without a profit, the best newspaper, the best movie studio, the best publisher cannot continue to exist. Different media have different ways to survive financially. Even the so-called public media—public television, public radio—have to raise money.

When you decode the media, you need to ask yourself, Who paid for this? What's the economic structure underpinning this piece of work? When the producer or the writer or the director chose the subject and went to work producing it, how did the financial constraints affect his or her choices?

Mass media do not speak to individuals but to groups of people, in fact, to demographic markets. You are a part of several demographic markets—young people, men or women, Washingtonians, people with your particular hobby, and so on. The more money you have to spend within any particular demographic, the more valuable you are to mass media's marketers. Different media have different capacities to access different demographics. For instance, network television reaches most people in America but isn't very good at targeting small demographics. *Modern Maturity,* the magazine of the American Association of Retired Persons, reaches almost everybody older than fifty.

Mass media's commercial implications also involve who owns the mass media. In the past decade, a long process of concentration of ownership has been speeded up dramatically. If the same company owns a record company, a movie studio, a cable service, network television, videocassette recording, and book and magazine publication (as does Time Warner), it has a powerful ability to control what is produced, distributed, and therefore seen.

### 5. Media contain ideological and value messages.

A media literate person is always aware that media texts carry values and have ideological implications. (*Ideology* in this sense means the set of assumptions for what we think is normal.) A media literate person does not complain that something is biased; he or she searches out the bias, the assumptions, the values in everything that's made. It's all made by people, after all, who interpret the world according to their values and assumptions. Most often, the media affirm the world as it is, the status quo, the received wisdom, whatever is thought of by the media makers as the consensus. And they become reinforcers of that status quo as a result. Here are some values that media typically deal with: the "good life," and the importance of affluence in achieving it; the proper roles for women; proper authority; patriotism.

Because media mostly reinforce the status quo, the fact that they carry values may seem almost invisible, or ordinary, or not worth noting. It becomes clearer that they carry those values when you disagree with them. A woman executive may object to a sitcom that makes women look dizzy; a Latino professional whose family has lived in the Southwest since before Anglo settlers got there may object to news coverage that represents Latinos as impoverished new immigrants; a welfare recipient may be outraged at the absence of media images that reflect her life. Because the reinforcement of the status quo is typically done in subtle ways that may simply be part of the producer's own image of reality, it may seem petty to pick on small background images, particular word choices, the amount of time or space or placement given to an news item. But the media shape values not only by the explicit message delivered but by the entire context in which they're presented.

6. Media have social and political implications.

Because media construct reality, under economic terms that shape their messages, and powerfully transmit values, they have important social and political effects. Some of these are more obvious than others. For instance, in the 1950s the average time a campaigning politician got uninterrupted to speak on television was almost a minute. Now it's a few seconds. That has a direct effect on how the public sees political issues in debate. On the other hand, it may be harder to judge the social effect of having the television on in people's homes more than seven hours a day. Surely, leisure patterns, babysitting arrangements, and family activities have changed, but they're not so easy to measure. Surely, if most of the top-ten children's books are (as they usually are) product- and particularly toy-related, that shapes the habits and appetites of young kids, so that they're plugged into a commercial universe at the beginning of their reading experience. But measuring how different that is from reading

Sesame Street books (which also have characters for sale on toy shelves) or the Disney Golden Book of Cinderella may be hard.

Social scientists in communication use a variety of ways, both quantitative and qualitative, to measure the social and political effects of the media. They do social science experiments, they conduct surveys and polls, they analyze popular texts. Whatever their method, what they share in common is a realization that the media have social and political effects. What that means is that the (mostly commercial) media have an effect on our lives together in society, and as members of the public.

As citizens and as members of our various local and national communities, we all have something in common that we do not simply share as consumers. Rich or poor, men or women, from all our different cultural backgrounds, we all live together and must work together in a democracy. That is, we all experience as the public the effects of our local, state, and national governments and the economic interests that shape our economy. A democracy depends not on elected representatives alone, but on an active public (not one that just votes) that is out there understanding, arguing about, and doing something about its own interests. For instance, a development corporation may ask a city council for a waiver to build a new development. But the road system isn't adequate. Where is the public interest? Is it in building new roads? (More traffic, more pollution, less park and farmland.) Is it in halting development? (Fewer new homes, less new work.) Is it in a different kind of development? (More first homes, fewer luxury homes, renovating downtown homes.) Citizens don't have to raise or answer these questions. If they don't, the developer and the city council will decide for them. But if they do, they will bring to the problem their model of reality built on the media. They will depend on the media's coverage of these issues. And they will have to use the media.

In the United States the media are protected by the First Amendment, saying that government will not infringe on the freedom of the press. The reason the First Amendment is there is that the Founding Fathers recognized that the media have social and political effects. They saw the media as a place where the public could get information the government might not want to give them.

There are many questions to address about the social and political effects of the media. Some examples are: How powerful in shaping expectations are different kinds of media? Does government ever legitimately exercise censorship control over any of the media? Are economic forces constraining media also a kind of censorship of unpopular views or views that are held by people who aren't interesting to advertisers or marketers? Some specific ways those questions have been brought to bear in media debates are: Should one company be able to own both the major newspaper and a television station in the same town? Should the government require commercial broadcasters to air programs for children? How important is violence in, say, TV programs or rock lyrics or pornography in affecting people's values, and is it serious enough that the government should take action? There are of course many more, coming up each day.

7. Form and content are closely related in the media.

Each medium has its own distinctive characteristics. You will get a very different experience of a major event by reading the newspaper, watching TV, listening to the radio, going to a movie, or reading a book about it. A media literate person asks, What about the form of this medium influences the content? Is that formal capacity being exploited well, or is it being wasted? What about the form limits the content?

8. Each medium has a unique aesthetic form.

A media literate person does not destroy his or her ability to enjoy a medium, because of an increased ability to analyze it. In fact, understanding how to read the media also means understanding that they are each art forms as well as information transmitters. We pay attention, in writing, to the well-crafted phrase, the vivid quote, the tightly structured argument. We appreciate editing that sharpens contrasts and makes our heart skip a beat in audio, video, and film. We understand the power of a camera to shape our own point of view, on entering a scene. When we see how media are constructed, we are able to judge their aesthetic value. We ask two sets of related questions: Did it entertain me, keep my attention, involve me, and how did it do that? Did it tell me more about the world, human affairs, and my part in it, and how did it do that?

## Note

Consultancies with the Aspen Institute and the Ford Foundation contributed to this work.

## References

Aufderheide, P., ed. 1992. *Beyond PC: Toward a Politics of Understanding.* St. Paul: Graywolf.

Giroux, H., and R. Simon. 1989. "Popular Culture and Critical Pedagogy: Everyday Life as a Basis for Curriculum Knowledge." In *Critical Pedagogy, the State, and the Cultural Struggle,* ed. H. Giroux and P. McLaren. Albany: State University of New York Press.

Gitlin, T. 1997. "The Anti-Political Populism of Cultural Studies." *Dissent:* 77–82.

Grossberg, L., C. Nelson, and P. Treichler, eds. 1992. *Cultural Studies.* New York: Routledge, Chapman and Hall.

Masterman, L. 1985. *Teaching the Media.* London: Comedia.

Ontario Ministry of Education. 1989. *Media Literacy Resource Guide: Intermediate and Senior Divisions, 1989.* Ottawa: Author.

Trend, D. 1990. "Critical Pedagogy and Cultural Power: An Interview with Henry A. Giroux." *Afterimage* 18 (4): 15–17.

———. 1992. *Cultural Pedagogy.* New York: Bergin and Garvey.

# Does a

# Librarian Need

# Multiculturalism?

*By the '90s, multiculturalism had been built into many mission statements with-
out looking much different from any other piety about pluralism and was under attack from the Right. Thanks to the indefatigable networking of Barbara Abrash and
Catherine Egan at New York University, I was invited to give a keynote address to
librarians attending the 1994 meeting of the Consortium of College and University
Media Centers. These were the people who ran the audiovisual libraries for their
schools, and who were in a key position both to purchase and help patrons learn
and teach pluralism, tolerance, and ordinary curiosity, using the burgeoning supply of independently produced films and videos.*

Multiculturalism. Everybody's talking about it, half of them are mandating it, and most of us would be happy to do it . . . only what does it mean
really?

A lot of people seem to think they know what it means. People like
Dinesh D'Souza, the author of *Illiberal Education,* are sure it means rob-
bing students of truth and beauty in the service of political correctness.
Meanwhile, many people whose voices have long been marginalized are
deeply suspicious. They're convinced this is another elite ploy to pacify
them.

But multiculturalism—or whatever jargon word we use next—actually holds a great promise: the revitalization of democracy in a polycultural society. It means the recognition of difference, in a positive way. It means you and I can work together for the public good—even though in private and within our very different cultural experiences we differ profoundly. It means not only can we work together, but we can work better because we can draw on each other's differences to come up with better answers. It means we don't have to go on pretending that we're all really the same under the skin or the accent or the attitude. But we don't have to write each other off either, because of the skin or the accent or the attitude.

In fact, some of the people who might benefit most from multiculturalism are those who oppose each other most extremely in this debate—the people who talk about essential truth and beauty, and those suspicious folks on the other side. Just imagine, if before they went into battle, they could see each other's viewpoints as culturally shaped and deeply felt and still find ways to communicate instead of hunker down in self-righteous positions. Then they could disagree, and even fight, constructively.

That's an exciting prospect. And it's also terrifying, when you start. I'm not talking about something that's easy at the outset. I don't want to be a Pollyanna about this. If it were easy to do this, we'd have a vital, living, contestatory, grassroots democracy now, instead of having to fight for it. That's where media can come in. Media can engage people and also allay their terror as they begin to explore difference.

For me, multiculturalism isn't just about making sure African American or Latino or Asian American or indigenous American voices get heard by white Americans—or, to complicate it, German Americans, Italian Americans, Anglo Americans, and other ethnic groups. That's important. Once we say "white" and "black," we're talking skin color, and if we're opposing people of color to white people, we're ignoring important felt realities and experiences.

It's critically important that people whose voices have not been heard much in mainstream media get heard. And heard in a way that doesn't make people who may never even have thought of them before to renounce their own cultural viewpoints—or, more likely, pretend to renounce them. What I understand by multiculturalism is a project that puts at its center power and its relation to American democracy.

The problem in American democracy is this: the political promises of equality of opportunity and equality before the law rest ultimately on economic and cultural bases. They assume—they don't give—an equality of access, an equality of understanding, an equality of treatment. But you only need to look at what poverty does to literacy, or what racism has done to voting, or what pregnancy without family leave does to women's working lives to know that the democratic promise can be fatally flawed in practice.

Multiculturalism at its best is a tool of democracy. It's not about celebrating Hmong tapestries and Chicano contributions to American cuisine. It's not about shifting the blame, or increasing the guilt, or lowering the standards. It's about difference, in both positive and negative senses. It can't avoid the fact of conflict—social conflict. Conflict over social resources, access to the political process, representation in the media. But it describes that conflict while offering ways to solve the problems it's created, with the all-important tool of cross-cultural perception.

The need for that perception may be patent in the case of America's ethnic minorities. But what about the cultures of rural Appalachia, of working-class Republicans, of Bret Easton Ellis–type preppies, of New Agers, and children of merged families? You don't have to like any of those cultural experiences to know you need to know about them to get any further.

I'm not asking for the categories of the "sacred three"—race, class, gender—to be infinitely expanded. I'm saying that once you grasp the concept of a culturally bounded worldview, you can become curious about people very different from you. And if, for a Jewish middle-class male that means sympathetic curiosity about African American lesbians, maybe it also means sympathetic curiosity by a Detroit Yemeni steelworker about the culture of a rural Iowa doctor trying to decide whether or not to offer abortions.

And why do I care about that? Because in a democracy, we need to understand both our differentness and the value of a political process that lets us keep that differentness while also carving out space in public to solve our problems of living together. And until you can see people as not that imaginary creature, the "individual"—just another marble in a bag of marbles—but as members of a variety of groups that shape that individual's expectations, you'll be spouting your sixth-grade civics cant. You won't really be able to work with them to figure out how we can live together and also live our separate lives.

There are many forces militating against that dream today. Of course, there are the traditional inequalities. And there's also the false consensus of national, commercial, entertainment-driven media. Dan Rather, *The Simpsons*, MTV. The mainstream commercial media pull us together, but not as citizens. Instead, they unite us as consumers of the products they pitch. And that includes the ultimate product: commodity consciousness, or, you are what you buy.

So the challenge of multiculturalism is to reposition cultural difference, not as a threat or as a demand to capitulate before someone else's viewpoint, but as an invitation to discovering difference. That can be a road to power for "the public"—all those people who differ so profoundly, one group from another, and within different groups, but who have in common the need to live together. We can teach our students not only to open their eyes to others, but to the fact that they themselves live in a culture. And through that realization, we can offer them the skills they need to participate effectively in a multicultural public.

That's the job of an educator. Educators are privileged people in society because we don't—at least not directly—have to bow to the whims of commerce and power, and we must undertake the grave responsibility of shaping future citizens.

As teachers and media selectors, we often know that special role as one of powerlessness—our budgets are small, our bureaucracies are slow, our old habits are entrenched and reinforced by the lack of market pressure that, say, business has. But it's also an exciting place on the social landscape, one where we have the freedom to experiment. And as the whole debate over multiculturalism and the curriculum has revealed, that freedom is not a pleasant luxury, but a necessity to build a strong society. In a society like ours, with so many pressures against a civic consciousness, we are playing a crucial role. Look around you and ask, if we don't do it in schools and universities, who will?

There's a clear place to start, for those who want to plunge into the task of shaping a multicultural consciousness: in a recognition of the *Other*. That's a fashionable term. By it, I mean the whole categories of people's experience that we contrast with whatever we think is normal. Now that category of the Other will differ depending on where you stand. For someone like me, it's likely to be the army of college graduates who went so eagerly to work in Washington, D.C., for the Reagan administration, and maybe people who watched as much television as they wanted to when they were kids. I learned about the Reaganites as I worked in Washington communications policy. And I learned about latchkey-TV from my students. If you're a struggling Puerto Rican entrepreneur, it'll be something different, maybe middle-aged bankers. If you're a poor single mother, it's something else again, maybe the culture of social workers.

Whatever it is, The Other is not a person. It's not about those other people, but the fact that you have a category in your mind that lumps a bunch of people together as somehow less real than your experience. Nobody is an Other to themselves. So it's a cultural viewpoint, a way of seeing the world and excluding some of it; it's about values and priorities. When you start to think about The Other, and you start to realize how different reality is from your imagination and your elimination of part of it, it involves a recognition that other people may not only be different from you because they're individuals, but also because they exist within a different cultural context. And only when you understand that can you begin to work against, on, and maybe even with those people.

It's hard work because it goes against the grain of American individualism. It's easy to say, "Skin color doesn't matter to me—you can be blue or green." That is, until the African American says, "It matters to me."

It's hard because it means overcoming hurdles of guilt and anxiety.

It's hard because it means having patience, most of all with yourself, to exit from the world of zero-sum games, in which if I'm right she's wrong, and if she's right then I must be wrong.

And because it means coming to a recognition of your own social self, a part of your person that goes beyond your consumer status and may even involve taking some political action as a small *d* democrat. It means seeing yourself as a culturally bound person, with limits on your own perception—limits that structure your life and are helpful as well as not. But if you want to see beyond them, you need to enter into dialogue with others, learn how to be conscious and curious, and seek out that dialogue.

People often don't want to do that, especially when they're threatened with the idea that they might have been wrong. The easiest, most familiar resort is denial. One small example: One professor of economics I worked with really wanted to use films by Asian, African, Latin American filmmakers to illustrate problems of development. He kept asking me, "Why are all these films so depressing? Can't you recommend any with happy endings?" Well, we'd all like happy endings.

But what happens if we say, "There can be a happy ending, but getting there means understanding why this person doesn't see a happy ending in the current situation"? What happens if we invite people to ask questions rather than looking for the correct answers?

Public life, that's what happens. That messy, pragmatic process whereby very different kinds of interests find common ground.

But you can't get anywhere unless you overcome denial. In overcoming that first step of denial, media has some salient advantages:

• It's one step removed: it's a vicarious experience. It's not like an African American and a non–African American talking about their different perceptions of the same action, like, say, the Los Angeles police beating. It's safer.

• Media has authority unlike the presence of an individual. It's not just a person talking, it's a public statement.

• It's familiar in form; it offers some familiar points of reference, even when its message is very different.

• A video is not just a logical argument (and usually not even that); it's a gestalt, a way of seeing, a perception. It offers lots of information that an argument doesn't have.

So that's where I start getting excited about seeing the interlock between media and multiculturalism.

That said, I think integrating media into a multicultural curriculum has some hurdles to overcome:

(1) Media selectors, whether they want to or not, are often on the front lines here. The teachers may be comfortable with their old routines; the students may be comfortable thinking the teachers are old fogeys. And they won't necessarily know what kinds of media are being made—especially by the kind of people they categorize as The Other and therefore don't think of at all.

When I say media selectors are on the front lines, I mean they may be having to rethink the traditional approach to collections. Maybe instead of making sure the library has *x* number of videos on African American experience, the librarian says, "What are the problems people have in perceiving those experiences, and how can media help?" Maybe the librarian or media selector has some materials in the collection that vividly illustrate misunderstandings and that can provoke an exciting discussion. Maybe the collection needs new materials, and to find them the librarian needs to have conversations with people very different from themselves, and to go to places where they can encounter them. And maybe the first conversations are a little awkward. Maybe they need to brainstorm with the faculty about how to approach multiculturalism as a positive challenge. But above all, it means a media selector has to take the initiative to reformulate the issue.

(2) Even once you've found the stuff, media won't solve the problem. Without a problem-solving approach, even a stimulating video will fall

on misinterpreting ears and eyes. The teacher has to be willing to address the issue; showing a video won't do the job for the teacher.

I have often used a clip from Marlon Riggs's provocative look at racist kitsch, *Ethnic Notions*. When I first showed it, one thing my students immediately said was, "These are ugly stereotypes from the past, and we shouldn't be bringing them up again." How important, then, for a communications professor to talk about how we can recognize and identify them as stereotypes and thus show that they live on in people's minds. How important for a history professor to show the link between pop cultural kitsch and historical decisions made easier by public acceptance of stereotypes. How important to acknowledge discomfort, and the fear of the anger of the Other, and to reinforce the reality that it can't be overcome by burying its existence. How important to raise the doubts that many African Americans had about resurrecting old stereotypes when they saw the video.

(3) Media must be used creatively, interactively. You must learn to see within even familiar images something new, and that means searching for the revealing. Consider the first few minutes of the well-worn classic *The African Queen*. I ask my students to look at the introductory few minutes not for Humphrey and Katherine, but for the movie's portrayal of the natives and the assumptions behind it. I ask them to locate the Africans and to note very specifically how they are represented. We ask questions such as, What's in the foreground and what's in the background? What meaning does a pan connote here? Whose names do we know?

(4) You have to know something about the media in question. You have to know who made it and why, and for whom. We look in class at a reworking of *Butch Cassidy and the Sundance Kid* by a Mexican woman filmmaker, Gloria Ribé, in her short video, *De Aca de Este Lado*. She made it for a Mexican audience, on the subject of the mutual misperceptions of Mexicans and North Americans. Seeing our media reinterpreted suddenly helps us see another point of view. It's also important to realize that the primary audience was Mexicans, and it's interesting to think about why this filmmaker thought they needed to think about this. It's also important to realize that many more Mexicans saw *Butch Cassidy* than saw *De Aca de Este Lado*.

What does this mean for teachers and for media selectors?

It means that the interlock between media and multiculturalism is a natural. The media part is pretty easy—for some more than others, admittedly. For some of us, it's been made more easy by the fact that our students can't sit still without a little video, so we're used to throwing something—sometimes anything—into the breach. That doesn't mean professors are often willing to see media as a tool like print that requires analysis. And I think the only thing that helps there is something like a strongly recommended media training seminar for teachers, to get them into a classroom and see how much more interesting visual media gets when you look at it, and look at it again.

The hard part, the really hard part, is the multiculturalism. Partly because the debate has been infused with self-righteous moralism and defensiveness, partly because we're dealing with long-standing social inequality, partly because our democratic process is so often the shell of democracy that we're not used to actively thinking in problem-solving ways.

It means for media selectors and teachers that we have to think, not in terms of the media themselves but the problems and miscommunications that media can address, and then we have to think about how to use the media creatively and interactively to address them. This takes the issue past collections policy and into creative learning strategies. It means we rethink how we present our existing collections to faculty and students as much as it means adding to those collections.

But in the process, you get to indulge yourself in the great adventure of crossing beyond your boundaries, to learn and find yourself a bigger, less embattled person as a result. It's work that, once you begin to do it, you become so eager to share with other people that you get a tremendous burst of energy. And then they give it back to you again.

# Conversations

# in Latin America

*By the time I was asked to host a Latin American tour of a package of U.S. in-*
*dependent films, I thought I had grasped the fundamentals of cross-cultural con-*
*fusion. But I traveled in 1985, at the height of Reaganism. The neoimperialist*
*triumphalism of that moment put a new spin on familiar issues in intercultural*
*relations. The trip was also a chance for me to put to the test my great hopes for*
*media as a cross-cultural bridge. The report card was mixed.*

"Thank you for coming," the wiry fifty-year-old Panamanian poet said to
me. "I've never had a real talk with a North American before. I never
wanted to before."

It was a terrific conversation, and it was also part of my job. In a six-
month trip throughout Latin America, I met with intellectuals and organizers in eleven countries, all dubious of the category "Latin American"
but united around the notion that at least they were not North American.
In each, I confronted the question of the Americas that Americans don't
see—both North and South.

Northern ignorance—and the ignorance of North Americans about
Latin America is virtually absolute—is only puzzling if you think about
the cost of knowing. If you want to live in peace in a prime-time empire,
you have to become expert at what Daniel Ellsberg called controlled

stupidity. Since the Pentagon Papers days, controlled stupidity may have become the defining feature of modern American life in the white middle class.

For Southerners, Northern ignorance has long been a favorite literary theme, and some Latin American savants have made international reputations by dwelling on the peculiar miscommunications among the peoples of our hemisphere, insisting that more is here and at stake than can be handled by even the best of State Departments. And our plugged-in culture has honored them in our way. We've turned them into media stars. Mexican author and diplomat Carlos Fuentes seems to have been nominated ambassador to the culture of the wilfully blind, while V. S. Naipaul seems its honorary adopted son, and Mario Vargas Llosa the fashion designer for imperial curiosity.

Archconservative Octavio Paz told Enrique Fernández of the *Village Voice*, "You don't understand us. I'm fed up with your country." And then, he launched into an analysis of North Americans' "extraordinary capacity not to see":

> This sort of blindness is not due to a lack of talent—North Americans are very talented—nor to a lack of sensitivity. . . . Instead, I think that it conforms to a historical pattern which is also reflected in their foreign policy and in their vision of the world, particularly of Latin America. Perhaps the explanation lies in the very origins of the American nation. The Founding Fathers wanted to build a utopia outside of history and Americans have had to adjust themselves to history. And not only to history, but to being an empire. They have the responsibility of an empire, which in their hearts, they would rather not have. They are Romans in spite of themselves. (Fernández 1985, 39)

More than a decade after my initiation into insight and blindness in Latin America, I was returning once again. My mission on this latest of many trips southward: to convince Latin Americans that a culture other than the one in James Bond and Rambo movies exists; a culture that lives in history, not in myth; a culture of subcultures, of conflict; a culture that intends to have as much to say about America's future as anything cooked up in the State Department or Madison Avenue.

I was doing it with a batch of American independent social-issue films, ranging from *Rosie the Riveter* to *Word Is Out* to *Americas in Transition* to *Killer of Sheep*. Women, gays, leftists, blacks. The series, called La Otra Cara/The Other Face, had been organized by a joint committee of North American and Latin American political filmmakers who had the kind of faith in "alternative" culture you need in order to keep on making it.

The previous few years had been tough, politically and economically, in Latin America. Every country we went into was still in the throes of crisis, whether monetary or political. Every host assured us—with a wry pride—that his country was the worst-off in Latin America. Our conversations were conducted, typically, in an atmosphere of impending political and economic chaos, whether in a Peru beset by Sendero Luminoso, or a Costa Rica in the midst of a governmental campaign against the Sandinistas, a Panama shaken by an IMF loan controversy, an Argentina rocked by scandal in the military, a Bolivia in the midst of a state of seige. Political institutions and alliances were fragile and fluctuating, and their economic underpinnings rotted. It's as if the passion to define, to assert, to name, to describe were rushing in to fill a vacuum in the political process, dominated by a few and lacking stable institutions and channels through which those voices could reach power. And everyone wanted to know whether in the world we were showing on screen, there was any realization that below the border people exist in an intimate and uncomfortable relationship with a behemoth to the North.

Anti-Americanism was where we would start talking, in the eager groups of critics and intellectuals who first received us. Maybe people felt I was vouched for by my left-leaning hosts, and thus fair game; certainly, they delighted in the chance to assert their own sophistication. But more than expressing their anti-Yankee spirit, they were putting into play a conversational ball, and waiting to see how I would pick it up and send it back. The fierce opening attacks, remarkably similar in different countries, had all the earmarks of a linguistic convention, a kind of "How are you?" once you knew how to hear it.

Political attacks on the United States were only a small—and, once I got incorporated into the group, not a very interesting—part of conversations that covered a wide range of political realities. It was all grist for one of Latin America's finest art forms and perhaps its most popular sport, the conversation. It was both an exercise in social life and a heroic effort at asserting and establishing one.

*Social* is the key word here. People talked big, stretching themselves in company. The subject was always society—civil society, the quality of civilization, historical grandeur and debacle and, its lessons for today, the obstacles to and mechanisms of social progress. Politics was not something you left to professionals, and not something that ended at the office. And if it was not a forbidden topic, neither was it a weighty—in the sense of leaden—one.

The discussions would go on late into the night, with film exhibitors, poets, admen, teachers, and the kind of entrepreneur who prides himself in relationships with an artistic world, and would evolve into a kind of macho stand-off to see who would stay out the latest and order the last round of drinks. We would move from an exchange of information to a shared experience of understanding; with our words, we would undertake a reshaping of our social universe.

The night was always long in a way that defied the regime of common sense and reasonable care of the body and mind. It made a kind of sense. Who needed reason, a cool cost-accounting approach to life, when business sense and reason got you the chaos, the cruelty, the absurdity of a day in underdevelopment?

I was moving through societies where free speech was often embattled, and just as fiercely defended. And not just the legal right but the quality of the act was constantly analyzed. We heard the harshest criticisms reserved not for the far-off Yankees, but for the quality of education in one's own country, for the inveterate subversion of the level of public debate by factions and cliques, for the damage done to society by repressive forces smothering the will to talk. "I'm not happy with the reaction to the films," a programmer told me in the backlands of Uruguay, which had only months before emerged from thirteen years of brutal dictatorship. We had just concluded an after-film discussion that had seemed reasonably active to me. "People have been so terrified for so long they're afraid to speak out. And I'm afraid that the government's brainwashing has worked—they're all afraid of communists under the bed." That didn't stop her from organizing film showings to reinvigorate what, before the generals' rule, had been routine community debates.

In each country, the first few days were a crash course in the intricacies of local political parties, in mastering the flavors and distortions of each of the newspapers and electronic media, in memorizing the names of local heroes most likely to appear on statues and tossed into casual references. We had to learn quickly in order to play the liveliest game in town. All information, it seemed, was regarded as interesting, to be challenged, to be savored even in its diabolism if necessary and then answered.

The profound separation between private and public, between profession and leisure life, between official and personal realities that neatly divides an American life the way kids' plates keep the vegetables away from the meat did not exist in these conversations. In fact, the very notion was part of the harshest criticism people had of the North.

"Americans don't know how to live," people would tell me again and again. They meant: Americans don't know how to talk. They don't know the ardent passionate game of conversation. They aren't interested in anything but their own stability, their own image, their own story. "Patricia, though, she's communicative," they would pronounce with a generosity that was also a command to join in, not to inform but to argue, to prove by doing that we were in the same realm of discourse.

People might turn to me for a point of information on American life—often as a belated gesture toward my mission as exhibitor—but they didn't want a lecture. Sometimes they didn't even wait for the answer. Truly outside information—explaining the workings of the two major political parties, for instance—would have just brought the conversation to a halt. And we had, as they say on the sports commentaries, come to play.

The thirst for culture, for theory, for argument was general. Foucault, Marx, Derrida would dot the conversations of Costa Rican theater folk and Colombian admen. At a late dinner in uplands Argentina, I met the wife of a film buff, a biologist. When I told her I had studied colonial Latin American history, she said she had just finished reading Alexander von Humboldt's eighteenth century journeys in the Amazon basin. She was looking for further training outside Argentina.

"The best places are in the United States," she told me, "but I could never go there." Why? "Because work isn't enough for me. All the American engineers I meet, the only thing they can talk about is their research. That's all they're interested in. I need more than that. In Europe I can be a whole person."

I loved being invited into—no, challenged to have—these conversations. But long before the party would be ready to break up, I would beg, exhausted, to go home. It wasn't just that I wasn't used to the social demands. It was also that unlike my hosts, I would never arrive at that moment of resolution when the enemy forces would be definitively named, isolated, targeted. Naming would never be enough to arm me to confront my own society's contradictions.

So I would plead the next day's obligations, and my duty to my mission. "Patricia's a good kid," they would say. "But she works too hard. That's Americans for you." And as I left, they would be regaling each other with hilarious parodies of the IBM salesman whose stiff gait could never accommodate a samba beat, or the U.S. visiting scholar who had encamped in a library and never savored the world the library recorded.

Critical as they invariably were of Northerners, of their technical wizardry and their stunted humanity, these intellectual flames weren't really very interested in seeing "the other face," as our tour was called, of America through film. Independent films from America's "minorities and marginals"—this is how our films about and by women, working people, Hispanics, blacks, and gays were described—conformed to some of their grimmest expectations about American social life. The embattled stands of independent filmmakers and the social groups they described looked to them like one more way that North Americans specialize and segment their humanity.

The notion that subcultures have their own languages and values, not comprehended by even so global a political analysis as that offered by Marxism, ran counter to every principle on which their flamboyant conversations were conducted. *Word Is Out,* a set of sixteen interviews with homosexual men and women about their coming out, was widely excoriated for being self-indulgent and even decadent. The decadence was not so much in sexual activity but in the self-conscious styling of an alternative culture, a deliberate separation from the larger work of building civilization and progress and, yes, civil society. "Are there really so many homosexuals today in the United States?" people would ask in every country. "Doesn't this increase reflect the general decay of social values there?" They wouldn't have agreed with Pat Robertson's or Jerry Falwell's take on homosexuality. Indeed, all over Latin America fundamentalists were regarded as a similar example of rot in our social system—because they too were seen as separatist, militant, and in some way selfish for espousing a sectarian position in social life. Even in Latin artistic communities, where homosexual behavior is much more prominent than in most other circles and where the film drew more genuinely curious audiences, the film was coolly received as self-indulgent.

*Rosie the Riveter,* about women working during World War II and losing their jobs thereafter, made many uncomfortable in the same way. Again and again we heard: in our country women and men work side by side and support each other; we see no future in championing women's rights; we think this is more evidence of the lonely, self-defeating isolationism that we see in Americans' behavior everywhere.

And the black films we brought, films that were made by blacks in a neorealist style about black urban life, often elicited the criticism that such films reinforced racism by not providing an analysis of the wider society and the forces maintaining inequality. For instance, when we showed *Clarence and Angel* in Ecuador to a group of students—like everywhere in Latin America, many of them were middle-aged political activists—the film raised a scandal. In the movie, an African American kid and a Hispanic kid learn from each other what they cannot learn in the authoritarian and impoverished public school system of New York.

The audience was appalled that virtually all authority figures in the film were black. "This film looks like a racist expression to me," said one student angrily. "Where are the whites? Why is there no analysis showing what the context for this poverty and authoritarianism is?" The notion that the film is dominated by black characters because the world of our inner cities is not integrated racially was not sufficient. In fact, the notion of de facto segregation on that order was plain baffling. But even if the Ecuadoran students had been able to accept that as reality, I wonder if they would not still have faulted the film for not providing an explicit analysis of racial discrimination. For them, naming had a reality far more acute than any neorealist expression.

*Killer of Sheep*, a neorealist film set in Watts, both shocked Latin Americans ("Aside from a few street signs, you'd never know it was in America; it could be in any Third World country") and appalled them. "Why can't whites and blacks just set an agenda and work together on it?" asked a Uruguayan political organizer in a question that was really an accusation.

Our fiercely analytical friends were imagining U.S. marginalized cultures in their own image. The notion that a North American black would not have a Latin American political consciousness and still be able to lay claim to an authentic representation of his community was just inconceivable. As well, for many it presumed intolerably to ask them to learn even more about us and our problems, as if they didn't have enough of their own.

That films about and by these cultures could be made and seen in the United States put a wrinkle in their neat dichotomies between Latin and North American cultures. In cultures where information was hotly contested on every street corner, where people read between the lines of letters to the editor, people were familiar with censorship and repression. If at least one of our films had been suppressed at home, we would have gotten much better box office abroad.

Much of our time was spent with people who watched movies in their cinematheques for the same reasons that people in the United States watch "high culture" on public TV. Largely professionals, technicians, and academics, they wanted to lay down the highest-quality carpets in their intellectual homes. They wanted, it seemed to me, to consider themselves cultured, usually in a European sense. They wanted to kill the awful insecurity associated with the phrase "the New World," locating themselves in a cultural tradition that elevated them from the invidious status of small and economically shaky nations.

Often in their talks with us, a nostalgia would surface for a world in which politics does not have to be dominant in the consciousness. And it was there that we heard positive comments about U.S. film—not ours, but the professional big time. Film buffs would praise the quality and creative potential of Hollywood, and American TV.

Their genuine affection, it seemed to me, was related to an ambition for their own lives, to carve out a space in which all aesthetic activity didn't have to be judged on its social relevance, in which truly independent media could flourish, as well as art for art's sake and technical expertise distanced gently from politics, in which reason would not seem a tool of higher irrationality. Film critics would search for the latest news of film festival favorites, for gossip from the mainstream production centers. "What is Arthur Penn's latest film like?" asked a film club volunteer, an accountant in an upriver Argentine town. The favorite angle of inquiry for big-city critics was, "Tell us more about how America has sustained a cinema of such energy and quality."

And for all my irritation with an approach that I often found stifling, I admired the thirst for knowledge, the curiosity, a demand even, to be part of a dialogue that, from the vantage point of the United States, we didn't even know we were having. That desire to communicate cut across class and national lines but was expressed in different forms. Our movies found their most receptive audiences among the disenfranchised—the poor, students, the political opposition, unions, women organizing for their rights. Among these groups, our conversations tended to be pointed toward the question of social action rather than toward elegant social models or consumer preferences.

In Peru, we met with members of the prestigious film magazine *Hablemos de Cine,* a group of men in their fifties who had been captivated by the French New Wave and its promise of individual aesthetic expression and since established a tight coterie of film buffs who focused their search for civilizing influences on innovative cinema. For them, the problem with our films was precisely that they deal with social themes. After discovering that the films were unlikely to make festival waves, the men never showed up again, except for the one film on an issue that touched many of them—the gay rights documentary.

But when we took our films to a slum on the outskirts of Lima, the reaction was dramatically different. The slum, established fourteen years before on a sandy beach by emigrants from the mountains, had been organized in a way that would have warmed the hearts of the Paris Communards. Its communications committee hosted our film showings and organized discussions. We showed *Clarence and Angel* to a group of teachers, teachers aides, and students, who acted as if they were in the movie while they were watching it—laughing, sighing, cheering. Afterward, they launched into a lively discussion of pedagogy and the oppressed. Although they referred to me and the film—"Is corporal punishment a common part of educational policy in the United States?" "Why are all the teachers also black?"—they mostly talked to each other, defining their rights and responsibilities, the problems that each faces, the need for education. There it was again: the desperate need to know, the need for civilizing influences, the need to create rather than merely to consume.

In Ecuador, we met with a group of feminists who watched *La Operación*, a documentary about sterilization of Puerto Rican women. The film provoked a discussion about similar and other birth control practices in the Andean highlands, and the connection between development policies and contraceptive policies. But what mattered most to me was the way it ended. The woman who organized the affair, a middle-class social worker, stood up and said, "Thank you for coming and sharing this film with us. We're working hard here to confront forces that threaten our livelihoods and lives. And we know it's hard. But it seems to us that it must be much harder for you, in the United States, to fight within the center of power. We want you to know that we're supporting you, and we admire you."

The flattery was welcome. And the speech reinforced the importance of public speaking in our many Latin American presentations—as a statement underlying social solidarity, its subtext always, "Here we are, all together, talking about how to be all together." Just as impressive, however, was what it demonstrated: the will to imagine what problems we in an entirely different political and economic environment face, and the generosity of spirit to acknowledge it.

In Bolivia, a group of successful and aspiring filmmakers hosted our stay and held a workshop analyzing the style of our documentaries. They were all members of the white minority culture in this country divided between white and Indian—a division that typically is also between rich and poor—and between those in the "civil society" and the "marginals." "Too much like what TV's already done well," was the short form of their verdict. These were the same people who, in an apartment whose floor-to-ceiling window overlooked half the majestic city of La Paz, solemnly decided to wait and see whether the economic austerity measures "will work"—concentrating their own capacities for controlled stupidity in order not to notice that if they do, it will be because the poor die more quickly than they can mobilize a protest.

On the other hand, we took *Americas in Transition* into a slum at the edge of La Paz, where Aymara, not Spanish, is the language spoken. It was the night before a state of seige was announced, and the men were off planning political actions. Only illiterate women and their children attended the screening. They didn't understand my introduction in Spanish to this film that describes U.S. intervention throughout Latin America, and they thought the Mexican intellectual Carlos Fuentes—who in the film points out that political instability in Latin America is more effect than cause of U.S. intervention—was some American diplomat. But they attentively watched the film, patiently waiting through a power failure, and launched a discussion afterward through a translator. Questions about the current U.S. stance toward Bolivia and about the prevalence of U.S. evangelical groups in the highlands peppered the discussion. But a few people asked specifically about the film. They wanted to know who had made it, and why—who in the United States criticized U.S. interventionism.

"I don't think I understood much," one woman said. "But what the film seems to say is that in every Latin American country, the military oppresses the people, and the U.S. government is helping the military." That pretty much summed it up, too.

*Americas in Transition* was by far the most popular film in the series, for the simple reason that it was the only one about U.S.-Latin relations. The film also prompted the toughest questions, where suddenly I was both inside someone else's conversation and irrevocably on my own territory.

In the impressive Cinemateca Uruguaya, a conversation I had just had in Argentina repeated itself. "Was this film censored?" asked the young man who runs the alternative distribution wing of the cinemateque. No, I said, far from it. In fact, the film was shown on commercial television, as a result of a regulation mandating that stations air more than one view on controversial issues.

"So the film was seen widely by Americans?" Yes, of course. "And so they know what their government is doing—and they still do nothing to stop its actions, they approve the funding of the contras, they pay no attention to its military aid to repressive governments?"

Well, yes, that's true, I said. And it's true that *Americas in Transition* is one twenty-nine-minute film, while the Reagan White House got to send out daily press releases on electronic mail. José went on, carefully deliberate, in a speech he'd obviously prepared:

> Please tell me your opinion. We are uninformed on your political processes. There are those of us who say that fascism is a very great possibility in your country—not old-fashioned fascism, but a fascism born of a will not to know, of a system of disinformation that isn't purely political but is built on commercial mass culture, on advertising, on popular movies, on the huge structure of information-for-sale. I believe that. My friends tell me I'm paranoid. They say that democracy won't allow that process. And yet we watch what Reagan is doing. And we have to wonder.

So do I. I'm hawking these offbeat visions of American culture knowing that most of my fellow Americans have never seen them and most likely never will. I ran into two UCLA film students in Uruguay, who eagerly jotted down the film schedule. "I've never heard of any of these films," said one. He was planning to write a thesis on leftist independent documentaries of the '60s and '70s. In the end, neither of them managed to make it to any of the screenings.

I returned to the United States brimming with plans for cultural exchange programs that went both ways. But La Otra Cara/The Other Face had by this time dissolved, having completed its project; the original filmmakers and funders were spinning off to new projects, new aspects of their respective careers. I began reconstructing mine, hawking bits and pieces of my Latin American "material" as a freelance writer, looking for niches and corners of the American publishing market interested in offbeat angles of what, while I had been there, was a pulsating, conflicted experience.

One day I dropped in to visit my friends, an exiled Chilean journalist and a Bolivian diplomat, who had started the only Spanish-language bookstore in town. They told me they were moving. "We're going to Madrid," said Berta. "It's just too hard to live here. We can't live—really live—the way we could there. Those late nights in the bars, the street life, the talk. Here, we're building a center for Latin culture. But we don't want to build it. We want to live in it."

I understood perfectly. It made me tremendously sad. I could see why they needed to go, and I knew I couldn't go with them. Their Madrid would never be my Madrid, although a part of me longed to deny that. Of course, my Washington would never be theirs either; but they felt no similar regrets.

And why should they? Their cultures owned a crucial piece of ours inevitably, claiming and reclaiming it in their own styles. The contradictions and clashes, the raw energy, the improbable possibilities hinted at by our "other faces"—the ones they only dimly saw—are part of a conversation North Americans will have to conduct on our own territory.

### Reference

Fernández, E. 1985. "Body Language: Octavio Paz in Pieces." *Village Voice,* March 19, p. 39.

# Doing Business

# with the

# Democrats

It was December 1992, and I felt like a *Doonesbury* character. I finally got it. I got The Call.

Actually, I just got a call. A brisk, generic, very young person asked me if I could show up for a meeting with the presidential transition team, to discuss the immediate future of a federal agency. Well, sure I could. I'd spent the Reagan-Bush years at ground zero, where public interest advocates like me had been cheerfully treated as beneath contempt. I'd even gotten used to it. It had come to seem almost normal, or at least a sour personal fate, that our crowd should spend its adulthood on the sidelines in the biggest power game around, occasionally throwing a spitball or issuing a Bronx cheer but mostly being ignored. When the right wing would get cranked up about the liberal threat, it was actually kind of touching—at least somebody noticed us.

So this was big news, the kind of occasion where I woke up thinking about What to Wear.

There was, in the event, no reason to bother about the niceties. The transition team worked out of several floors of a downtown Washington office building, where it seemed not a single person had had a moment to so much as tape a family photo to the wall. It was a rabbit warren of paper, desolate desks, and impromptu equipment arrangements. Vending machines offered an eerie simulacrum of sustenance. Once ensconced, it was possible to believe you might never figure out how to get out.

But getting in was a scene. There was an airport ambience. Security gates were up, with very unfunny people guarding them. They channeled a steady, seemingly nonstop stream of visitors spilling out of the elevators. Files, documents, and briefs in hand, they all stepped out ready to give their best policy recommendations to the teams, clusters, liaisons of the transition.

This was definitely not the lockstep look of the passing era. The diversity of the crowd looked more like what you might encounter at a bus stop than at a Washington policy conference. The buzz was infectiously enthusiastic, uncool. It was policy input gone retail—the K-Mart of political reform. We were all there with our blue-light specials, our little piece of the answer. Happy to serve.

Once we all got our badges and our escort, we wove our way up and down staircases, down corridors, and finally into a conference room increasingly crammed with people with Something to Say. That's when the transition team guy explained what we were there for. After us, he explained, the briefing book team would meet with trade associations and industry groups. Our conversation would, he claimed, guide their next one.

The team's big question for us: "We need to find out ways for this agency to get all kinds of input justly and fairly represented, not just from people with money." Say what? It's been so long, people can't quite believe their ears. The honcho goes on to belabor the obvious: "Frankly, the corporate community has a lot more money than all the people in this room." So very true. The librarian and disabled spokesperson and children's advocate and public interest computer programmer and the rest of us acceded without a peep.

Then the honcho explained that another top-down directive was to figure out how to get the agency's staff itself to reflect the demography of the American population. The equal opportunity mandate was, according to him, one of "Bill's" priorities. We listened, trying hard to make sense of it. The words just sounded funny. It had been a long time since anyone in power spoke our language.

Then we all got to work, resolutely trying to rein in impulses to tell horror stories. They leaked out anyway. We couldn't quite believe we were talking to people who wanted to know how this agency had sabotaged its mandate, buried basic data, hidden and charged for basic procedural documents, cavalierly ignored or dismissed our properly filed and entered interventions, for twelve years in which things have gone from bad to worse to grisly.

We warmed to the task. We began to feel like maybe we had to tell them how the archival staff insulted us; we wanted to rehearse for them the petty civic indignities that have rubbed salt into our wounds. But we weren't going that far. Suddenly, it was all over. The transition team was driving this afternoon like a bus, and we'd arrived at our destination. No one offered to lead us out of temporary office hell. We bumped into a few vending machines and left. But not without reeling a bit, even getting a tad giddy, from the shock of an approach that some of us had never, in our little policy lives, even imagined.

That kind of experience—being given the thrill of recognition, the promise of being seen, understood, respected, represented in the most traditional way politically—turned out to be what the Clinton adminstration did best. It wasn't even just Clinton himself, although he was the past master of mass-marketed empathy. The minions we met with, who were many levels below dealmaker, also had it in their own workmanlike way.

Of course, the follow-through on the promise, in terms of policy action or appointments, was vastly disappointing; it could even reinforce your cynicism. But it was impossible for me to forget that shock at the very idea that one might be taken seriously. It was a tip-off for me about what remains so sadly lacking in ordinary political process, and also a signal about the sources of populist anger at government. It helped me to think about the personalization of the presidency, accompanied in the Clinton era by the Gennifer-Paula-Monica type of scandal, as a consequence of the distance between the practice of politics and the promise of connection. Clinton's strategy, of not just feeling our pain, but awakening our entirely justified sense of public neglect, was risky, especially in the absence of action. We need a connection to politics as members of the American public, not to gossip and scandal as members of the American audience of political life.

# Oh,

# Grow Up

When I belatedly became a mom after a harum-scarum career as a free-lance arts critic and college teacher, I wondered uneasily if I could cope with a baby after a life that had been pleasantly obsessed with word work. Different rhythms, different demands, different responsibilities—the very thought of all this in an anything but virtual reality was daunting.

But soon after I had my first child, I discovered what I suspect is an open secret among those of us in the intellectual service professions: when you care for a baby, you suddenly realize you've been dealing with them all your life, only they've been *disguised* as grown-ups. And it's a lot easier to deal with a real one.

The world of the working intellectual turns out to be great training for mothering. Consider the parallels. As (in my case) a freelance journalist, you're ever at other people's behest and have to be ready for their complete indifference to you—except when they want you, all of you, right then. Success is about juggling—finishing the turnaround rewrite on a break from the first draft of a second project, pitching a third, and adding up last week's parking receipts while the fact-checker leaves you on hold. You make fine plans for your day that get knocked into a hat by 11 A.M. Oh, and nobody ever says thank you. Go ahead, moms, tell me this doesn't sound like life with a toddler.

But nice as it has been to find I actually did bring to my new job a backpack's worth of skills, it has been more of an adjustment than I had counted on to go back to work. There are the obvious reasons, which may or may not (you be the judge) be related to the lack of national standards for parental leave.

But for me the greatest challenge has been recovering a saving patience with my colleagues. Take your basic baby: he's wet, he whines. You change him, he's happy. Now, take your underpaid, underpromoted assistant editor, chafing for a chance to flaunt that elaborate package of knowledge from the best schools and to demonstrate mastery over *some* situation. After a tortuous pretense of mutual consultation over a five-hundred-word article, it turns out that the object is not finding a solution to clumsy writing. It is not even the writer's capitulation to a total rewrite. That would be too easy. The goal is for the writer to grasp, truly grasp, just how much work the unsung editor has had to go through to get to this point in the conversation.

Or consider the toddler's demand for juice in a cup—no, he means milk in a bottle. Actually, he really really wants a straw in the special blue glass, and he wants it now. These are all concrete, if conflicting, desires, testable in the present; and the passion is right there on the table along with the spilled juice. Compare this to the all-morning meeting in which staffers from disparate wings of an organization reenact family pathologies as they struggle toward consensus over the brochure they're pretty sure they want you to write. Or maybe it's a pamphlet, or a special issue of the magazine. Or maybe there's no budget for it after all. The executive director believes all these things, at different times of the day. It all makes terrible-two indecision look transparently simple.

How about the young child's impatience with mommy's moods, and the frank demand, "Mommy, look *happy!*" That's a lot more direct than the suffocated huffiness that comes over the phone when the fact-checker discovers that dinnertime is not the most convenient moment in the world to recheck the stats on the Argentine national economy, or that, still worse, you are on another line.

It's so much harder these days to sit through the boring parts of meetings, knowing it would be more fun and undoubtedly more instructive to be home watching somebody learning to pour honey. The other day a colleague actually stamped his feet in a faculty meeting when he discovered he hadn't been assigned to a particular committee. It's a good thing he's not in our play group, I thought automatically. Then I realized with despair that he was.

And while there's a certain inevitability in mopping up spilled milk three times at lunch or changing a just-changed diaper, my tolerance for students who want to know, yes, again, exactly how long their paper should be—not because it's not in the syllabus, not because I didn't write it on the board or mention it in class, but just because they feel better if I say it again—seems to have shrunk alarmingly.

If I'm going to act like a responsible grown-up, is it too much to ask the people I'm working with to do the same? Well, yes, as a matter of fact, it is. I know that, when I'm not too sleep-deprived. I do hear from my mom friends who went to work after growing their families that eventually the skills become two-way again, and you learn to reapply your child-rearing experience more efficiently and gracefully to your grown-up interactions. After orchestrating a particularly contentious conference, my seasoned friend smiled when I complimented her on her ability to negotiate the thicket of querelous passions. "Navy wife," she said crisply. "Three kids."

# Selections

# from

# Interviews

*It has been one of the great privileges of a career in cultural journalism to meet creative, thoughtful people who take time out of their working lives to talk to me. These excerpts from interviews over the past decade or so include some of the remarks that linger with me.*

Spalding Gray, actor, performance artist, and storyteller

I personally see culture as a piece of art, a man-and-woman-made design imposed over cosmic, meaningless nature. Wherever you look, you will see signs and stories. Some people call that paranoia. But the difference between paranoia and art is when you see that the signs are synchronous with the culture. I'm interested in the theater of culture, the way people behave and speak, all the little things I see where I'm working.

Hanif Kureishi, book author, playwright, and scriptwriter

I am always in search of my audience, as someone who is between cultures myself. For me, England is both a foreign country and home. You just have to make it there, I figure—that's where you are. But I do have a Pakistani community I respond to. The way I dealt with showing that community, warts and all, in *[My Beautiful Laundrette]* was by confusing the issue, bringing in the homosexual theme.

Donald Freed, coscriptwriter with Robert Altman of *Secret Honor,* about Richard Nixon

In spite of being lied to for some forty-odd years, the American people still have some impulses intact. They know there are two Americas, a secret and a democratic government, and they are not paranoid. They understand there are elected representatives and vested interests: that is not shocking. But if you play the Wizard of Oz with the American public, then they will focus on conspiracies, they will read the UFO articles in the *National Enquirer,* they will read horoscopes, and they will find their feelings exploited in sometimes bizarre ways.

Reading a horoscope is not a contemptible impulse. What is contemptible is to have everyone watching the spectacle of going to the moon on TV, while keeping them away from any scintilla of involvement in the gigantic process of space travel, or for a few to arrogate to themselves the power of technology for "Star Wars" and to give the ordinary person computer dating.

Mike Leigh, British television and film director

It's healthier to have four television channels than, say, fifty. With fifty channels, it's like a room with so much food you can't decide what to eat. . . . The audience's relationship with a play or a football game is more a true relationship when the number of relationships available is contained. In the cinema you can sit with other people and experience something together. The sheer fact of being able to laugh together is important. TV doesn't work like that. But to be able to talk about it the next day, to have a discussion, that is what I'm most interested in. I suppose that is why I am so interested in working in the cinema. When I grew up in the '40s and '50s, going to the pictures was something you did several times a week, at the local cinema in Manchester. It was very important. It remains important. There's nothing better. Apart from all the other things, it was going into a place designed for you to concentrate. That's very important in this distracted age. I feel more and more urgent about it.

John Sayles, U.S. independent director and Hollywood scriptwriter

I don't regard anything I do as art. That's a foreign world to me. I regard it as a conversation. The story has to be well told for people to stay. Most of my movies have had a guide who makes it easier for an audience to walk into it with. In *The Return of the Secaucus Seven* I had one guy who was very straight, and many people told me later that they could identify with him, that they at first didn't like these people who were hippies, who were clannish, who were snobbish, but because those people were nice to him they began to like them. In *Lianna* there was Lianna's best friend who really likes Lianna but can't deal with her being gay all of a sudden. With *Brother from Another Planet*, he's from another planet because I wanted people to go to Harlem, but I wanted them to have a guide who would be accepted as black so people wouldn't act different like they do to whites. But because he's not from this planet, he knows even less than they do. In *Matewan*, Joe Kenehan starts out as a guide, but I think then people realize that they actually have more in common with the people of West Virginia.

Because I write genre movies for other people, I know what works, and I resist it in movies I write for myself, because in a way it's too easy, and because it's about the machine. You raise certain expectations and then you pay off. And in the movies I direct and in my fiction, I raise certain expectations and I don't pay off, and then I try to show them some of the reasons why the easy way of thinking about this thing won't work. I want people to go to my movies, but not enough to lie to them. That's the line I walk. I write a line in a movie and say, I just lost a million dollars. And then you go back to the drawing board and say how much is this movie going to cost? I'm just doing what I want to do. I get to write a book and make a movie. I'm very lucky because I also write fiction, which doesn't require money.

What I want to do is to tell stories to people and get them across. If I work for a studio and can't do it the way I want to, there's no attraction. I don't need that much money. You get too much for writing crummy exploitation movies anyway. And that's how I do my living.

Movies made just for entertainment are not bad. What distinguishes good entertainment movies is the question of not being condescending. I worked with Spielberg on something that didn't get made, and I think a reason why they were so successful is that they made movies they would like to see. They haven't been making stuff that they said, What's good product, what will those suckers go for? I don't know him or Lucas well, but I know they will take time to make the movie better even though they don't have to. Both have had failures. Spending the extra $2 million only makes sense if it's gonna make another $10 million, but they'll do it because they want to make a better movie for those people in the audience. And that's what I respect about those guys. I have different tastes, and maybe different values, but I never feel condescension there.

The most successful movies, no matter how schlocky, have that quality.

Russ Meyer's attitude, you know: "Americans like square chins and big tits and I do too." Movies are not necessarily about what they say they're about. There can be communist Westerns, fascist Westerns, and Westerns that are just about horses. Sometimes I watch movies that way. I was thinking about the difference between theater and movies. There's still something magical about all that light shining through colored light shining through plastic.

Denys Arcand, Canadian filmmaker, on the release of *Decline of the American Empire*

What I am doing is hyperrealism, ethnography. The only thing that interests me is life. I'm not making a criticism of media. Let's take *Network*, one of many bad films but a good example. This is not an accurate description of how a network is run. The characters are cardboard. It becomes very easy to denounce them, and to denounce TV. But in fact, it is a way of despising people. You think of those millions of people as the morons who listen to TV every night—you try to reform them, it's an elitist position. Why are all those people looking at TV every night? Because it's very well made, by people who sold out but who have a lot of talent. The best talent in the world is working for the U.S. networks. Then the picture becomes very complicated. Why have they sold out? How can we talk to those people? How can we change that? You can't just preach about it.

Walter Bernstein, once-blacklisted scriptwriter

Anybody's best work is done when they are fully expressing themselves. If you have the kind of political orientation I have, it's tough [to work in Hollywood]. The problem you have to deal with is your self-censorship. You always have to deal with accommodation: on what level do you accommodate, are you accommodating before you have to? I find myself constantly in conflict with myself: "Gee, is this going to be too strong, what's the point of spending much time on this because nobody cares anyway. . . ?" You're constantly between Scylla and Charybdis, risking going too far to make something palatable.

It's like with runners—you hit a wall. Then the choice has to be made. Are you going to take it on, or are you going to veer off and do more of what you know is acceptable and what you know?

Bill Couturie, documentary film director

I'm not trying to make a blanket antiwar statement [in *Dear America: Letters Home from Vietnam*]. I'm not saying that we should not fight wars. I think it would be great if we didn't, but I don't see it in the cards for human beings. But I did want to make a movie that says, Look at the cost and the pain. This is what war means. It means young men die. Look at the cost, the pain, and then ask yourself, is it worth the price? because this will be the price.

Gabriel Figueroa, Mexican cinematographer

My style came from painting. The Flemish painters understood lighting, and especially Rembrandt. Also, of course, Vermeer. I believe the first Impressionist was Turner—those incredible skies!

When I started out, I tried to get the skies quite in the tone that I visualized, and the clouds and the trees and ocean and the waves, but I was not satisfied, because what my eye had seen I didn't see on the screen. So I said, I must improve, and I started studying. I got a book of Leonardo da Vinci, in which he pointed out that it was very important for painters to take into consideration the color of the atmosphere, the air. I said, Oh my God, the color of the air, what is that? Color comes from the mountains, the oceans, it's a reflection. But the lenses were more intelligent than my eye. So I started trying filters—I'm talking about black and white—I tried with filters to get sharpness and distance, and depth. Because afterward, you can diffuse it, but first you must have that. So I got it with infrared filters, a combination of green and red. The filter gets into the fog that is invisible for us, the haze. That was the first advantage, and it also gave me the color I wanted in the sky; I could get beautiful clouds. In Europe after I won several different prizes, they started to use the term "Figueroa skies."

Black-and-white requires volume. With color it's different. Color separation already gives you roundness. Black-and-white is more the experience of a dream. Color is closer to reality. You are there with people. It's hard to be sharply, socially critical—*strong*—in color. Look at *Guernica*, Picasso's only political painting, and done in black and white basically. Now color has advanced, and it's more artistic.

Marcel Ophuls, documentary filmmaker

I never construct a film for a European or an American audience. Both in my own head and even contractually I make sure that you don't aim at specific audiences. That would transform the film into some form of propaganda. It's not what a documentary should be. The film that gets made should be just as legitimate to a French or a German audience. That is a challenge—that is one reason my films are long. You have to try to be clear enough on complex and ambiguous material like that, so that the necessary information is conveyed to people who know a great deal and also people who do not.

I believe that if I can convey it coherently and use logic and rational analysis, the tools of my trade, then in the end what interests or surprises me or makes me laugh or think will have the same effect on others. The filmmaker is not talking to collective groups or surveys but individuals.

One of the reasons *The Sorrow and the Pity* did well [in 1971] was that we were still under the influence of the '60s, both in France and in the United States, and the people who saw the film at the time—mostly young people—were still wondering about the relation between protest and resistance in their own lives. I don't know if that can happen today. I watch the exhibitionism on TV in the morning—yesterday it was about incest and today about grave robbers—and they are all complicit in the attitude that if it makes money, then we just feed off each other. Greed, I suppose. I don't think you just get it at the political level or in the White House. If the climate has changed, and there is no longer necessarily the same sympathy for my essays, which if we were to be honest about it are rather puritanical in the Judeo-Christian tradition, there may be no more understanding for that.

When my father's last film, *Lola Montez*—which is now seen as a masterpiece, but then it was a dismal flop—came out, my old man said, "This one-to-one relationship with the audience, if it breaks down, it means that you are no longer with it, and there is no longer a bridge between you as an individual and the spirit of the times. When that happens, you are just out of luck."

## Raoul Peck, Haitian filmmaker

I don't make a film as a Haitian filmmaker, but as a filmmaker with Haitian, German, and French experience. I'm part of a generation that for the first time had access to production possibilities, to film school—I studied in Berlin. We were the first to grow up inside the *metropole*, the heart of empire, the first who understood the system from the inside. On my first feature, I didn't have a model I could follow.

The important people for me have been [Ethiopian filmmaker and Howard University professor] Haile Gerima and [African American feature filmmaker] Charles Burnett. My generation includes Caribbeans, Indians, young Britons from India and Africa, young Africans, young Chinese, Arabs. The New African, Arab, and Latin American Cinemas [which flourished in the 1970s] were important models, too. I had heroes like [Argentine polemical filmmaker] Fernando Solanas, who made *Hour of the Furnaces,* and [Cuban documentarist] Santiago Alvarez.

I was always attracted by memories, by the moment when you discover you are somebody, that you exist and that you have made your contribution to world history and it was not recognized. Consider, for instance, that the Haitian revolution helped the U.S. independence struggle because the French and English were weaker as a result. Consider that the French were willing to sell the [Louisiana Purchase] to the United States because they had lost Haiti.

I accept myself as a product of my own biography, and it's not necessary to define it. More interesting is to see the result of this, to see the capability of having different perspectives. I am as familiar with my being as a Third World person, as a mainstream American, and as French. I am as familiar with Lucille Ball as with any French characters on TV. That gives us an enormous advantage.

In my generation, I see more and more people who have these characteristics. If I have to name names, then people like Hanif Kureishi, John Akomfrah, David Achkar, and Felix de Rooy come to mind. We are different from the pioneers—although they have done a great job, and I respect them for that. You can see the difference between the New Arab Cinema and my generation. The first stage was to recover our identity, and now we are going further, not only that we have our identity but that this identity should not be used to marginalize us.

*Abbas Kiarostami, Iranian filmmaker*

I have hundreds of small sources of inspiration throughout the day, just watching people in daily routines. I think what happens in real life is more important than cinema. My technique is similar to collage. I collect pieces and put them together. I don't invent material. I just watch and take it from the daily life of people around me.

Also, I'd rather look at the positive side of daily life rather than the negative, which makes me sleepless and nervous. So I look around and I select the things that seem to me the best. I collect and put them together as a package and sell it.

I'm not the only one who does this, you know. Florists do the same thing. They don't make the flowers—they just find the best arrangement.

Some people go after beautiful things. And in cinema it's been made easy for us. We have this camera, which is very sensitive and registers all the details. All that's left is for us, the film directors, to decide when to register them. There's also a personal satisfaction in it—we are the first consumer of what we tell.

I can't put out of my mind an image that was formative for me—it haunts me. One snowy day I was going to work and saw a mother walking down the street, holding a small child, a baby really, wrapped up in her chador. The baby was clearly burning up with fever, and its eyes were nearly shut.

I happened to be walking behind them, and I was staring at the child and waving my hand, the way you do to little children. I thought he couldn't even see me, his little eyes were so swollen up. And the mother didn't even know I was there. When we got to the intersection, I saw to my astonishment that the child with great effort pulled out his hand and waved back at me. Well, it shocked and touched me, and it also struck me that nobody was around us to see this scene. And I thought, there should be a way to show this moment to people.

Then, this is what happened: That moment was repeated in the second part of the trilogy [And Life Goes On], with the child with the broken arm. I waved at him, and this scene happened again—he waved back.

I enjoy so much watching good films with a human touch and emotions, and I don't get that kind of pleasure when I see violent movies.

# Permissions

"New Latin American Cinema Reconsidered" originally appeared as "Latin American Cinema and the Rhetoric of Cultural Nationalism: Controversies at Havana in 1987 and 1989," *Quarterly Review of Film and Video* 12, no. 4 (1991): 61–76. Used by permission of Harwood Academic Publishers.

"Grassroots Video in Latin America" originally appeared as "Beyond Television: Grassroots Video in Latin America," *Public Culture* 11, no. 4 (winter 1993): 579–92. Used by permission of Duke University Press and the author.

"Making Video with Brazilian Indians" originally appeared as "The Video in the Villages Project: Videomaking with and by Brazilian Indians," *Visual Anthropology Review* 11, no. 2 (fall 1995). Reprinted by permission of the American Anthropological Association. Not for further reproduction.

"Memory and History in Sub-Saharan African Cinema" originally appeared as "Memory and History in Sub-Saharan Africa: An Interview with David Achkar," *Visual Anthropology Review* 9, no. 2 (fall 1993). Reprinted by permission of the American Anthropological Association. Not for further reproduction.

"Why and How to Teach Media Literacy" originally appeared as "Media Education in the 90s," *Afterimage: The Journal of Media Arts and Cultural Criticism* (September 1992). Used by permission of *Afterimage*.

"Does a Librarian Need Multiculturalism?" was originally delivered as a keynote address to the Consortium of College and University Media Centers in 1991.

"Conversations in Latin America" originally appeared as "'The Other Face': Conversations in Latin America," *Massachusetts Review* 27, nos. 3/4 (fall/winter 1986). Used by permission of the author.

"Doing Business with the Democrats" originally appeared as "On the Transition Team," *In These Times* (December 1991). Used by permission of the publisher.

"Oh, Grow Up" originally appeared as "Stealth Infants Abound in a Mother's Working Life," *Newsday* (September 14, 1997): B4. Used by permission of the author.

**Patricia Aufderheide** is professor in the School of Communication, American University, and a senior editor of *In These Times* newspaper. She is the author of *Communications Policy and the Public Interest: The Telecommunications Act of 1996*, and the editor of *Beyond PC: Toward a Politics of Understanding*. She has been a Fulbright and John Simon Guggenheim fellow and has served as a juror at the Sundance Film Festival. She serves on the film advisory board of the National Gallery of Art and on the editorial board of a variety of publications, including *Communication Law and Policy*.